The
BARBRA
STREISAND
Companion

The

BARBRA STREISAND

Companion

A Guide to Her Vocal Style and Repertoire

Linda Pohly

Companions to Celebrated Musicians
Michael Meckna, Series Adviser

GREENWOOD PRESS
Westport, Connecticut • London

Library of Congress Cataloging-in-Publication Data

Pohly, Linda, 1954–
    The Barbra Streisand companion : a guide to her vocal style and
repertoire / Linda Pohly.
        p.   cm.—(Companions to celebrated musicians)
    Includes discography, bibliographical references, and index.
    ISBN 0–313–30414–9 (alk. paper)
    1. Streisand, Barbra—Criticism and interpretation.   I. Title.
II. Series.
    ML420.S915P64   2000
    782.42164'092—dc21   99–31631

British Library Cataloguing in Publication Data is available.

Library of Congress Catalog Card Number: 99–31631
ISBN: 0–313–30414–9

First published in 2000

Greenwood Press, 88 Post Road West, Westport, CT 06881
An imprint of Greenwood Publishing Group, Inc.
www.greenwood.com

Printed in the United States of America

The paper used in this book complies with the
Permanent Paper Standard issued by the National
Information Standards Organization (Z39.48–1984).

10 9 8 7 6 5 4 3 2 1

Contents

Photo Essay follows page 160.

Foreword

Musical creation is a two-fold endeavor. Traditionally music scholars have concentrated on that most Romantic of geniuses, the composer. Rightfully revered as keeper of the flame, he (and it usually is a man) inspires books, articles, portraits, and legends. However, what good is a piano sonata without a pianist? A song without a singer? Without performers music does not come to life. Whether always fulfilling the composer's original intentions or not, musicians bring music to us, applying their talents to the notes and to the silences between them. In our day these artists have become the most publicized members of the music community, yet they typically receive little scholarly attention. As interpreters of music, performers deserve more than the ephemeral applause of an audience and trivial treatment by the sensational media.

The Greenwood Companions to Celebrated Musicians series is devoted to these musicians whose genius, technique, and style have combined to produce unforgettable music. Included will be performers from both vernacular and cultivated traditions. While there may be a volume on a pre-recording era musician, the subjects will most likely be drawn from the enormous pool of twentieth-century luminaries. Lovers of music will, *Deo volente*, eventually have companion books to musicians such as the Andrews Sisters, Leonard Bernstein, Maria Callas, Pablo Casals, Bing Crosby, Ella Fitzgerald, Vladimir Horowitz, Harry James, Liberace, Yo-Yo Ma, Ignacy Paderewski, Niccolo Paganini, Luciano Pavarotti, Itzhak Perlman, Arthur Rubinstein, Frank Sinatra, Georg Solti, and Arturo Toscanini.

For the present though we have this Companion to Barbra Streisand. Carefully researched and genially written by Dr. Linda Pohly, this book will appeal to an educated but not necessarily academic readership. Anyone interested in Streisand's unique vocal style and wide-ranging repertoire will find all they need and more in the following pages. "Excellence is in the details," Streisand once said to Larry King, and regardless of level of expertise, students, teachers, performers, musical hobbyists, and fans will find an abundance of details in this Companion. Additionally, both public and academic libraries will also want to enrich their collections with this thorough treatment of an American musical icon.

Michael Meckna, Series Adviser

Preface and Acknowledgments

... excellence is in the details.[1]

This book probably began during the late 1960s and early 1970s when my musical tastes were developing. The power of Beethoven's music impressed me, many hymns inspired me to sing, and my years in high school band were satisfying. But I also was intrigued by the sound and style of the Beatles and various Motown artists, and a voice I heard on the radio kept grabbing my attention. I soon noticed that the disc jockey always said the same name after I heard a song that stopped me in my tracks: Barbra Streisand. I did not own many phonograph records at that time, but one of my first was the cast album from *Funny Girl*. (I actually had purchased the wrong thing, not realizing there was a Broadway show of the movie I had just seen. I quickly bought the soundtrack, too.)

Over the years my eclectic interests in music continued, and as I started college, I enjoyed learning additional repertoire and more about music history and theory. But I noticed that much of my personal listening was different from the material I was studying in the classroom and in the rehearsal room. Some of my teachers occasionally referred to popular music in class or in informal settings; I wondered if they listened to it, too. I remember hesitantly asking a voice teacher if she had ever heard Barbra Streisand's album of classical songs. To my surprise she had, and she liked it.

Although raised in the American education system, my first formal study of American music came in the late 1970s—in graduate school. I was excited to learn about different styles and genres, including jazz, folk, blues, rock and roll, and so on. This experience did not introduce a new world to me, but it surely influenced the professional paths I have chosen. As is well known, studying and teaching the "vernacular," "popular," and "ethnic" musics of America and the world have become more commonplace in the last quarter of the twentieth century.

With its many branches and styles, "popular music" is difficult to define or delimit, but it is quite clear that the scholarly attention paid to popular music in the 1980s and 1990s primarily has focused on jazz and rock, with secondary emphasis on pre-1950s material, rap or hip hop, and country. Musical theatre also has received academic notice, but mostly with regard to composition. In other words, the type of popular music covered least often by serious, scholarly study is that which is sometimes called "the second generation of Tin Pan Alley" or the "Golden Age of popular song"[2] and its later cousin, variously called contemporary pop, adult contemporary, easy listening, or mainstream. Similarly, the techniques of songs stylists who sing this literature have not been studied to any great extent.[3]

As my own career developed, I began to teach collegiate classes in American music and in popular music. In retrospect, I realize that I too emphasized rock and jazz, even though my personal listening interests in popular music were theatre and pop vocalists. Collecting material about Streisand and absorbing the sound of her albums and compact discs still occupied a portion of my time, and I often found myself making connections and associations between observations I made about her singing and other material I was studying and teaching—but only at home, not in the classroom. I clearly remember a long car trip with a colleague during which I had a Streisand cassette playing. This friend asked me something about the song, and the floodgate opened—she got more than she ever wanted to know. Many minutes had passed before she could interrupt, and when that moment came she said something like, "You know, you really should write that down." I stammered but asked, "Do you really think anyone would be interested?" Her answer was revealing: "Well, the information is interesting, but your enthusiasm really sells it." I spent the rest of the trip telling her about many of my ideas and observations as that cassette and others played on. I ended the conversation by saying, "But I'm not sure I'm confident enough to write about Barbra, having never seen her perform in person. That would be an important link—and it doesn't appear that public performances are on her agenda." My friend agreed.

Shortly thereafter, in the fall of 1993, her management announced that Barbra Streisand would be performing publicly for the opening of the Las Vegas MGM Grand Hotel and Casino on 31 December 1993 and 1 January 1994 (see chapter 5). Many die-hard Streisand fans were surprised, and the ticket frenzy began. I didn't plan to try to get tickets, knowing what the demand would be, but an advertisement in *USA Today* about the MGM Grand and her appearance there caught my eye. To my surprise, it included an 800 number to call for information. Fortunately, my phone call was answered at a time when, according to the operator, a few additional seats had been put up for sale following a rearrangement of the seating plan. Having no idea about transportation to or housing in Las Vegas (especially during a holiday) or about my credit-card balance, I boldly ordered two of the $300-level tickets. All the arrangements fell into place, and it was an unforgettable experience—both in terms of the music and the atmosphere surrounding the event. I took notes during the concert (to the bewilderment of the woman seated next to me!), but still had time to enjoy it. Streisand's subsequent tour in the spring of 1994 included a stop in Detroit, where I was able to attend another concert.

Almost immediately after the Las Vegas trip, I responded to calls for papers from several professional organizations whose members I thought might be interested in hearing about Streisand the singer. After several proposals were accepted, I realized that there was an audience for this information, and I began to formulate analytical ideas and organize my thinking and observations more carefully. A bibliographical study revealed that, as I suspected, little had been written about Barbra's vocal style beyond individual recording reviews. Even the few books that dealt generally with popular-music singers focused on her biography, offering little detail about technique or repertoire. My years of listening and collecting were beginning to make sense and to play a part in my professional activities.[4]

The Greenwood Press series, "Companions to Celebrated Musicians," emphasizes that the creativity of performers of music is equally important to that of composers, and that the techniques, repertoire choices, and impact of performers deserve careful attention. The list of proposed subjects for the series is varied as to representation of musical style and historical setting from Sinatra to Solti, Fitzgerald to Paderewski, and Paganini to Streisand.

I hold Barbra Streisand's abilities as a singer and lyric interpreter in high regard, and I want to respect her as a person (although we have never met or talked), not just as an artist or a historical phenomenon. This book is "positive" in its tone; beyond my own admiration of Streisand, I contend that her name would not be on Greenwood's "Companions" list if it were not for her talents, influence, and success. Nonetheless, I continually have tried to maintain an objective, professional outlook—even though a scholar or a historian rarely is totally devoid of some sort of personal attachment to or opinion about a subject. Composer, conductor, and arranger David Shire wondered aloud as to whether the "academic filter" was the best for studying this music with its "oral tradition" characteristics.[5] I kept that in mind as I wrote. I hope the subjective nature of much of my work is balanced by the analytical approach.

The primary sources for this study include my own analysis of Streisand's commercial recordings, critical reviews of her recordings published in various print sources, audio interviews Streisand has given, and words she has authored over the years. Secondary sources include comments from popular and classical vocalists I interviewed, other musician friends from whom I sought counsel, and the many biographical articles and books written about her. My approach to analysis is described below; transcription examples are not included as they do not serve the purpose to best advantage.[6] Each chapter begins with a quotation from Barbra that comes from the time period covered by the chapter and is relevant to the material discussed therein. Streisand's words that open this preface served as a goal for me.

Chapter 1 provides an overview of her life and career. Chapters 2 through 5 contain commentary on her singing style and repertoire choices divided into periods: the early years (to 1967 and *Simply Streisand*); transition, experimentation, and tradition (through 1973 and *Barbra Streisand and Other Musical Instruments*); eclecticism and maturity (through 1984 and *Emotion*); and coming full circle. Conclusions and an assessment of Streisand's historical significance and influence appear in the final chapter. Even though the decision invites some repetition, I made the choice to discuss the albums and her repertoire in chronological order (as opposed to by topic, i.e., lyrics, diction, rhythm) because readers likely will not read the chapters consecutively, instead referring to certain songs, albums, or periods individually. Reference information, including a substantial discography (of both albums and individual songs) and a bibliography of reviews, then follows.

The analytical portions of the middle chapters contain detailed comments about many recordings and songs, and summaries of the style or technique exhibited in others. Musical elements, such as instrumentation and orchestration, melody, harmony, rhythm and time, dynamics, and form, are the basis for the study, although not every element is mentioned in every circumstance. (Streisand has released more than fifty album-length recordings averaging about ten songs each, so commentary on *every* song is not practical or necessary. See discography and appendices.) I also discuss and describe Streisand's application of concepts and techniques specifically related to singing, like diction, phrasing, timbre and tone, inflection and embellishment, and text interpretation. An examination of Barbra's repertoire choices reveals much about her interests, abilities, and style. I describe the results of this study where appropriate and include pertinent information on social, historical, and technological context. The analytical remarks are based primarily on my own investigation of the singing heard on her commercial albums and compact discs, although, as evident in the notes that follow each chapter, I consulted many critical reviews of individual recordings in search of varied opinions. I also studied videotaped performances (especially those that had wide release and contain concert singing), and a majority of the comments about Barbra's 1994 tour concerts come from my own observations as an audience member. Information about Streisand's singing in films, on singles (45-rpm records or cassettes), and on television are included where necessary for comparison or substantiation.

Henry Pleasants has identified several conventions of American popular-song performance that are assumed at the outset: use of microphone, text emphasis, flexible approach toward written melody and rhythm, and lyric phrasing based on conversational English. He also wrote, "It's as easy to have rhetorical fun with Barbra Streisand's excesses as it is difficult to identify and define all the facets of her vocalism and phrasing that have made her a great singer in spite of them."[7] Indeed, the goal herein is to identify and define those facets of her singing.

Understanding the importance of first-hand information, I requested an interview with Miss Streisand and with several of her closest associates and collaborators including Martin Erlichman, Stephen Sondheim, Alan and Marilyn Bergman, Marvin Hamlisch, and Barry Gibb. For various reasons, these interviews did not transpire. Speaking for himself and Miss Streisand, Mr. Erlichman cited the likelihood of future autobiographies where they will share their reminiscences. David Shire, the assistant conductor for *Funny Girl* on Broadway and conductor for her albums entitled *Simply Streisand* and *Live Concert at the Forum* graciously recalled his experiences. The photographs were enthusiastically provided by Anthony Andrich of *Barbrabilia Magazine*.

No project of this magnitude is accomplished alone. I have many people and institutions to thank, especially Ball State University in Muncie, Indiana. Kristi Koriath and others in the BSU Office of Academic Research and Sponsored Programs helped acquire funding, and the Provost's Office supported me in many ways. Several administrators, colleagues, and friends in the College of Fine Arts and School of Music assisted me in my work: thank you to Phil Repp, Greg Steinke, Joe Buttram, Robert Kvam, Nancy Baker, Heather Platt, Cynthia Miller, Phil Jackson, Don LaCasse, Raphael Crystal, Fritz Mountford, Doug Amman, Maureen Miller, John Hines, and the School of Music staff for their time and efforts. Student assistants Laura Ward, Bridget Nelson, David Rodenberg, and Cory Estby contributed considerable (and very accurate) leg work. Ball State University Library personnel provided valuable aid, particularly Deb Dolak, Suzanne Rice, Carrie Bartels, and the Interlibrary Loan staff. Dr. Fritz Dolak and Kim Ferguson offered remarkable assistance with copyright details. Jeni Elliott at the Hal Leonard Corporation was very helpful.

Copy and content editors and persons serving as sounding boards for ideas and questions are always vital to the research and writing processes. Several colleagues and friends deserve a huge acknowledgment: Patricia Martin Gibby, Dr. Christina Lamb, Dr. Douglas Lee, Dr. William Miller, Prof. Janet Polvino, and Dr. Suzanne Snyder. Family members and friends helped and supported me in a variety of ways; among them were Atcha

Nolan, Jan Hedge, Katie Hedge, George Pohly, Louise Pohly, and Nancy Dain. I also want to thank Greenwood Press for its instigation of this series. Editors Pamela St. Clair and Dr. Michael Meckna have been patient and helpful in responding to my questions, ideas, and revisions.

NOTES

1. Barbra Streisand, interview by Larry King, *Larry King Live*, CNN television, 7 June 1995.

2. These phrases are associated with Charles Hamm, *Yesterdays: Popular Song in America* (New York: W. W. Norton and Co., 1979), and Allen Forte, *The American Popular Ballad of the Golden Era, 1924–1950* (Princeton: Princeton University Press, 1995). Hamm's venerated book deals with many styles and years of song history in textbook fashion, and Forte's is highly analytical based on the composer's printed music. Several textbooks designed for studying popular music in college classrooms were published in the 1990s, and popular music is discussed at conference fora and paper sessions. But my experience with these sources and at these events indicates that they emphasize rock and jazz, as mentioned above (*Yesterdays* is the exception). This notion is supported by a review written of three books on Frank Sinatra by Keir Keightley for *American Music* 15, no. 1 (Spring 1997):101–110. He begins: "While jazz and rock have attained varying degrees of acceptance as subjects for scholarly analysis, the world of pre-rock pop remains *terra incognita* within the academy" (101). He also notes that the books on Sinatra do not include references to similar academic research, this being further evidence that "pop singers like Sinatra have fallen into the crack between the academic institutionalizations of jazz and rock" (106). Some authors are skeptical about scholarly studies of popular music, see Terry Teachout, "Taking Sinatra Seriously," *Commentary* (September 1997): 55–58.

3. My own experience and anecdotal information from colleagues indicates that one of the drawbacks to studying popular music is the copyright-permission issue. In the minds of publishers, the lyrics of popular songs, in particular, are tightly regulated so that a scholar either has to use isolated words out of context or tackle the confusing, time consuming, and potentially expensive task of obtaining permission—often from various sources for a single lyric. Likewise, commentary on vocal style and technique might best be presented in a format that allows immediate aural examples (such as CD-Rom), but licensing concerns are formidable. When granted, permission is gratefully acknowledged, but the process slows down, and in some cases thwarts, study and published commentary that certainly is not intended to encroach upon the livelihoods, rights, or privileges of the creators.

4. I own many of the biographies written about Streisand and have read all or parts of most of them. I purposely have not gone back to study them in preparation for this book. My interests center on her singing style and repertoire choices; the myriad details of her life are only at issue when they play a significant role in her musical choices.

5. David Shire, interview by author, Muncie, Indiana, 4 March 1998.

6. David Shire remarked, confirming of my own view, that it is not possible or practical to notate exactly what Streisand does with her voice.

7. Summarized in Steven Petkov and Leonard Mustazza, eds., *The Frank Sinatra Reader* (New York: Oxford University Press, 1995), 75–76. See also Henry Pleasants, *The Great American Popular Singers* (New York: Simon and Schuster, 1974), 361.

Chapter 1

Introduction: The Road to Stardom

Oprah Winfrey: Do you listen to your own music?

Barbra Streisand: No, because it takes so much work again to get it right. . . . I'm sick of it by the time it's released. . . . It takes me about ten years to appreciate what it is I've done.[1]

This response from Barbra Streisand came after she had spent more than three decades as "an intimidating force on the pop scene."[2] Even when her other interests have occupied significant amounts of her energy, or when other performers and styles temporarily have grabbed the spotlight, Barbra's commercial and artistic success in popular music rarely has been questioned—regardless of her own ambivalence toward her singing evident in the quotation above. Her longevity in an industry characterized by change, her natural vocal abilities, and her unique interpretive skills place her near the top of any list of America's most significant song stylists. Who might have imagined that the girl born on 24 April 1942 to Emanuel and Diana Rosen Streisand would, in twenty short years, be on her way to becoming a one-woman entertainment force at a level perhaps unparalleled in modern history?

There are many dimensions to Barbra's life: she is an actress; a film director and producer; a singer and recording artist; a record producer; a composer and lyricist; a popular-culture icon; a woman, daughter, mother, and wife; and a philanthropist and political activist. Like most human beings, she is complex and evolving, hard to describe accurately and completely, and wary of being misrepresented and misunderstood. But since the early 1960s, her name has appeared regularly before the public, and her various endeavors have brought her living-legend status.[3] Streisand's legion of faithful fans secures her financial drawing power, while at the same time she attracts scathing personal and professional criticism from many directions.

It is fitting that so complex a person, who might be studied from a number of angles, also should be seen in light of one overall, yet multifaceted, perspective: the vantage point where contradiction, paradox, duality, and unconventionality all come into view. Although these words are not synonyms, and one is used more properly than another in a given instance, they can elicit related feelings—feelings that something is not as concrete, simple, clear, or predictable as it might seem upon first glance. This perspective frequently applies to Barbra Streisand and to the reactions that others have toward her. For example, on the surface she seems able to reinvent herself as musical styles and trends evolve. Closer inspection reveals that many of her most personal musical traits have remained consistent over the years. Indeed, what has changed is the musical material (repertoire, accompaniment style, vocal flavoring, etc.) surrounding and supporting her vocal technique. Even when it appears that Barbra is moving in a new musical direction, the foundation of her style and her ability to put a personal stamp on her repertoire remain intact. The most contradictory and deceiving nature of her singing, at least to the uninitiated, might be this: her attention to every detail and her complete absorption of her material allows Streisand to create a feeling of spontaneity in the final outcome—the willful and intended inducing the natural and instinctive. In fact, this apparent contradiction is not one at all; this approach is the essence of much artistic creation.

The beginnings of Streisand's professional life set the stage for a career full of paradox. She wanted to be an actress, but found work as a singer first. Consequently, singing is where she began, and it brought her first large-scale success. But in a 1969 interview, Streisand commented that singing was real work for her, that her interpretations came from deep inside and were "slightly painful."[4] She surmised that this very element is what drew people to her; therefore, pain was necessary to achieve the desired result, satisfaction was a companion of suffering. Through the years, when she could have rested on her laurels or taken the safe route, Streisand usually has chosen the challenging path, whether that be recording Broadway songs when others saw no market there (the conventional taking on the role of unconventional) or facing her fear of public performing (in great measure, a fear of the audience's expectations) by launching a high-profile concert tour.[5]

Barbra's fans and collaborators are well aware of the incongruities in her life and work,[6] and she frequently has acknowledged (with no apology) the conflicting characteristics of her personality, shying away from trying to categorize herself. After decades of public scrutiny and considerable commentary from the star, the press, devotees, and colleagues, it would be easy to think of this perspective as cliché or even passé, but any serious discussion of Streisand inevitably, and rightfully, leads in that direction.

But even the tendency toward contradiction is countered by one consistent theme in Streisand's life: a strong social consciousness. Her interest in social and political matters emerged in the late 1960s and reached a zenith in the 1990s. Her commitment to several issues (based on a liberal position) and her use of stardom as a tool of advocacy are prominent in Barbra's life and career. While this consistency suggests an interesting contrast to her otherwise contradictory nature, her work as an activist apparently provides her with a foundation and a way to enrich her soul in a capricious world. Through her social consciousness, the star finds a sort of grounding in life's reality.[7]

Although contradiction and social awareness play important roles in the totality of Streisand's work and persona, this book focuses on her singing, taking into account examples of how these themes affect and support it. Moreover, the book provides information about and analysis of her album-length recordings, style and technique, repertoire choices, and place in American song history. The other major aspect of her professional life, film work, is touched upon when it bears on her singing. Similarly, events of her personal life are mentioned when they provide necessary context or pertain directly to her rise in fame and her singing, important considerations since there clearly are autobiographical messages in many of her commercial recordings.[8] Further information on the arrangement of the book and my approach to analysis is found in the preface.

The girl with the special voice was born in Brooklyn in 1942 of Jewish parentage. Barbra's father held advanced degrees, was a teacher of English literature, and was a practicing Jew. Emanuel Streisand's premature death, when Barbra was fifteen months old, profoundly affected his daughter, both personally and professionally. Her mother, Diana Streisand Kind (remarried to Louis Kind after Emanuel's death), reportedly has a lovely voice and, at one time, desired a singing career. Both mother and daughter have commented at various times on Diana's limited support of Barbra's show-business aspirations and subsequent triumphs.[9] Indeed, neighbors knew young Barbara (as her name appeared then) to have a fine singing voice, and she and Diana each recorded acetate, limited-use records in 1955. Barbra selected "Zing! Went the Strings of My Heart" and "You'll Never Know," the latter of which was released publicly many years later on her 1991 *Just for the Record* retrospective boxed set.[10] In the lengthy booklet that accompanies that set, Streisand wrote that, even in this first recording, she had specific ideas about the arrangement of the accompaniment (that it should not be too elaborate) and a natural tendency to embellish the melody (the penultimate note with a note above). Her performance also exhibits other Streisand traits the listening public soon would come to know: using breathy timbre and slightly irregular tempo to color and emphasize certain words, and phrasing in places other than punctuation points of the text.

Emanuel and Diana Streisand also had a son, Sheldon, born in 1935. He consistently has remained out of the glare of the spotlight that surrounds his younger sibling. A daughter, Roslyn, was born to Diana and Louis Kind in 1951. Roslyn achieved a modicum of success in the 1970s as a singer and recording artist. Reviewers and colleagues found the similarity of her voice to that of her sister's to be both positive and negative in their assessment of her work.[11]

Barbra Streisand participated in vocal music in Erasmus Hall High School in the 1950s, an experience that later influenced her philanthropy and the sound she wanted to create on her 1967 album of Christmas songs.[12] She also began to take acting lessons and part-time jobs, such as ushering in theatres, where a world of purposeful fantasy appealed to a young lady seeking an escape from reality. Her high school career ended with a high grade average and early graduation in 1959.

In 1960, after winning a talent show sponsored by The Lion, a Greenwich Village nightclub, Barbra landed an important professional singing job, opening at the more up-scale Bon Soir for comedienne Phyllis Diller.[13] Streisand's popularity there led to return bookings over the next few years and to local television appearances on *The Jack Paar Show* and *P.M. East* with Mike Wallace. In between she secured singing engagements at the Caucus Club in Detroit and the Blue Angel in New York. A review of one performance at the Blue Angel appeared in the 25 January 1963 issue of *Time* magazine. It read in part, "But when she sings, everyone knows exactly what she means; even with a banal song, she can hush a room as if she really had something worth saying."

In 1963 Streisand performed in Las Vegas as an opening act for Liberace and sang at several California venues. National exposure was inevitable with her appearances on *The Tonight Show* with Johnny Carson in 1962 and 1963, *The Ed Sullivan Show*, and *The Judy Garland Show*. Of course, the latter brought immediate comparisons between the two singers, and at that time, there was some similarity in their style and sound. Both women sang showtunes; had bright, nasal vocal timbres; and were known for exhibiting great emotion. Videotape of their 1963 performance allows comparison of one legend too near the end of her life and another legend in the making.[14] Young Barbra sensed the paradox of the situation as Judy-the-star held on to her tightly during their duet. Only years later did she begin to understand the kind of anxiety that can come after years of "showbiz" pressure.[15]

Martin Erlichman was Streisand's manager during this developmental period, and he has retained that position for most of her career. Beyond business considerations, selecting and rehearsing additional repertoire was necessary during those years of increasing exposure and opportunity. In this regard, Barbra was helped and influenced by her friend and colleague Barry Dennen.[16] She focused on literature appropriate for club settings (showtunes and standards), steering clear of the musical styles (like contemporary pop, country, and rock) that were occupying the energies of many popular-music performers of the day. Typical of the duality that attends her career, Streisand's look and mannerisms might have said unconventional or off-beat, but her repertoire did not. Early on she became enamored of the work of Harold Arlen, counting him and George Gershwin as her favorite composers.[17] Her success with this repertoire clearly was indicated when Arlen, Richard Rodgers, Jule Styne, Harold Rome, Cy Coleman, Jerry Herman, and Burton Lane joined in a May 1969 Friars Club tribute to twenty-seven-year-old Streisand. A few weeks later and a world away from this literature and musical style, tens of thousands of young people gathered in Woodstock, New York. That crowd and Streisand shared the same generation—if not musical tastes.

Barbra's first significant theatrical work came concurrently in 1962 with the musical *I Can Get It for You Wholesale*. The show ran for about eight months and, although Barbra played the part of a secondary character, Miss Marmelstein, it brought her rave reviews and considerable attention. *Wholesale* also introduced Barbra to her future husband, Elliott Gould, who had one of the leading roles. They were married in Carson City, Nevada, on 13 September 1963. A cast album of the show was released, allowing her voice to be heard beyond the theatre and club dates. These professional opportunities were stepping stones leading in the direction that Streisand and Erlichman had planned. In 1963 Streisand signed her first solo recording contract, sang for President Kennedy, and landed the starring role in the upcoming Broadway musical *Funny Girl*. Her unconventional style bewildered some, but her talent impressed many.

Columbia Records, through the leadership of Goddard Lieberson, decided to take a risk on young Streisand after some other labels had rejected her sound. She remarked that the most important part of the contract was the clause "giving me the right to choose my own material. It was the only thing I really cared about."[18] In a 1964 interview with jazz author Leonard Feather, Streisand said, "In these days of novelties . . . I'm the first singer to sell with straight-forward music."[19] She went on to state her belief that any "genuine" music will be commercially successful and that some of her repertoire (like "Who's Afraid of the Big Bad Wolf?") was selected because it challenged the expectations of the audience.

Streisand's first two albums were released in February and August of 1963, and they began an important collaboration between Barbra and arranger/conductor Peter Matz. *The Barbra Streisand Album* received Grammy Awards in 1964 for Album of the Year and Best Vocal Performance—Female.[20] Several of the same songs also were released as 45-rpm singles (some of which became available as collectibles in the 1990s), but the singles usually were performed with an arrangement and orchestration different from that heard on the album version. In general, the accompaniment on the singles is more cabaret-like (perhaps with some instrumental lines added after the fact) while the album versions have a decidedly Broadway sound. Keeping in mind that all of the performances were recorded within a short period of one another, Barbra's style or approach on the singles might be described as free or spontaneous (and therefore preferred) by some listeners. Others might find the clarity and control of interpretation and sound that is heard on the albums to be preferable. Nevertheless, except for minor variations in vocal inflection or melodic fill, her performances of the basic melodies and rhythms usually are quite similar from recording to recording.[21]

Singer and comedienne Fanny Brice is the subject of *Funny Girl*, and Fanny's son-in-law Ray Stark produced the show. Bringing the part-biographical, part-fictional story to the stage was, typically, a drawn-out process (beginning long before the star had been signed), but Barbra found the process of rehearsing and finalizing the show, with all the necessary experimentation, very appealing. The process probably also served as a school of sorts for the minimally experienced leading lady. Among the musicians involved with the production was rehearsal pianist Marvin Hamlisch, who collaborated again with Streisand years later as composer and conductor.

Funny Girl opened at New York's Winter Garden Theatre on 26 March 1964 and featured Streisand until December 1965.[22] Shortly thereafter, Barbra opened in a London run of the show, but her overseas performance schedule was cut short by the impending birth of her son. Jason Emanuel Gould was born on 29 December 1966. The success of *Funny Girl* brought Barbra to the attention of an even wider audience. She appeared on the covers of both *Life* (22 May) and *Time* (10 April) in the spring of 1964, and despite the unconventional wardrobe she wore in early club engagements, she was named to the International Best Dressed List in 1965 (a fact she chose to include among the awards listed in the 1991 *Just for the Record* booklet).

Streisand signed a contract in 1964 with CBS for several television specials, which meant that she was well on her way toward conquering all of the media available for singers and actresses.[23] In April 1965 she starred in *My Name Is Barbra*, which was unusual in style and format (three one-act segments, the first two with story-line themes and the last a miniature concert) and lacked guest stars. The show garnered Emmy Awards that fall, including one for Outstanding Individual Achievement by an Actor or Performer for Barbra. A second special for CBS was broadcast on 30 March 1966; its title, *Color Me Barbra*, reflected new technology of the day as color television made its way into American homes. Other television specials followed in 1967 and 1974. *The Belle of 14th Street* allowed Streisand to stretch her acting muscles (both physical and vocal) while playing a variety of characters in vaudeville-like sketches. *Barbra Streisand and Other Musical Instruments* was perhaps ahead of its time musically in presenting her familiar repertoire in unusual multicultural stylings. Neither of these specials attracted the critical acclaim of the first two, and both included guest stars. Jason Robards participated in several *Belle* scenes, and Ray Charles joined Barbra for a duet in *Instruments*. These would be the last Streisand specials originally designed for television until her behind-the-scenes production efforts in the 1990s. (Some of her sporadic concert work appeared after-the-fact on television and as videos as that format became more common.)

Looming on the horizon was another forum for Streisand to tackle. Since her youth, an important goal had been to appear in the movies, and that opportunity came as a multi-picture deal with *Funny Girl* producer Ray Stark. The first project was a film version of that same Fanny Brice story—with her stage experience, who better than Barbra knew the character and the show? The movie was released in September 1968, and in what was becoming a pattern of first-time success, Barbra received an Academy Award for Best Actress the next spring (there was a tie between Streisand and Katherine Hepburn in *The Lion in Winter*). Streisand's other film commitments (*Hello Dolly*; *On a Clear Day You Can See Forever*; and a non-musical *The Owl and the Pussycat*) were released in quick succession under the Rastar banner. In the midst of this flurry of activity, Barbra's marriage dissolved.[24]

Streisand accepted a few public singing engagements and appeared occasionally as a guest on television in the late 1960s and early 1970s. These performances included a massive outdoor concert in Central Park in 1968 (later aired as a television special), a short stint in Las Vegas at the International Hotel in 1969, and *The Burt Bacharach Special* in 1971. The International engagement was for the opening of that hotel and casino, and Barbra began her show with "I've Got Plenty of Nothin'," an incongruous theme to associate with Las Vegas and with Streisand's rapidly rising salary scale.[25]

Increasingly Barbra's attention and energies were aimed at the privacy and limited time frame of recording studio and film work.[26] Her movies of the 1970s included comedies such as *What's Up Doc?* and *The Main Event*, musicals such as *Funny Lady* and *A Star Is Born*, and love stories such as *The Way We Were*. Barbra became more involved with the financial and behind-the-scenes details of film making with *Up the Sandbox*, which was produced in 1972 by First Artists, a company she formed with Paul Newman and Sidney Poitier in 1969. The film's plot focused on concerns of women in the 1970s. It was not successful at the box office, but Barbra remains proud of the work and the message.[27] Deeper involvement in film production came with *A Star Is Born* and her relationship with paramour Jon Peters in the mid-1970s. Barbra won her second Oscar for composing the love theme for *Star* entitled "Evergreen," with words by Paul Williams.[28] Her technique with composition and notation is unclear; she uses musical vocabulary correctly in interviews but often remarks that she does not read music, an unexpected idea to associate with someone outspoken in her concern for detail.[29]

Many of Streisand's movies were financially successful, elements of her film work were praised by a number of sources for their artistic merit, and her fan base remained faithful. On the other hand, some industry insiders and some critics were vociferously uncomplimentary in their reactions, creating a rift between them and Barbra throughout the 1980s and 1990s. This conflict and her lack of success with personal Academy Award nominations for *Yentl* and *The Prince of Tides* (some would say "snubs"), have been the subject of many articles and press reports. The complicated interaction between the commentator on the one hand and the performer on the other comes into clear relief in Streisand's relationship with reviewers. She criticizes them for focusing on her life and personality in exclusion of her work; they find fault with what they view as inconsistent quality in her products. They scold about her propensity for control and perfectionism; she declares that her fans deserve her best and complete energies. She states that she finds the directorial role to require soft-spoken nurturing of all involved; they accuse her of too much camera focus on her own character. The debate goes on, and apparently it is not something Streisand can ignore. She often comments and writes about it, even going so far as to include some of her thoughts in her vocal repertoire.[30]

Although her public vocal performances virtually came to a halt in the 1970s and 1980s, new Streisand record albums and compact discs appeared regularly.[31] Various popular-music styles and distinct experimental ventures are evident during this period, and Barbra began a string of successful duets with partners whose individual singing styles varied greatly (Neil Diamond compared to Donna Summer, for example). High industry chart ratings for two songs, "The Way We Were" (1973) and "Evergreen" (1977), both love ballads, brought Streisand her most significant radio exposure since "People" in the mid-1960s. Her first foray into the music-video arena (a natural extension for an actress and film director) is seen in "Left in the Dark" from her *Emotion* album of 1984. Despite this new attention to inter-arts communication, she retained her interest in melody-based songs with meaningful and sensitive lyrics that could be acted. As with her films, listeners can observe Barbra's greater inclination to include messages of advocacy in her recordings after 1969. At the same time, hints of autobiographical information become increasingly prevalent in songs and liner notes, regardless of her preference for privacy and infrequent interviews.[32]

During the 1970s, the financial rewards of her career afforded Barbra more time and material resources to delve deeply into her hobby of buying and redecorating houses.[33] The results of her efforts with her New York and California homes were shown to viewers of *House Beautiful* in August 1974, *Architectural Digest* in May 1978 and December 1993, and *The Barbara Walters Special* on ABC television in the fall of 1976. In the 1990s Streisand made a concerted effort to cut back on some of her material goods with a Christie's sale of many of her art deco and art nouveau pieces and Tiffany lamps. The sale reaped more profit than had been predicted, topping $5 million on the first day.[34] Shortly thereafter Barbra donated the twenty-four acres and multiple houses of her Malibu compound, valued at $15 million, to the Santa Monica Mountains Conservancy.[35]

Fewer Streisand movies reached the screen during the 1980s and 1990s as she was being more selective in her projects and more involved in their drawing-board-to-final-edit creation. The prime representative of this approach from the 1980s was *Yentl*, a film she co-wrote, produced, and directed, and in which she starred. *Yentl* is worthy of comment on many levels and for many reasons. It is a musical on a rather serious subject (a young woman in early-twentieth-century Eastern Europe has a desire for education and other freedoms prohibited by tradition, but also is interested in love and family) in which only the main character sings. The music is used to convey inner thinking, an appropriate technique since the Yentl character, a young woman, masquerades as a young man. The score contains no potential pop-music hits and no flashy dance numbers; the music is tightly woven into the overall fabric. *Yentl* also was very personal for Streisand in its themes about the joy of learning, Jewish traditions, women's rights, and longing for the support of a father.[36] Some of her other films (both as star and director) also dealt with serious human relationships (*Nuts*, *The Prince of Tides*), but romantic comedies were not neglected (*The Mirror Has Two Faces*). In 1992 Barbra received a Crystal Award for her significant contributions to the entertainment industry; she also received other film honors, including a Golden Globe for directing *Yentl* and the ShowEast Filmmaker of the Year award in 1996.[37]

Beginning with the release of *The Broadway Album* in 1985, Streisand embarked on a purposeful return to the musical roots of her repertoire: ballads, standards, and showtunes. Although record executives were skeptical about the financial viability of such a collection, it quickly climbed the sales charts and brought Barbra her first Grammy for Best Pop Female Vocalist in twenty-four years.[38] In 1992, after releasing a four-compact-disc, retrospective boxed set entitled *Just for the Record*, Streisand renewed her recording contract with Sony Music Entertainment, then the parent company of Columbia Records. Her thirty-year relationship with Columbia had proved profitable, and an article in *Billboard* reported that the new deal was worth at least $60 million over five years. The writer also noted:

At 50, Streisand is now in a league with a younger generation of superstars. . . . [But] unlike Madonna [and Michael] Jackson . . . Streisand's career was launched in the pre-Beatles era . . . just as rock'n'roll was becoming the pop sound of choice among youth.[39]

Her secure preeminence in the popular-song domain was further acknowledged by her receipt of the Grammy Legend award in 1992, a Lifetime Achievement award from the National Academy of Recording Arts and Sciences in 1995 (at age 53), and critical and popular acclaim for her return to the concert stage in 1994.[40] In 1997 the Recording Association of America listed Streisand as the female artist with the most gold and platinum records. Although perhaps still anxious about her own vocal work in the 1990s, she remarked several times on the satisfaction and joy that she received through coming to terms with her fear of returning to public performance, the audience's warm reception for her singing, and the consistent support of her fans. This period of her musical life may have brought her commercial achievements and her artistic success into a happy convergence.

Since the late 1960s, Barbra publicly has voiced her views on political and social issues.[41] Contradicting a 1966 article in *Time* where she reportedly admitted to knowing little about Vietnam or black power because of the time she spent on her career,[42] Streisand has become a staunch and financially supportive Democrat. She actively champions concerns related to children, human rights, health issues such as AIDS, and the environment. In fact, most of her rare live performances over the years have been in support of political and social issues: a concert for presidential candidate George McGovern in 1972, participation in the celebration of Israel's thirtieth anniversary in 1978, and the *One Voice* concert given at her Malibu home on 6 September 1986 to raise money for Democratic congressional candidates. In the mid-1980s she formed the Streisand Foundation to provide monetary assistance for liberal causes and used her considerable drawing power to bring attention to other fund-raising events. Her beliefs and her desire to raise social awareness were the impetus behind the verbal links connecting the songs of her public concerts in 1994, even though she acknowledged that it was probable that not everyone in the audience shared her point of view.[43]

Barbra's interests in learning and study led to financial support for (among others) the Emanuel Streisand School of the Pacific Jewish Center, an endowed chair in cardiology at the University of California at Los Angeles, a professorship of gender studies at the University of Southern California, the establishment of the Virginia Clinton Kelley (mother of President Bill Clinton) Breast Cancer Foundation at the University of Arkansas, and a Jewish Women's Studies Center at Brandeis University.[44] Realizing the educational potential of television movies, Streisand also lent her behind-the-scenes skills and name to productions such as *Serving in Silence*, a 1995 film based on the story of Margarethe Cammermeyer, who was dismissed from the military for her sexual orientation.[45]

Although usually rather reclusive, speaking publicly only in promotion of her films and recordings or as an advocate, Streisand granted several interviews in the mid-1990s.[46] Likewise, as her social consciousness blossomed and became better known, she spoke at the Women in Film celebration in New York in 1986, and she delivered a speech entitled "The Artist as Citizen" at the John F. Kennedy School for Government at Harvard University on 3 February 1995.[47] These appearances, in part, seem related to Streisand's developing maturity, to her growing sense of spirituality and comfort with herself, and to the urgency she felt about many issues.[48] Barbra embarked on a new personal relationship with actor James Brolin as she was finishing work on her film *The Mirror Has Two Faces*. They were married two years later, on 1 July 1998. Music related to their relationship appeared on Streisand's *A Love Like Ours* compact disc, which was issued by Columbia in September 1999.

Barbra Streisand has achieved a great deal in the decades since she stepped into the international spotlight. While not without her detractors, her talents and stamina brought acknowledgment as a propitious film maker, an influential societal leader, and the singer that many young women want to emulate in their musical-theatre aspirations.[49] Her commercial and artistic success is marked in a variety of ways, from a long list of industry awards, to indisputable financial tallies, to flattery in the form of imitation, to expanded marketing of Streisand memorabilia in the 1990s. Indeed, her success might even be substantiated by the depth and callousness of the criticism she evokes; interestingly, the criticism often stems from her choice of or approach to a project rather than her talents.

In music, Streisand acquired her superstar status without the usual steps to fame (frequent public performances and top-40 radio hits), accomplishing it instead through the sale of albums and compact discs and by injecting her music with very personal stylistic traits and interpretations. Despite her youthful goal to become an actress, and although her recordings are enhanced by her acting and directing skills, Streisand's historical significance might prove to be based more on her singing and her rapport with a concert audience than on other facets of her work. Nevertheless, the consistency of her performance style amidst constant change around her, the multiplicity of her activities (both professional and social), her commercial success, and her forceful celebrity status play major roles in the overall assessment of her historical and artistic place. Streisand's life and career clearly exhibit two philosophies that might be stated: *I'll do it my way—I'll be faithful to my own truth no matter the consequences* and *Keep them wanting more—don't give away too much too soon*. These beliefs, in fact, both attract and repel the public; many appreciate but many dislike her vulnerable and insecure, yet strong, risk-taker image. Through it all, her fans consistently are drawn to her work and to her personality, probably for reasons as varied as the fans themselves. According to Oprah Winfrey, who is similarly famous and influential, Barbra exudes the kind of quest-for-her-best image that is inspirational to others. Streisand's own response to talk of her "star" or "legend" status is to call herself a "perpetual student" or "a work in progress," underscoring her need for continued work, growth, and support despite past accolades.[50]

NOTES

1. Barbra Streisand, interview by Oprah Winfrey, *The Oprah Winfrey Show*, ABC television, 11 November 1996.

2. Dave Marsh, *The New Rolling Stone Record Guide* (New York: Rolling Stone Press, 1983), s.v. "Barbra Streisand," by Stephen Holden.

3. A survey indicates Streisand is among the top-ten people mentioned in gossip columns for both 1996 and 1997. See Frank DeGiacomo, "New York's Most Wanted," *New York Observer*, 22 December 1997, 1, 57, 61–63.

4. Barbra Streisand, interview with unidentified reporter, compact disc, *Barbra Streisand Rarities* vol. 5 (private release by *Barbrabilia*, Arlington Heights, Illinois, 1997).

5. Of course all performances, whether they are presented in public or in the recording studio, are "live." Succinct terminology is difficult when writing about Streisand, and in some cases it has not yet evolved in popular-music scholarship in general. Some of her concert performances, which could be called "public" (to distinguish them from studio work), were actually for rather limited audiences of invited guests—in other words, not really public. Herein the term *public* will indicate a concert performance open to all (usually for the price of admission), and *live* will indicate either a public performance that is limited in audience scope or a reference to a concert taped for later recorded sales (such as Streisand's *Live Concert at the Forum* album). The term *live* often is used more widely than this in popular-music discussion, even though the implication of its proper meaning is rather ludicrous. It indicates a performance that was not done in the privacy of a studio and perhaps one that is intended for wide-scale commercial release as a recording.

6. An essay about Streisand by Jerome Robbins, production supervisor for *Funny Girl* on Broadway, has a subheading: "Consider Her: a tug-of-war goes on in all departments." He goes on to enumerate many conflicting sides of her personality, her mannerisms, and her rehearsal techniques, all of which are heightened by her undeniable talent. See Roddy McDowell, ed., *Double Exposure* (New York: Delacorte Press, 1966), 51–53.

7. Streisand certainly is not alone in her interests in political and social concerns. Many celebrities lend financial and "star-power" support to various causes, and in an era of pervasive media influence, politicians find their efforts and visibility useful. Perhaps no celebrity has drawn as much praise and criticism for this kind of work as Barbra Streisand has in the 1990s.

8. Wherever possible, insight into her personal life and thoughts will come through Streisand's own words from videotaped or televised interviews or words

she has written. She dislikes being misquoted and suggests that much print material about her is rehashed (often incorrectly) from one article to the next. See Barbra Streisand, interview by Larry King, *Larry King Live*, CNN television, 6 February 1992. While Streisand has not penned an autobiography, more than twenty books have been written about her life and film career, although none is authorized. See the bibliography for a selected listing.

9. Judy Klemesrud, "Barbra and Rozie's Mother Used to Hope for Her Own Name Up in Lights," *New York Times*, 24 February 1970, L:2; Diana Kind, interview by unidentified reporter, compact disc, *Barbra Streisand Rarities* vol. 5 (private release by *Barbrabilia*, Arlington Heights, Illinois, 1997); Barbra Streisand, interview by Jane Pauley, "The Way She Is," *Dateline*, NBC television, 12 November 1996; Barbra Streisand, interview by Katie Couric, *Today*, NBC television, 12 November 1996.

10. Barbra decided early in her career to keep her own name, but changed the spelling of her first name. See Arthur Alpert, "Barbra Sticks by Her Name—Wants Friends 'To Know It's Me,' " *New York Telegram and Sun*, 24 May 1961, B:2. The two songs Barbra recorded in 1955 were hits in the 1930s, 1940s, and 1950s. "You'll Never Know" was recorded by Alice Faye, Betty Grable, Dick Haymes, and Ginger Rogers among others. "Zing" was recorded by Judy Garland and Doris Day. Diana Kind is heard singing "Second Hand Rose" on Barbra's 1991 *Just for the Record*. See also Barbra Streisand, accompanying booklet for *Just for the Record*, compact disc 44111 (Sony Music Entertainment, 1991), 7. The year 1955 also saw the rise of the first national rock-and-roll hit, "Rock Around the Clock" by Bill Haley and the Comets. Barbra's musical interests would remain out of step with many of her young American peers.

11. Huvert Saal, "Lion's Cub," *Newsweek* (29 December 1969): 59; Rick Mitz, "Sibling Rock," *Stereo Review* (December 1976): 88–91; David Shire, interview by author, Muncie, Indiana, 4 March 1998.

12. Her high school yearbook mentions Freshman Chorus and Choral Club under her photo and name, see James Spada, *Barbra: The First Decade* (Secaucus, New Jersey: Citadel Press, 1974), 10. Barbra Streisand, interview by Larry King, *Larry King Live*, CNN television, 7 June 1995; Sherma Brizan, "Barbra Streisand's Generous Donation," [online] http://ns2.con2.com/~erashum/Streisand.html, 27 March 1997. See also an article on her 1994 donation to Detroit's Remus Robinson Middle School cited in *Detroit News Index 1994* (Ann Arbor: UMI, 1994), 1066.

13. Other information about these New York nightclubs is found in James Gavin, *Intimate Nights: The Golden Age of the New York Cabaret* (New York: Grove Weidenfeld, 1991). See pages 4 and 5 in particular, where the Blue Angel is described as "a lavishly upholstered room" featuring non-jazz performers, and the Bon Soir is described as "a mafia-owned cellar club" with "a gay bar inside the room that existed through police payoffs." The Lion also was a gay bar, a fact that Streisand did not realize when she entered the contest there. A part of her faithful following for years has been from the gay community, which is one of the similarities between her career and Judy Garland's. See Kevin Sessums, "Queen of Tides," *Vanity Fair* (September 1991): 174–179, 228–235 (especially 228). Barbra made similar comments about the Lion during an interview on the French television show *A La Una* during a *Yentl* promotional tour in the spring of 1984.

14. *Judy Garland and Friends*, videotape 338293 (Warner Bros., 1991).

15. Barbra Streisand, accompanying booklet for *Just for the Record*, compact disc 44111 (Sony Music Entertainment, 1991), 19. For a history of the show, the duet pairing, and the repertoire, see Coyne Steven Sanders, *Rainbow's End: The Judy Garland Show* (New York: William Morrow and Co., Inc., 1990); Mel Tormé, *The Other Side of the Rainbow* (New York: William Morrow and Co., Inc., 1970).

16. Many years later Dennen wrote a book entitled *My Life with Barbra* (Amherst, New York: Prometheus Books, 1997). It contains very little detailed discussion of music or her singing.

17. Barbra Streisand, accompanying booklet for *Just for the Record*, compact disc 44111 (Sony Music Entertainment, 1991), 29; Barbra is heard on an Arlen album, *Harold Sings Arlen (with Friend)*, as noted in Appendix C.

18. Barbra Streisand, accompanying booklet for *Just for the Record*, compact disc 44111 (Sony Music Entertainment, 1991), 17.

19. Leonard Feather, "Wild Girl, Wild Sound," *Melody Maker* (1 February 1964): 12.

20. Details on Streisand's personal Grammys and those won in connection with her recordings are found in Thomas O'Neil, *The Grammy Awards for the Record* (New York: Penguin Press, 1993).

21. These singles often are listed on Streisand memorabilia or discography internet sites such as the Barbra Streisand Music Guide (see bibliography). See also Steve Thacker, "Her Name Is Barbra," *The Record Collector* (October 1997): 77–85; Nellie Bly, *Barbra Streisand The Untold Story* (New York: Windsor Publishing, 1994), 336–337. I thank composers/arrangers Raphael Crystal and Cynthia Miller for their comments comparing the early singles with album versions.

22. Many articles were written about her success and her career-to-date after the opening of *Funny Girl*. See for example, "She's a Calculated Kook," *New York Daily News*, 26 April 1964, II:12; John S. Wilson, "A Kook from Madagascar," *High Fidelity* (May 1964): 43–45, 103. The reference to Madagascar comes from the imaginative biographical note Barbra wrote for the *I Can Get It for You Wholesale* playbill. Her creativity caused a stir, as was noted in "The Playbull," *Theatre Arts* (November 1963): 9. According to that source, Streisand threatened to insist on blank space in the program for *Funny Girl* if not allowed to submit biographical material of her choice.

23. An article in *Time* relates that her ten-year contract (the longest in television history to that date) was worth $5 million, that it called for her to work as little or as much as she wanted, and that she retained artistic control: see the issue from (3 July 1964): 62. The writer also reported that Barbra seemed rather indifferent about her salary figure. Under Martin Erlichman's leadership, and often in partnership with him, Streisand has established a web of companies that are related to the publishing and production facets of her work. For example, Emanuel Music is named for her father and holds the copyright for several songs she recorded.

24. Elliott Gould achieved considerable fame in the movies in the 1970s, especially with the films *Bob & Carol & Ted & Alice* and *M*A*S*H*. See Judy Klemesrud, "Now Who's the Greatest Star?," *New York Times*, 5 October 1969, D:15.

25. Streisand's pay increases can be logged by tracing articles in *Billboard* and *Variety* magazines. A writer for *Billboard* learned from Martin Erlichman that Barbra earned $250 per week in 1961; $23,000 in 1962; $225,000 in 1963; and an

estimated $500,000 in 1964; see (11 July 1964): 20. By 1969, writers for *Variety* reported that she would earn $250,000 per week at the Las Vegas International Hotel and wondered what impact this would have on performer's salaries in other hotels; see (19 February 1969): 1, 76; (14 May 1969): 1, 74.

26. The 5 August 1969 issue of *Los Angeles Times* (IV:1, 4) includes a review of and an article about Barbra's International Hotel engagement. Charles Champlin found that the show had improved immensely over its run, that Barbra's concert was "a scintillating display of her gifts," and that she was beginning to fear the expectations of live audiences, preferring to be on a movie set instead. See also the bibliography.

27. Barbra Streisand, accompanying booklet for *Just for the Record*, compact disc 44111 (Sony Music Entertainment, 1991), 53.

28. This was not the first nor the last time Streisand would don the hat of composer or lyricist, see discography.

29. Composer, arranger, conductor David Shire suggests that, as a singer, Streisand's "incredible ears" help her to learn a song faster than reading notation would allow and that she always has been a composer and arranger, so to speak, for her own material, working out ideas with collaborators who can take care of the technical matters (David Shire, interview by author, Muncie, Indiana, 4 March 1998). Perhaps this is how she approached composition as well. It also may be a case of semantics (what is meant by "reading music"?) or of image or myth projection.

30. Her recordings of "Don't Believe What You Read" and "I'm Still Here" on *Superman* and *Barbra: The Concert*, respectively, are examples.

31. Streisand participated in sporadic benefits like one for the Special Olympics held at the Kennedy Center for the Performing Arts in association with the 1975 premiere of *Funny Lady*. The show aired on ABC television as a special entitled "Funny Girl to Funny Lady."

32. Several articles attempted to point out the changes Streisand was experiencing in her personal life during her late 20s and 30s. See for example, Grover Lewis, "The Jeaning of Barbra Streisand," *Rolling Stone* (24 June 1971): 16; Lawrence Grobel, "Playboy Interview: Barbra Streisand," *Playboy* (October 1977): 79–107, 193–200.

33. Astute listeners will find what might be a subtle reference to this hobby in Streisand's recording of "The Man I Love" on *Back to Broadway*. At one point the original lyric indicates "he'll" build a house, whereas Barbra's version claims "we'll" do the building!

34. Barbra Streisand, interview by Barbara Walters, *20/20*, ABC television, 19 November 1993; Barbara Kantrowitz, "Out Goes the Nouveau," *Newsweek* (7 March 1994): 69; Andrew Decker, "The Way She Was," *New York* (7 March 1994): 60–61; "Streisand Goods Fetch $5.8 Million," *USA Today*, 4 March 1994, D:2.

35. Typical of her actions, this gift fostered praise, criticism, and debate, especially regarding stipulations for use of the property and related financial matters. See articles that appeared over several months in the *Los Angeles Times* beginning on 18 November 1993. Several years later, the bequest still attracted comment. Walter Scott's "Personality Parade" in *Parade Magazine* of 24 May 1998 mentioned that the Conservancy continued to face economic problems, but that they were partially offset by the popularity of tours of the property.

36. *Yentl* drew considerable attention from the press, in part because of Streisand's multiple responsibilities and in part for its storyline. Many articles were written that went beyond the typical publicity interview or critical review. See for example, Andrew Sarris, "Yentl Schmentl—Sing, Barbra," *Village Voice* (29 November 1983): 55; Stephen Wiest, "Streisand and Women's Ordination," *Christianity Today* (10 August 1984): 68; Marcia Pally and Harlan Jacobson, "Kaddish for the Fading Image of Jews in Film," and "Singer, Not the Song," *Film Comment* (January–February 1984): 49–55; Joseph Gelmis, "Hollywood's New Heroines," *Detroit News*, 11 March 1984, 7E; Garrett Stewart, "Singer Sung: Voice as Avowal in Streisand's *Yentl*," *Mosaic* 18, no. 4 (1985): 135–58.

37. A filmography is included in the "Barbra Streisand Special Issue" of *The Hollywood Reporter* (18–20 October 1996), as are other articles on her films. As with her recordings, critics and colleagues have been both extremely complimentary and very harsh in their reactions to her work. There rarely seems to be a middle ground.

38. A documentary about this album, entitled "Putting It Together: The Making of *The Broadway Album*," was aired on HBO television in January 1986 and later was released on video by CBS/Fox.

39. Bev Lichtman, "Barbra/Sony Pact," *Billboard* (26 December 1992): 5, 99.

40. There has been considerable debate, especially in the press among critics, about the meaning and validity of the Grammy Awards given by NARAS. See for example Jon Pareles, "How to Win a Grammy, or at Least a Nomination," *New York Times*, 23 February 1992, 2:31; Robert Hilburn, "Grammy Perspective," *Los Angeles Times*, 23 February 1992, CAL:8 (he writes that the Academy favors "mainstream" bestsellers); Steve Morse, "Grammy List Runs From Class to Camp," *Boston Globe*, 6 January 1995, 49; Richard Harrington, *Washington Post*, 26 February 1995, G:4; Steve Dollar, "Grammys Changing but Daring They're Not," *Atlanta Journal Constitution*, 26 February 1995, N:1. These representative articles come from the two years Streisand was given special awards, although she is not the focus of any of the articles. While acknowledging that this debate is important and relevant, the giving and receiving of Grammy Awards remains one barometer of success in the recording industry and is pertinent to Streisand's career.

41. Barbra's name is listed in an advertisement for a "one performance only" gala entitled *Broadway for Peace 1968* printed in *New York Times*, 12 January 1968, 22. The ad mentions that the show's proceeds will support the campaigns of congressmen who oppose the war in Vietnam.

42. "Stars Poifect," *Time* (19 August 1966): 64.

43. A chart tabulating her giving and use of music in support of political issues is found in *Variety* (21 October 1996): S48.

44. Streisand received an Honorary Doctorate from Brandeis in 1995.

45. Streisand also produced *The Long Island Incident*, the story of Congresswoman Carolyn McCarthy. The 1998 film criticized the National Rifle Association and advocated strong gun-control legislation; it provoked a heated rebuttal from Streisand's fellow actor Charlton Heston, then a candidate for the NRA's presidency.

46. Perhaps one of the most emotional interviews was Streisand's appearance on *The Rosie O'Donnell Show* on 21 November 1997 on NBC television. O'Donnell is an unabashed Streisand fan, as had been O'Donnell's late mother.

47. Much was written by columnists and editorialists, mostly negative, about her speech at Harvard. See for example, Andrew Ferguson, "From the Mouth of Babs," *National Review* (20 March 1995): 84; Margaret Carlson, "Of Barbs and Barbra," *Time* (13 February 1995): 51; Kristiana Helmick, "Barbra Streisand Brings Her Advocacy to Harvard," *The Christian Science Monitor* (6 February 1995): 14. The text of the speech was available for many months at www.artsusa.org. Barbra responded to criticism of her involvement with political issues in taped and print interviews such as Robert Scheer, "Barbra Streisand, Breaking Another Barrier Mixing Politics and Hollywood," *Los Angeles Times*, 23 May 1993, M:3, and Barbra Streisand, interview with Larry King, *Larry King Live*, CNN television, 7 June 1995. See also Clarke Taylor, "Streisand: Women in Film have 'Special Role,' " *Los Angeles Times*, 3 May 1986, CAL:1. The text of Streisand's "Film" speech is printed in her 1994 concert tour program and in *Premiere* (Women in Hollywood Special Issue 1993): 27. That magazine also provides interesting insight into Barbra's perceived power in Hollywood politics by way of a chart by Christine Spines entitled "It's the Women, Stupid." The chart has columns of information concerning four of the leading political groups in Hollywood and subheadings for topics such as "membership" and "accomplishments." One of the subheadings is entitled "Streisand connection."

48. Claudia Dreifus, "Life Like a Love Song," *New York Times*, 11 November 1997, B:1. See also Barbra Streisand, interview by Barbara Walters, *20/20*, ABC television, 19 November 1993. During that interview, Barbra comments on selling her art collection and donating her Malibu compound as ways to simplify her life, her own philosophies on trusting God and using film to reveal messages about life, and her desire to be of service to humanity.

49. Bill Reed, interview by author, telephone, Muncie, Indiana, 24 June 1997.

50. Barbra Streisand, interview by Oprah Winfrey, *The Oprah Winfrey Show*, ABC television, 11 November 1996; Barbra Streisand, interview with Barbara Walters, *20/20*, ABC television, 19 November 1993; Barbra Streisand, acceptance remarks for Grammy Legend Award, "The Thirty-Fourth Annual Grammy Awards," CBS television, 25 February 1992.

Chapter 2

The Early Years: An Actress through Song

On the way to the audition [at the Bon Soir], I remember very clearly walking to the subway thinking, "This is the beginning of something."[1]

A study of Barbra Streisand's vocal career necessarily begins with a brief historical overview and a discussion of related style terminology.[2] The complex history of American popular song in the first half of the twentieth century might be summarized thus: the turn-of-the-century Tin Pan Alley sheet music era (with its ragtime and ethnic elements); the so-called "jazz" and theatre influence on songs of the 1910s and 1920s as promoted on radio and phonograph; and the Golden Age of popular song, especially those heard during the 1930s and 1940s in musical theatre and film, played by big bands (or dance bands), and broadcast on shows like *Your Hit Parade*. In each period, works that soon would become standards came from the creative minds of Jerome Kern, Irving Berlin, Cole Porter, George and Ira Gershwin, Richard Rodgers (with partners Lorenz Hart and Oscar Hammerstein II), Harold Arlen, and many more.

The popularity of rhythm and blues (and then rock and roll) significantly altered the musical scene of the late 1940s and 1950s, especially with its characteristic instrumentation and rhythm, intense vocal delivery, and aggressive lyrics. But the importance of song stylists continued in the widely varied approaches and repertoire of Bing Crosby, Frank Sinatra, Nat King Cole, Ella Fitzgerald, Patti Page, Harry Belafonte, and Judy Garland among a host of others. Likewise, an emphasis on smoother vocalization was prominent in the recordings of some of the rock-and-roll idols of the late 1950s and early 1960s such as Paul Anka. Radio and phonograph records were the major commercial media for performers, with the contrast between musical styles sometimes reflected in the record market's two main factions: the pop single versus the long-playing record (or album).[3] Programs like *Your Hit Parade* eventually became irrelevant as listeners wanted to hear a specific performer, not just any singer's version of a popular song.

Whether she was aware of it, this is the popular-song heritage of Barbra Streisand growing up in Brooklyn in the 1950s. In 1959, the year of her graduation from high school, the first phase of rock and roll ended, and America's more subdued and varied listening interests are indicated by the top-40 singles and the best-selling albums of the day. "Mack the Knife" by Bobby Darin, "Battle of New Orleans" from Johnny Horton, and Frankie Avalon's "Venus" topped the charts, and popular albums included soundtracks from *Gigi* and *South Pacific* and compilations by the Kingston Trio and Mitch Miller.[4] Jazz characteristics also flavored popular music in works like the theme from *Peter Gunn* by Henry Mancini and "Misty" recorded by Johnny Mathis. As Streisand began to make her mark in popular song in the 1960s, the commercial mix comprised a number of styles and an integration of stylistic markets. The styles included folk-pop, rock, country and western, Motown, Broadway, and a continuation of the Tin Pan Alley legacy with singers like Sinatra, Garland, Mathis, Andy Williams, and Tony Bennett. In most cases, the song continued to be important, but so too was the individual singer's interpretation.

Nomenclature for and the stature of this popular-song repertoire changed between the 1950s and 1960s and continued to evolve throughout the rest of the century. The evolution is observed in various situations, from the way indexes like *Reader's Guide to Periodical Literature* listed (or chose to ignore) critical reviews of pop albums, to an expanded number of *Billboard* charts and Grammy categories, to radio-format and critical-review terminology. The simple but too-inclusive moniker "Popular Music" was swept away in the 1960s and 1970s by other imprecise terms like Top 40, Middle of the Road, Hot 100, and Sweetheart Pop.[5] This change indicated in part the commercial power of popular song, and *High Fidelity* announced in its February 1977 issue the addition of a new "Backbeat" section to provide greater coverage for the growing contemporary popular-music scene. In the 1990s, some of Streisand's music (and that of other singers like Barry Manilow, Linda Ronstadt, Billy Joel, Neil Diamond, and the veteran Mathis) was identified by radio-format and trade-paper terms like Adult Contemporary, Mainstream, or Easy Listening, or might be promoted with advertisement phraseology such as "relaxing favorites of the seventies, eighties, and nineties," and "soft rock."

A vein of traditional popular song also continued in other Streisand recordings and in those of singers such as Michael Feinstein, Harry Connick Jr., and Natalie Cole. Although a considerable portion of the media and market-place attention of the second half of the twentieth century was aimed at rock, country, and rap, the popular-song consumer (for both contemporary and traditional styles) remained a potent force. This was particularly evident in the 1980s and 1990s by the number of previously released pop albums successfully re-issued in the compact-disc format, the "crossover" into the traditional popular-song market of singers not usually associated with that repertoire, and the renewed popularity of singers like Tony Bennett.

The sales figures related to Barbra's recordings and the faithfulness of her large international fan base precluded any belief that her style of performance (and in many cases, her preferred repertoire) had become passé.[6] During the early years of her career, those covered by this chapter, her repertoire focus was on "quality theatrical standards and nightclub songs," or put another way, the songs "of the American show-biz tradition . . . Broadway ballads and nightclub standards."[7]

In the years between 1962 and 1967 Barbra Streisand was finding her voice and her musical style, much of the time in full view of theatre, nightclub, or television-studio audiences. Barbra's choice of material and basic show format were not unusual for those settings, but her musical preferences (influenced by her desire for an acting career) ran counter to those of many her age.[8] In fact, one author suggests that she "outrebelled the rock revolutionaries by rebelling against rock."[9] On several occasions Streisand has acknowledged listening to *Your Hit Parade* as a youth, and she has mentioned Helen Morgan, Billie Holiday, Ella Fitzgerald, and Judy Garland as important singers of their day, but she apparently never has commented on any direct influence or inspiration.

For descriptive and cataloging purposes during this period of her career, Streisand's repertoire can be divided into four large categories.[10] These categories are malleable as to their definitions and content, allowing songs to fit simultaneously under more than one heading, or to move from one heading to another, depending on the musical circumstances and the intent of the analytical discussion. Likewise, a category heading remains intact, even if the musical style of the material included within it changes over time. For example, a love ballad written in the 1940s might have significant musical differences from a love ballad written in 1975, but the two still could exhibit basic similarities. Or, Streisand might sing a ballad in a manner causing it to be placed under the character-song heading. The text of a song could determine its categorization, the musical content or arrangement can suggest placement, or Streisand's individual interpretation might point to a certain category—the plan merely allows further organization of a vast quantity of material. A broadly conceived description of the four categories follows:

Character songs: those that she clearly approaches as an actress playing a specific role (novelty or serious), whether the song is actually from a show, like "Who's Afraid of the Big, Bad Wolf?" (see Discography Appendix B for album location and composer information).[11]

Belt or *Torch songs*: those that require a fullness of tone and dynamic level and an attitude of defiance, sarcasm, or submissive or unrequited love, like "Cry Me a River" or "My Man."[12]

Lyric songs: those that differ from the pop norm in formal plan, orchestration and arrangement, melodic demand, or textual content, for example "Jenny Rebecca." Many lyric songs rarely receive top-40 radio broadcast time since they do not meet usual expectations of length, content, or performance style.[13]

Love ballads: not narrative tales as in folk music but rather slow, legato romantic songs, often with an unobtrusive beat, such as "Why Did I Choose You?"

Streisand's primary consideration in selecting repertoire is whether a song text lends itself to character development or character interpretation. Any song, placed under any of the categories outlined above, will likely contain some element of characterization in her interpretation and performance. This observation was noticeable immediately in her career; already in 1963 on *The Second Barbra Streisand Album* liner, composer Jule Styne concluded that Streisand's ability to find a character within each song (through careful attention to the lyric) was similar to the finesse necessary for a quality presentation of a full-length play. Many years later, after recording "With One Look" from Andrew Lloyd Webber's *Sunset Boulevard*, Barbra wrote, "When I first heard this song, I was immediately taken with its strong melody. I couldn't wait to sing it—act it. The lyrics gave me the chance to play the character."[14]

Streisand's work in two Harold Rome shows in 1962, *Pins and Needles* and *I Can Get It for You Wholesale*, led to her first recording sessions. *Wholesale* opened on Broadway on 22 March 1962, and Barbra, in the secondary role of a secretary, was the highlight of the show.[15] The secretary, Miss Marmelstein, sings in several ensemble songs including "The Ballad of the Garment Trade," "I'm Not a Well Man," and "What Are They Doing to Us Now?," and has one solo number, "Miss Marmelstein." Reviewers commented on Streisand's fine presentation of the distraught Girl-Friday Marmelstein,[16] and indeed upon listening to the cast album, several points are worthy of mention. Her solo is clearly a character song. Streisand's delivery of the complicated, wordy lyric is admirable and is helped by its short textual phrases. She achieves timbral variety through interspersed spoken words or lines, a touch of vocal growl, and an impassioned, almost disgusted forcefulness on the final word, *bust*. In fact, when compared to the regularity of the rhythms in the printed vocal score (realizing that the printed source often follows rather than precedes performance), her recitative-like approach allows Barbra to sing with considerable rhythmic freedom.[17] She places some words off, rather than on, the beat or reserves the final word of a measure until the chord change of the next. Her consistent (if often gentle) enunciation of the final consonant sound helps with textual clarity and rhythmic definition. Underscoring Barbra's singing, Sid Ramin's orchestration begins simply, but expands later to support the secretary's growing frustration over her lack of sex appeal in the office.

Equally interesting is Streisand the ensemble singer in "What Are They Doing to Us Now?" As her character begins the robust finale, the opening tempo is slow, again allowing her considerable rhythmic flexibility with the sarcastic text set in an angular melody. As two-part melodic patterns are presented by the voice, the English horn interrupts while beginning an upward sequence of melodic fragments that harmonically heightens the sense of distress. A short-lived change to a major harmony occurs on the word *hoping*, and Streisand expands her sound into a full dynamic level and rich tone on this melodic climax. Her skill in coloring individual words for emotional or story development is apparent on words such as *quizzical*. On other words (for example, *say*) she quickly moves to and stays with the second of the paired vowel sounds of the diphthong, but the long "e" sound is not brighter or more nasal than the others surrounding it. As the tempo increases and the meter changes to five beats per measure, the chorus joins, but Barbra continues as vocal leader with an easily identified timbre. The irregular meter helps underscore the questions, insecurity, and ridicule of the text message.[18] Later Streisand sings alone on a harsher melodic section that continues with Eastern-European-like pitch and rhythmic flavors brought about through hints of modality and unsettling rhythms. She deviates from the printed vocal line by sliding off notes or with brief melodic inflections. As this section of the song continues, the melodic range moves upward through modulation, and eventually Barbra must hold a high E for several beats.[19] The note seems a stretch for her voice in the belt register, especially with the natural brightness of the second half of the *a* diphthong in the word *hey*, but is perhaps acceptable for the moment. Her voice sounds young and undeveloped, from the wistful introduction to the powerful belt sections, but the song aptly shows off her early comfort with style shifts.

Several songs from *Pins and Needles* involved Streisand, and again she was called upon as soloist, featured singer within a chorus, and ensemble singer.[20] The similarity between songs of *Wholesale* and *Pins* establishes Harold Rome's compositional framework. For example, Barbra solos on "Nobody Makes a Pass at Me," and the title makes clear that this character's desire for attention and affection remains unfulfilled, much like Miss Marmelstein's. Streisand delivers the text with clean diction, cast in a nasal Brooklyn accent, and uses word coloring and some spoken text to provide variety. On the second and fourth verses of the song, a guitar countermelody adds to the combination of melancholy and disappointment. Like the ending of "Miss Marmelstein," this song ends with a sarcastic, disgusted tone from the singer, especially on the word *pure*, which is underscored by a triplet-rhythm, kick-line-style accompaniment and spoken text. Earlier, as she switches from speaking to singing, Streisand allows a soft high note to crack, an effect that helps project the frustration of the character. Nevertheless amidst all of the character traits there are moments of rich warm vocal tone.

A different technique is required on the quartet (Barbra plus three men) "Four Little Angels." The mocking, ironic lyric about peace and the domination of one country or one people over another is parodied with a sweet vocal style (sometimes in stereotyped ethnic dialect—hers is oriental) and a waltz meter. Streisand's timbre and volume are restrained; she matches the overall sound well enough to be part of (rather than leader of) the ensemble. "What Good Is Love" offers a chance for Barbra to sing a blues-inflected torch song with a cabaret-type accompaniment (the whole album uses only a rhythm section for instrumentation). Her low range on the first chorus is full throated and reedy, and a hint of soon-to-be-characteristic Streisand phrasing is heard near the end as she melds one text phrase into the next, avoiding a breath at the punctuation point. "Doing the Reactionary" and "Sitting on Your Status Quo" exhibit Barbra's fast, narrow vibrato (usually placed at the end of long notes that conclude a phrase) and the interpretive variety she achieves with repeated words, as when those of the titles return intermittently.

Columbia Records released Streisand's first solo album, entitled *The Barbra Streisand Album*, in February of 1963.[21] It included an assortment of her club material arranged and conducted by Peter Matz.[22] The repertoire emphasizes character songs, belt or torch songs, and lyric songs (from the types outlined above) as borrowed from theatre and cabaret fare.[23] "Who's Afraid of the Big, Bad Wolf" affords the opportunity to play with a familiar tale full of interesting characters. Barbra begins with a child-like tone, but later switches to a robust timbre, opening her throat fully on some of the loud and high passages. There are many words to be sung, and she presents them cleanly with a variety of colors suitable for individual moments in the plot. Matz's arrangement for the band also supports the narrative, reminiscent of the orchestral piece *Peter and the Wolf* by Sergei Prokofiev, in which instruments represent characters of the story. Other character songs on the album include the obvious ("Come to the Supermarket") and the less obvious (her playful approach to "My Honey's Lovin' Arms" or "Keepin' Out of Mischief Now"). "My Honey's Lovin' Arms" was composed by Joseph Meyer and contains some of the jazz flavor often found in songs from the 1920s—a trait that fuses nicely with Streisand's characterization and rhythm and Matz's arrangement.

The belt or torch song mode is required for "Cry Me a River," a piece that also appears later on *A Happening in Central Park* and *Just for the Record*. This early arrangement by Matz for the album begins with Barbra and plucked string bass. Shortly, strings and brass and a rhythm section join, but the piece is divided into theatrical-like sections to better portray the bitter emotion. Near the end the meter is almost suspended allowing Barbra (backed by minimal instrumentation) to play with the text rhythmically in a sort of parlando style (leaning toward speech declamation).[24] The song ends with full ensemble and belt tone, although controlled dynamic gradations are frequent.

Careful study of Streisand's delivery of individual words illuminates the diversity of her palette as related to diction. Words ending in *er* (*river*, *never*) are sung as though spelled "uh" or "ah," a technique that many choral directors prefer. This approach may simply be natural dialect for Barbra, considering her birthplace.[25] Vowels or vowel combinations stretched over several beats go through a metamorphosis; they are almost "chewed" (in a non-pejorative sense). For example, *tear* is heard approximately as "ti-ee-er-ah."[26] She produces a throaty, catched release (without much pitch or tone) for some words to add a hint of a crying or choking effect, and her jaw sometimes closes before the end of a long note causing a change in the final vowel or soft-consonant sound.

"I'll Tell the Man in the Street" by Lorenz Hart and Richard Rodgers fits the description of lyric song with its long sweeping melody and more classical-style (as opposed to big-band) accompaniment. Barbra's clean and clear diction is created by making ending consonants distinguishable or by momentarily stopping the breath before initiating a new word that begins without a crisp sound (such as between *man* and *in* from the title words). Words like *shout*, *old*, or *sweet* are treated individually to help paint the picture, and Streisand's ability to project a musical tone (and a muffled vowel) even with her mouth virtually shut is noticeable again at the end of some long notes. To further establish the mood, she produces a sweet, less-nasal quality and considerable dynamic contrast.[27] Overall, her sound might be described as youthful but with a surprisingly seasoned control. Other lyric songs on the album include "Soon It's Gonna Rain" and "A Taste of Honey." The latter provides marked contrast to belt songs by exhibiting an almost folk-like sound, a fact noted in a review by John Indcox.[28] *The Barbra Streisand Album* also contains Barbra's unique slow version of "Happy Days Are Here Again," which would later become one of her signature songs. The idea for the slow arrangement came from Ken Welch for Barbra's 1962 appearance on *The Garry Moore Show*, and it allows her to play with the contradiction and irony of text and tempo.[29]

In 1964 Streisand commented that, in hindsight, her first album sounded as though she had felt a "desperate" need to express something and that she had given too much in giving so much emotion.[30] In the meantime, she had observed in Frank Sinatra what she thought was a healthy tendency to hold something back in performance; she believed that an audience desires more if a performer does not give too much too easily. Nevertheless, Streisand took home her first Grammy award in 1964 for this album; it turned out to be the first of three in a row—it preceded one in 1965 for "People" and one in 1966 for *My Name Is Barbra*.

Columbia took advantage of Streisand's sudden popularity and released *The Second Barbra Streisand Album* in the fall of the same year, 1963. This album also was arranged and conducted by Peter Matz, and it includes several songs by Harold Arlen. More than one writer has commented that Arlen's blues-inflected melodies and harmonies and his personal vocal style, one that focuses on text interpretation, were influential in Streisand's early career.[31]

On this album Barbra offers extremes from a less-than-two-minute rollick through "Gotta Move" to three songs that exceed four minutes, which likely would prevent them from getting radio broadcast time. Generally, there is an air of greater assurance with the second album (even though chronologically it came just months after the first), and perhaps this is even reflected in the liner photograph of Barbra by Wood Kuzoumi. Her first album had featured an incomplete, shadowed view of her face with her microphone and herringbone vest with white blouse more visible.[32] The second album photo projects her face with a girlish but grown-up look, her chin placed on a bare shoulder set off with her trademark page-boy hair style.

The listener hears Streisand's growing experience in the belt numbers of *The Second Barbra Streisand Album*, including "Any Place I Hang My Hat Is Home," "Like a Straw in the Wind," and "When the Sun Comes Out." A similar emboldened sound is heard on her fiesty "Down with Love" and "Lover, Come Back to Me." Her fast vibrato and bright, forward timbre are evident, as is her breathing. It often is possible to hear Streisand inhale between phrases even though that sound could have been removed from the final edited version.[33] Perhaps this sound was retained to add an air of intimacy, as in a club setting, for the record listener who is removed from personal contact with the performance. These brisk numbers are supported by a dance-band instrumentation with prominent percussion and brass. Barbra's voice is recorded to be very forward in the mix. "Lover" has a jazz-influenced vocal style, but without any scat. The accompaniment style and the tempo force her vocal decorations and extended notes to be more calculated so that they fit into tiny spaces between the short, choppy lyric phrases.[34] In fact, in the Romberg/Hammerstein II composition, many of the short text lines begin just after the downbeat of a measure. Barbra varies her temporal initiation of the lines: some come as written, others begin with the first word treated as a pick-up note from the previous measure into the "proper" measure, and others start right on the opening beat.

"Who Will Buy?," the poignant song from *Oliver*, and "Right as the

Rain" provide complete contrast. For the former, Barbra uses a child-like, white tone (meaning without much overtone or vibrato) appropriate to the original intent of the song in the show. In both songs she breathes in places other than logical punctuation points in the text, often stretching a phrase from the end of one sentence into the beginning of the next.

"My Coloring Book" fits the description of a lyric song and offers a chance for a comparison of her performances in differing arrangements because the song is heard on this album and two privately released recordings: a reissue of the 45-rpm single and a tape from a performance at the hungary i club in California.[35] The single was arranged by Robert Mersey with a triplet-like rhythm that creates a country or folk sound, and it omits the verse that opens the other recordings. The club version (probably arranged by Peter Daniels) sounds almost non-metrical, reflecting the freedom that comes with simple arrangements and minimal back up. The album rendition, arranged by Peter Matz, is the most refined and elaborate with a compound duple meter and 1940s movie-score harmonies. The use of high and low string countermelodies helps paint the visual story of a woman who has lost her man.

The text of "I Stayed Too Long at the Fair" might remind the listener of situations in Barbra's own life, although she seems never specifically to have commented about it: "Oh mother, dear, I'm sure you're very proud, your little girl in gingham is so far above the crowd. Oh daddy, dear, you never could have known that I would be successful yet so very much alone."[36] (In later periods, autobiographical references become more prominent in Streisand's recordings.) The rhythm and meter of Matz's arrangement support the story-telling aspect of the mid-section; for example, there is a change to a three-beat pattern to accompany the text about a carnival.

The chart success of Streisand's first two albums, with repertoire and a style that many in the industry predicted would be too unconventional for a wide demographic market, confirmed her growing appeal. Despite the commercial success of Barbra's second album, John F. Indcox, who had written a complimentary review of her first album for *High Fidelity*, decried what he found to be boring and overdone on the second (see bibliography for a list of reviews). He may have been predicting her next move.

Relatively speaking, *The Third Album* and *People*, both of which were released in 1964, could be called "subdued." In contrast to the first two albums, these albums contain arrangements by several musicians including Matz, Ray Ellis, Sid Ramin, and Peter Daniels (who arranged material for and accompanied Barbra in her club and television performances). Mike Berniker, the producer of *The Third Album*, remarked that Streisand's sound was more controlled on this album, that she had taken away the "edge" from her high notes, and that these tracks reflected a serenity when compared to her earlier recordings.[37]

Third and *People* continue Barbra's focus on songs that allow characterization, but belt and torch songs now take a back seat to love ballads. Streisand creates various moods by coloring her voice with breathiness in some cases or with less vibrato, to create a transparency, in others. Both techniques can be used to create a child-like or innocent tone. As mentioned on the liner notes of *Third*, Barbra's version of "Just in Time" was arranged by Leonard Bernstein for the wedding of musical-comedy lyricist Adolph Green and Phyllis Newman. It is based on J. S. Bach's Prelude No. 1 from *The Well-Tempered Clavier* and therefore has an arpeggiated keyboard accompaniment and rather strict rhythm (chordal strings are added for richness). Barbra's timbre is gentle with less vibrato than she projects on forceful numbers. Contrary to Bach's original style, toward the middle of the piece more rhythmic flexibility is heard in the accompaniment and in her text delivery, so that some back phrasing occurs (holding back the beginning of a new text section until after the accompaniment has begun). The listener also hears Streisand's ability to steadily control the pitch, vowel, and timbre on the long, soft final word, *day*, where she does not settle on the second vowel of the combination sound.

For variety, "Taking a Chance on Love" has a blues flavor with piano and muted trumpet. The melodic range necessitates some register change from chest to head voice, and this is one of the few Streisand recordings where that change is noticeable. Likewise, her otherwise clean diction is slightly muddled in the higher range. Her approach to the word *love* is interesting; she moves quickly to the "v" sound, extending it rather than the previous vowel, contrary to expectation. The piece closes with a bit of scat singing, although that performance technique never has become a regular feature of her recordings.

Streisand's vocal technique plays a strong enough role in her text painting that a listener can almost visualize what is happening. A case in point comes from "Bewitched, Bothered, and Bewildered" where the word *I* goes through three vowel sounds (vaguely: "ah-ee-uh"), as the open space of her throat is closed off, then opened by tongue and jaw. Similarly on "Never Will I Marry" her defiant tone in the middle of the song clearly sounds as though she is singing with her jaw clenched shut—a very unusual singing method, one that would prevent many singers from maintaining a musical tone. Reminiscent of her earlier albums, this song ends with a long note on the word *dead* that Barbra produces in a strained, out-of-control-sounding manner. Her concern with text considerations taking precedence over proper tone is evident. "Make Believe" exhibits her reedy low tessitura and the extent of her overall range with full, open-throated higher notes. Again some sentences are phrased into the next with no breath; her lack of precision with the "th" ending sound on some words is notable because it is uncommon for her.

According to Barbra, "Absent Minded Me" on *People*, her fourth album, was written for her by Jule Styne (it was cut from *Funny Girl* before the Broadway opening), and it is in a style she finds reminiscent of "Draw Me a Circle" from her third album.[38] Streisand also remarked that she was aware that Ethel Waters had recorded "Supper Time," but she chose not to hear Water's version lest it cause her to hesitate to sing it herself. Barbra nonetheless recorded it for this album.

A careful study of her phrasing on *People* reveals more inclination toward breathing and phrasing in places other than text punctuation points. Examples are found in "Will He Like Me?", "My Lord and Master," and "Absent Minded Me." "How Does the Wine Taste?" has hints of Spanish rhythm in the accompaniment and a concomitant more-aggressive vocal style than other songs of this collection. The triple repeat of the title words at the end provides ample opportunity to hear Barbra's method of interpretive coloring. With the help of rhythmic and metrical placement, she emphasizes *how* and *taste* the first time, *does* the second, and finally *wine*. "Love Is a Bore" helps balance the gentle nature of much of the album by allowing her to use a big, belt voice against a full accompaniment. Her characterization is seductive and confident, and some dialect is included in places where quote-like material is included in the story of the lyric.

The title track of the *People* album, of course, comes from her successful Broadway show of the same time period, *Funny Girl*. In what is certainly a Streisand signature song, her vocalization of the word *people* clearly shows her ability to make a musical tone where other singers struggle. The final syllable of the word is difficult because of its unclear vowel—especially when it appears on a rather long note. In performances of the song by others, many singers create an "uhl" sound back in the throat or try either an "ahl" or "el" sound, which comes across as unnatural and affected. Streisand produces a mix of those choices, or actually treats the *l* (with the tip of her tongue touching the roof of her mouth) as the vowel, or puts a hint of a nasal "n" sound in with the amalgam, all of which work for her individual style.[39]

In his review of the album, John Wilson proclaimed that, "The same skill that made her early innovations seem valid makes these straight presentations just as brilliant."[40] Streisand's interpretive skills and wide tonal spectrum were allowing her to offer the listener a diversity within a limited repertoire framework.

The daily obligation of *Funny Girl* and two specials for CBS television occupied Streisand's time in 1964 and 1965. The rehearsal and out-of-town preparations for *Funny Girl* were long and tedious, and in fact, more than twenty songs by Jule Styne and Bob Merrill were not retained in the final staged version.[41] The timing of the production was beneficial to Barbra, however; it came at an important point in her career and appeared just before the late-1960s shift in musical theatre tastes away from traditional popular-song-filled new shows. After the premiere and her debut, a reviewer for *Variety* had this to say regarding Streisand's singing in *Funny Girl*:

The star can, of course, belt across a song with a crescendo of power. . . . Experience will bring improvement in her enunciation, which isn't invariably clear on song lyrics, and in such things as variation and change of pace, the nuances of underplaying, and greater quality of relaxation and repose.[42]

Commonweal of 24 April 1964 (Barbra's birthday) printed this assessment by Richard Gilman: "[Streisand is] beyond doubt the most talented all-purpose performer to have emerged in many years, a virtuoso of astonishing range and infinite nuance."

A review in *Time* mentioned that, "Her voice is too nasal to be winningly melodic, but she uses it like a jazz instrument, improvising a jumping rhetoric of sound. She can bring a song phrase to a growling halt, or let it drift lyrically like a ribbon of smoke. Her lyrics seem not to have been learned by rote, but branded on her heart."[43] And a writer for *Newsweek* added, "[Streisand] also has a protean voice that can be lowdown and growly ('Cornet Man'), clean and simple ('People,' 'Don't Rain on My Parade'), funny ('You Are Woman'), and pure Fanny."[44]

Compliments on Streisand's versatility and virtuoso technique also abounded during the brief run of the show in London in 1966. Opinions about the cast album, one of Barbra's few recordings on a label other than Columbia (in this instance, Capitol) were mixed.[45] Streisand was nominated for a Tony award for her work, but ironically lost to Carol Channing for the role in *Hello, Dolly* that Barbra would later create on screen.

Streisand's album *My Name Is Barbra* is not an exact soundtrack from the television special of the same name, which aired on 28 April 1965. The album includes some songs from the childhood segment of the show and some from its closing concert segment, but fifty percent of the album material was not part of the television program.[46] In *The Barbra Streisand Scrapbook*, Allison Waldman rightfully points out that the album, apart from its connection to the show, could be considered Barbra's first "theme" album.[47] This approach to album production was new in the rock arena of the 1960s (there called "concept album") with the Beach Boys' *Pet Sounds* and the Beatles' *Sgt. Pepper's Lonely Hearts Club Band*, but quite natural for someone with a theatre background. Research on the recording career of Frank Sinatra indicates that he was an earlier innovator in concept albums, establishing a mood and text sequence for an album beginning in the 1950s.[48]

The album art establishes the theme with a childhood picture of Barbra on the front cover and a grown-up picture (remembering she was only twenty-three at the time) on the back. Added to the television childhood material (which includes "A Kid Again" and "I'm Five") are other songs about youth, such as the lyric song "Jenny Rebecca." A big-band arrangement of "I've Got No Strings" and "My Man," songs about relationships, then usher the listener into the adult stage of life. Streisand sang the latter as part of the television special following a medley of songs from *Funny Girl* (which was playing on Broadway concurrently), but made it clear that "My Man" was not in the stage show even though it had been a hit for Fanny Brice.

The album entitled *My Name Is Barbra, Two* . . . was released on the heels of Emmy awards for the television show. It contains the medley from the fashion-show segment of the special, which places songs about poverty in opposition to the elegance of the Bergdorf-Goodman store, in addition to other songs. In an interesting marketing strategy, side 1 of the album contains full-length versions of "I Got Plenty of Nothin' " and "Second Hand Rose," which both occur again on side 2 as part of the fashion medley. The other songs on this album may, in fact, be thought of as continuing the theme of the *My Name Is Barbra* album. "He Touched Me," "The Kind of Man a Woman Needs," and "All That I Want" allow Streisand to showcase the many sides of love.

From a historical point of view, the television broadcast of *My Name Is Barbra* was important because it was the first time a large public audience could both hear and see Streisand sing. For analytical purposes, the subsequent videotape of the special is the earliest full-length visual and aural material available for study, and an examination leads to several observations, some of which have been noted previously but are mentioned again to indicate consistency or to emphasize technique.[49]

- The animation of her jaw, lips, tongue, and mouth contributes significantly to her diction and vowel production as witnessed in the many long notes of "Why Did I Choose You?" or on the word *I* in "My Man," which approximates "ah-ee-uh."

- She generates several contrasting timbres appropriate to differing styles, from pure, child-like with no vibrato ("My Name Is Barbara"); to nasal child ("I'm Five"); to sweet and simple, without being shallow (the beginning of "Second Hand Rose"); to strong belt with considerable volume and vibrato ("Plenty of Nothin' " and "The Best Things in Life Are Free"); to jazz style ("Lover, Come Back to Me"); to a tone-filled parlando, setting up the story of a song (the beginning text of "My Man" or "Much More").

- Coloring individual words for text interpretation is equally common and important.

- While her voice can elicit many moods, her facial expressions support the characterizations. Streisand's performance of "We Could Make Believe" is intimate and almost nonchalant, as though the listener is hearing the singer's private, unspoken thoughts.

- In public performance settings (even though these were taped, and likely partially pre-recorded and edited, for broadcast), she is inclined to decorate a melody with small inflections or add filler notes between words more readily than on her studio-produced albums ("Lover, Come Back to Me"). In contrast, some of the emotional cries that ended earlier recordings of songs (discussed previously in this chapter) are gone in these renditions (for example, the *now* at the end of "Lover Come Back to Me" becomes a verbalized stinger on the last beat).

- Her overall tone, at this stage in her career, is quite nasal and forward in her facial mask, as witnessed in the words *gone, store,* and *more* in "Much More" or *came* and *same* in "When the Sun Comes Out."

- She vocalizes some consonants, such as *L, R, NG,* or *N* with a nasal hum or with shadow vowel sounds (in "People" on the words *feeling* and *world*).

- Streisand's large mouth, a trait of many fine singers, and her willingness to open it and her throat fully, especially on loud, belt passages, contribute to the free, rich timbre she projects (seen and heard on *last, go,* and *love* in "Why Did I Choose You?"). Most voice teachers would be pleased with the open throat, but Streisand also tends to curve her shoulders inward and allow them to hunch a bit, a posture generally frowned upon for classical singing. Her unconventional physical approach contradicts the freeness of her sound, which seems in large part to be created through deep rib breathing (as opposed to chest or shoulder breathing).

- Her tendency to overlap the musical phrase with a textual phrase is becoming more pronounced. Clear examples are heard in "When the Sun Comes Out" (for example, the connection of *should* to *love*) and "Where Is the Wonder" (joining *then* to *oh* but then breathing after the title words). Usually, she has enough breath control to sing long phrases, but even if her breath is running out, she uses that slight gasping sound to add drama to the end of a phrase ("The Music That Makes Me Dance").

The *My Name Is Barbra* special also introduces the listener to some personal situations from Barbra's life. For example, during the childhood sequence background voices echo "crazy Barbra" as she moves from song to song and from one play situation to another. Streisand has commented several times on feeling like a misfit as a child. Equally interesting is the scene that shows Barbra playing a celesta. An article about the special in the 30 April 1965 issue of *Time* mentions that she is taking piano lessons, which perhaps contradicts her claim that she does not read music. Similarly, at one point she blurts out August 29th as her birthday. Actually that date marks the birth of her husband, Elliott Gould. (On the album, she corrects this date to be her own birthday, April 24th).

The *Color Me Barbra* album is like the *My Name Is Barbra* album in that it contains material from the television special of the same name (her second), but with some additions. Likewise, the format of *Color* is similar to the first in having three acts: an art gallery segment, a circus segment, and a concert segment. Much of the creative team of the first special was retained for the second, including executive producer Martin Erlichman, director Dwight Hemion,[50] and production-number designer Joe Layton. Many song titles, words, and comments about style and technique applicable to this collection could be substituted into the summary list about the first special provided above. One technique becomes increasingly noticeable: when singing "Starting Here, Starting Now" Streisand drops her jaw slightly for the R that ends words like *here, near,* or *year,* which creates a brief "ah" or "uh" shadow vowel rather than the typical "er" sound. David Shire, the composer, reports that he had originally written "Starting Here" for Robert Goulet, but that Barbra became interested in it during an otherwise unsuccessful repertoire-hunting session. The dramatic modulation on *now* was added to fit her style and turned the song into a "super aria."[51]

Color Me Barbra also introduced the public to Barbra's interest in spoken and sung French; "Non c'est rien" was presented in its entirety on the television special with no translation or subtitles. Her facial expression, her tone and demeanor, and the minimal set and staging told the English-speaking audience all it needed to know. A reviewer for *High Fidelity* criticized the subsequent album for not translating better from the television screen to vinyl even though he was impressed with the versatility of her vocal stylings.[52]

The generation of female, popular-song singers preceding Streisand included Edith Piaf. Barbra initially ventured into the French chanteuse's territory with "Non c'est rien," but that experiment blossomed with *Je m'appelle Barbra* (1966), another album title based on her name. The origins of two songs on this album are of interest. "Ma première chanson," as the title states, was Barbra's first composition; the French lyrics, about the birth of a love song, were written for her melody by Eddy Marnay. "Le Mur" actually was written for Edith Piaf, who died in 1963 before singing it. The creators then decided to withhold the song from other French singers in favor of Streisand. "Le Mur" also has been transcribed as "I've Been Here" in English; both versions are on the album. Like earlier albums, the liner contains a testimonial to Streisand's abilities, this one from Maurice Chevalier (who describes her as a "miracle"). Most of the songs in the collection are arranged and conducted by Michel Legrand, who would collaborate with Barbra many other times in the future. His orchestrations received praise from Morgan Ames in *High Fidelity*.[53]

Barbra's French is admirable most of the time. She occasionally adds a diphthong where it should not be, and sometimes her mute *e* is a bit flat (in pronunciation, not pitch), typical problems for English-speaking singers. Likewise on "Clopin Clopant" the first syllable of each word has an "o" sound that is too closed (as in *boat* rather than *other*) for French pronunciation, possibly exaggerated because the song mixes French and English texts. These characteristics add an American pop flavor to the overall mix.[54]

Typical of this period of Streisand's career, the album contains character songs ("What Now My Love?"), belt or torch songs ("I've Been Here"), lyric songs ("Autumn Leaves"), and love ballads ("Speak to Me of Love"). But characterization and pictorial interpretations through phrasing, dynamics, timbral contrasts, and word coloring play an over-arching role. The album is indeed "French," which could suggest experimentation or a new direction for Streisand, but the repertoire and her approach are similar to those heard on earlier albums. Barbra might have been seeking diversion through new challenges and inspirations, but she had not wandered too far afield. Her fan base, which was becoming more international, had little reason to be uncomfortable with this repertoire. Nonetheless, *Je m'appelle Barbra* was not a commercial failure, but it was the least profitable of her albums to that point.

The first period of Streisand's recording career ends with the transitional *Simply Streisand* released in 1967.[55] *Billboard* reported on 11 November that Columbia Records intended to give the album an additional "Christmas push" after its highly successful entry into the market with nearly 250,000 copies sold in the first two weeks. Earlier, in a "Pop Spotlight" mini-review, *Billboard* had proclaimed, "Another Streisand, another winner."[56] The relatively inexperienced vocalist had, in short order, recorded a significant body of American popular song, and the young woman who had wanted to be an actress had become one through song. In many ways, her accomplishments resulted from a personality and a career path that belied the norm. Barbra's artistic and commercial successes of a mere five years were admirable and undeniable; the question was about the future—a future during which the Tin Pan Alley legacy (traditional or classic pop) took a back seat to folk revival and rock music.[57]

Barbra's musical future is not previewed in stark and startling ways, but rather in the details of *Simply Streisand*.[58] There are fewer belt/torch songs in the collection, and fewer character songs, although characterization of songs is still important, and six of the set are from shows or films with music by Rodgers and Hart, Fields and Schwartz, Frank Loesser, Hammerstein II and Kern, Martin and Blane, and Hammerstein II and Romberg. David Shire, the conductor for the album, states that the album's title sends the message: "Let's just get some good old standards, and not gussie them up too much, and just kind of sing."[59]

"My Funny Valentine" is a representative example. It begins simply and ends with a kind of belting, but the belt sound is more refined, perhaps being mixed with the head voice. Head voice alone is used smoothly on the high note of the first syllable of *favorite* after the narrow-range melodic opening. The simple voice and cello contrapuntal opening, on the verse that is rarely sung, shows that Barbra does not have to be supported by full instrumentation to be effective.[60] The color added later by the harp, strings, and woodwinds adds to the richness. Vocal techniques like those previously described are found in this example as well: moving to the "e" sound of the *day* diphthong, making a vowel sound and tone on the *ble* syllable of *unphotographable* (probably the tip of the tongue on the roof of the mouth for the *l*), and coloring important words such as *don't* or *laughable*. The bridge exhibits Streisand's penchant for altering written rhythms; Richard Rodgers had written brief rests after the sequential leaps for *fig-(ure)*, *mouth*, and *o-(pen)*, but Barbra's rendition does not include his exact repeated rhythms or rests in those places. In the concluding measures, she stays in her high range throughout rather than dropping down to the range of the song's opening as it was written to create an AABA form.[61] Similar techniques are noticeable in "All the Things You Are" composed by Jerome Kern. Streisand sings the opening verse to establish the mood, and solves the *you*-to-*you* text challenge, which occurs between the last written word of the verse and the identical word that opens the chorus, by singing only one long *you* with harmony and instrumentation assisting in the transition. Kern's thrice-repeated rhythmic motives that begin the verse are no longer identical in her recitative-like delivery.

In contrast, "Lover Man," written in 1942, the year of Barbra's birth, begins with a restless accompaniment that complements the agitated, rougher sound she produces for this text. In fact, hints of what might be described as a "soul" sound creep in beginning on the word *sweet*. Gentle flutes and strings add a contrasting flavor. The piece fades away at the end with Streisand providing improvisatory repetitions during the fade, a trait of many contemporary pop songs.

Finally, a hint of the contemporary pop sound that would occupy Barbra in the next period of her musical career is evident in "The Nearness of You," a love ballad. The rhythm is established immediately with a soft backbeat, but her vocal line is not strictly with the beat, especially on words she chooses to inflect and color like *thrills*, *feel*, and *enchant*. Her tone is far away and somewhat breathy, which matches the relaxed "oo" vowel of the word *you*. She slides slightly from one note to the next, finally centering on a pitch. After an orchestral interlude, she projects a much stronger and louder tone with additional rubato, but ends softly.

"The Early Years" are marked by the number and frequency of Streisand's recordings and by her focus on theatre songs and standards arranged for and presented in various venues: at a club or cabaret, on the theatre or television stage, or in concert performance. By happy historical coincidence or by tailor-made musical opportunity, Streisand's style, as described in the preceding analytical comments, lends itself perfectly to the nature of this vast repertoire. The overall musical characteristics of this literature, most of it written before 1960 or with techniques common to that period, can be summarized thus: verse-chorus structure (with the verse being important to the story but the chorus able to stand alone on its musical and emotional strengths),[62] a sectional and repetitive form (often AABA) that allows evolving melodic variation, a sense of forward motion or development in the goal-oriented phrases, imaginative harmonies especially in the release (or B area) that heightened the drama, rhythmic vitality provided by syncopation and interruption of expected beat divisions (like 3 in the place of 2), and texts with personal emotions.

Streisand's vocal performances reveal several specific and related characteristics: overt emotionalism; clean diction aided by easy skill in controlling her tongue, jaw, and breath; contrast of sound from belt to girlish but with an overall bright, forward, and nasal timbre; [63] development of her unique phrasing patterns; coloring of specific text words through multiple means to highlight the story development; [64] an ease with flexible but not formulaic rhythms; and an inclination toward jazz inflections. Her repertoire centers around songs that allow characterizations and evolving stories or situations, and the songs conform to the song types defined at the outset, although some clearly could fit more than one category simultaneously. As subtly suggested in *Simply Streisand*, the next period of her vocal career departs from the first in wider exploration of musical styles and repertoire and in her move into the Hollywood film world.

NOTES

1. Barbra Streisand, accompanying booklet for *Just for the Record*, compact disc 44111 (Sony Music Entertainment, 1991), 15.

2. Many sources will provide more details, including definitions of "popular music." See for example, Charles Hamm, *Yesterdays: Popular Song in America* (New York: W.W. Norton and Co., 1979); Marvin E. Paymer, ed. *Facts Behind the Songs* (New York: Garland Publishing, 1993), s.v. "Popular Song," by Allen Sigel.

3. Ken Barnes, *Sinatra and the Great Song Stylists* (London: Ian Allan Publishers, 1972), 33.

4. For further information see Bob Gilbert and Gary Theroux, *The Top Ten 1956–Present* (New York: Simon and Schuster, 1982). For information on Mancini's jazz style in *Peter Gunn* see Mark Evans, *Soundtrack: The Music of the Movies* (New York: Hopkinson and Blake, 1975), 191–193.

5. Michael Barackman, "Pop Duets: A Top-10 Marriage," *Los Angeles Times*, 26 November 1978, CAL:7; Ken Barnes, "Top-40 Radio" in *Facing the Music*, ed. Simon Frith (New York: Pantheon Books, 1988), 8–50; Arnold Shaw, *Dictionary of American Pop/Rock* (New York: Schirmer Books, 1982). In 1977 Streisand received the *Billboard* Top Easy Listening Artist award. See Barbra Streisand, accompanying booklet for *Just for the Record*, compact disc 44111 (Sony Music Entertainment, 1991), 64. Further discussion of vocabulary will appear where appropriate to Streisand's recording history.

6. This statement contradicts the belief of David Lee Joyner who wrote, "Soft rock continued to flourish in the 1980s. Barry Manilow and Barbra Streisand had

run their course, but a variety of artists came to take their place." See *American Popular Music* (Madison, Wisconsin: Brown and Benchmark, 1993), 313.

7. Dave Marsh, ed. *The New Rolling Stone Record Guide* (New York: Rolling Stone Press, 1983), s.v. "Barbra Streisand," by Stephen Holden; Anthony DeCurtis and James Henke, eds., *The Rolling Stone Record Guide* (New York: Straight Arrow Publishers, Inc., 1992), s.v. "Barbra Streisand," by Paul Evans. See the discography herein for information about songs Streisand has recorded that are from theatre shows.

8. Barbra was 20 years old in 1962. Although inexperienced she was adventuresome in her approach. Her concerts sometimes began with a slow ballad, rather than the more customary up-tempo attention getter.

9. Roy Hemming and David Hajdu, *Discovering Great Singers of Classic Pop* (New York: Newmarket Press, 1991), 206.

10. These song categories first were introduced in Linda Pohly, "Barbra Streisand and the Theatricality of Popular Song: Vocal Technique and a Director's Eye," *The American Music Research Center Journal* 6 (1996): 69–86.

11. Streisand was not the first or the only singer to approach a song as though playing a character. This same technique is found in the work of the French singer Edith Piaf, although her vocal sound is quite different from Streisand's.

12. Although there can be a distinction between a belt song and a torch song (the former a vocal approach, the latter a textual consideration), the two can be connected in performance, as in several recordings by Judy Garland. For further information on the torch song, see John Moore, " 'The Hieroglyphics of Love': The Torch Singers and Interpretation," *Popular Music* 8, no. 1 (1989): 31–57.

13. Another possible term for lyric song would be "popular art song." Some authors borrow the term "art song" from the classical domain to refer to a popular song of musical distinction. The category headings are of my own design, and my choice of the term lyric song is intended to denote a song's breadth or complexity. The headings may or may not apply to other singers or popular music in general. Another category, Advocacy and Autobiography Songs, will be added in subsequent chapters.

14. Barbra Streisand, *Back to Broadway*, compact disc 44189 (Columbia, 1993), liner.

15. This study focuses on her commercial albums and compact discs, with secondary attention paid to videotaped performances of concert singing. See Henry Hewes, review of *I Can Get It for You Wholesale*, in *Saturday Review* (14 April 1962): 28; Howard Taubman, review of *I Can Get It for You Wholesale*, in *New York Times*, 23 March 1962, L:29. A selective list of reviews of performances and recordings appears in the bibliography. According to Steven Suskin, Harold Rome fashioned "Miss Marmelstein" and "What Are They Doing to Us Now?" to Streisand's talents after signing her to the part, see *Show Tunes 1905–1985* (New York: Dodd, Mead & Co., 1986), 342. Although originally in a minor role, Streisand's subsequent rise to fame brings continued interest in this show. When the cast album was reissued by Columbia many years later (see discography), Streisand's character was the only one pictured on the liner, but her first name was misspelled (to include three As) in one instance in the Act II song list.

16. While acknowledging the differing goals and procedures between criticism

and scholarship, critics nevertheless play an important role in popular culture, and their comments will be considered.

17. The songs with piano accompaniment are available from Florence Music Co. (publisher's number 5502–199), sole selling agent Chappell, New York. Streisand has remarked that she does not read music, as has been noted. This might call into question the validity of commenting on printed music in a discussion of her technique. Whether the notation precedes or follows her performance or whether she or anyone involved in her performance uses it with precision, the printed notation is the visual source available for study or for learning the song in most cases. It also is useful as a point of comparison. This fact was made clear to me when a colleague, who teaches musical theatre, heard Streisand's recording of "Don't Rain on My Parade" and came to understand why his students never seemed to sing the piece "correctly" when they used it in class or for an audition. The teacher was thinking about the notation, assuming it to be the basis from which an interpreter might depart. The students were thinking about what they had heard as the model. This conflict is on-going in music history and in the study of popular music. An article entitled "Studying Nineteenth-Century Popular Song" contains a discussion of the validity of studying sheet music compared to the usefulness of studying performance. See Paul Charosh's work in *American Music* 15, no. 4 (Winter 1997): 459–492, especially pages 462–463.

18. I thank Professor Janet Polvino for her observations and comments.

19. No attempt will be made to use classical-music octave indications. General references will be made to Streisand's range, which falls approximately between the F below middle C and the E a tenth above middle C. She is able to maintain a belt sound for her high C and D, although it often is mixed with her head voice at that point. Therefore, the listener does not hear register shifts as she moves to a higher range. David Shire, interview by author, Muncie, Indiana, 4 March 1998. According to New York City vocal teacher, Bill Reed, a belt sound in that range has a psycho-acoustic effect that causes a pitch to be perceived to sound higher than it really is; female belting around those C and D pitches appeals to the ear like an operatic tenor in that very same range. He believes Streisand to have been one of the first to use this technique (belting consistently over her range achieved through a belt mix) and that, for her, it was quite natural, as opposed to learned. Bill Reed, "Singers on Stage Workshop," Ball State University, 21 September 1996. Other comments about the importance of and connection between timbre and register and Streisand's type of belting are found in Aaron Frankel, *Writing the Broadway Musical* (New York: Drama Book Specialists, 1977), 87–89; Conrad L. Osborne, "The Broadway Voice: Part 1," *High Fidelity* (January 1979): 57, 62–65. Osborne writes that Streisand was one of the few Broadway singers to successfully integrate, equalize, or mix belt with "legit" singing. He notices, as do I, that while her range is typical of a lower female voice, her voice quality suggests lyric soprano, and that over the years she became increasingly able to "thin out" the belt mix in her upper register, adding more head voice, when that sound was desired. The term "belt" is not used in conjunction with classical music, although many vocal teachers understand the meaning of the term. It is a part of the argot of popular vocal music and is described in sources such as Arnold Shaw, comp., *Dictionary of American Pop/Rock* (New York: Schirmer Books, 1982) in addition to those by Frankel and Osborne cited above. The word typically appears in several forms: belt as a verb

or an adjective, belter as a noun, and belting as a gerund. The terms "head voice" and "chest voice" are described in classical singing as the intermediate and lower pitch ranges of the female voice, respectively. The terms head and chest do not imply the part of the body where the sound is produced; instead, they refer to the area where sympathetic vibrations often are felt by the singer. The head voice is characterized by a light quality and the chest voice by a heavier quality. The two voices are produced and mixed in a variety of ways by different classical-voice types. For further information, see Richard Miller, *The Structure of Singing* (New York: Schirmer Books, 1986), chapter 10; William Vennard, *Singing, The Mechanism and the Technique*, rev. ed. (New York: Carl Fischer, 1967), 250.

20. The original *Pins and Needles* revue was staged in the 1930s and reflected political thoughts on union struggles of that time. Streisand was involved in the Twenty-fifth Anniversary production. Her participation in political events to send a musical social message would become more prominent beginning in the late 1960s. Although more renowned as a soloist, it is important to reflect on her early experience as an ensemble singer since later she recorded a series of duets. Moreover, the use of another singer, a backup chorus, or an instrumental countermelody sometimes seems to draw more energy out of Barbra's performance. This was even noticeable in 1994 when she sang duets with herself (via videotape) during her tour concerts.

21. Several Streisand singles also have been issued over the years, some exactly like the album track of the same name, and others with different arrangements. This study focuses on albums and compact discs, but occasionally a single will be discussed to point out contrasts of style or technique. The singles are listed in James Spada, *Barbra, The First Decade* (Secaucus, New Jersey: Citadel Press, 1975), 89; Stephen Thacker, "Her Name Is Barbra," *The Record Collector* (October 1997): 81–82; and on internet sites concerned with Streisand memorabilia such as The Barbra Streisand Music Guide (see bibliography).

22. Barbra called on Matz at the suggestion of Harold Arlen. See Barbra Streisand, accompanying booklet for *Just for the Record*, compact disc 44111 (Sony Music Entertainment, 1991), 17. A scholarly study of the work and influence of arrangers of popular song is needed; the contributions of popular song composers and performers only recently have begun to be studied. Occasionally, comments on an arranger's skills and influence are found in record reviews, see for example, *High Fidelity* (January 1966): 106 regarding Peter Matz and Claus Ogerman, who worked with Streisand in the 1970s. See also Jennifer Ember Pierce, *Playin' Around* (Lanham, Maryland: Scarecrow Press, 1998) for information about session musicians of Nashville, which might serve as a model. One source for information on composers is David Ewen, *American Songwriter* (New York: H.W. Wilson Co., 1987), and biographical studies of some songwriters are available. One of the few analytical books about a singer is Will Friedwald, *Sinatra! The Song Is You: A Singer's Art* (New York: Scribner, 1995).

23. This observation is supported by a quotation from Streisand in "Coming Star," *New Yorker* (19 May 1962): 35. There she explains that it is difficult for her to find songs she likes; she does not like "mooshy" love songs.

24. In an interview with Leonard Feather in 1964, Streisand remarked that four of the songs on her first solo album "weren't even in tempo," indicating that she

was aware of the fluidity with which she approached rhythm. See "Wild Girl, Wild Sound," *Melody Maker* (1 February 1964): 12.

25. Many of her pronunciations likely are based on what for her is natural English dialect, as would be expected in popular music. However, this discussion of her vocal pronunciation takes on added meaning over the course of Streisand's career, because in later years her New York accent is not nearly as prevalent in her singing or in her speech (although she can slip into that accent quickly and smoothly). The technique remains a part of her singing, whether planned or natural.

26. The IPA phonetic symbols will not be used; many readers may be unfamiliar with them, and they create typesetting difficulties.

27. The listener hears switching from her belt voice to her head voice on isolated words during "I'll Tell the Man." It is unclear whether this is purely for dramatic effect (it heightens the drama especially when accompanied with dynamic contrasts) or whether her ability to smoothly mix and switch voices, so prominent and controlled later, is still undeveloped.

28. See *High Fidelity* (June 1963): 84.

29. The version of "Happy Days" issued as a single consists of a cabaret-sounding accompaniment and perhaps a more tentative vocal approach. Theatre composer and arranger Raphael Crystal suggests that the contrast to the album arrangement might, in fact, reflect Streisand's working style. As she gets increasingly comfortable with the lyric, and gets her characterization securely established, the accompaniment can be more complex and can support better her emotional intention. This can cause a "mannered, theatrical" presentation that will please some listeners and displease others. Likewise Crystal notes considerable back phrasing in her singing of "Happy Days." In his experience some singers do this with great skill for rhythmic and harmonic variety, others seem to use it as a technique to hear the harmonic foundation before committing vocally. Raphael Crystal, interview by author, Muncie, Indiana, 5 February 1998. "Happy Days" on *The Barbra Streisand Album* ends with loud, high notes during which Streisand does not use a belt/head voice mix, causing them to sound strained.

30. Barbra Streisand, interview with unidentified reporter, compact disc, *Barbra Streisand Rarities* vol. 5 (private release by *Barbrabilia*, Arlington Heights, Illinois, 1997).

31. John S. Wilson, review of *Harold Sings Arlen (with Friend)*, in *High Fidelity* (June 1966): 97; Charles Hamm, *Yesterdays: Popular Song in America* (New York: W.W. Norton and Co., 1979), 355–356.

32. Barbra comments that she designed the herringbone outfit for her earlier club dates. See Barbra Streisand, accompanying booklet for *Just for the Record*, compact disc 44111 (Sony Music Entertainment, 1991), 15.

33. According to an interview in *Playboy*, Streisand asked editors not to clean up the sound of the breathing; she wanted a more natural sound. See Lawrence Grobel, "Playboy Interview: Barbra Streisand." *Playboy* (October 1977): 81.

34. Columbia released a single of "Lover, Come Back to Me" arranged by George Williams. It begins with a Basie-style piano introduction at a break-neck speed. Only a few instruments are used throughout, and the fury is balanced by a sweet string line above. Barbra's vocals sound more relaxed than on the album version. The author thanks Raphael Crystal and Cynthia Miller for their observations. Writing about the album for *High Fidelity*, reviewer John Indcox found her

up-tempo treatment of this otherwise "tender love song" to be less than admirable (December 1963): 104.

35. Barbra Streisand, compact disc, *Barbra Streisand Rarities* vols. 1a and 4 (private release by *Barbrabilia*, Arlington Heights, Illinois, 1997). See the list of recordings and videos in Appendix C.

36. "I Stayed Too Long at the Fair," by Billy Barnes.

37. John S. Wilson, "A Kook from Madagascar," *High Fidelity* (May 1964): 45, 103. Peter Daniels also worked with other singers, including Lainie Kazan, who was Streisand's understudy in *Funny Girl*. See John S. Wilson, review of *Lainie Kazan*, in *High Fidelity* (November 1966): 48.

38. Barbra Streisand, interview with unidentified reporter, compact disc, *Barbra Streisand Rarities* vol. 5 (private release by *Barbrabilia*, Arlington Heights, Illinois, 1997).

39. This is similar to the Tone Syllables concept of choral conductor Fred Waring (1900–84). He recognized that many letters have more than one sound, especially in their American English pronunciations, and that some consonants (especially L, M, N, and NG) can be pitched or given tone. See Fritz Mountford, "Fred Waring and American Choral Singing: His Career, Philosophy, and Techniques" (D.M.A. diss., University of Missouri—Kansas City, 1992), chapter 8.

40. See *High Fidelity* (January 1965): 94.

41. Ken Bloom, *American Song, The Complete Musical Theatre Companion*, vol. 1: A—S, 2nd ed., 1877–1995 (New York: Schirmer Books, 1996), 353. Other comments about finding a suitable leading lady are found in Theodore Taylor, *Jule: The Story of Composer Jule Styne* (New York: Random House, 1979). Styne died in 1994 just shortly after Streisand's tour; he attended one of her performances in New York and was the dedicatee of her performance of "People" that evening.

42. "Funny Girl," *Variety* (1 April 1964): 80.

43. "On the Rue Streisand," *Time* (3 April 1964): 54.

44. "Full Throttle," *Newsweek* (6 April 1964): 76–77.

45. In my own study of the cast album, I concur with the comments about her faulty diction (especially on "I'm the Greatest Star" and "Cornet Man"), and agree with comments on her versatility. The photograph on the back of the album clearly indicates how large Barbra's mouth is and how open her throat is when singing, both of which aid her sound production and resonance. In 1966 Streisand was scheduled to go on an American concert tour after the London run of *Funny Girl*. It was reduced by sixteen concerts, however, because of her pregnancy. Robert Sobel suggested in 1965 that Streisand had not yet adequately conquered the large, outdoor, stadium-size concert setting as evidenced by her West Side Tennis Club concert on 8 August, see *Billboard* (21 August 1965): 16, 47. By the following year, Streisand's camp announced that a new concept, "theater in the ballpark," would dominate the planning of Barbra's forthcoming tour. Her production team (including producers Alan King and Walter A. Hyman) invested more than $250,000 in a sound and light system designed by Ralph Alswang and Myles Rosenthal. It was to include a "Zemon," a lighting device that tracked the performer as she moved about the stage. Additionally, 300 spotlights and 10 tons of sound equipment would help create the illusion of intimacy for a large audience. Peter Matz was hired to conduct the thirty-five piece orchestra. See Mike Gross, "Miss Streisand to Bat Out Tunes in Theater Meant for Diamonds," *Billboard* (23 July 1966): 18.

46. See the discography for a complete listing of the album's contents. Typical of the time period, little information appears on the liner, unlike the trend after the 1960s to include all kinds of detail about the material and the performers on the liner and record or compact disc sleeve. Streisand's own recordings from the 1970s and later contain more information, some of it personal and autobiographical. It is always rewarding to look for the visual details that attend Streisand's work. *My Name Is Barbra* begins with her in an empire-waist gown with a sailor collar and tie. As the show unfolds into the childhood sequence, Barbra is wearing a romper with the same sailor collar and tie motif.

47. Allison J. Waldman, *The Barbra Streisand Scrapbook* (New York: Citadel Press, 1995), 42–43.

48. See Will Friedwald, *Sinatra! The Song Is You: A Singer's Art* (New York: Scribner, 1995), 286.

49. There apparently were several versions of the special's audio from which the editors of the videotape could select; those chosen may reflect Barbra's preferences as to technique and sound. See Tony Seideman, "Streisand TV Programs Released by CBS/Fox," *Billboard* (1 November 1986): 42.

50. Hemion also was involved in the direction and production of Frank Sinatra's successful special entitled *A Man and His Music* in the mid-1960s.

51. David Shire, interview by author, Muncie, Indiana, 4 March 1998.

52. John S. Wilson, review of *Color Me Barbra*, in *High Fidelity* (July 1966): 92–93. See also a lengthy article by Rex Reed entitled "Color Barbra Very Bright" in *New York Times*, 27 March 1966, 25. On the reissue of the video in 1986 (see list of recordings and videos in Appendix C), Streisand introduced the special by discussing the art gallery segment, which was taped in the Philadelphia Museum of Art. Apparently the crew had thirty-six hours to film it from closing time on Saturday to opening time on Monday. Production was hectic, compounded by the fact that two of the brand new color cameras broke down (so new that no replacement parts were available), causing the blocking to be changed to accommodate one-camera shots.

53. See issue dated February 1967, page 124. Ames points out the conflict that many of Barbra's fans felt about her commercial offerings of the mid-1960s. Sometimes they as individuals loved her work, but at other times they railed against it, vacillating as often as Barbra changed character and style.

54. Patricia Martin Gibby, interview by author, Muncie, Indiana, 6 July 1997.

55. Of the nine non-cast albums released by Streisand between 1963 and 1967, only one (*People*) does not have her name in the title in some fashion. Perhaps this was a message to those who suggested that she change her real name in favor of a professional moniker. On 11 October 1967, CBS television aired Streisand's special entitled *The Belle of 14th Street*. According to an article in *Monsanto Magazine* (October 1967): 1–5, Streisand and company completed taping more than fifty hours of footage in April. It was then edited to fit the one-hour October show schedule and included sketches in the style of a late-nineteenth-century vaudeville show. Three songs from the special were eventually released on *Just for the Record* in 1991: "A Good Man Is Hard to Find" (partially done with a Mae-West type accent), "Some of These Days," and "I'm Always Chasing Rainbows." The latter is particularly instructive for studying Barbra's phrasing: as the title words are repeated, she often breathes after *always* but then carries the phrase past *rainbows*

into the next text line, and on occasion the opening *I'm* is not the beginning of a phrase, but is part of a carry over from the preceding text line. The tune is based on the Fantaisie-Impromptu in c# minor, op. 66 by Frederic Chopin.

56. See two issues of *Billboard* (11 November 1967): 11; (28 October 1967): back cover. Also in November, Columbia was pushing *A Christmas Present . . . and Past* by Paul Revere and the Raiders, which was "geared to the teenage rock 'n' roll and hippie markets."

57. Charles Hamm, *Yesterdays: Popular Song in America* (New York: W.W. Norton and Co., 1979), 457.

58. Although I view this album as hinting toward transition, other writers viewed it as harkening back to the style and material of her first two albums. One writer called it "a return to her vintage style" and another mentioned *Simply Streisand* was her "best album of standards since the *Third*." See Anthony DeCurtis and James Henke, eds., *The Rolling Stone Album Guide* (New York: Straight Arrow Publishers, Inc., 1992), s.v. "Barbra Streisand," by Paul Evans; Dave Marsh, ed., *The New Rolling Stone Record Guide* (New York: Rolling Stone Press, 1983), s.v. "Barbra Streisand," by Stephen Holden.

59. David Shire, interview by author, Muncie, Indiana, 4 March 1998. Shire mentioned that he thinks Barbra's vocal timbre is much like that of an oboe. According to him, her voice is not particularly loud (like a classical singer's), but it projects because of the intensity of the vibrato and overtones even in a complicated arrangement. He calls her voice "laser-like" in its ability to cut through.

60. The song is from the show *Babes in Arms*, and "Valentine" is a male character. The verse is interesting in its use of uncommon, sophisticated words like *doth* or *thy*, which are then opposed near the end by a more colloquial *dopey*. For discussion of these words and many other popular-song lyrics see Lehman Engel, *Their Words Are Music* (New York: Crown Publishers, Inc., 1975).

61. For more detailed analyses of the composer's version of this and many other ballads, see Allen Forte, *The American Popular Ballad of the Golden Era, 1924–1950* (Princeton: Princeton University Press, 1995).

62. As Charles Hamm points out, this is similar to the use of recitative and aria in opera composition; see his other summary comments in *Yesterdays: Popular Song in America* (New York: W. W. Norton and Co., 1979), chapter 14. Streisand often performs an opening verse with many recitative-like traits, such as simplified accompaniment, vaguely metrical rhythms, and a declamatory approach to the text. The verse often is omitted by many other performers and arrangers.

63. Although this book focuses on Streisand's music rather than details of her personal life, it must be noted that the variety of adjectives used to describe her wide-ranging tonal palette (as noted throughout this chapter) is similar in quantity but contradictory in tenor to the variety of words used by reporters and critics to describe her personal appearance. Especially in these early years, many writers commented unfavorably about her looks, using words like *gawky*, *plain*, and even *ugly* and *frightful*. Others saw a kind of beauty in Streisand, one that came through in her artistry, and recognized that this perhaps began to alter the conventional notion of the term. In retrospect she seemingly has learned to deal with continuing references to her physical features (whether applicable to the given professional situation), but to be subjected to this kind of barrage as a young woman must have been a difficult challenge. The effects resonate throughout her career (see reviews

of her 1996 film, *The Mirror Has Two Faces*). Her success in spite of this negative commentary has provided hope for and instills loyalty in many of her fans.

64. Similar comments have been written about Frank Sinatra's style: "He phrased with a conscious regard for the logic of the lyric," and "he 'read' the lyrics with uncanny clarity and emotional directness." See Terry Teachout, "Taking Sinatra Seriously," *Commentary* (September 1997): 56.

Chapter 3

Transition, Experimentation, and Tradition: Popular Song in Flux

It's so difficult to constantly have to top yourself. It's a pressure that's put upon you by the outside world.

I just pick my own songs, and I record what I want to sing.[1]

This phase of Barbra Streisand's vocal career begins with the release of her album of Christmas songs in 1967. The attitude she expressed in the second statement above continued to play a significant role during this period, even though Barbra was encouraged by Columbia Records personnel to venture into new musical territory. Streisand recorded a wider variety of repertoire between 1967 and 1973, but many of her basic vocal techniques and stylistic traits remained consistent.

A Christmas Album manifests many points of interest, the lack of critical commentary notwithstanding. The album includes conventional repertoire, like "Have Yourself a Merry Little Christmas" and "O Little Town of Bethlehem," but also contains some non-Christmas material ("The Lord's Prayer") and some unusual arrangements of familiar songs ("Jingle Bells" at a break-neck speed with jazz-like interpolations and "I Wonder as I Wander" presented as an elaborate lyric song rather than as a simple folk song).[2] It is, of course, interesting to consider the incongruity of a clearly Jewish songstress releasing such a collection—one that does not focus on secular aspects of the season, but Streisand seems never to have commented on this.[3]

Although many of the vocal characteristics heard on Barbra's earlier recordings still are evident, her tone on this album generally is softer and less nasal with a more discreet vibrato—as though she approached the repertoire as something other than pop. Similarly, her diction, especially with some concluding consonants, might be described as more "classical." For example, words that end with an *er* are not given the dropped-jaw "ah" sound, but are produced to create an "ah(r)" effect, with just a touch of the final consonant added. Some "r" sounds in the middle of words are rolled in the style of Latin or Italian pronunciation. Adding to the semi-classical feeling, a number of the arrangements employ background choirs and orchestrally oriented accompaniments, a few including the harpsi-chord. The arrangement for "The Lord's Prayer" seemingly was motivated by Hollywood film scores to include full orchestration, lush harmony, and dramatic dynamics. Streisand personalizes some familiar melodies with her usual mannerisms: considerable embellishments, maneuvering away from expected melodic lines, and word coloring through timbral changes. But on the classically influenced arrangements, she is more true to the published or traditional melodic line.

The soft-tone approach mentioned above is contrasted by her perfor-mance of "The Lord's Prayer," which progresses from a focused, refined sound to a full-toned belt with its attendant nasal timbre and fast vibrato. Within the song, Barbra mixes refined diction techniques (a tiny break be-tween *be* and *thy*) with pop characteristics (placing an "h" sound in the middle of vowels that change pitch (*be* becomes "be-he" or *kingdom* be-comes "ki-hing-dom"). Her pop tendencies help her create a natural mix of "i," "u," and "l" sounds on the second syllable of *evil*, which usually forces most classical singers to go with a true "short i" vowel, even though spoken English gives that syllable a sort of "ul" sound. The song also stretches her range, exposing the reedy quality of her low chest register.

Ironically, during "Sleep in Heavenly Peace" (also known as "Silent Night") Streisand maintains the traditional awkward phrasing between *bright* and *round* in the line "all is calm, all is bright round yon virgin mother and child," rather than creating typically unique phrases. Especially in this case, new phrasing might make more sense of that text line. The arrangement by Ray Ellis calls for Barbra to repeat the opening verse's text, rather than progressing through the other stanzas. On the other hand, she sings the less-familiar, introductory verses for "Have Yourself a Merry Lit-tle Christmas" and "White Christmas," perhaps in the interest of estab-lishing a story line for the song.[4] Streisand's rendition of "Jingle Bells" allows her to play with a characterization created through tempo changes and even some New York dialect. Her growing propensity for leaping up-ward (often to the octave) to emphasize certain words is heard during *know* and *many* on the text repeat of "The Christmas Song" ("Chestnuts Roast-ing on an Open Fire") and in other songs on the album.

Streisand encounters the same stumbling blocks that many English-speaking singers face when performing the Latin text of "Ave Maria"—adding diphthongs where a purist would not and making "o" sounds, as in the word *Dominus*, too long and round (rather than using the preferred mix between an "oh" and an "ah" sound). However, she produces a pure and gentle "oo" vowel on the word *tu*. This song and other material of the set stretch Barbra's range from her low, darker sounds to her pure head voice for soft, higher notes—she sometimes chooses not to use her belt mix for high C, D, and E.

A Christmas Album also supports the reasoning for the fifth category of repertoire, autobiographical and advocacy songs, those in which the text, performance situation or venue, or associated liner information reveal something of personal interest to Streisand. Although she usually guards her privacy and that of her family and close associates, it is possible to learn much about Streisand's thinking by looking for messages in her recordings. Musically these songs might well be included under one of the other headings (character song, lyric song, torch or belt song, and ballad), but her frequent inclusion of this kind of material and her comments about it make a separate category pertinent and useful. In this case, "The Best Gift," a song about the joy of a child's birth, comes just after the birth of her son, Jason. The minimal accompaniment provided by Marty Paich allows a very personal performance (almost a lullaby) with considerable parlando singing and word coloring.

Thirty years after its release, an advertisement ranked the album "among the best-selling holiday albums of all time," by "one of the most popular and successful singers of our time."[5] Whatever her reasons for recording *A Christmas Album*, it was a wise financial decision. Her extended range, finesse with diction, and variety of tone color are striking even after repeated listening, and the listener is reminded of the importance of sophisticated microphones and recording technology throughout Streisand's career. The album serves both to introduce this period of transition and experimentation and to anticipate her 1976 *Classical Barbra* album. Her quasi-classical approach to some of the holiday material is balanced by and blended with her pop style, making clear the meaning of Aida Pavletich's statement that Streisand possesses "a voice that cannot be mistaken for anyone else's, even though she often takes her style wherever she finds it."[6]

Its 1968 release date suggests that the next album for consideration is *A Happening in Central Park*, but its material actually comes from a concert Streisand recorded on 17 June 1967. The event was presented as a free public concert while Streisand was on leave from the set of *Funny Girl*. She rehearsed in New York during the early morning hours of the 17th and that evening presented more than two hours of music to an audience estimated at about 135,000. Editors subsequently trimmed the video and audio tape to fit both a one-hour television special and a Columbia album. The special aired fifteen months later in mid-September 1968; the album was released at the same time, resulting in Barbra's first "live" album (see discography).[7]

The subsequent commercial videotape of the concert is instructive for watching Streisand's methodology, but the sound quality on both the video and the album are less than perfect (not surprising for an outdoor event recorded with full orchestral accompaniment on a windy and humid evening). In fact, in one uncomplimentary review of the album, the writer noted that some unidentified audience members had a hard time hearing because the sound equipment was geared toward recording, not just amplifying.[8] On the other hand, a writer for *Variety* complimented Rheingold beer (the concert's sponsor) for supplying a sound system adequate for the difficult setting. A pull-away camera shot near the end of the show reveals that the front rows of the audience were not seated particularly close to the stage. This could have been for security concerns, for equipment practicalities, or for some other reason.[9] Of course, the illusion of closeness and intimacy are possible with the video, despite the large crowd and Streisand's apparent distance from the audience.

Many of the songs on the *Happening* album already would have been familiar to Streisand fans; she emphasized character and belt numbers with monologues and humorous bits of song in between.[10] Only "Love Is Like a Newborn Child" and "Natural Sounds," both lyric songs, were completely new. "Sleep in Heavenly Peace" was part of the New York concert, but its recurrence in her performance history is convoluted. The song was new to August 1966 attendees of her concert in Newport, Rhode Island, and to June 1967 Central Park concert goers, but before the 1968 release of the *Happening* album, "Sleep" already had become familiar to a wider Streisand audience through its inclusion on her November 1967 Christmas album. The incongruity surrounding this Christmas repertoire was further magnified by its performance during summer months. Streisand later wrote that her intended focus with "Sleep in Heavenly Peace" in 1967 was "peace," since the Six-Day War was being fought at the time.[11] Despite the unusual programming, the videotape indicates that Barbra received a standing ovation from the Central Park audience at the conclusion of the carol.

Several observations about her vocal technique during *Happening* deserve comment. For "Love Is Like a Newborn Child," Streisand uses her soft, breathy tone (as opposed to soft and pure), and the word *child* goes through a metamorphosis, something close to "cha-i-l-d," where she again treats the letter *l* as a vocalized sound. Words ending with *ng* (*song* and *strong*) take her back to a rather nasal vocal quality. "Natural Sounds" places her in a low register, again with a soft, breathy tone. One of the comic segments, "Value," which comes from a show entitled *Another Evening with Harry Stoones* in which Streisand was cast in her youth, displays her ability to move with ease from character dialect and speech-like delivery to a full, resonant musical tone.

Even though "Cry Me a River" was included on previous Streisand albums, *watching* her sing it by means of videotape transforms this belt song into a character song, as her facial expressions and body language act out the message. Similarly, on "I Can See It" the audience can see her reaction as she nearly runs out of breath before the end of a musical phrase. To compensate, she twists her body as though wringing out one last ounce of breath, but all in character with the text. In general her posture is quite upright with her shoulders comfortably back as compared to earlier videotaped performances. "He Touched Me" affords the opportunity to hear Barbra's stylings with minimal accompaniment and nonchalant rhythm at its beginning, and to see her wide-open throat and flat tongue on its rousing conclusion. Throughout the concert, Streisand's casual but effective use of the microphone is a lesson for singers who move it about so much that it becomes a distraction.

Much has been written about Barbra Streisand's film debut in *Funny Girl* in the fall of 1968. Although record, television, and theatre critics had not given her exclusively rave reviews for her previous work, her relationship with the press seems to have taken on a negative tone during the filming of this, her first movie. Reporter's views on her interaction with director William Wyler, co-star Omar Sharif, other crew members, and the Hollywood community became the substance for many articles. Wyler suggested that this negativity was based on Barbra's cool reaction to the Hollywood press; she did not make a "fuss" over them or stop work to be interviewed as they might have liked.[12] In spite of the fact that the reviews for the movie often were critical of the plot, the production, and the obvious focus on its leading lady, Streisand's performance generally was hailed as remarkable. The film was nominated for an Academy Award as Best Film, and Streisand won her first Oscar for Best Actress. Notwithstanding all of this media commentary, little was written about her singing as though its quality was unquestioned.

The score for the film contained several of the Jule Styne/Bob Merrill songs from the stage version including "Don't Rain on My Parade," "You Are Woman," "I'm the Greatest Star," and, of course, "People." Some comic songs for the show-within-a-show segments of the film were changed to include "Roller Skate Rag" and "The Swan." The most notable substitution was the use of Fanny Brice's torch-song hit "My Man" for the film's powerhouse finale (it partially was filmed and recorded live, not lip synched after the fact[13]), which purposely had been excluded from the stage show. Interestingly, Streisand has never recorded all of the original lyrics of that song, omitting those portions that reveal the "man" to be physically abusive and unfaithful. A comparison of the 1964 cast album and the 1968 soundtrack clarifies that Barbra's voice was slightly less nasal and strident in the later recording, that many of her vocal stamps and interpretive techniques remained consistent, and that her confidence as an actress was growing. The latter is particularly evident in "You Are Woman," where she sounds more playful or nonplussed (even though the character is innocent) than in the version presented on the cast album. A similar effect is heard during her film performance of "I'd Rather Be Blue," where Fanny's growing confidence is a part of the song's purpose in the plot. More than one recording reviewer noted that the accompanimental subtlety of the film-score orchestra was advantageous over a theatre pit orchestra (see bibliography).

Since "Don't Rain on My Parade" occurred in both the stage show and the film, and because Streisand continued to sing it in later concert settings, a few analytical comments are appropriate. The published arrangement that appears in the *Funny Girl* Vocal Selections[14] is only vaguely related to her vocal arrangement. The former includes an opening verse that is omitted in all of Streisand's recordings, and the order and content of the text often differs between the printed version and her performances. Nevertheless, her earliest rendition (on the cast album), despite the re-ordering of several phrases, is more faithful to the published melody and rhythms than her later performances. For example, Barbra sings *don't* after beat 1 (as written) on the cast album, but places it squarely on beat 1 for the soundtrack, which certainly emphasizes the meaning of the word with greater potency. Several of the melodic phrases end on a low note (G below middle C in the Selections), and she sings a note in that range on the cast album. On the soundtrack and on her 1994 *Barbra: The Concert* compact disc, only about fifty percent of the phrases end with her on the low note; other phrases end with a repeat of the higher penultimate pitch. The later recordings also contain more changes of tempo and meter to include brief half-time or double-time sections, which add to the intensity of this belt number. The bridge or release of the chorus exhibits the most change from recording to recording as to when and where words are placed in the temporal scheme of the accompaniment. This is an effective strategy since the purpose of the bridge is to provide contrast. Interestingly, the rendition that varies *least* from the print version is the bridge from *The Concert* performance, a recording that dates from nearly thirty years after *Funny Girl* reached the Broadway stage. But the tag repeat of that section on *The Concert* then is altered rhythmically to vary the *most* of all her recordings from the printed score, making any summary of style progression impractical.

Streisand's presentation of the long last note of "Don't Rain on My Parade" allows further observation of her technique over the years, but again without suggesting concrete patterns. During the eight beats assigned to the second syllable of *parade* (according to the printed music), her Broadway recording has about four beats given to the first half of the "a" sound while the other four are reserved for the ensuing "e" sound of the diphthong. Barbra's film version exhibits less "e" sound, saving it until very near the end of the note. Her 1994 concert version also has less "e" sound than her original Broadway recording, and the final d is punctuated with its closing shadow vowel ("dah"). All in all, the different performances may indicate that, while her basic technique remained consistent, she gained confidence and agility with melodic decoration, she acquired greater finesse in adjusting to harmonies as she displaced melodic segments within the metrical scheme, her voice matured to a darker sound with an increasingly controlled vibrato, and perhaps she learned to reserve some drama and passion for later sections of a song.

The release in 1969 of Streisand's *What About Today?* album further indicates that she was in the midst of a transition, as was terminology describing popular song. As various styles of vocal music, influenced individually or collectively by rock, jazz, soul, folk, the Tin Pan Alley legacy, or any sub-categories of these branches, were performed and recorded, commentators sought new verbiage to identify what was happening. This resulted in rather amorphous labels and descriptors, some of which were applied to Barbra Streisand's recordings. For example, the term "classic pop" began to denote the older style of popular song, those from Broadway shows, movies, and nightclub acts from the 1920s into the 1960s, by composers and lyricists of the ilk of Jerome Kern, Harold Arlen, Frank Loesser, and Oscar Hammerstein II.[15] Author Deborah Winer suggests, in fact, that standard or classic pop is closely related to jazz and show music, the difference often determined by the liberties the singer takes with melody or rhythm.[16] Indeed, this was the repertoire and the style with which Streisand was most closely associated in the 1960s.

The material of the newer generation of popular-song composers (as varied as Burt Bacharach, Paul Simon, Jimmy Webb, and many others) needed classification as well, causing several terms to be coined. Often the simple moniker "pop" was used to distinguish a sound that clearly was neither rock nor classic-pop. The occasional lack of distinction between rock and pop and the frequent lack of distinction between new pop and older pop come into clear relief in reviews written in the early 1970s. For example, an author for *Rolling Stone* in 1972 mentioned that Streisand is more comfortable with "pop" music than rock, but offers "On a Clear Day You Can See Forever" as an example—a song that otherwise might be referred to as classic pop.[17] Similarly, in a 1973 review entitled "The Merging of Pop and Rock" about recordings by Streisand, Bette Midler, Peggy Lee, and others, Patrick Merla suggests that rock of the 1960s had "rejuvenated" pop and that rock had already split into many categories.[18] He went on to claim that, "The surest indication of where rock is really going probably comes from successful pop singers who have made either rock albums or albums of all-rock material *sung in their own styles* [italics added]." An article entitled "Today's New Rock Crooners" from 1972, began, "Over the last few years a type of rock figure has appeared whose roots go far deeper than those of rock." Streisand's name is included in the author's list of exemplars who fit the "age-old tradition of the 'star.' "[19] Furthermore, he declared that her *Stoney End* album (from 1971) deliberately featured a "pop" sound (meaning not quite rock) and that she "willingly submitted her great, wild talent to the disciplines of pop . . . despite her torchy theatrical success." The amorphousness of the terms is obvious.

For purposes herein, terms and phrases like "classic pop," "traditional pop," "theatrical pop," or "Tin Pan Alley legacy" will refer to the Broadway, movie, club, and jazz-inspired standards or ballads, many from the 1930s and 1940s, like those Streisand recorded in her early years. "Contemporary pop" and "soft rock" will refer to the work of composers and arrangers with clear rock, soul, or folk-rock orientation and to the newer works of already-established composers who were being influenced by their younger counterparts. Further musical descriptions follow where pertinent to Streisand's transitional and later periods.

Barbra's *What About Today?* album contains material from a variety of composers and lyricists, including several associated with contemporary-pop and folk-pop/rock or rock: John Lennon and Paul McCartney, Paul Simon, Buffy St. Marie, Jimmy Webb, and Burt Bacharach and Hal David.[20] Streisand's supposed change in repertoire was highlighted by Columbia's pre-release advertisements, and in her first personal comments on an album liner, Barbra (at age twenty-seven) dedicated the collection to young people who sought a better future and who wrote and performed "songs of today."[21]

But those who would label this album a watershed in her oeuvre or suggest that Streisand had wholly entered the soft-rock arena overlook the fact that much of the repertoire is arranged and conducted by familiar colleagues (Peter Matz, Don Costa,[22] and Michel Legrand), and that composers and lyricists from the traditional or theatre style still are represented, including Legrand, David Shire, Alan and Marilyn Bergman, and Harold Arlen. In fact, several of the album's songs that make political and social statements are from this group: "That's a Fine Kind of Freedom" by Martin Charnin and Arlen, "Ask Yourself Why" by Legrand and the Bergmans, and "The Morning After" by Shire and Richard Maltby Jr. These songs draw attention to contemporaneous issues but are arranged to allow Barbra to use her old belting skills to add passion to the protest. Transition is indicated by the touch of shout or soul style that can be detected during moments of "Freedom."

By way of contrast, Lennon and McCartney, writers from a more contemporary, rock-influenced style, are represented by two songs that Streisand performs as playful character songs with dialect and a touch of humor: "Honey Pie" and "With a Little Help from My Friends" (although the latter has been arranged by Michel Legrand to include thick and dissonant harmonies that create a sense of ambiguity). Further contrast of style occurs in "Until It's Time for You to Go" by St. Marie, which Barbra also presents with her soft, floating tone supported by a string orchestra and varied dynamics. A similar gentle sound is used for the ballad "Goodnight" by Lennon and McCartney and the political poem "Little Tin Soldier" by Webb.

"Alfie" from Bacharach and David represents the love ballad category. Streisand had been asked to sing the song earlier; she "loved it," but had rejected the idea because the demonstration version recorded by an English singer was, in Barbra's opinion, good enough that she thought it should be promoted.[23] That English single never was released in the United States, so Barbra acquiesced and recorded the song for this album. She traverses Bacharach's characteristic melodic leaps with ease, but her rubato rhythms provide stark contradistinction from the soft-rock approach of Dionne Warwick's well-known version. Streisand also infuses some of her characteristic overlapped textual phrases into "Alfie," which results in some very long melodic segments sung on a single breath.

The repertoire of *What About Today?* also manifests many points of contrast between and within arrangements, and there sometimes is contradiction of style between text and accompaniment. For example, contemporary pop sounds are heard in the rhythmic layers and active bass lines of "What About Today?" and "Ask Yourself Why," even though the rest of the orchestration is quite theatrical with sweet strings and pyramiding brass. The occasional use of a backbeat and duple subdivision of each beat mean that Barbra has less flexibility with her customary rhythmic meandering. Some songs exhibit modern pop form through multiple verse-chorus format, fade-away conclusions, and harmonic modulations during vamped endings. Unlike most of Streisand's previous albums, this one contains places where some of her words, especially in the higher range, are hard to decipher. Her tendency to close her mouth and lips while continuing the musical tone is noticeable on the final *m* of *freedom*, which is not out of the ordinary, but the technique also is heard at the end of the *o* of *go*, adding a new final consonant.

In hindsight, composer/conductor David Shire wondered if the energy and repertoire of *What About Today?* were meant as a counterbalance to the subdued nature of *Simply Streisand*, her previous straight popular-song album. He, as composer of the title track, had hoped its release might net him a "Streisand hit," but he eventually wondered if neither the contemporary pop nor the classic pop audiences knew how to receive *What About Today?*, which straddled the two styles.[24] In Shire's experience, one of the main differences between the aesthetics of the two styles is that contemporary pop lyrics often start and end in the same emotional place, whereas theatre pop songs have more depth and a larger story to develop. His observation concurs with a strong feeling Streisand had regarding her repertoire choices throughout her career.

The soundtracks for *Hello, Dolly* and *On a Clear Day You Can See Forever* closed one decade and ushered in another for Barbra. Many film-goers would have been familiar with the music of *Hello, Dolly* from the popularity of the Broadway show and subsequent cast albums.[25] The re-cording of the title song by Louis Armstrong was a top seller in 1964, the same year Streisand had a hit with "People." The music from *Clear Day* had been available since the 1965 opening of the show on Broadway, but none of it climbed the pop charts in the same manner as the music from *Dolly.*

Casting young Streisand in the lead role of Dolly Levi was a surprise to many who had become accustomed to the character played as an older woman. In an interview given near the time of the movie's premiere, Barbra acknowledged amusement when she first learned of the possibility—she thought Elizabeth Taylor would make a more appropriate Dolly—and also wondered if this style of movie was going to be out of touch with the times.[26] Committed to the job by contract, she decided to search for facets of the role on which she could comfortably focus. She determined that it could be the story of any woman who loved but had been left a widow, no matter her age (a relevant issue with the Vietnam conflict current at that time), or of a woman who struggled to determine whether to live life as she found it in the present or as she remembered it from the past. Opin-ions of critics and the public varied as to whether the goal was accom-plished.

Barbra believed the title song to be the least effective of the score, but enjoyed singing a duet with Louis Armstrong during his cameo appearance in the rousing "Hello, Dolly" production number. She purposely chose to perform its opening verse slower and more out of tempo than previous singers had so that she could linger among the various restaurant waiters Dolly encountered on her return to Harmonia Gardens. Streisand also de-cided to present "So Long, Dearie" as fast as the words could be sung, in contrast to recordings by others. That song and "Just Leave Everything to Me" show off her precise enunciation in songs with many words and fast tempos. The audio of the latter perhaps indicates how hard Barbra is work-ing as both her quick breathing and even-quicker swallowing are heard on the track. Although Streisand's character and voice are primary in the show and on the album, it is particularly interesting to listen to songs on the soundtrack where she is part of an ensemble, such as "Put On Your Sunday Clothes." Her vocal timbre and the recording levels allow Barbra's voice to cut through the other voices and accompaniment, and her vitality seems to be boosted by the surrounding musical layers. When the range of the melody exceeds her capabilities, she moves to a harmony part, but still is identifiable. "Before the Parade Passes By" exhibits her on-again, off-again singing with and around the beat in a song where the meter and tempo cannot fluctuate as the music literally marches by.

Readers familiar with the re-incarnation story of *On a Clear Day You Can See Forever* realize that it provides the actress playing Daisy Gamble with many opportunities to display skills with contrasting dialects and personalities.[27] The film's opening song, "Hurry! It's Lovely Up Here," has Daisy singing to flowers, causing them to grow at unusual speeds—one of her secret and somewhat magical gifts. Streisand's rendition of the lilting, disjunct melody comes across as somewhat tongue-in-cheek, but mostly charming and warm. On words like *here* and *fill* a listener can detect her increasing habit, especially on light songs, to close off to an "n" sound at the end of the word—even when that sound is not part of the word. She continues to color and musically decorate certain notes to enhance the meaning of some words; for example, she slides up to and settles on the proper pitch during the quick word *up*. Other picturesque or sensory words, such as *hot, rosy, spread*, or *wake*, are slightly emphasized by means of extra breath around the tone, pitch inflections and slides, brief volume changes, or abrupt rhythmic stress. The text "fondled and sniff'd by millions who drift by. Life here is rosy, if you're a posy" is presented with no breath between *by* and *life*, but with one occurring after *here*.[28] This interpretation perhaps places more emphasis on the word *life* than it would otherwise receive as a relatively short note. Many measures of the song (as noted in the printed vocal score)[29] contain the rhythm in Example 1. Barbra often sings behind the beat and turns the measure into something approximating either Example 2 or Example 3. The former vaguely retains the short-long-short feeling of the printed score, but the latter creates a different kind of syncopation.

Example 1:

Example 2:

Example 3:

"Love with All the Trimmings" underscores a past-life, seduction-over-dinner scene, and Streisand uses her soft, breathy tone until the robust release and codetta. The tune itself has only a few pitches as many of the notes are repeated in a speech-song manner, a style Barbra often uses to present a text. (It is possible that the notated sheet music is an attempt to duplicate the rhythm and pitch that she sang in the film.) The sheet music indicates that the contrasting release is to be performed with a "Gentle Rock beat," but Barbra's full-throated sound is more prominent than the rhythm line. A subdued tone is heard on "He Isn't You," where she creates very long phrases for herself according to where she chooses to breathe. For example, nine measures are grouped together by not breathing after *you* in the text: "He isn't you. Mem'ries may fade in the shadows behind me."[30] These tender words contain many places where the meaning easily could get muddled, but by making slight breaks in her sound at potentially slippery moments, she is quite clear: "he^isn't^you."

Other pieces from the film are character songs mostly sung by the contemporary Daisy (not the past-life Daisy). "Go to Sleep" has Barbra singing a sweet, comic duet with herself, and her sound is more nasal than for other songs on the soundtrack, an appropriate color for the New York City character. On the other hand, "What Did I Have That I Don't Have?" is a fiery, multiple-section, dramatic character song. It begins with a hesitant opening, where Streisand is able to keep a musical tone as the character stammers through her thoughts. The opening is followed by a confused, slow torch section (presented as though talking to herself) and an angry, defiant conclusion. In the printed music, the lyrics of the second and third sections are printed underneath the same music (in verse 2 and verse 3 format), but any interpretation matching Streisand's would require considerable flexibility with the printed tempo and rhythm—not a simple repeat. She also sings some of the text in a higher range the final time.

The movie's title refrain, with its text full of pitfalls for singers, has become a Streisand signature song that provides plenty of opportunity to hear her treatment of vowels and vocalized consonants. At least three renditions of "On a Clear Day" appear on Streisand albums, including one from her 1994 tour (see discography and appendices). Barbra sculpts the word *clear* in a variety of ways approximating: "cah-l-ee(r)"; "clee-(r)eh"; "cle-eh-ee(r)" with pitch change in the middle; and "clah-eer-ah." She takes a similar approach to the word *here* vocalizing the ending as "r-eh" (with a shadow vowel) or closing off the *r* to a nasal sound. In contrast, the *r* of *ever* nearly is missing as the word is pronounced "ev-ah." She avoids the potentially blurred transition between the words of the line "see who you are" by inserting slight breath impulses.[31]

Streisand's rhythm for the melody of "On a Clear Day" also is interesting. The opening eight measures are flexible and speech-like against minimal accompaniment. The beat becomes more defined for the second eight bars as additional instruments join the mix. She lengthens the word *clear* from two beats in the printed version to four, moving *day* to beat 1 of the following measure. A similar procedure takes place with the words of the next two measures. During the following four measures, Barbra places several words or syllables squarely on beat 1 as notated: *glow*, *be(-ing)*, *(out)-shines*, and *star*. Shortly thereafter she takes considerable rhythmic liberty, stretching several words and beats and even repeats *never* of "never heard before." Near the end, she leaps up to emphasize the rather insignificant word *a*, but then waits until after the accompanimental chord is sounded before she sings *clear*, giving the word emphasis through syncopation. The following *clear* is decorated with a lower neighbor note. As noted previously, Barbra often breaks her sound slightly before initiating a word with a vowel, but here she ties the *d* of *and* to *ever*, which helps mark the downbeat. The final syllable of the song (*-more*) is difficult vocally as there is no clear vowel to elongate. Barbra's approach is to add a bit of an "r" sound to the *o* early and vocalize them together, but not to close off to a solid *r* for the ending. At the same time, her fast, loud, belt vibrato is very evident.

Morgan Ames noted that Streisand went "all out Broadway" for the title song, but that much of her other singing was appropriately restrained, adding to the effectiveness of the album separate from the film.[32] He also complimented Nelson Riddle's arrangements for their help in achieving this same effect. Co-star Yves Montand was the only other singer heard on the album. A single version of "On a Clear Day" was released, which is supported by a different arrangement and accompaniment—sounds appropriate for use outside the dramatic context of the show. However, the text is tied so strongly to the show's story that the song may not work as an independent piece, becoming instead a song-for-song's-sake (albeit an effective belt number). Interestingly, when Barbra chose to include it on her 1994 tour concert, she used the show arrangement rather than the arrangement heard on the single. In that performance situation, "On a Clear Day" came at the end of Act 1 of her concert, which was presented as a series of autobiographical vignettes—in other words, as a story.

In the meantime, Columbia released Streisand's first "greatest hits" album in 1970. While this type of album eventually became commonplace in the popular-music market, it should be noted that, of the eleven songs on *Barbra Streisand's Greatest Hits*, only "People" had made it onto the top-10 singles charts.[33] Her commercial success in the recording industry continued to be based on album sales rather than on single hits and was accomplished without much concertizing. The album was not an immediate best seller, but it eventually was certified multiplatinum (a "platinum" designation indicates that more than one million units have sold). *Greatest Hits* contains all of the song types (except advocacy and autobiography songs, which will become prominent later in the 1970s), with emphasis placed on the character and belt categories: character songs—"Second Hand Rose" and "Sam, You Made the Pants Too Long";[34] belt or torch songs—"My Man" and "He Touched Me"; lyric songs—"My Coloring Book"; and ballads—"People."

The albums *Stoney End* and *Barbra Joan Streisand*, both released in 1971, can be viewed as a pair that clearly took Streisand in new directions, at least in terms of repertoire.[35] "Newness" was illustrated by the personnel of the production team, perhaps the most important being Richard Perry as producer. According to the *Just for the Record* booklet, Barbra already had begun recording songs for an album to be entitled *The Singer*, but Clive Davis, the president of Columbia Records, asked her to record an album of contemporary pop songs and to work with Perry.[36] As *Stoney End* came to fruition, Streisand noticed that this was the first time she was the same age as the other musicians at the recording sessions rather than being younger—a sign of further transition.

The musical style of several of the works on *Stoney End* reflects a contemporary mode of composition. A backbeat, an eight-part division of the four-beat measure, and an active prominent bass line are important. Forms often fit an extended AABA arrangement (going beyond a 32-bar chorus) or some variation thereof, and several are formatted into multiple verses with or without repeated refrains. The accompaniment features a rhythm section, electronically produced sounds, and back-up singers (several of whose names would appear on many Streisand albums in the future—Clydie King and Vanetta Fields, for example). Streisand's approach to vocalization reflects a greater inclination toward soul- or gospel-influenced passages, but in terms of lyrics, the previously established song categories still pertain.[37]

"Hands Off the Man" by Laura Nyro and "Maybe" by Harry Nilsson both fit the description of a character song. During the former, the rhythm section is balanced by traditional Streisand instrumentation—high sweet strings and punctuating brass. The moderate but unwavering tempos of "Hands Off" and "If You Could Read My Mind" seem to put Barbra in a casual vocal mood. She does not project her customary dramatic style, and in fact, seems rushed by the tempo of "If You."[38] Nevertheless, she still decorates certain notes with brief embellishments or inflections.

"I Don't Know Where I Stand," by Joni Mitchell, is presented as a lyric song with pastel, impressionistic-like accompaniment from arpeggiated strings and electronically produced woodwind sounds. During one interlude between verses, Barbra plays a part in the orchestra, adding a distant-sounding hum. Her timbre is light and pure (her "white" tone, meaning without much overtone coloring); gentle vibrato colors longer notes. Her enunciation of certain words is typical: going to the *n* of *stand* and briefly stopping the sound between *my* and *hair*.

The aforementioned gospel influence is heard in Streisand's singing of

"Just a Little Lovin' " by Barry Mann and Cynthia Weil, which also has some characteristics of a slow torch or belt song. Its three-beats-per-measure meter, active bass line, and triplet subdivisions from the piano and other instruments add to its contrasting nature. Barbra sounds as if she relishes the slower tempo, inserting even more melodic decorations, word coloring, and emotion than usual. Interestingly some of the same musical techniques are heard on the bluesy "Let Me Go," but it is delivered in a character-song fashion. That piece is accompanied by rhythm section plus organ.

The title song of the album, by Laura Nyro, is the most soft-rock oriented song in the collection and was released as a single, earning Streisand her first million-selling single as well as a gold album.[39] A tambourine provides the eighth-note pattern, the backbeat projects clearly, and the electric bass is prominent and active. The multiple verse/chorus format comes to a close with a fade-out. A bright tempo permits Barbra to combine text lines into long phrases like (^ indicates a breath and + indicates no breath): "Mama cradle me again.+I can still remember him^with love light in his eyes."[40] William Ruhlmann has suggested that Streisand virtually copied Nyro's own recording of "Stoney End," but that the success of the single helped launch Streisand into a new decade.[41]

"I'll Be Home" by Randy Newman is a simple ballad made effective with minimal accompaniment. Although newly composed, it recalls an older love-ballad musical style, and at the same time, foreshadows the success Barbra will have in the 1970s with contemporary film ballads. In this performance, Streisand uses her breathy soft tone and, more than elsewhere on the album, plays with word coloring in the flexible surroundings. The intimate setting is reinforced by the sound of her breathing, which is not heard on the faster, louder tracks. Naturally, two words that occur frequently in the song are *home* and *I'll*. During the former, she moves quickly to the *m* and sustains that sound with pitch or mixes in a bit of nasal "n." Barbra avoids the "long e" sound of the *i* vowel in *I'll*, possibly to retain the tender mood. The word comes across as "ah-l" with both parts vocalized. The lyric also contains several words that begin with soft consonants (*h*, *wh*, and *y*), which makes them difficult to initiate clearly. She begins some of these words with a good aspiration before the beat, causing the vowel to occur on the beat thereby providing rhythmic definition (a common choral technique). Other words lacking crisp beginnings almost seem devoid of the opening sound, the text repetitions making them nonetheless intelligible. Because of the relative simplicity and repetition of the lyric and melody, the song provides ample opportunity to hear Streisand embellish and interpret what the composer/lyricist has provided. Her phrasing and some of her rubato and word coloring are indicated below (^ means breath taken; underlined words are accented; a letter in parentheses means it is vocalized; ~ indicates melodic decoration; and / indicates a slide into pitch).[42]

/   (m)   (m)   *rhythmic delay (l)*   (n)
I'll be home,^I'll be home^when your nights are troubled and you're all alone;^

                        slur   *inflection*   /   *slur*
when you're feeling down^and need some sympathy;^nobody's around^to keep

inflection
you company.^

                              ~   *rhythm drag   / stretch*
Remember baby,^you can always count on me.^ I'll be home,^I'll be home,^I'll be

(m)
home.

            inflection, (m)   *drag (m)*
    Hmm,^I'll be home,^wherever you may wander,^wherever you may roam.^

quiver   *stretch*   *inflection*   *intense, drag*
You'll come back^and I'll be waiting here for you.^ No one else will ever love

            gentle, breathy
you^the way I do.^

loudest   ~   / *stretch*   (m) *drag*
I'll be here^to comfort you and see you through.^ I'll be home,^I'll be home,^I'll be

(o)
home.

Although Barbra obviously does take rhythmic and melodic liberties, as would be expected, she retains the short breath phrases inherent in the compositional structure rather than applying her customary text/phrase overlapping.

Reviews of *Stoney End* were mixed, with some critics finding the material or arrangements not strong enough for the singer's abilities.[43] Some decided the titular song really did "rock" and that some selections had "soul" (although perhaps too precisely done), but that other performances in the collection were mediocre. Alec Dubro, writing for *Rolling Stone*, noted the conflicting historical difference between her earlier material and this; with the former being composed by professionals for professionals and the latter related to the folk or oral tradition. Rex Reed, who in the past had been rather vitriolic, thought that Streisand had made a satisfying transition to rock- and folk-influenced music.[44]

Barbra Joan continued to mix Streisand's fledgling new contemporary pop sound with some of her older theatrical sound. Richard Perry served again as producer, and Gene Page and Nick DeCaro assisted with some of the arrangements. Careful attention to the liner information reveals that an increasing number of female names appear among the list of composers and musicians,[45] and three songs by Carole King, who was experiencing significant chart success with her *Tapestry* album at the time, are included: "Beautiful," "Where You Lead," and "You've Got a Friend." Multi-track and other technology allows Barbra to sing duets with herself on some songs and to have the sound of seagulls and ocean waves added to "The Summer Knows."

Barbra's gospel or soul style is heard even more clearly on this album, and both the upper and lower ends of her range are needed.[46] Billy Preston, known for his gospel, soul, and rhythm-and-blues experience acquired through work with Mahalia Jackson, Sam Cooke, and Little Richard, plays the organ on some selections. But this soul sound is contrasted with gentle contemporary ballads like "I Never Meant to Hurt You" by Laura Nyro and "Love" by John Lennon. A hint of autobiography might be represented in Streisand's selection of Lennon's acidic "Mother" for the set, and "Space Captain" by Matthew Moore is performed as a futuristic character song.

The contemporary pop repertoire is joined by ballads set in a traditional style, such as her medley "One Less Bell to Answer/A House Is Not a Home" by Burt Bacharach and Hal David and orchestrated by Peter Matz. Similarly, Streisand includes "The Summer Knows," which was written as a movie theme song by Michel Legrand and Alan and Marilyn Bergman. The torch song "Since I Fell for You," written by Buddy Johnson in the 1940s, provides additional contrast and indicates how much variety was available in the popular-song arena. Barbra recorded the song simply because she wanted to sing it.[47] Although its composition antedates those of other songs on the album, the arrangement by Gene Page suggests contemporary soul.

Critics reviewing *Barbra Joan Streisand* commented on several points: the eclectic and uneven nature of the collection, how Barbra's acting and interpretive abilities either could add new layers of meaning to a lyric or cloud its meaning, and her willingness to try new material without losing sight of her vocal strengths. Morgan Ames noted in the 6 January 1972 issue of *High Fidelity* that her simpler style was appropriate for most of the material. In *Rolling Stone* of 6 January 1972, Stephen Holden concluded that the mixture of material was designed to appeal to as wide an audience as possible (see bibliography). In my own listening, the reissue of the album on compact disc affords greater opportunity to hear minute details in Streisand's vocalization. For example, during "Since I Fell," she uses various means to color both significant and minor words (*leave*, *such*, *loved*, and *for*), adds a guttural sound to the short word *in* at the song's dramatic high point, and after opening to a full tone on *I*, gasps slightly before starting *guess*.

The album art for both *Stoney End* and *Barbra Joan Streisand* is full of mysterious ambiguity. The former pictures Streisand on an elegant couch placed in the bed of a classic old pick-up truck with scrubby terrain all around (two matching chairs are visible in the distance). Barbra is only a minor part of the scene, a situation rare among her album jackets, and her face is small and shadowed so that it is hard to detect her expression. Many interpretations are possible, one conceivable choice being the idea of feeling lost or insignificant within the whole scheme of life. *Barbra Joan* has a dark brownish cover with Streisand's name in relatively small letters across the top. Only her face and shoulders are pictured, again in a rather shadowy fashion, and her expression is one of confusion, uncertainty, or maybe slight fear. While the photograph might seem curious at first glance, nothing is really unusual about the cover—in fact, it might be viewed as a companion to the dark quality of the *Stoney* photograph. But when the *Barbra Joan* jacket is reversed, a totally different mood is evident. The back of the jacket has her name across the top in the same location, but it is spelled "Barbara Joan Streisand." Her expression is mischievous, contented or, perhaps, childlike. The viewer is left to wonder about the message. Is it simply enigmatic art, or is it autobiographical, perhaps revealing that the "professional" Barbra has some serious questions about life? Although Streisand never has commented about this situation, perceptive fans will notice a significant change on the reissue of *Barbra Joan* on compact disc many years later. In that format, the cover photo and name remain the same, but the back-cover photo has been moved inside the CD booklet and the original spelling of her name (with three a's) is gone. The new back cover lists the songs on the album; the mysterious message has disappeared.

In 1972 Streisand participated in a concert to raise money to support the presidential campaign of Senator George McGovern, who later lost the election to Richard Nixon. Her performance marked her first large public concert since 1967 in Central Park.[48] Also included on the concert docket were folk-rock singers/composers Carole King and James Taylor. Shortly after the event, an album of Barbra's material entitled *Live Concert at the Forum* was issued by Columbia. David Shire, who had conducted her *Simply Streisand* album in 1967, served as the conductor for this concert, and Richard Perry produced the album.

An article by Peter Reilly in *Stereo Review* about *Live Concert at the Forum* began: "So why should you buy this album? After all, almost everything in it has been recorded by the same artist under perfect studio conditions. . . . The answer is that you should buy this album because it contains a full charge of the old-fashioned star-type electricity, that's why."[49] He went on to report that the star garnered six standing ovations ("explosions of enthusiasm") in her forty-five-minute set. Similar thoughts were expressed by Jon Landau in *Rolling Stone*, who also noted that she, like Elvis Presley, could overwhelm a song by her artistry, but surmised that her artistry was what the listener long remembered. In contrast, Henry Pleasants found her penchant toward "blowing up the songs emotionally beyond what a slender subject and a slender musical frame can support or sustain" noticeable in her version of Jim Webb's "Didn't We."[50] He also noted that she often exposed a "duality" in public performances, ranging from "delightful" to "egregious." Clive Davis recalled that Lou Adler, one of the concert's organizers, had suggested that Carole King close the concert on the strength of her *Tapestry* album. Streisand's manager, Martin Erlichman, objected strongly, and Streisand retained the closing slot. Davis quickly realized that they had made the correct choice, observing that Barbra had the audience "in the palm of her hand," and that "the evening belonged to her." By word of mouth, *Live Concert at the Forum* reached gold sales status immediately.[51]

This entire album could be placed under the autobiography and advocacy heading because of its political overtones. Similarly, Streisand's references to music from *Sesame Street* are a result of her son's influence. Nevertheless, musically the album contains mostly love ballads and belt songs. Some of her older hits, like "Don't Rain on My Parade," are performed with slightly new arrangements that reflect a contemporary style in terms of instrumentation and rhythm. (In hindsight, they draw further attention to notions of duality and unconventionality, in that the expected or old is presented in unexpected or new ways.) Her new-found gospel-oriented sound is heard on the "Sweet Inspiration/Where You Lead" medley. Similarly, Barbra's "oh yeah" ending on "Starting Here, Starting Now," her monologue about marijuana, and her character-song interpretation of the torch song "My Man" add an up-to-date air to the album. Likewise the album photographs reflect a contemporary-looking Streisand. Because Barbra was not one to simply imitate someone else's style, always placing her own stamp on material, one writer used the phrase "personality pop" to describe her overall approach.[52]

Perhaps Streisand's immersion in her film career in 1972 and 1973 (*What's Up Doc?*, *Up the Sandbox*, and *The Way We Were*) caused her fourth special for television (fifth if the Central Park concert is counted) to come across to some viewers and some critics as an innovative idea not carefully executed. *Barbra Streisand and Other Musical Instruments* aired on CBS on 2 November 1973. Much of the production team from the earlier specials remained intact (Martin Erlichman, Dwight Hemion, and Joe Layton), but Ellbar Productions no longer was involved as Barbra's marriage to Elliott Gould had ended in the interim.

Other Musical Instruments features many of Streisand's signature songs set in new ethnic settings, again revealing unconventionality and duality. Likewise, varied approaches to music composition common to the third quarter of the century are portrayed sporadically through the use of electronic and other modernistic sounds. Barbra's skills as an actress and a comedienne help weave together the story line and musical travelogue. But as several reviewers (of both the show and the soundtrack) noted, the ethnic and modern flavors are just that—flavors, not substantive ingredients. During some scenes it is difficult to ascertain whether the approach is serious, in jest, or an uncomfortable mixture of the two. Reviewers also suggested that the best part of the television show involved the guest star, Ray Charles. Streisand's duet with Charles on "Crying Time" and his solo number were not included on the album that Columbia released from the special in 1973.[53]

Even without the aid of the visual show, musical characterizations abound in the *Musical Instruments* repertoire. Several of Streisand's usual vocal techniques are apparent and are wrapped in a growing mature sound—mature in the sense of a darker, less nasal timbre and an increasingly refined control, especially pertaining to dynamics. Barbra's ability to change tone color for character and to blend with accompanimental harmony are paramount as contrasting timbres from various instruments and non-traditional harmonies must be complemented. Her clean diction with both the patter-song style of "Piano Practicing" and the placid nature of "The Sweetest Sounds" and "Glad to Be Unhappy" is clear.

One of the most interesting songs on the album, from a vocal point of view, is "I Never Has Seen Snow" by her old friend Harold Arlen and Truman Capote. (It was written for their 1954 show *House of Flowers*, which had a plot set in Haiti—hence the dialect.) Alec Wilder found the melody of "Snow" more impressive "than the song-arias from *Porgy and Bess*," and believed that Arlen, even more than Gershwin, wrote music of high quality while staying within popular-music boundaries.[54] Streisand's lengthy version (more than five minutes) has a blues quality established near the beginning with the harmonica. She uses considerable portamento and vibrato throughout, a full round "o" on words like *snow*, and the closed-mouth vocalization of some final consonants. Her controlled breath support provides a good foundation for several lengthy phrases and individual sustained notes, including a remarkable fifteen-second, soft *like* near the end. Barbra's ability to manage her breath and sound production allows her to break sensitively between *I* and *never* of the title words so that the second word gets a slight accent. More than most, this lyric song exhibits her skill in mixing classical finesse with popular dialect and emotion. Although it probably would never get broadcast time on top-40, mainstream, or light-rock radio stations of the 1970s, it is a Streisand exemplar.

In retrospect, Streisand might have been ahead of her time by presenting a multicultural program, and Peter Reilly rightfully noted that only a star of her stature could or would attempt such a production. Nonetheless, *Other Musical Instruments* has never been released on video.[55] By now it was clear that rebellious young Barbra had become part of the establishment, despite her attempts to modernize her image.[56] This period in her recording career was about experimentation and transition, but it ended with a nebulous view of exactly what she had discovered and where she was headed.

NOTES

1. First quote: Barbra Streisand, interview with unidentified reporter, *Funny Girl 30th Anniversary Video* (private release by *Barbrabilia*, Arlington Heights, Illinois, 1997). Second quote: Barbra Streisand, interview with unidentified reporter, "Hello, Dolly" interview, compact disc, *Rarities* vol. 5 (private release by Barbrabilia, Arlington Heights, Illinois, 1997).

2. For analytical and organizational purposes, Streisand's repertoire is grouped into song types as described in chapter 2: lyric songs, love ballads, character songs, belt or torch songs, and autobiography or advocacy songs. *A Christmas Album* also contains "My Favorite Things" from *The Sound of Music*. That song is not oriented specifically toward Christmas, but the movie soundtrack (featuring Julie Andrews) did make the top album lists of 1965, 1966, and 1967. It certainly is typical of Streisand to include theatre and film repertoire on an album, even if the choice did not fit the Christmas theme specifically. Her gentle rendition of "My Favorite Things," as opposed to the bouncy version heard in the film, reveals her attention to textual detail—every word and every sound matters. Her ability to paint a visual picture by vocally coloring selected words is prominent, once again lending a sense of characterization to the song. For further information on Streisand's history with the song, see James Spada, *Streisand: Her Life* (New York: Crown Publishers, Inc., 1995), 62. "My Favorite Things" has become a "Christmas song" in the oral-tradition manner. It also is included on Christmas albums by such diverse performers as Andy Williams (1965), Diana Ross and the Supremes (1965), Herb Alpert and the Tijuana Brass (1968), and Kenny Rogers (1981). See Jeff Green, *The Green Book of Songs by Subject*, 4th ed. (Nashville, Tennessee: Professional Desk References, Inc., 1995), s.v. "Christmas."

3. See Andrew Sarris, "Films," *The Village Voice* (10 October 1968): 53–55 for commentary on Streisand's portrayal of "Jewishness" in her career to that date. The topic continued to occupy the thoughts of some writers as noted in "The Streisand-Midler Connection" from *The Jewish Journal* of 2 January 1992, which was reprinted in *Diva: Barbra Streisand and the Making of a Superstar* (New York: Boulevard Books, 1996), 141–146. There is, of course, a long history in American popular music of musicians releasing Christmas-oriented albums and compact discs. The repertoire, whether sacred or secular, is presented in varied styles from jazz to country to children's song. The performers involved come from equally varied ethnic and religious backgrounds. Raphael Crystal suggests that Streisand's repertoire may not be unusual or unexpected from her point of view (being outside the Christian tradition) or from the point of view of many 1950s and 1960s amateur musicians. Raphael Crystal, interview by author, Muncie, Indiana, 6 April 1998. Other

questions that I am not able to answer come to mind: Did Columbia pressure her to record a Christmas album? Did she record it *because* it would not be expected? Would she do it again in the same way?

4. "White Christmas" was written by Irving Berlin and eventually was used in three films: *Holiday Inn* (1942), *Blue Skies* (1946), and *White Christmas* (1954). Bing Crosby did not sing the opening verse in any of the films. See Stanley Green, *Encyclopaedia of the Musical Film* (New York: Oxford University Press, 1981), 300.

5. Wireless Audio Collection catalog (Holiday 1997): 11.

6. Aida Pavletich, *Sirens of Song: The Popular Female Vocalist in America* (New York: DaCapo Paperback Press, 1980), 41.

7. In 1987, Streisand's company, Barwood, released the *Happening* special on CBS Fox videotape. Barbra introduces the program and explains that they had expected a crowd at the post-midnight rehearsal but that no one came. This puzzled and worried her, in spite of her established star status, until she learned that Central Park was closed after midnight. Her fears were assuaged when tens of thousands were already staking out claims on the lawn when she arrived for a sound check in the late afternoon.

8. Gene Lees, review of *A Happening in Central Park*, in *High Fidelity* (February 1969): 126; "Nothing Could Follow Barbra's Freebie in Central Park Except Sanitation Dept.," *Variety* (21 June 1967): 58. Barbra later complimented Phil Ramone on his technical abilities with sound for the "Happening" in an article about Ramone by Paul Verna in *Billboard* (11 May 1996): PR-10. She is quoted therein as saying he used the state-of-the-art tape-delay techniques of the day.

9. Security was a concern. The Six-Day War was being fought in the Middle East, and *Funny Girl*, even before its completion, was causing a stir in Egypt where many objected to Egyptian Omar Sharif and Jewish Streisand sharing the screen. See Alta Maloney, " 'Funny Girl' Banned in Egypt," *Sunday Herald Traveler* (Boston), 29 September 1968, Show Guide: 1, 6.

10. Interestingly, the monologue on the video is slightly different from what is heard on the album. Reviewers were mixed in their assessment of her banter between songs and rapport with the audience. See bibliography for a list of reviews.

11. Barbra Streisand, accompanying booklet for *Just for the Record*, compact disc 44111 (Sony Music Entertainment, 1991), 34.

12. Marjory Adams, "Wyler, Streisand Hit It Off OK," *Sunday Boston Globe*, 29 September 1968, A:9, 11. See also Axel Madsen, *William Wyler* (New York: Thomas Y. Crowell Company, 1973), 387–394. "Building a Dowry for Funny Girl," *Business Week* (28 September 1968): 82–84 contains information about the marketing and advance boxoffice sales for the film.

13. James Spada, *Streisand: Her Life* (New York: Crown Publishers, Inc., 1992), 208–209.

14. The Vocal Selections book is available from Chappell and Co., New York. See bibliography.

15. Roy Hemming and David Hajdu, *Discovering Great Singers of Classic Pop* (New York: Newmarket Press, 1991), 2. Charles Hamm refers to this group as the second generation of Tin Pan Alley composers in *Yesterdays: Popular Song in America* (New York: W. W. Norton and Co., 1979), 329.

16. Deborah Grace Winer, *The Night and the Music* (New York: Schirmer Books, 1996), 82–83. She believes there to be significant crossover between jazz and pop: Ella Fitzgerald was a jazz singer who recorded pop standards, Sarah Vaughan was a jazz singer who had pop hits, Peggy Lee sang jazz repertoire but was a pop singer, and Billie Holiday sang jazz without many jazz techniques.

17. Jon Landau, review of *Live Concert at the Forum*, in *Rolling Stone* (21 December 1972): 62.

18. Patrick Merla, *Saturday Review* (January 1973): 54.

19. Joel Vance, *New York Times*, 10 December 1972, D:36–37.

20. Bacharach and David are described by Michael Campbell as " 'Brill Building'-style" songwriters who were part of an attempt to "bridge the gap between rock 'n' roll and traditional popular song." See *And the Beat Goes On* (New York: Schirmer Books, 1996), 240.

21. Some observers might see an additional anomaly in the front liner photo of Streisand compared to that found on the back. The front perhaps suggests an old-time star image, and the back a sultry, contemporary look—in the same way the music is both old and new. Both photos feature Barbra with a short, curly hair style, one that she will use again in *A Star Is Born* in the mid-1970s. Streisand had been involved in some political events before the release of *What About Today?*; she performed in a 1968 concert to raise funds for congressional candidates opposed to the fighting in Vietnam. Her awareness of and interest in contemporaneous political issues becomes increasingly important later in her career.

22. Don Costa's arrangements for Frank Sinatra, as the singer was trying to adapt to new repertoire from the 1960s, are discussed in Richard Ackelson, *Frank Sinatra: A Complete Recording History* (Jefferson, N.C.: McFarland, 1992), 337–343. Costa's soft-rock background was helpful, and his skillful arrangements often featured busy rhythm lines, a quickly established medium beat, heavy strings, no breakstrains, a layered multi-track but soft overall sound, a form other than verse-chorus AABA, fadeout endings, and non-verbal vocals added to the orchestration.

23. Barbra Streisand, interview by unidentified reporter, "Hello, Dolly" interview, compact disc, *Rarities* vol. 5 (private release by *Barbrabilia*, Arlington Heights, Illinois, 1997). The name of the singer is hard to discern from the interview; Streisand may have been referring to a 1960s British singer named Cilla Black.

24. David Shire, interview by author, Muncie, Indiana, 4 March 1998. Shire wrote "What About Today?" with Peter, Paul, and Mary in mind, incorporating a simple folk-like quality. They were not interested in the song because it was not "folk" enough; Streisand's arrangement by Don Costa was much different from Shire's original concept, but he now thinks of the song in the "Streisand style." See also Tim Murphey, "The When, Where, and Who of Pop Lyrics: The Listener's Prerogative," *Popular Music* 8, no. 2 (1989): 185–193 for a discussion of the open-endedness of pop lyrics and the wider interpretive options available to the *listener* in these songs.

25. Commentary on the various recorded versions is found in Kurt Gänzl, *The Blackwell Guide to the Musical Theatre on Record* (Cambridge, Massachusetts: Basil Blackwell Ltd., 1990), 406–407. The film *Hello, Dolly* was completed in 1968, but its release was held until the Broadway show completed its run.

26. Barbra Streisand, interview by unidentified reporter, "Hello, Dolly" interview, compact disc, *Rarities* vol. 5 (private release by *Barbrabilia*, Arlington

Heights, Illinois, 1997); Barbra Streisand, accompanying booklet for *Just for the Record*, compact disc 44111 (Sony Music Entertainment, 1991), 39. She was correct in her assessment of the movie's style. Although her talents lent themselves to traditional musical theatre and musical film, public interests were going to insist that these genres evolve. Barbra's dilemma was to choose between heading in a new direction or risking getting lost in the transition. The decision was made easier by her desire to focus on her film career and studio recordings. In the same *Rarities* interview, Streisand remarks that a writer recently had described her as both "aristocrat" and "street urchin." She agreed with this perception of the conflicting sides of her personality.

27. In the story, the Daisy character goes to a hypnotist to help her stop chain smoking. During these sessions, her past lives are discovered. Joseph Morgenstern reviewed the film in *Newsweek* (29 June 1970): 78–79. He complimented Streisand's ability to play such a varied part: "She's alive and at home in any period, any accent the movie requires of her. . . . She's a thoroughbred clotheshorse for Cecil Beaton's costumes. She flashes lightninglike between Melinda's airs and Daisy's earthiness."

28. "Hurry, It's Lovely Up Here," lyrics by Alan Jay Lerner, music by Burton Lane.

29. The Vocal Selections book is available from Chappell & Co., Inc., New York. See bibliography.

30. "She Isn't You (He Isn't You)," words by Alan Jay Lerner, music by Burton Lane.

31. "On a Clear Day (You Can See Forever)," lyrics by Alan Jay Lerner, music by Burton Lane.

32. Morgan Ames, review of *On a Clear Day You Can See Forever*, in *High Fidelity* (October 1970): 136.

33. Of course, the idea of a "greatest hits" or "best of" album would have been impractical before the development of long-playing records in the late 1940s. An early successful example was *Johnny's Greatest Hits* by Johnny Mathis released in 1958. Sometimes a "greatest hits" album indicated a declining audience or a waning career, but Elton John, in particular, turned that notion around in the 1970s. See Donald S. Passman, *All You Need to Know About the Music Business* (New York: Simon and Schuster, 1991), 99.

34. The song "Sam, You Made the Pants Too Long" had been excerpted as part of a circus medley (sung to penguins) on Streisand's *Color Me Barbra* television special, and she released the entire song as a single, but it was not found in its entirety on any of her albums until *Barbra Streisand's Greatest Hits*. This marketing strategy of including new versions of older material or previously unreleased material on a "greatest hits" collection will continue during Streisand's career.

35. Streisand already had been experimenting with a rock-oriented sound, albeit soft rock. About 1968 she recorded three singles that did not appear on commercial albums; they are contained on Barbra Streisand, compact disc, *Rarities* vol. 1A (private release by *Barbrabilia*. Arlington Heights, Illinois, 1997). "Our Corner of the Night" is unique in presenting Barbra almost buried in a "girl-rock" arrangement in the style of Leslie Gore or Petula Clark. Her recording of "He Could Show Me" features Latin rhythms and considerable "Sergio Mendes-sounding" vocal backup. She performs "Frank Mills" from *Hair* as a sweet, humorous teeny-bopper

character song (much like it occurs on the cast album), but Streisand's accent suggests a timbre and dialect amalgam that might be described as "Second Hand Rose" meets "Grease."

36. Barbra Streisand, accompanying booklet for *Just for the Record*, compact disc 44111 (Sony Music Entertainment, 1991), 45. Other information about Streisand's recording career is found in Clive Davis, with James Willwerth, *Clive: Inside the Record Business* (New York: William Morrow and Co., Inc., 1974). Columbia Record's "middle-of-the-road" (MOR) inclination and Streisand's role in that style in the 1960s are discussed on pages 3–4; the renegotiation of her Columbia contract in 1966 is described on pages 50–53; Columbia's attempts to find a balance between an MOR and a rock stable of performers is retold on pages 104–105; and Streisand's move into the contemporary pop scene and Davis's suggestion of Perry as a collaborator are described beginning on page 218.

37. Additionally, "Free the People" by Barbara Keith could serve as an advocacy song or autobiography song. It is the second song on the album that contains religious references (the other is "Time and Love").

38. One reviewer thought "If I Could Read Your Mind [*sic*]" was the best song on the album because Streisand "plays it straight." See Alec Dubro, review of *Stoney End*, in *Rolling Stone* (1 April 1970):50.

39. Irwin Stambler, *The Encyclopedia of Pop, Rock, and Soul*, revised edition (New York: St. Martin's Press, 1989), 655.

40. "Stoney End," words and music by Laura Nyro.

41. See Michael Erlewine, Vladimir Bogdanov, and Chris Woodstra, eds., *All Music Guide to Rock* (San Francisco: Miller Freeman Books, 1992), s.v. "Barbra Streisand," by William Ruhlmann.

42. "I'll Be Home," words and music by Randy Newman.

43. This is related to David Shire's comment that, to him, one of the distinctions between "pop" and "theatre music" is that the former begins and ends in the same emotional place, whereas the latter usually has greater emotional development. David Shire, interview by author, Muncie, Indiana, 4 March 1998. Streisand's sound on *Stoney End* is called "a wailing pop-rock vocal style that was suitable" in Dave Marsh, *The New Rolling Stone Record Guide* (New York: Rolling Stone Press, 1983), s.v. "Barbra Streisand," by Stephen Holden.

44. Several reviews of *Stoney End* and *Barbra Joan Streisand* are listed in the bibliography. Notice once again the varied use of popular-music terminology in these titles and in other reviews.

45. This trend is not maintained with Streisand's subsequent albums.

46. Henry Pleasants came to a similar conclusion, noting that Streisand occasionally sounded like Aretha Franklin and Mahalia Jackson. See *The Great American Popular Singers* (New York: Simon and Schuster, 1974), 364.

47. Barbra Streisand, accompanying booklet for *Just for the Record*, compact disc 44111 (Sony Music Entertainment, 1991), 48.

48. Between 1969 and 1972 Streisand had a few singing engagements in Las Vegas and appeared on a Burt Bacharach television special. Music from these events was not released commercially, although a few selections from her Las Vegas performances in July 1969 and from the Bacharach special are included on *Just for the Record* (see discography). Her 1969 engagement in Las Vegas improved over its run, according to Charles Champlin. This experience with an audience (her first

nightclub engagement in six years) left Barbra frightened, even though audiences warmed to an "ecstatic" state once the show was refined. See the bibliography and Charles Champlin, "Streisand: A Scintillating Show of Gifts," *Los Angeles Times*, 5 August 1969, IV:1, 4. Allison Waldman points out that even the visual differences between Streisand's 1969 and 1970 Las Vegas performances were indicative of changes in her life. For the earlier shows she wore designer gowns and wigs, while the next year she wore pants suits and long, straight hair. See Allison Waldman, *The Barbra Streisand Scrapbook* (New York: Citadel Press, 1995), 50. Eliot Tiegel points out that her 1972 concerts at the Las Vegas Hilton were a mix of her old hits and her newer contemporary repertoire, including the duet with herself (on tape) of a medley of "One Less Bell to Answer" and "A House Is Not a Home" from the Bacharach special. He found it a "treat" to watch her compete with herself. See *Billboard* (15 January 1972): 16. (The medley also appeared on *Barbra Joan Streisand*. See discography).

49. Peter Reilly, review of *Live Concert at the Forum*, in *Stereo Review* (March 1973): 89–90.

50. Jon Landau, review of *Live Concert at the Forum*, in *Rolling Stone* (21 December 1972): 62; Henry Pleasants, *The Great American Popular Singers* (New York: Simon and Schuster, 1974), 360–363.

51. Clive Davis, with James Willwerth, *Clive: Inside the Record Business* (New York: William Morrow and Co., Inc., 1974), 221–222. He also recounts that the advertising campaign for *Stoney End* had, in part, backfired, offering as an example an article in *Rolling Stone* that described her as "an old-style movie-star type living in the glittering Hollywood Hills and *incongruously* wearing dungarees" [italics added]. Davis concluded that, although the visual images did not match, Streisand "was able to mix both worlds of music as few other artists could." See also Grover Lewis, "The Jeaning of Barbra Streisand," *Rolling Stone* (24 June 1971): 16.

52. Roy Hemming and David Hajdu, *Discovering Great Singers of Classic Pop* (New York: Newmarket Press, 1991), 210. (The assessment of the similarity between Streisand's version of "Stoney End" and that of the composer, Laura Nyro, notwithstanding.)

53. "Crying Time" was recorded as a Streisand solo (actually she sings a duet and trio with herself) on *ButterFly* in 1974. The television duet with Charles is included on *Just for the Record* (see discography).

54. Alec Wilder, *American Popular Songs: The Great Innovators, 1900–1950* (New York: Oxford University Press, 1972), 286.

55. Peter Reilly, review of *Barbra Streisand and Other Musical Instruments*, in *Stereo Review* (July 1974):93.

56. Dichotomy and change even were noted in an article about *Barbra Streisand and Other Musical Instruments* in *TV Guide* (27 October 1973): 12–14. The writer remarked that "second-hand," thrift-shop clothes were no longer a part of Streisand's wardrobe since she had become prosperous enough to dress like a "first-hand Nefertiti."

_____ *Chapter 4* _____

Eclecticism and Maturity:
Personalized Products

I believe in the audience. . . . I believe they are the greatest barometer
of the truth.[1]
   I'm not interested just in good technique. I don't know how I sing
or why I sing like that.

Under the heading "Barbra Streisand," an author for *The New Rolling
Stone Record Guide* stated: "But Streisand was never able to sing hard
rock convincingly, and on the eccentric *ButterFly* . . . she sounded way out
of her depth. *The Way We Were*, however, was more on the mark."[2] These
comments introduce the first two albums in the next period of Barbra's
recording career, and the albums manifest the eclecticism that would typify
her commercial recordings between 1973 and 1984. Yet Streisand abandoned neither her musical heritage nor her earlier style; instead, she brought
her theatrical approach to contemporary pop ballads, which were newly
written but reminiscent of pre-rock standards. Bruce Pollock has pointed
out that popular music of the early 1970s was marked, in many instances,
by a return to melody-oriented songs, a trait that went hand-in-hand with
Streisand's lyrical style. Equally important at that time was the growing
tendency toward writing theme songs specifically for films, especially non-
musical films. Alan and Marilyn Bergman were at the forefront of this
movement, and their poetic texts matched Barbra's penchant for word coloring and characterization. Pollack concluded that "the miracle of the well-
written, well-sung song, one that could sustain many interpretations over
the course of years, happened frequently in the seventies, at least in the

early part."[3] Some of the songs on *Barbra Streisand: The Way We Were*, to be discussed shortly, fit that description perfectly.

Pollock also observed that the later 1970s were characterized by the "fragmentation" of the marketplace, by the overriding importance of "the beat" in ubiquitous rhythm and dance music, and by the inclination toward "crossover" recordings from many labels and many artists.[4] This crossover, related to eclecticism, also would become a hallmark of Streisand's recordings during the 1970s, as she ventured into previously unexplored territory like classical music, pop duets, and beat-dependent disco. At the same time, she found her musical maturity through the natural process of aging—her voice began to acquire the refined timbre of a thirty-year-old, which allowed her to show off her meticulous control of pitch, timbre, and dynamics with greater distinction. She adapted traits of several contemporary styles and new repertoire to fit her own musical interests, vocal technique, and performance style; and ever unconventional, she bucked tradition by keeping to the confines of the recording studio. Indeed, the 1970s saw Streisand retreat from public vocal performance (except as part of isolated "benefit" concerts), even though she continued to influence other soft-rock singers who were making their way in the club and cabaret circuit.[5]

The Way We Were serves as the title of four separate entries in Barbra Streisand's oeuvre: the name of her 1973 Columbia Pictures *film* directed by Sydney Pollack and co-starring Robert Redford; the title for the *theme song* of that film with music by Marvin Hamlisch and lyrics by Alan and Marilyn Bergman; the name of the *soundtrack* from the film on which she sings the title song (arranged by Marvin Hamlisch); and the name of an *album* of Streisand songs featuring the single of that name (arranged by Marty Paich).

"The Way We Were" is a contemporary love ballad that harkens back to a style suitable for the movie's plot set in the 1940s and 1950s. The Bergmans have acknowledged the importance of understanding popular-song history in their own approach to writing, suggesting that an awareness of the style and technique of writers like Rodgers and Hammerstein and the Gershwins helps them to connect contemporary pop with traditional standards.[6] They have succeeded in making that connection with "The Way We Were," which garnered an Oscar and a Grammy and accolades like "superior and enduring"[7] (both characteristics of a standard) in an era replete with musical sub-styles.[8] Likewise, the Bergmans have reflected on the challenge of serving multiple masters when writing for a specific dramatic situation and specific singer, a scenario applicable with this film, song, and star. Although not citing Streisand specifically in this instance, Alan Bergman remarked that, "When you have a singer with a real instrument, you have to be sure that you're always putting open sounds on high notes, and that you're never giving the singer 'mouthfuls,' so they will have the chance to open up and sing."[9]

A careful examination of "The Way We Were" reveals how the Bergmans put their words into action (figuratively and literally). The lyric contains many words set to short melody notes, but the tempo is slow enough to allow clean and clear enunciation—especially with a singer who has a propensity for good diction. The picturesque text and tempo complement Streisand's tendency to treat texts in a free-flowing rhythmic manner and to color words with accents, timbre changes, and decorative pitches. The highest pitches of the song come in the extended and altered return to A (actually A¹ in an AABA¹ form) on the words *to*, *we*, and *whenever* allowing the singer to settle on the vowel sounds "oo," "e," and "eh," the first and last of which are easy, open vowels. Several of the song's phrases conclude with words ending in *er* or *re*, for which many pop singers would create a nasal or tight-throat sound. In typical fashion, Streisand softens or almost omits the "r" sound altogether, so that, for example, *were* becomes "weh-(r)ah," "wuh-(r)ah," or "we(r)(ehn)," with the latter hinting of a slight nasal hum at the end that sounds as if it might be created by arching the tongue toward the roof of the mouth forcing greater quantities of air into the nasal passages. Also typical of her now-familiar technique, Barbra sings the rhythms much differently than they are printed on the sheet music.[10] This is especially noticeable in the bridge where the words *can*, *or*, *if*, and *all* each are printed on beat 1 of a measure, but Streisand puts only *all* in that specific metrical place. Similarly, many notes printed as whole notes occupying a full measure are instead sung beginning on beat 2 or beat 3 after she has stretched out words in the previous measure for emphasis. At the return to A¹ from the bridge, she does not take a breath, tying together *we* and *memories*, which sets up a long musical phrase of fifteen seconds. Listeners might recall that both the movie and single versions begin with Streisand humming almost a full verse of the melody. This effect was used again during her 1994 concert tour; "The Way We Were" opened Act 2, with Barbra beginning the hum off stage.

The other repertoire on *Barbra Streisand: The Way We Were* is a conglomeration of songs from younger composers (Carole King, Stevie Wonder, and Paul Simon) and established composers (Michel Legrand and Irving Berlin). In addition to the title song, Alan and Marilyn Bergman supplied the lyrics for three additional songs in the set, each time teaming with Legrand as composer (see discography).[11] In terms of the song categories established in chapter 2, love ballads and torch or belt songs are the most clearly represented, the former with "The Way We Were" and "What Are You Doing the Rest of Your Life?", and the latter with "The Best Thing You've Ever Done" (although several moments of that song suggest character song as well). Some of the other songs straddle the boundaries, mixing love texts and lyric qualities with characterizations and perhaps even personal messages ("I've Never Been a Woman," "All in Love Is Fair," and "Summer Me, Winter Me").

The texts of "Being at War with Each Other"[12] and "Something So Right" blend ideas about relationships and social awareness, as though the composers (King and Simon, respectively) are intertwining 1960s "message lyrics" with 1970s "love lyrics."[13] These songs are placed first and second on side 1 of the album, and their styles might remind a listener of Barbra's *What About Today?* from 1969.[14] Rock-like instrumentation and rhythm layers are most pronounced on "Being at War" and "The Best Thing" (both produced by Nick DeCaro who had worked on *Barbra Joan Streisand*); full orchestration with only light percussion is heard on others. Interestingly, the backbeat of "Pieces of Dreams" is interrupted (eliminating its intent) whenever Streisand wants to deliver text passages in a parlando style for dramatic effect, which nonetheless is a serviceable amalgam with the bluesy harmonica and piano accompaniment. Other modern traits also are heard: the pungent piano harmonies near the end of "Being at War" that are resolved and followed by a saxophone fade-out solo; the verse-chorus, verse-chorus, bridge, verse-chorus form of "Something So Right,"[15] and Legrand's slithering harmonies and jazz inflections of "What Are You Doing."

Streisand's overall sound is polished and mature; the passion remains, but its impetuous vein has been tempered, perhaps through deeper understanding and experience. If adapting terms from classical, or at least established, voice pedagogy, Barbra, more than ever, might be described as an alto, a contralto, or a mezzo-soprano in her vocal range, but the lightness and flexibility of her voice recall a lyric soprano. Her lyric qualities are balanced by her capabilities as a belter, and she continues to mix her upper belt and head voices for power with higher notes. She uses her full cache of tone colors and vocal stamps (fast vibrato on loud passages, abrupt dynamic changes, *er* becoming "ah," vocal growl, closing off the ends of words to a hum-like sound, settling on the second sound of a diphthong vowel, overlapping musical and textual phrases, etc.) on each individual performance, but they are especially noticeable in "The Best Thing You've Ever Done."[16] Her previous soft-rock style and timbre are conspicuous enough on "All in Love Is Fair" that the song might have been recorded earlier than others of the set.

The 1974 album *ButterFly* displays a different kind of repertoire mix through its inclusion of works by a multiplicity of writers: Bob Marley, Bill Withers, Paul Williams, Paul Anka, Graham Nash, David Bowie, and Buck Owens. The album was produced by Jon Peters, then involved in an amorous relationship with Streisand. His influence in repertoire selection and in the studio allows this entire album to be catalogued as autobiographical; some individual songs also might be quite personal. The album liner is full of photographs of Streisand and Peters in the studio, which added fuel to the fire when some critics and media commentators pounced on Peters's lack of previous experience in the recording industry. Others applauded her adventuresome spirit and earthiness (see bibliography). Although the album is certified gold, many years later Barbra commented (without elaboration) that *ButterFly* was the album she might like to withdraw.[17]

Many of the songs on *ButterFly* were arranged by Tom Scott who blended electronic pop-rock instrumentation with traditional strings, and in some cases, punctuating brass.[18] Significant contrast is provided by the piano, harp, and cello accompaniment and fragmented countermelodies of "Simple Man," a song which again proves that Barbra is sometimes best left to do her interpretive work against minimal backup. In fact, she almost approaches classical diction with this piece by not going as quickly to the second vowel sound of the diphthong (for example, on *time*) and by using minuscule breath breaks between words to set up clean enunciation. Otherwise Streisand's timbre choices run the gamut from a gentle, restrained clarity (in some instances mixed with a bit of seductive teasing, for example, on "Love in the Afternoon") to an intense delivery, created in part through substantial use of her upper range and dynamic changes.

Gospel or rhythm-and-blues inflections and short melismas (perhaps from the influence of Aretha Franklin) are heard on several pieces including "Grandma's Hands" and "Since I Fell for You." The latter is cast as a slow rock ballad with three subdivisions on each beat of the arpeggiated accompaniment, but often Streisand is off or behind the beat. This song makes clear her gentle-to-intense timbre scale as she moves from opening verses to bridge to final verse. The gospel nature of "Jubilation" by Paul Anka is underscored through the use of electric organ. This piece shows Streisand's expansive range parameters, even noticeable on just one word, *sorrow*, as she alters it on repetitions of the chorus.

"Crying Time," by Buck Owens, includes a hint of country guitar near the end, and the vocal line (with Barbra singing a duet and trio with herself) exhibits significant country-like sliding in and out of pitches, but Streisand does not go as far as southern dialect (nor is there dialect on the reggae-influenced "Guave Jelly"). In fact, a gospel-like vocal style continues to predominate and is heard on the third repetition of the "Crying Time" chorus during her one-woman trio.

Most of the song categories are represented on *ButterFly* through her renditions and the arrangements: belt or torch song—"Since I Fell for You"; character song—"Simple Man"; and love ballad—"I Won't Last a Day Without You." In Barbra's hands, David Bowie's "Life on Mars" defies categorization, reflecting from moment to moment several style traits. "I Won't Last" exhibits the usual Streisand vocal techniques, including music and text phrase overlapping, word coloring (*hard, best, you*), and timbral variety for character development. The song is constructed in an AABA form with each A constituted by a verse and a chorus. Streisand's ability to add minute interpretive variations is clear, especially on the repeated chorus text, where each repetition is altered a bit more than the previous (heard on the words *rainbow* and *madness*, for example). Several reviewers commented that this was among the best performances on the album because the song allowed Streisand to do what she does best—create an emotional story even though the text does not contain obvious dramatic development.

The 1975 album entitled *Lazy Afternoon* put Barbra in the hands of one primary arranger and composer—Rupert Holmes, whose work as composer and performer she had heard previously on his own albums. Although there are contemporary qualities in some of the repertoire, in the lush orchestral/electronic arrangements, and in her vocal delivery of several of the songs, the album also suggests a return to earlier times and to Streisand's earlier singing. This mix of styles, in fact, might cause this album to be the one that squarely places her in the middle of the middle-of-the-road faction, between rock and pop on the one hand, and between old pop and new pop on the other.[19] Several of the songs are written with a theatrical bent, allowing Barbra to play roles as she sings. Likewise, her appreciation of lyrics that change meaning, that evolve as the song unfolds, is fostered by a love ballad (or maybe "modernistic torch song," in the sense of resolute rather than desperate emotions) from her own pen "By the Way," which she co-wrote with Holmes. During that song, the repeat of the prepositional phrase title usually is used to suggest a conversational nonchalance, especially in connecting thoughts about a vacillating or uncertain relationship. By song's end, a climactic rhetorical question is posed, asking why *love* sometimes cannot (or should not) be made to simply slip "by the way." The accompaniment varies from full orchestra to simple guitar arpeggios, although Barbra seems uninterested in singing straight eighth notes to match the eighth-note guitar patterns near the end.

The title song of the *Lazy Afternoon* album was written for the 1954 musical *The Golden Apple*. Its poetic text, supported by an impressionistic electronic accompaniment and her floating, breathy tone, provides many words ripe for coloring; her rendition suggests the song's placement in the lyric-song category. Streisand's personal liner notes about each song make the album strongly autobiographical, and two songs clearly have personal meaning for her: "Widescreen," about the difference between "real" life and "screen" life, and "My Father's Song," which resonates with her feelings about her own father's premature death.[20] Belt or torch songs are represented by the cabaret standard from 1929, "Moanin' Low," and the contemporary "You and I," by Stevie Wonder. Wonder's contribution stretches Streisand's range in both directions, and again, she uses the repetitions of the title words to good advantage with a variety of word-coloring choices. The word *world* is interesting to observe as she spreads it so that every possible sound (vowel or consonant) is vocalized; a similar result is heard on *celluloid* and *avoid* in "Widescreen." The final few measures of "You and I" show her control with sudden dynamic changes and her fast, narrow vibrato on loud, high notes. "Moanin" contains octave leaps to emphasize certain words, and Barbra changes timbre frequently and quickly between loud and soft sections and high and low pitches. A touch of early disco, with the requisite four-part division of each beat in the measure, is heard in her version of the Holland-Dozier-Holland Motown song, "Wake Me, Shake Me." Her performance proves she can sing directly on beat 1 when necessary. "Wake Me" is the only rhythm or dance song of the set; perhaps the "lazy" title here reflects just that mood, in the same way the 1967 title *Simply Streisand* indicated a relaxed-sounding album. Interestingly, the critics were more contradictory of one another than usual in their assessments of *Lazy Afternoon* and of individual tracks (see bibliography), but several writers acknowledged Streisand's pre-eminence in America's popular-music arena of the 1960s and 1970s.

Two musical films starring Barbra Streisand opened in 1975 and 1976: *Funny Lady*, the sequel to her Broadway and film portrayal of Fanny Brice, and *A Star Is Born*, her updated version of the familiar *one star ascends while the other star falls* story. The two films display both her musical maturity and her willingness to borrow from many sources, and they exemplify the transition occuring in the musical-film genre at that time. The former is old fashioned in its style and story, but *A Star Is Born* shows how contemporary popular music, in the broad sense of the definition, was wresting its way into movies. This trend eventually would have a significant impact on the recording industry as pop-and-rock-laden soundtrack albums (that would appeal to a large and young audience) added to the studio's and the record-label's coffers.[21] Herbert Ross, who had been the choreographer and "Director of Musical Numbers" for *Funny Girl*, directed and choreographed *Funny Lady*. Ray Stark again served as producer for this second phase of Fanny's life story dealing with her relationship with composer/producer Billy Rose. The *Funny Lady* score contained new musical numbers by John Kander and Fred Ebb and others from the 1920s and 1930s credited, in part, to Billy Rose.

A television special entitled "Funny Girl to Funny Lady" was aired on ABC in March of 1975. It introduced the public to Streisand's latest movie and helped raise funds to support the Special Olympics program. Guests at this event in the Kennedy Center for the Performing Arts in Washington were entertained with a short concert by Barbra and saw the premiere of the film. Television viewers witnessed a pre-recorded interview with Barbra by host Dick Cavett and saw the concert "live." It truly was presented live, in fact, the introductions of Special Olympics officials at the end were cut short because broadcast time had expired. Streisand engaged Peter Matz to conduct the orchestra for the performance, which included some of her signature hits (the love ballad "The Way We Were" and the belt/torch songs "Don't Rain on My Parade" and "My Man") and some material from the movie (the Streisand/James Caan duet-medley "It's Only a Paper

Moon" and "I Like Him/I Like Her," and her sarcastic character song "How Lucky Can You Get"[22]). Once again, Barbra's rapport with an audience—here a mix from Hollywood, Washington, and the Special Olympics—was outstanding; her nervousness, after several year's absence from the stage, was evident at first but certainly not debilitating. A comparison of a videotape of this performance and her 1968 concert in Central Park indicates that she still has a tendency to curve inward slightly at the shoulders, but that the nasality of her overall sound has decreased. The modern Barbra, in terms of wardrobe and hair, also is evident.[23]

Interestingly, a similar flair and energy can be heard in the songs on the soundtrack of *Funny Lady* (supervised by Peter Matz) that are part of the show-within-a-show segments of the film. This provides another indication that, despite her hesitancy toward public performance, Barbra is energized when presenting material in a show format, whether there actually is an audience present.[24] For example, her characterizations and dialects in "I Got a Code in My Doze," "Blind Date," "Am I Blue," and "So Long, Honey Lamb" (based on Fanny Brice characters and the film's plot) are comical and engaging, while at the same time possessed of admirable vocal control. In contrast, Streisand's new-found comfort with gospel-inflected styles adds a strength Fanny Brice could not have mustered to "Let's Hear It for Me" and "It's Gonna Be a Great Day" (although the latter has a brief middle section set in a harder gospel-rock style, and Barbra sounds and looks ill at ease). To accommodate needs of the plot, several of the songs are sectional; for example, the fox-trot-like beat and "boom-chick" accompaniment of the opening bars of "How Lucky Can You Get" give way to a quick-tempo, jazz-style accompaniment. Additional contrast is apparent in her gentle version of the love ballad "If I Love Again" with its recitative-like opening, clean diction, floating tone, and unadorned piano accompaniment. A similar floating tone is heard on "More Than You Know," which also displays Streisand's extreme rhythm maneuverings, heard most clearly during the release of the AABA format when compared to the set rhythmic performance of the A sections. Her delivery of the title words, "If I Love Again," is indicative of her interpretive style: in one instance, the preceding phrase is connected directly (with no breath) to a phrase containing the title words, while in another setting, a breath is taken after *if* to emphasize it, and the word *love* is accented. Therefore, what was written as the hook, or the most identifiable portion of the song, has been presented in ways that could obstruct its intended function. On several occasions, Streisand chooses not to end words with a stop of her breath, and shadow vowels are heard as a result (*day* becomes "da-ee-ah" and *him* becomes "hi-m-ah"). Her usual attention to every note is evident, most ironically in the word *incidently* from "I Found a Million-Dollar Baby." Indeed, that word, which means "parenthetically," is sung the first time in a casual-but-tone-filled fashion with no accompaniment, but on the repeat, it is given a forceful, declarative presentation underscored by a harmony change. Several words in "Million-Dollar Baby" end with an *r* or *re* (*store*, *more*, *four*), and Streisand's habit of closing the "r" sound to a nasal "n" hum is prevalent.

The *Funny Lady* story is set during the "Golden Age of Popular Song," and although some contemporary musical effects creep into the score, the overall musical style of the period and of the film's repertoire give Streisand plenty with which to work—musically at least. An article published before the release of the film quoted Streisand as saying, "These two films are a set of bookends. My Fanny Brice syndrome, 1964 to 1974, is ending."[25] In fact, she already was contemplating a more up-to-date musical film.

Even before the December 1976 premiere of Streisand's version of the film *A Star Is Born*, press reports and rumors abounded about its production process and potential for success. While Barbra had had a tense relationship with the press as far back as *Funny Girl*, *Star* seemed to aggravate the situation. It had been almost a decade since her remarkable movie debut and she was a top box office draw in 1970, but Streisand's stature and reputation in Hollywood were still a mystery. Was she by now an insider, a part of the establishment (as she was in music), or did her persona, film productivity, and unconventionality sustain her outsider status?[26] Whatever her standing in Hollywood, Barbra's fans remained loyal, and the *Star* film and the soundtrack proved to be commercially successful. On the other hand, the film reviews ranged from scathing to excited, touching both on the final product and on perceptions of her work habits. The soundtrack was released about a month ahead of the film, and both media indicate Barbra's increasing control over her career and products. She is listed as "Producer" of the album (with Phil Ramone) and "Executive Producer" of the film, and it was during this period of her life that many of Martin Erlichman's managerial duties were assumed by Jon Peters. The soundtrack remained a top seller for several months.

The Streisand/Peters setting of the film's familiar story was intended to contemporize it within a Hollywood music-industry setting. The story would be about a rock star, whose career was on the decline, and his relationship with a female singer (with a decidedly soft-rock or pop style, appropriate for Streisand), whose fame was about to blossom. Exactly what constitutes "rock" is subject to many opinions and musical sub-categories (and is a subject worthy of consideration because of the stated goal of Streisand's production), but few on the musical team of *Star* had strong and clear ties to what might have been labeled "hard rock." Eclecticism, for right or wrong, ruled the day. Paul Williams served as Musical Supervisor for the soundtrack, Kris Kristofferson played the ravaged John Norman Howard, and Clydie King and Vanetta Fields, who had sung back-up on other Streisand albums, contributed as "Esther's" singing partners. The songs were crafted through the efforts of a diverse group: Williams, Rupert

Holmes (of *Lazy Afternoon*), Kenny Ascher, Leon Russell, Donna Weiss, Kenny Loggins, Alan and Marilyn Bergman, and Barbra Streisand. Streisand's contribution, "Evergreen," brought her into the "singer-songwriter" fold of popular music of the 1970s, even if her work in that area was sporadic (see discography).[27] She has stated several times that her music for "Evergreen" developed out of the guitar lessons that she took for authenticity in some scenes in the movie. Phil Ramone, who had worked on the sound for Streisand's 1968 Central Park concert (see chapter 3), assisted with the soundtrack production and with recording the concerts where parts of the movie were filmed. Stanley Green wrote that the "documentary reality" of these concerts helped in "ably conveying the excitement of Esther's [Barbra's] first appearance before a large crowd and the anguish of the performance after her husband's death."[28] His comments again point to the value of Barbra in front of an audience.

Ironically for the "rock" movie, the most enduring song from the score is "Evergreen," the love ballad written by Streisand and Williams. Since she composed the music, it is interesting to compare the printed sheet music (supposedly the blueprint presented to aid subsequent vocal performance) with any one of her vocal renditions (see discography and appendix B). Barbra takes as many pitch and rhythm liberties with her own creation as she regularly does with songs by others. Her control of breath and phrasing, pitch, and sustained vowel sounds (when that is the result she wants) is apparent during the final long *-green*. In some performances she does not hold the final note for its fully notated 32-beats, instead repeating the final (title) word about two-thirds of the way through that timespan. Attendees at her 1994 New-Year's-Day performance in Las Vegas witnessed that she can hold the long note in concert settings with control and finesse. "Evergreen" also has been recorded by Streisand in several languages, including Spanish, Italian, and French, and its popularity even prompted marching band arrangements.[29] The song brought Streisand her second Academy Award; she seemed particularly thrilled to win an award that went beyond the dreams of her youth.

Other songs from the film fit the categories previously established: "Lost Inside of You" is a love ballad;[30] "Queen Bee" is a character song with a women's advocacy point of view; the lyric song "Everything" also serves as an autobiographical song for the Esther character; and the "With One More Look at You/Watch Closely Now" medley is a type of torch/belt song.

The promotional barrage from Warner Brothers for *A Star Is Born* included a television interview special entitled "Barbra, With One More Look at You," produced by Kaleidescope Films. The program revealed several interesting behind-the-scenes glimpses of Streisand-the-musician at work. She hones in on a wrong pitch in the synthesizer during one recording session for "The Woman in the Moon," worries about the timing of her entrance and the tempo of the bridge on "Watch Closely Now," and suggests the key of that song be changed. During the interview, Barbra commented on a variety of topics: that her approach to pleasing an audience, paradoxically, comes from pleasing herself—even though she is riddled with self-doubt; that she still preferred the work of her art over the celebrity lifestyle it brought; and that she, like many women, wanted to fulfill multiple aspects of her life, both personal and professional, even though she realized the inherent difficulties.

New paths of musical exploration were not difficult to find, however, as Streisand's next commercial album proved. Although some tracks apparently had been recorded many months earlier, February 1976 marked the debut of *Classical Barbra*. She has said little about the album since its release, but Barbra's awareness of classical music often is evident in interviews and on liner notes she has written. At that time, releasing an album of classical repertoire recorded by a pop-music singer was unconventional, but in many ways, the classical songs Streisand selected centered around popular repertoire of that milieu.[31] Most of the songs are French, a language she had previously sung, and they provided the purchaser with new renditions of familiar songs.[32] Equally important are the imagery and poeticism of the lyrics she chose.

On the other hand, some of the repertoire comes from composers who preferred that the voice and accompaniment be treated as equal partners (a fact stated in the liner notes), which is a contradiction to the approach in most of Streisand's recordings. Several components of the classical songs allow Barbra to use her best skills, such as the long phrases of "Dank sei dir, Herr" and the soaring, lyrical melodies of "Beau Soir" and "Pavane." She does not take advantage of her ability to deftly ornament melodies on "Lascia Ch'io Pianga" from Handel's opera *Rinaldo*, where it would have been appropriate during the da capo repeat, especially on "e che sospiri (let me sigh)." Streisand avoids some of her usual pop inflections, staying away from adding an "h" sound in the midst of vowels on slurred pitches and remaining longer on the front half of diphthong vowels.

In general, the arrangements place Barbra in the upper area of her register, where she can produce a light, even tone with less vibrato than she often uses. In fact, she stays rather consistently with this white tone. That simple, clear tone color might be appropriate for some songs, like the first two verses of "Mondnacht" (which sound uncomfortably high for her) that tell of the quiet of the evening, but perhaps is not as appropriate for the dignified passion inherent in "Lascia," a lament.[33] The album liner credits Claus Ogerman with producing, conducting, arranging, and accompanying Streisand; he also composed the one English-language song of the set, "I Loved You," based on an Alexander Pushkin poem. Ogerman had acquired considerable popular-music experience years earlier and had worked previously with Streisand on *Stoney End*. Interestingly, a review of *Watusi*

Trumpets by Claus Ogerman and His Orchestra, states that his reputation was based on his "rock 'n' roll recordings," which were having a positive influence on his "big-band arrangements."[34] That in mind, his choice to provide Streisand with full orchestral arrangements for some of these classical pieces that were written originally for voice and piano alone (for example, "Beau Soir") might be explained but still questionable. As has already been noted (with "I'll Be Home" on *Stoney End*, "Simple Man" from *Lazy Afternoon*, and "If I Love Again" from *Funny Lady*), Streisand does not need full accompaniment to supplement her voice, as Ogerman surely learned through the delicate piano accompaniment used for his own composition on *Classical Barbra*. Likewise, the slight microphone-amplification quality of the whole album adds an incongruous air—to the repertoire if not to the singer.

A comparison of Barbra's performances and the printed vocal music (a relevant exercise with nineteenth- and early-twentieth-century classical music, for which the expectation is that the performer will faithfully recreate the score, since it supposedly represents the composer's specific intentions) reveals that she makes several adjustments in her usual arsenal of interpretive techniques, a few of them already cited. But some of her pop characteristics still are evident. The rhythmic notation of "Beau Soir" indicates that the composer, Claude Debussy, has created a conflict between a triple division of the beat in the accompaniment and duple divisions in the voice. At times Streisand sings the rhythm as notated, but at other moments she too sings triplet rhythms or stretches one of a group of eighth notes, thereby bunching the remaining notes together on a later beat. She also overlaps text and musical phrases, for example (+ indicates carry over, ^ indicates breath; text by Paul Bourget): "Un conseil de goûter le charme d'être au monde,+Cependant qu'on est jeune^et . . ." The printed score ends with the singer's note of five beats followed by two measures of solitary accompaniment. Barbra keeps the vocal sound going, ending (with a slight close of the lips to a nasal hum) after the orchestra has already initiated the final chord of the concluding measure.

Gabriel Fauré's rhythm for "Après un Rêve" is just the opposite, with triplets in the voice against duple eighth notes in the accompaniment. The "dreamy" lyrics make Streisand's wandering, uneven triplets acceptable, although a strict rhythmic approach would be followed by most classical singers. The range of this song encompasses an eleventh; around the exclamatory *Helas*! the melody quickly spans that parameter with the intervals octave down, octave back up, continued up a fourth, octave down. The dynamic is to be loud, and Streisand stays with her belt-mix voice. In other places, she sings upper-register notes with her head voice. This song also exhibits some personalized phrasing, creating a very long passage beginning with the text (by Romain Bussine), "Je t'appelle, ô nuit, . . ." and another near the end on the long notes of "Reviens,+ô nuit^mystérieuse."[35]

Among the many writers who commented on and reviewed this album were two classical musicians (see bibliography). Pianist Glenn Gould had many positive things to say regarding Streisand-the-singer in general and specifically about *Classical Barbra*. He commented on her diverse timbral palette, her complete awareness of the text, her exacting intonation (especially on "In Trutina"), and her very personal approach to the French. But he also was disappointed in the moderation of tempo, dynamics, and emotional range on this album. Composer Ned Rorem concurred about the weakness of the repertoire's match to Streisand's style and voice, suggesting that she had proven she had the technical skill to do first-rate renditions of the pieces, but that she might not have fully comprehended the material—an unusual comment to make about her. He also noted the popularity of the selected songs and that she sounded as though she thought "classical" meant "restrained."[36] Many years later Streisand revealed that she felt "compelled" to take risks with her music and that she found this album difficult because of the disciplined nature of classical music. She reported that she learned the repertoire by listening to other singers.[37] Barbra was nominated for a Grammy for Best Classical Vocalist—Solo for her *Classical Barbra* efforts, but in a crossover irony, she lost to opera singer Beverly Sills singing showtunes of Victor Herbert.[38]

Barbra's next two albums, *Streisand Superman* and *Songbird*, reflect how she comments on personal issues of her life readily and clearly through the albums of this period, and how she continued to be willing to borrow from a variety of new and old sources for her repertoire, all the while maintaining a studio light-pop sound.[39] Even the album liners and artwork address autobiographical topics. *Superman* shows Streisand dressed in shorts and a tee-shirt displaying the super-hero's logo, and the liner contains printed and hand-written notes by Barbra about the songs and the album's production, including a note of thanks to her fans for their support of *A Star Is Born*. Several of the song texts advocate women's rights (a paradox to the "Super*man*" theme) or explain personal concerns. "Don't Believe What You Read" was written by Streisand, Ron Nagle, and Scott Mathews to counter a press report that she had an aviary inside her home; the song garnered a range of comments from reviewers about its rock sound and its text, a text that continued to ring true two decades later (see bibliography). She reports that "Answer Me" had been written for *Star*, but had been cut from the film. Its lyric, again in part written by Streisand, contains several twists on the title words; the final repetition of the words indicates the singer's hope that she (the "me" of the song) will be the "answer" to her hoped-for lover's longings. "My Heart Belongs to Me," "Lullaby for Myself," and "Cabin Fever," as the titles imply, all reflect varied facets of women's experiences with relationships; the music also displays variety, ranging from heavy rock rhythm in "Cabin" to the gentleness of "Lullaby." In contrast, "Superman" and "I Found You Love" are breezy, upbeat love songs, and Billy Joel's "New York State of Mind" (another text containing a play on words) is presented as a cabaret belt number. "Love Comes From Unexpected Places," by Kim Carnes and Dave Ellingson, offers a long, thoughtful text (something for the actress to develop) set as a lyric song with minimal accompaniment.

Writing for the *Los Angeles Times*, Robert Hilburn found the eclecticism of *Superman* to be its downfall, suggesting that Streisand's dramatic voice was enhanced when given songs that could live up to its power (a feeling expressed by reviewers of previous Streisand albums, see bibliography). Dave Marsh also found the album to be a "pastiche" lacking focus, but her "best since *Stoney End*."[40] In a lengthy interview published in *Playboy* in 1977 around the time *Superman* was released, Streisand made several comments about music that indicated her awareness of present and past female vocalists. She acknowledged admiration of Aretha Franklin's ability with high notes, Joni Mitchell's beautiful voice and poetry, and the sounds of Lee Wiley, Ethel Waters, and Billie Holiday. Barbra also remarked that she prefered the current mellow nature of her own voice over her younger sound.[41]

The cover of *Songbird* features photographs of Barbra and several of her dogs at her Malibu home, but fewer personal messages are contained in the song texts. Although still aimed at a pop audience, the selections harken back to her interests in ballads and nightclub material, even though they are updated with polished, and perhaps over-produced and over-rehearsed, studio arrangements. Most of the previously described song categories are present: "You Don't Bring Me Flowers" (her solo version) is a love ballad with considerable characterization,[42] "Honey, Can I Put on Your Clothes?" is a lyric/character song more than five minutes long, and "One More Night" is a torch/belt number. "Stay Away" also is a belt song, and it shows Streisand at her cabaret best: her voice sounds relaxed and controlled as she decorates several notes, stretches frequently into her high range for intensity, and creates several elongated triplet rhythms against the duple accompaniment. The title words again provide a twist in meaning near the end, a common feature on the two albums under consideration. Several of the same vocal traits are heard in "Deep in the Night."

A modernistic approach to the traditional torch song once again is found in "I Don't Break Easily," whose text tells of a woman scorned but surviving. The title song, "Songbird," could be partially autobiographical; it is a poignant anthem for those who have reached the summit of their chosen field but find they still need someone to turn to: "My song sets you free, but who sings to me? I'm all alone now. Who sings for Songbird?"[43] "A Man I Loved" has an enigmatic text, one that might hint at some religious or spiritual meaning (similar to "Free the People" on *Stoney End*), and the music of the song ends inconclusively. Streisand's version of "Tomorrow," from the musical *Annie*, departs from what the listener expects.

It is devoid of the youthful belt sound so strongly associated with the song's appearance in the show. Instead, Streisand presents the song as a restrained, mature statement of confidence in the future. Several active rhythmic layers in the accompaniment provide energy. (Previously this technique was used in her version of "Happy Days Are Here Again," where she turned a quick-tempo ditty into an emotional signature song.)

As with *Streisand Superman*, the songs of *Songbird* reflect several musical styles ranging from the relaxed-but-rich beauty of "You Don't Bring," to the casual dance or pop style of "Songbird" and "Love Breakdown," to the gutsy, rhythm-and-blues or soul flavors of "Stay Away" and "Deep in the Night." Ernie Watts, a saxophonist on the latter, felt that, at the time, Streisand had been listening to Aretha Franklin, Marvin Gaye, and some of the Motown artists, drawing inspiration from their style and then "molding it" to match her own mannerisms. In most instances he also observed her "sailing over the top, rather than in, the beat," once again "mixing the stage thing and pop."[44]

Since her previous "greatest hits" album at the end of the 1960s, Barbra had recorded several albums, but only a few of her singles—ballads like "The Way We Were," "Evergreen," and "My Heart Belongs to Me"—had done well on record charts. Having already established the practice of re-leasing such an album with or without singles hits, Columbia released two "best of" or "greatest hits" Streisand collections in November 1978 and November 1981, each in time for that year's holiday buying season.[45] In addition to previously recorded songs, both albums also contained some new material; therefore, fans had to buy *Barbra Streisand's Greatest Hits, Volume 2* and *Memories* to obtain a complete collection of her recordings. Each album's contents support the notion of eclecticism prevalent during this period of Streisand's career.

The first of two "new" songs on *Volume 2* is "Prisoner," which Barbra recorded expressly to be used as the theme song (following the tendency to use a pop song to help promote a non-musical movie) for the film *The Eyes of Laura Mars* produced by Jon Peters and starring Faye Dunaway. Streisand had no other connection to the movie, and thus, this recording turned out to be unique in her career. "Prisoner" was produced by Gary Klein (who also had produced *Streisand Superman* and *Songbird*), and has a familiar pop-rock feeling, with heavy electronic and percussive sounds and a full chorus in the background. Barbra's voice quality is intense, with several notes in her high C and D range, and she employs considerable vibrato throughout.[46] Perhaps these techniques are intended to highlight the "murder-mystery" element of the film. The tempo of the song is rather slow, so that all of Streisand's word-sculpting mannerisms are noticeable: *way* becomes "wa-ee," *eyes* is heard as "ah-eez," *wrong* is vocalized on the "ng" sound, every vowel sound in *voice* clearly is heard, and *love*, spread over two pitches, becomes "lah-huv." Additionally, a "chew" sound develops as *about* and *you* are ellided, a common occurance with most pop singers but not usual with Streisand.

The tale of how the Barbra Streisand/Neil Diamond duet of "You Don't Bring Me Flowers" (new on *Greatest Hits, Volume 2*) transpired is well known among her fans and is recounted by Barbra in the *Just for the Record* booklet. Both singers had made individual solo recordings of the song, but a disc jockey from Louisville spliced the two together into a duet as a parting gift for his ex-wife. The pairing was an immediate hit, causing Barbra and Neil to record a true duet. This would be the first of many duets, with both male and female partners, to appear on Streisand albums over the next several years.[47] Of equal interest is the birth of "Flowers" by Neil Diamond and Alan and Marilyn Bergman. The couple relates that the song is a result of Neil and television producer Norman Lear attending a dinner party where Diamond asked Lear if any new television-show theme songs were going to be needed for the upcoming season. They agreed that he should compose something for a pilot called *All that Glitters*, and Diamond asked the Bergmans to provide lyrics. The result was a 45-second "song" that would introduce a show about modern male/female role reversals. Eventually, the show's plot changed, the song was cut, and the Bergmans forgot about it. Neil Diamond continued to work on "Flowers" and included it on his tour to the delight of his audiences. This encouraged the three to work together again to complete the song.[48]

Besides the obvious addition of the male voice to Streisand's, the only other significant change between her solo version (on *Songbird*) and their duet lies in the accompaniment. The latter again features piano and strings, but the strings come in earlier. Streisand uses a slightly breathier tone in the duet and approaches the song even more clearly as a character song. Diamond's vocal style is quite different from Streisand's; he does not hold notes (especially those at the ends of phrases) as long as she does, and he is less comfortable than Barbra with the slow, legato melody. They rarely sing simultaneously during the song, instead trading lines and sections with one another or adding brief echo responses to each other's main part. The voices do come together at the very end with Barbra leaping up on the final syllable of *goodbye* and holding the note.

The "You Don't Bring Me Flowers" duet is repeated on Streisand's *Memories*, but the most appealing version is found on a videotape entitled *Grammy's Greatest Moments, Volume 1*. The story of Barbra's and Neil's surprise performance of the song at the Grammy Awards show is true Hollywood.[49] David Crosby, host of the video, recalls that Streisand and Diamond did not decide to perform until the night before the 27 February 1980 telecast; they supposedly then rehearsed over the telephone. Their appearance was not advertised, nor were they introduced—they simply entered opposite sides of the stage. After several moments of enthusiastic audience applause, Streisand visibly "gets into character" and hesitantly began to sing. She had momentary problems adjusting to the microphone, but then Neil's voice began, and it too was slightly muddled in the amplification.[50] The technology quickly was brought under control, and the duet progressed, much as it does on vinyl. Typical of a Streisand performance, the most intriguing part is to *watch* her presentation. The music and the voice were fine, but her acting added a compelling new dimension. Barbra obviously was nervous, which was set into clear relief by Neil's apparent ease with the whole situation, and her tentativeness added an appropriate wistful quality to her vocal timbre. As the song progressed, she moved closer to him, then he moved closer toward her, meeting at center stage. By the final segment they were standing side-by-side, and at an appropriately poignant moment, Barbra gently stroked Neil's face, bringing an outburst of applause and cheers. He kissed her hand, they sang together on the final few words, and the song ended. The audience appeared to appreciate and grasp not only the vocal performance, but the dramatic performance as well. Although "Flowers" brought the pair a Grammy that night for Best Pop Vocal Performance by a Duo or Group, the two Erasmus Hall high-school alumni did not sing together again. Musically, Barbra improvised more melodic ornaments in the concert setting than during their studio version, and the concert duo sang simultaneously more often on the title words and near the song's end than they did on the studio version. Otherwise the two renditions and arrangements are similar.

Four tracks from *Volume 2* were repeated verbatim in 1981 on *Memories* including the "Flowers" duet, "Evergreen," "My Heart Belongs to Me," and "The Way We Were." Other material for the album came from Streisand albums released in the interim. The liner for *Memories* contains photographs of Streisand and various music and film colleagues from this period of her life, adding to the sense of a nostalgic scrapbook or family photo album. Three new songs also are included on the set: a lyric song, "Memory" from *Cats;* a belt number, "Comin' In and Out of Your Life"; and a solo version of the love ballad "Lost Inside of You," which had been sung as a duet with Kris Kristofferson in *A Star Is Born.*

Andrew Lloyd Webber's aria-like hit from *Cats* was a natural for Streisand to record even though she had no connection with that theatre show (a harbinger of things to come). Its sweeping melodic line, orchestral accompaniment, and poetic, story-line text matched her style perfectly. The melody's low notes stretch her bottom range in a strong, mature way—she neither shies away from the notes nor tosses them aside lightly. "Lost Inside" features heavier electronic instrumentation and percussion mixed with 12/8 (or triplet) arpeggios and the pronounced sound of a strummed acoustic guitar. The dynamics of the song vary widely, and Streisand's breathing between phrases is heard clearly during the soft conclusion.

"Comin' In," written by Richard Parker and Bobby Whiteside, was produced for *Memories* by Lloyd Webber. The sheet music for the song appears nearly to be a transcription of what Streisand does vocally; its overall AABAB form is written out with no repeat signs, indicating the amount of variation that takes place from one A section to the next.[51] The melodic line reveals her rhythmic fluidity and parlando-like text delivery as well as her growing penchant to leap upward to emphasize a word or a moment in the musical line, especially in the bridge. Again the range, key, and dynamics are carefully selected so that the most intense part of Streisand's tessitura is featured at the dramatic moments of the bridge. In contrast, she uses her softer, breathy tone on the first A section.

A romantic comedy, *The Main Event*, followed *A Star Is Born* in Streisand's movie career. Its soundtrack, produced by Gary Le Mel, includes songs used to underscore various film scenes by pop-rock performers such as Frankie Valli and the Four Seasons, The Silhouettes, and Loggins and Messina; other background instrumental music; and two dance-style songs, entitled "Fight" and "The Main Event," which were performed by Barbra as a medley. The latter also was recorded in a ballad setting. Bob Esty prepared the "short" version of the medley (actually almost five minutes long—the "long" one exceeds eleven minutes) to play under the final film credits and to release as a single, which was a wise commercial move during an era of discotheques and aerobics classes. The single and the soundtrack both quickly were certified gold. The three arrangements exhibit three different vocal lines as Barbra varies the melody slightly in several places. The long version is extended by a lengthy hummed introduction, several instrumental breaks, and a modulation about two-thirds of the way through; it also has words and verses that do not appear in other versions. The strict and pronounced beat keeps Streisand more squarely in each measure, but she employs other means of decoration, like leaping to a higher note on accented syllables of *celebrate* and *one* (which frequently is heard as "wa-*hun*" so an accented syllable is created) and sustaining long notes, with a lot of vibrato, in her intense high, belt-mix range. The shorter version of the medley begins with a brief slow introduction and then picks up the disco tempo. It retains the extended high notes and intervallic leaps. The ballad version of "The Main Event" provides interesting contrast as it allows Barbra to deal with the melody and rhythm liberated from the heavy punch of the bass drum. Here the accompaniment is provided by acoustic strings and piano, and she soars above it with sweeping melodic lines that likely are of greater interest than the repetitive text deserves. In several instances, she recalls her other versions by maintaining the leaps to higher notes and by holding some long notes, but her overall tone is softer.

The word *wet* begins and ends Streisand's album of the same name. It is a concept album in the sense that all the songs make some reference to water; in "Niagara" and "After the Rain" the accompanimental instruments are used to portray swirling water or water droplets. A careful study suggests that the eclecticism of this repertoire occasionally hints at a return to musical material like that heard in earlier stages of her career, this in spite of the inclusion of "No More Tears/Enough Is Enough," her duet with the disco queen of the 1970s, Donna Summer.[52]

The opening title song, "Wet," could be labeled a lyric song, and B. Streisand is listed along with D. Wolfert and S. Sheridan as composers. Barbra uses her child-like, white timbre, with minimal vibrato, against the orchestral accompaniment. The tempo generally is slow, but contrast is provided by a brief quick-tempo mid-section with no backbeat. Several musical and textual phrases are overlapped, and the song ends with a sustained, soft *me*. Her precise enunciation of repeated consonants or final consonants preceding a vowel is particularly noticeable as she moves with no ellision from *wet* to *to* and *wet* to *is*. This song is followed by a Johnny Mercer/Harold Arlen standard, "Come Rain or Come Shine." The arrangement by Greg Mathieson is contemporary pop with a Latin rhythmic sense, and Barbra often rearranges accents and syncopations within or between measures (as compared to the published music),[53] as is customary for her. Arlen's original tune was designed around a four-section, 32-bar format (typically, each section has eight measures, but the form is quasi-ABAC). Mathieson's arrangement extends beyond that plan by means of an instrumental interlude and a repeat of the final two sections. Streisand begins gently but ends strongly with vocal improvisation and melodic variation on the repeat and final tag extention. Arlen's repeated-note melody, with the repeats serving as the song's hook, provides Streisand the opportunity to sing the text in a parlando fashion against the steady beat. He also included several octave drops, particularly on the words *sunny* and *money*, that Barbra follows—at least the first time through—and she adds others on words like *deep*.

One of the least effective songs in the set is her character-song arrangement (by David Foster) of Bobby Darin's old hit, "Splish, Splash." Its accompaniment has a contemporary four-part-division of each beat and a heavy electronic sound—heavier than the text or Streisand's vocal sound seem to warrant. Similar comments might be made about "I Ain't Gonna Cry" on side 2, which has a funky bassline and short, choppy phrases. These songs, like several others on the album, include brief instrumental interludes.

On the other hand, "On Rainy Afternoons" and "After the Rain" are gentle love ballads, both with texts by Alan and Marilyn Bergman, that allow Barbra to use her soft, breathy tone against a string accompaniment. Even amid a light backbeat, tempo fluxuations and dynamic and timbral contrasts add to the emotion of the lyrics. There are many words ripe for coloration, and "After" in particular shows how much sensuality Streisand can bring to an interpretation when supported by the right arrangement. It and other songs of the set cause her to reach down to the low reedy, but increasingly mature, part of her voice.

Side 2 begins with the eight-minute Streisand/Summer duet, which apparently was partly a result of Jason Gould's interest in Summer's recordings of the day. The song begins slowly with the children's chant "It's raining, it's pouring . . . ," but then continues with new adult lyrics, quickly moving into the disco tempo. Much was written about the meeting of the two "divas" in the recording studio; the result indicates they were mutually inspired. Donna's range generally is higher than Barbra's, but Barbra complements Donna with some notes at the upper-most part of her own range. As several reviewers have noted over the years, Streisand's voice can be chameleon-like when blending with various duet partners, and that seems to be true with "Enough Is Enough." Although the ear usually can distinguish which lady is singing, there are moments, particularly in the high range with full accompaniment, when it is difficult to identify one from the other—their timbres are nearly identical. This duet contains more harmony than Streisand's duet with Neil Diamond, and Barbra and Donna take turns with the secondary part. Twice Streisand sings a sustained note on the word *tear*, which is remarkable for its length and vowel clarity—the first time the word comes across as "tee-(r)ah," and the second time the "r" sound is delayed until the last possible moment and ceases with a stop of air. Occasionally Streisand's reluctance to sing on the beat is noticeable against Summer's accented rhythms.

The final songs of the album are "Niagara," a torchy love ballad with music by Marvin Hamlisch, and "Kiss Me in the Rain," a love ballad with ample opportunity for characterization. The sheet music of the latter (likely an after-the-recording transcription) reveals several compositional traits that are hallmarks of both Streisand's early style and her 1970s style.[54] The tempo is slow, and the opening verse (of an unusual A[8 measures]–B[11]–C[8]–B–D[11]–E[12] format) is replete with story-like words, the shorter notes bunched at the beginnings of phrases and sections. Many printed measures begin with the words commencing after the chord for beat 1 has been sounded, although a transcriber would be hard pressed to notate exactly what rhythms Barbra sings, and she sings momentary harmony with herself on the return of B. Several phrases and text lines begin with a low pick-up note that is completely tone-filled, even though short. The composition also provides several instances in which she can display her skill in holding long notes or where long-held words are given energy with a slur up the octave. Otherwise, these notes usually are not decorated with melismas, as might be heard with many other performers of the late 1970s through the 1990s. Streisand's ability to control tone, pitch, and breath have allowed her to stay away from excessive melismatic pyrotechnics.

Individual songs on these albums received rave reviews and considerable radio broadcast; in fact, in 1979 Streisand had three successful singles. The three certainly represent an eclectic mix but also reflect a contradiction in comparison to her accomplishments of the previous decade: "You Don't

Bring Me Flowers" (pop ballad duet), "No More Tears/Enough Is Enough" (disco duet), and "The Main Event/Fight" (disco movie theme). Her albums also were commercially successful by most standards, but it had been awhile since Streisand had released a smash-hit, critically acclaimed album. Barry Gibb and the Bee Gees were riding high in the late 1970s as a result of *Saturday Night Fever* and the disco phenomenon, but few might have guessed that Gibb would be the next composer, producer, and duet partner to work with Barbra Streisand—and that he would guide her to that desired hit album.

Guilty was released in the fall of 1980, nearly a generation after *I Can Get It for You Wholesale*. In general, Gibb's compositional style (in some cases with assistance from his brothers) provided Barbra with sweeping melodic lines, but also with more veiled or subtle lyrics than those to which she had usually been drawn. She remarked later that his style of working was new for her—most of the instrumental tracks were recorded before Streisand entered the studio.[55] The accompaniments often are electronically oriented, and the medium-tempo backbeat usually is evident within active rhythmic layers of varied styles, yet neither overpowers the gentle but penetrating tone Streisand chooses for much of the album. In other instances, sustained, ethereal strings support her vocals, and many of the songs have a light dance feeling without being disco music.[56] Her legato quality is contrasted nicely, not competitively or obtusely, by Gibb's choppy vocal approach and unique timbre. Their two playful duets ("What Kind of Fool" and "Guilty") have an air of characterization about them, as does her solo "Never Give Up." The duets have the singers echoing one another and occasionally singing together, but very little true harmony develops. The verses of "Never" almost approach patter songs with their rapid-fire texts and repeated-pitch melodies, and Streisand is in her low range employing considerable word coloring. The repeated chorus then provides contrast through its greater lyricism and by placing the singer in a higher range. The album's liner photographs of the two stars together take advantage of Gibb's popularity and help to emphasize his contribution to the project.

Despite their abstract nature, many of the texts on *Guilty* still can be placed into categories established previously. The title song and "Promises" are perky pop ballads.[57] "Woman in Love" is an advocacy song about a woman's right to find happiness. In this performance, Streisand produces a relaxed tone on the verses and a contrasting belt tone on the chorus; the word *right* is placed in a climactic moment of the melody, accentuated by Streisand's slide up into the note and word. "Run Wild" and "The Love Inside" have long phrases, instrumental interludes, and thoughtful texts that fit the lyric song definition, even though they are dissimilar in musical style.[58] "Inside" shows her willingness to use a thin, breathy (but tone-filled) sound both in the higher-ranged verses and during the bottom notes of words like *over*, *together*, and *forever*. In each case the *er* becomes a breathy "ah" sound. "What Kind of Fool" fits the description of a modern torch song.

On the other end of the spectrum, "Life Story" is lengthy, musically powerful, and challenging for the vocalist in terms of intervalic leaps and stamina. Although not clearly a story, its mysterious text, underscored by triplet-like rhythms, lends itself to development in the manner of a character song. During the choruses, Barbra's intense, almost defiant, tone is reminiscent of "Prisoner" on *Greatest Hits, Volume 2*. Similar comments apply to "Make It Like a Memory," which might be labeled a "lyric character song." It employs a large accompanimental ensemble, featuring the piano, and begins with a long introduction that leads to a recitative-like opening statement for the voice. Its several sections create an unusual formal structure, each distinguished by text, by rhythm and meter, by harmony and orchestration, or by overall style. Barbra is afforded the opportunity to use several of her timbres ranging from soft (especially on the verses) to a soulful belt sound during the title sections, and her range is stretched at both ends. Gibb's tunes and the appropriately expansive arrangements of these songs allow her to exercise her vocal technique (solid pitch, clean enunciation, melodic phrasing, dynamic contrasts) perhaps to a greater extent than her interpretive skills. "Make It" has much to offer those wanting to hear Streisand's technique and mature power, even though several critics found this to be the least effective song of the album. It also is unique among the hundreds of songs she has sung in that the last quarter of its seven-and-a-half-minute length is purely instrumental—in fact, the album draws to a close without its vocal star.

On *Guilty*, Streisand's technique of overlapping musical and textual phrases is evident, as is her usual approach to diphthongs. But she also sustains the initial sound of a diphthong, especially on long notes not set in a belt context: *wide* becomes "wah-(e)d" rather than "wah-eed." Several of the songs are in verse-chorus form with vamped fade-away endings, and Barbra provides variation or development of the melodies on the chorus and vamp repeats. The album was certified multi-platinum in sales, solidifying Streisand's long-sought-after younger fan base, and several individual songs were nominated for Grammy awards in various categories. The title single won a Grammy for Best Pop Vocal Performance by a Duo or Group with Vocal (in the year that Christopher Cross's self-titled album took home many awards). *Guilty* also did well in the international market; the album reached the top of charts in Britain, Canada, Australia, Holland, Belgium, New Zealand, and Sweden, and reached the top ten in Germany, Japan, and France.[59]

The high-tech pop sound of *Guilty* could not have been followed by greater contrast than the 1983 release of *Yentl*. The soundtrack from this, her much-anticipated, controversial, and very personal film, was also Streisand's thirty-second Columbia album.[60] Much already has been written about the film, its long gestation, and its meaning in Streisand's life and career. Some information was provided by a limited-release, hour-long interview entitled *The Legend of Barbra Streisand* issued by Columbia Records for radio broadcast in promotion of the film.[61] In addition to the statements that open this chapter, during the course of the interview Barbra revealed that she loves knowledge, study, and the process of learning; that she relished but respected her first official job as film director; that Johnny Mathis was her favorite singer; that her hesitation to sing in public came from a fear of the audience's expectation of constant perfection; that she felt singing should be a natural extension of speech; and that critical reviews of her albums (unlike those of her movies) are not problematic for her because of her greater confidence in that area. Likewise, Streisand expressed that she did not view *Yentl* as a particularly ethnic movie; rather she viewed it as one about the many facets of love (between friends, between parent and child, between husband and wife) and the universal struggle to make dreams come true. She acknowledged that an equally important theme of the movie was the power and value of learning and education (heard during "This Is One of Those Moments" as Anshel, her boy persona, is accepted into a yeshiva). Barbra confided that these themes also were relevant in her personal life; the experience perhaps sparked in her a revitalized interest in her Jewish heritage.

Geraldo Rivera also interviewed Streisand and Jon Peters for a special edition of ABC television's *20/20*.[62] The interview makes it clear that Peters was not completely enthusiastic about Streisand's immersion in the *Yentl* project (although he did assist with some aspects of the production, which originally was turned down by several Hollywood studios), and that he had suggested the time was right for her to accept some public singing engagements. It was during the production of the film that their relationship dissolved.

Continuing the publicity blitz, *Billboard* magazine devoted a special section of its 10 December 1983 issue to her career—with the focus on *Yentl*. The section, also entitled "The Legend of Barbra Streisand," contains retrospective articles and photographs, congratulatory notes from several colleagues and business associates, a story by James Spada on the birth and completion of the film, and an interview with Alan and Marilyn Bergman, Barbra's long-time friends and collaborators. The Bergmans penned the lyrics for Michel Legrand's score for *Yentl*. One humorous story they retell is of Barbra volunteering to anonymously sing "What Are You Doing the Rest of Your Life?" the theme song of the film *The Happy Ending*. The Bergman's did not quite know how to tell her that her voice is not exactly "anonymous" (she eventually recorded the song for *Barbra Streisand: The Way We Were*).[63] They also recount that Streisand originally did not think of *Yentl* as a musical, but that they eventually suggested the idea to her since the Yentl character was living a secret and would need a way to express inner thoughts.[64] The music could be used to enhance the film's format, but the question remained as to style—should it be ethnic or popular, classically or Broadway inflected, modern or historical sounding? It was determined that Yentl's character would be the only one that sings,[65] and most of the time the singing would be reflective and subdued. Indeed, there are no tour-de-force belt songs (until the optimistic ending with "A Piece of Sky") and no comic or dance numbers in the traditional musical-film sense.

The composer seems to have taken a middle road on the question of style; Streisand's mature timbre, control, and directorial interpretations are essential to make the numbers come alive. There are recitative-like vocal segments to move the story line and create a prayerful mood, and there are some characteristic Eastern-European augmented (or modal) melodic intervals, but the orchestration is lush and several songs lean toward a secular pop style.[66] This single-singer approach was effective for the story line, but some critics found that it made the soundtrack ineffective without the film's context (see bibliography). Perhaps to counter such concerns, studio versions of "The Way He Makes Me Feel" and "No Matter What Happens" (produced by Phil Ramone and Dave Grusin) also appear on the album, representing the ballad and belt categories of her repertoire.[67] Yentl collaborators received a few Academy Award nominations, and it won an Oscar for Original Song Score, but Streisand herself received no nominations. She won a Golden Globe award for her directorial efforts, and Yentl won for Best Motion Picture—Musical Comedy. Despite the critic's reservations, the soundtrack eventually was certified multiple platinum by the Recording Industry Association of America.[68] If Streisand's personal devotion to the film was not clear enough through her publicity comments, her long struggle to get financial backing for the production despite her "superstar" status, or her professional involvement as soundtrack producer, film star, director, producer, and co-writer, the dedication of the film to her own father's memory confirms the relationship.[69]

The final album of this period of Streisand's career is *Emotion* from 1984. Although she certainly was not a novice in the area of filmed stories, the album brought her first entries into the music-video arena with "Left in the Dark" and the title song, "Emotion." Naturally, both are elaborate in character-development, with "Left" depicted by a pair of love triangles set in intertwining 1940s-era and contemporary scenes. Barbra's co-star from *A Star Is Born*, Kris Kristofferson, also co-starred in this video opposite Barbra's nightclub-chanteuse role. While it is interesting to watch Streisand during the brief club-performance segments of the video, there is no "live" singing for analysis. The "Emotion" video was shot in London, and it portrays the fantasy life of a bored wife. Roger Daltrey (of The Who) plays the part of Barbra's husband, and Mikhail Baryshnikov glides through one of her dreams. The London setting allowed Streisand to play with several makeup and costuming schemes drawing on the punk scene of that city. The video's concept was developed by Streisand and Richard Baskin, her intermittent companion and colleague for several years.

Emotion continues Streisand's eclecticism in its assortment of songs and arrangements from disparate sources: compositions by Kim Carnes and John Cougar Mellencamp; a duet with Carnes (which, unlike the Donna Summer duet, clearly shows the timbral contrast between the two women's voices); backup singing from the Pointer Sisters; and production help from Richard Perry (of her early 1970s work) and Maurice White (of Earth, Wind, and Fire fame). Several of the pieces use heavy instrumentation, much of it based on the studio technology of the day; the credits frequently list the names of drum machine or synthesizer programmers. The heavy sound is particularly evident on "When I Dream," which otherwise could have been set as a meaningful lyric song. Streisand's own name is associated with various tracks on the album as producer, lyricist, or composer. Several critics commented on the stylistic confusion that so many diverse hands can bring to a project and, once again, on the fact that Barbra's dramatic tendencies and superior technique can quickly overshadow slight pop material (see bibliography). Awareness of some of the personal and professional situations of Barbra's life at the time contributes to speculation about the autobiographical nature of some of the song texts.[70] "Time Machine" and "When I Dream" are about having confidence in one's own decisions and personal dreams. "Best I Could" and "Heart Don't Change My Mind" are about a woman's right to seek "more" out of a relationship and about the struggle she faces to control her own emotions; both song's lyrics also evolve in a way that allows musical characterization. The final two songs of the group are "Clear Sailing" and "Here We Are at Last," both optimistic love ballads, the latter written by Streisand and Baskin.

While discussing the "Emotion" video, a writer for *Time* stated, "the way she is is never the way she was."[71] Indeed for the most part, Streisand personally was miles away from the past. But although her musical travels had taken her on many adventuresome and successful side trips, she never traversed too far from where she always had been or perhaps wanted to be.[72] An album inspired by an idea that she had formulated years before was about to come to fruition, in spite of the skepticism of others. Barbra's accumulated knowledge and experience, backed by her *I'll trust my own instincts* mentality, and her return to material that could withstand the weight of her talents, would yield great rewards.

NOTES

1. Barbra Streisand, interview by Mary Turner, *The Legend of Barbra Streisand*, produced by Westwood One, phonodisc A2S1779 (Columbia Records, 1983).

2. Steven Holden, *The New Rolling Stone Record Guide* (New York: Rolling Stone Press, 1983), s.v. "Barbra Streisand," by Stephen Holden.

3. Bruce Pollock, ed. *Popular Music, 1970–1974*, vol. 7 (Detroit: Gale Research Co., 1984), 65–70.

4. Bruce Pollock, ed. *Popular Music, 1975–1979*, vol. 8 (Detroit: Gale Research Co., 1984), 71–72.

5. Stephen Holden suggests her influence is heard in the work of Bette Midler and Barry Manilow, among others. See Dave Marsh, *The New Rolling Stone Record Guide* (New York: Rolling Stone Press, 1983), s.v. "Barbra Streisand," by Stephen Holden.

6. See *ASCAP's Art & Commerce Cafe, Meat & Potatoes*, "Alan and Marilyn Bergman on Songwriting, Part 2" [interview on-line]; available from http://www.ascap.com/artcommerce/bergman-part 2.html; Internet; accessed 1 December 1997.

7. Bruce Pollack, ed. *Popular Music, 1970–74*, vol 7. (Detroit: Gale Research Co., 1984), 65.

8. When studying the April 1974 *Billboard's Top LPs & Tape* list, Jon Landau discovered that five of the top-twenty albums were instrumentals, five were by women, only five were by "conventional rock bands," and four were rhythm-and-blues or jazz. This to him suggested the diverse "state of mass taste." See Jon Landau, "Top Twenty: The Times They Are A-Middlin'," *Rolling Stone* (6 June 1974): 66.

9. See *ASCAP's Art & Commerce Cafe, Meat & Potatoes*, "Alan and Marilyn Bergman on Songwriting, Part 3" [interview on-line]; available from http://www.ascap.com/artcommerce/bergman-part 3.html; Internet; accessed 1 December 1997. Other information about the Bergmans in the 1970s (including their relationship with Streisand and their importance in the movie-music industry) is found in Joyce Haber, "The Bergmans: The Way They Are," *Los Angeles Times*, 10 March 1974, CAL:19.

10. "The Way We Were" sheet music is available from Colgems Music Corp. in New York, #0055WSM.

11. Legrand had worked with Streisand as early as *Je m'appelle Barbra*, and the Bergmans contributed to *What About Today?* in 1969. The foursome would collaborate again in the future, most significantly in the early 1980s on *Yentl*. In his review of *Barbra Streisand: The Way We Were*, Stephen Holden suggests this album "allows Streisand to do what she does best: theatrical interpretations of 'legit' and nightclub music." See *Rolling Stone* (11 April 1974): 62. He also comments that her medley of "My Buddy" and "How About Me" draws on repertoire from Judy Garland's catalogue and that "Pieces of Dreams" might be aimed "toward the loyal gay contingent among [Streisand's] admirers." (The film *Pieces of Dreams* was released in 1970 by United Artists; it was a story about a priest who fell in love with a female social worker, and in his questioning of his faith and church, was accused of being gay.) Holden's *Rolling Stone* colleague Jon Landau took a different view of the album, finding it "disappointing." See "Top-Twenty: The Times They Are A-Middlin'," (6 June 1974): 67. Curiously, Landau points out that Streisand "no longer sings songs; she acts them out." I would argue that she has been doing that since before her first album; it is a hallmark of her style.

12. This song contains a curious moment near the end where it sounds as if

Barbra jumps in too quickly with an "s" sound which is then followed shortly with the word *so*. It is hard to imagine, if it is an error, why the "s" sound was not edited out. The spot is startling even with repeated listening.

13. Colman Andrews found "Something So Right" to be the best song on the album. He complimented Paul Simon for including in it "all of the finest attributes of good song writing" including a good blend of words and music, honest but ironic context, and freedom from conventional rhyme and rhythmic patterns. On the other hand, Andrews blasts the Bergman's lyrics generally as "dull." See his review of *Barbra Streisand: The Way We Were*, in *Creem* (June 1973): 66–67.

14. The album-cover photographs of *Barbra Streisand: The Way We Were* and *What About Today?* also exhibit a similarity. Although both albums contain contemporary musical material, the photos of Streisand, perhaps paradoxically, reflect an era gone by.

15. "Something So Right" also contains greater melismatic embellishment, especially on the word *me*, which is a sign of the gospel influence that will become more pronounced in Streisand's work and that of several singers and groups in the 1980s.

16. An "alternate vocal" of "The Best Thing You've Ever Done" is heard on Barbra Streisand, compact disc, *Rarities* vol. 1A (private release by *Barbrabilia*, Arlington Heights, Illinois, 1997). Compared to the album version, it includes stronger guitar and bass sound and more resonance on the voice track, where the timbre is somewhat darker and fuller. Some of Dave Grusin's *Rarities* orchestration also is slightly different, especially the brief woodwind countermelodies. Additionally, Streisand's treatment of the title words is altered: on the first statement, the word *thing* is emphasized, and on the second statement both *best* and *done* are accented (and *best* is sung on a higher pitch). Her clarity with pronunciations is evident as she moves from *free* to *of* where two vowels are adjacent, and between *of* and *all* where it would be tempting to ellide the "v" sound of the former into the second word.

17. Barbra Streisand, interview with Larry King, *Larry King Live*, CNN television, 6 February 1992. She includes other information about songs recorded during the March 1974 *ButterFly* sessions but subsequently omitted from the album ("God Bless the Child," "A Quiet Thing," and "There Won't Be Trumpets") in her accompanying booklet for *Just for the Record*, compact disc 44111 (Sony Music Entertainment, 1991), 57. Also of interest, two of the liner photos for *ButterFly* picture Barbra playing a keyboard, and the front cover photo is unusual in that it does not picture her, rather an unwrapped stick of butter with a fly resting on it. The title of the album on the front liner is printed: *ButterFly*:

18. Scott is credited, by William Ruhlman, as exerting the strongest influence on the album. Ruhlman suggests that Scott's "jazz-pop style" was perfected during work with Joni Mitchell earlier in 1974, and that he wisely shaped the *ButterFly* arrangements to fit Streisand's style rather than expecting her to "ape" performances of the repertoire by other singers. See *All Music Guide* (San Francisco: Miller Freeman Publishing, 1992), s.v. "Barbra Streisand," by William Ruhlman.

19. Rupert Holmes seems to have an affinity for styles of the 1930s and 1940s; during the 1990s he was one of the creators of the American Movie Channel series entitled "Remember WENN" about a World-War-II era radio station. Steven H. Bregman, writing a review of *Lazy Afternoon*, in *Listening Post* (March 1976): 25,

found Holmes's music less appealing. A writer for *Melody Maker* suggested that Holmes' music "has more in common with Broadway proper than the Brill Building." See review of *Lazy Afternoon* (24 January 1976): 26.

20. Streisand also writes that she contributed specific ideas regarding the arrangements for the album, suggesting the harmonica countermelody on "I Never Had It So Good" and the simple piano/voice version for the tender "A Child Is Born," among other things. The accompaniments on this album cover the spectrum from elaborate and full to simple and restrained. Streisand is able to work with both styles equally well, and the variety is a plus.

21. For more information on the influence of pop and rock on film music, see Mark Evans, *Soundtrack: The Music of the Movies* (New York: Hopkinson and Blake, 1975), chapter 7.

22. Alternate arrangements of "How Lucky Can You Get" are found on Barbra Streisand, compact disc, *Rarities* vol. 1A (private release by *Barbrabilia*, Arlington Heights, Illinois, 1997). One version (that was repeated from *Soundtrack Memories* from Arista Records #ABM2005/F) might be described as containing "more." There is more playfulness in the opening and more sarcasm during the second half. Except for minor inflections and phrasing choices, Streisand's renditions are very similar, indicating that she gets her basic interpretation of a song clearly set in her mind, and then only makes minimal spontaneous changes.

23. A person in the public, popular-culture eye would be expected to evolve with (or influence) ever-changing fashion trends. The point about Streisand's change is relevant because of the frequent dichotomy between and among her age, appearance, and musical repertoire.

24. Not all film critics agree with my assessment. Susan Stark felt that the theatrical sequences "demean both Fanny Brice and Barbra Streisand." See Stark's review of *Funny Lady* in *Detroit Free Press*, 12 March 1975, 4D. Charles Michener had a similar reaction in his review in *Newsweek* (24 March 1975): 59. Perhaps the film's "performances" served as vicarious "live" performances for many viewers.

25. "Brice Twice," *Newsweek* (15 July 1974): 83.

26. Other topics of interest, but outside the parameters of this study, are evident in the film: a real-life, more-personal image of Streisand related to her own period of self-discovery (she has stated that her early rise to fame cost her part of her adolescence, so that in her 30s, she was experiencing youth and maturity simultaneously) and advocacy for women's diverse potentiality and women's rights. These notions and beliefs already were being made clear in her recordings. Nevertheless, a review of the film in *Ms.* (May 1977): 39, is anything but complimentary.

27. Kris Kristofferson's talents as a composer ("Me and Bobby McGee," "Help Me Make It Through the Night") are not represented.

28. Stanley Green, *Encyclopaedia of the Musical Film* (New York: Oxford University Press, 1981), 267. Phil Ramone had a similar reaction to Streisand's concert performances. See Paul Verna, "Phil Ramone Salute," *Billboard* (11 May 1996): PR–24.

29. The sheet music is available from Warner Bros. Publications, Inc., #VS0766. Streisand's Spanish (Latin American) accent is commendable and her diction clear. Occasionally the proper syllabic accents of the Spanish do not match neatly with the music's metrical accents, causing a slight variation from normal or preferred

pronunciation, for example on *día*. Streisand's tendency in English to add soft consonants in the middle of words as she slurs pitches or ornaments notes also is evident in her Spanish. Professor Permilla L. Jenkins, interview by author, Muncie, Indiana, 7 January 1997. "Evergreen" also brought Streisand two Grammys: as composer for Song of the Year (in a tie with "You Light Up My Life") and as singer for Pop Vocalist—Female. See John Rockwell, "Grammy Award for Fleetwood Mac," *New York Times*, 25 February 1978, 16.

30. Streisand also composed the music for "Lost Inside of You," and that process was recreated in the scene in the movie with Kristofferson playing the real-life part of lyricist Leon Russell.

31. As a means of comparison, many of the classical songs Streisand recorded might be graded among literature appropriate for middle- to upper-level undergraduate vocal music majors. (Years before this Marilyn Horne had successfully straddled the classical/showtime boundary with recordings and concertizing. In the 1980s and 1990s, classical-to-popular crossover became more common. Opera singer Samuel Ramey recorded showtunes, and pop singer Michael Bolton recorded Puccini arias.)

32. The exception, from a vocal perspective, is "Pavane" by Fauré, sung by Streisand as a vocalise or vocal exercise without text. Nevertheless, the melody would have been familiar to many listeners. Of course, voice teachers vary in their selection and grading of repertoire for their students, but often Italian, the language of only one song on Streisand's collection, is an early target. As has been noted previously, Barbra had lost some of the nasality of her voice by the early 1970s. She could benefit from returning to a slight nasal sound on some of her French diction at this point. Likewise, some of her "classical" French is flavored with "popular" French pronunciation, but all in all, it is well done. I thank Patricia Martin Gibby and Dr. Maureen Miller, associate professor of voice at Ball State University, for their observations about Streisand's repertoire and technique. Interestingly no songs by Franz Schubert, the prolific *lied* composer of the early nineteenth century, are included. Barbra had sung (not completely seriously) his "Auf dem Wasser zu singen" as part of her 1974 *Barbra Streisand and Other Musical Instruments* television special. The date of that recording might be near to the dates of the studio sessions for the repertoire eventually placed on *Classical Barbra*.

33. Most classical vocal teachers probably would recommend a soft, pure head tone over Streisand's white tone.

34. Review of *Watusi Trumpets*, in *High Fidelity* (January 1966): 106.

35. Streisand may or may not sing these songs in the keys originally written by the composer. There is disagreement in the classical arena as to the validity of such adjustments, but "low," "medium," and "high" arrangements of many classical songs are published for teaching purposes. "Beau Soir" and "Après un Rêve" are found in Max Spicker, ed., *Anthology of Modern French Songs* (New York: G. Schirmer, Inc). See also Conrad L. Osborne, "The Broadway Voice: Part 1," *High Fidelity* (January 1979):57, 62–65. Osborne writes that, "Streisand is singing these songs [on *Classical Barbra*] in comfortable contralto keys" but that this low range requires her to avoid being too inappropriately heavy with her lower chest voice, causing a limitation in dynamics and coloring. On the other hand, he does not recommend pitching the songs higher for fear of losing her ease with the upper notes.

36. Ned Rorem, *Settling the Score* (New York: Doubleday, 1988), 223.

37. Stephen Holden, " 'This Is the Music I Love. It Is My Roots'," *New York Times*, 10 November 1985, 2:1. In light of my analytical comments, it is interesting that Streisand particularly noted the need for "specific" rhythms when singing classical music.

38. Allison J. Waldman, *The Barbra Streisand Scrapbook* (New York: Citadel Press, 1995), 55.

39. Gary Klein the producer of both albums has stated that the goal of *Superman* was to keep her on the "pop charts, not have people think of her as just an MOR [middle of the road] artist." He also comments on her "unconventional" and experimental ways in the recording studio. See Jim Spada, "An Interview with Producer Gary Klein," *Billboard* (10 December 1983): BS–16.

40. Robert Hilburn, review of *Superman*, in *Los Angeles Times*, 5 July 1977, IV:9; and Dave Marsh, review of *Superman* in *Rolling Stone* (11 August 1977): 68.

41. Lawrence Grobel, "Playboy Interview: Barbra Streisand," *Playboy* (October 1977): 96. The extended article, which begins on page 79, also has many comments about her film *A Star Is Born*.

42. The arrangement features piano and chordal string with no percussion. Streisand is allowed to tell the story unencumbered by strict time and supported by rich atmosphere. She is dramatic and heartfelt with a subdued and lyrical tone, providing a sense that the listener is privy to something quite private.

43. "Songbird," words and music by Steve Nelson and David Wolfert.

44. Ernie Watts, interview by author, Muncie, Indiana, 16 October 1997.

45. By 1991 the practice of adding "new" material on "greatest hits" albums was expected because of the financial advantages it brought. As Donald S. Passman stated, "It's becoming more and more customary to require an artist to record one or two new songs for a Greatest Hits package." See *All You Need to Know About the Music Business* (New York: Simon and Schuster, 1991), 100. Other Streisand albums were released in between *Volume 2* and *Memories*, but the two will be discussed here as a pair.

46. The intensity of the song (or of her performance) is created, in strong measure, by the tessitura and accompaniment and is probably its most identifiable feature. I recall years ago hearing a disc jockey come back on the air after playing the single saying something like, "and that was Barbra Streisand working very hard." The song also is available on the soundtrack from *The Eyes of Laura Mars* released by Columbia. Because the soundtrack is not really a Streisand album, it is not listed in the discography.

47. An article in the *Los Angeles Times* recounts other details about the inception of this pairing and about the trend towards "Sweetheart Pop" duets in the late seventies. During that period, duets by John Travolta and Olivia Newton-John, Johnny Mathis and Deniece Williams, and Roberta Flack and Donny Hathaway all were chart successes. The article also contains information about similar trends in the 1960s and earlier and about the benefits duets bring to new and to established singers. See Michael Barackman, "Pop Duets: A Top-10 Marriage," *Los Angeles Times*, 26 November 1978, CAL:7.

48. *ASCAP's Art & Commerce Cafe, Meat & Potatoes*, "Alan and Marilyn Bergman on Songwriting, Part 1" [interview on-line]; available from http://www.

ascap.com/artcommerce/bergman-part1.html; Internet; accessed 11 December 1997.

49. The videotape is from A*Vision Entertainment, 1994, #50740–3, see Appendix C.

50. The microphone was cordless, with a small power box and short antenna at the bottom. Its length (and perhaps weight) seemed to bother Streisand during the performance; normally the microphone seems natural and comfortable in her hand so that its presence is hardly noticed.

51. The sheet music was produced by The Entertainment Company of New York and published by Hal Leonard Publishing Corporation, Winona, Minnesota, #00353357.

52. Dave Blume came to a similar conclusion writing, "[O]f the successful tracks, five can best be described as . . . [having] a timeless quality that's neither old-fashioned nor contemporary." See review of *Wet*, in *Los Angeles Times*, 11 November 1979, CAL:79.

53. Many of Harold Arlen's songs are found in David Bickman, ed., *The Harold Arlen Songbook* (MPL Communications, Inc., 1985) distributed by Hal Leonard.

54. The sheet music is from Cortlandt Music Publishing, Inc., Emanuel Music Corp., and Songs of Bandier-Koppelman, Inc. This shows Streisand's increasing involvement in all products related to her work as Emanuel Music is under her purview, as is Diana Music (named for her parents). She has been associated with several companies over the years: Ellbar, a partner in the production of her early television specials; First Artists, the film company that produced *The Main Event* but stopped being involved in film work shortly thereafter; and other production (especially Barwood) and publishing connections. Beginning with *A Star Is Born*, as has already been stated, her name became more visible in the production credits of films and recordings.

55. Barbra Streisand, accompanying booklet for *Just for the Record*, compact disc 44111 (Sony Music Entertainment, 1991), 71. A Vocal Selections book for *Guilty* is available from Hal Leonard Publishing, see bibliography.

56. One of Barry Gibb's talents is writing creative rhythms and rhythmic layers. His name is mentioned in the "Rhythm Hooks" section of Gary Burns, "A Typology of 'Hooks' in Popular Music," *Popular Music* 6, no. 1 (January 1987): 1–20.

57. "Promises" and several of Barbra's other dance numbers also were recorded in "extended version" format for promotions and as singles. Her vocals usually are quite similar from version to version except on improvised repeats during a final fade. Often the extension is accomplished through a longer introduction, instrumental interludes between text verses, repeats of choruses, and vamp-to-fade endings.

58. "The Love Inside" was the only song on the album not expressly written for Streisand. See Paul Grein, "Gibb Pleads 'Guilty' to Being a Streisand Fan—Especially Now," *Billboard* (28 February 1981): 6, 11, 62. He writes that Barbra also worried that some of the text of "Woman in Love" might be too strongly feminist for a pop song, but the single was successful.

59. "Streisand Disks Dominate Global Charts," *Billboard* (6 December 1980): 4.

60. The partial greatest-hits collection, *Memories*, was released in 1981. It is discussed earlier with *Greatest Hits, Volume 2*. Some writers have criticized Strei-

sand and Columbia for repeating so many tracks from one "greatest-hits" collection to the next.

61. Barbra Streisand, interview by Mary Turner, *The Legend of Barbra Streisand* produced by Westwood One, phonodisc A2S1779 (Columbia Records, 1983).

62. Barbra Streisand and Jon Peters, interview by Geraldo Rivera, *20/20*, ABC television, 17 November 1983. Further comments on Peters' connection to *Yentl* are found in Frank Rose, *The Agency: William Morris and the Hidden History of Show Business* (New York: HarperCollins Publishers, Inc., 1995), 382–384.

63. James Spada, "An Interview with Marilyn and Alan Bergman," *Billboard* (10 December 1983): BS-13.

64. Isaac Bashevis Singer, the author of the original short story, apparently was not fond of the addition of music to the tale. See "I. B. Singer Talks to I. B. Singer about the Movie 'Yentl'," *New York Times*, 29 January 1984, 2:1.

65. Streisand made this choice even though co-star Mandy Patinkin is known for his fine voice.

66. The Eastern-European, modal flavors are especially noticeable during the candle scene of "Papa, Can You Hear Me?" and the grave-side scene after Yentl's father has died. David Sills, interview by author, Muncie, Indiana, November 1997.

67. A "single" version of "Papa, Can You Hear Me?" also was recorded and is found on Barbra Streisand, compact disc, *Rarities* vol. 1B (private release by *Barbrabilia*, Arlington Heights, Illinois, 1997). It begins with a brief dramatic orchestral introduction and uses voices as part of the sustained accompaniment. Streisand's vocal line is nearly identical to the soundtrack version, except that she may sing an occasional longer phrase by not breathing as often.

68. Record executives suggested the brisk sales of the soundtrack were helped by Streisand's loyal fan base and by the album's release in time for holiday sales. Like the soundtrack for *A Star Is Born*, the *Yentl* album was in the stores before the film was in the theatre. A video of "The Way He Makes Me Feel" also was available for broadcast. See Richard Gold, " 'Yentl' Soundtrack A Hit, Ethnic Bent Doesn't Hurt Sales," *Variety* (18 January 1984): 1, 108. Although her fans felt that Streisand was snubbed by the Academy that year, two years later Barbra was the presenter for the Best Director category. The introduction for her segment included clips not only from the nominated films, but also from the work of other directors and her own movies (both as actress and director). This all was underscored by her recording of "Putting It Together." (She presented the award to her long-time friend and colleague Sydney Pollack for *Out of Africa*.)

69. Parts of Streisand's "audition" tape of songs from *Yentl*, which was used to explain the film's concept to Hollywood executives, are included on *Just for the Record* (see discography).

70. Continuing her habit of putting personal messages on the liner, Streisand thanks the Pointer Sisters, Mastering Supervisor John Arrias, and three persons only identified by their initials (but likely her son, Jason; Jon Peters; and Richard Baskin).

71. "People," *Time* (5 November 1984): 51.

72. An article by Stephen Holden, which includes a review of *Emotion*, tackles the issue of "mature stars" seeking ways to keep a "mass appeal." Ironically (for where Streisand was headed next), one of the albums he discusses is Linda Ron-

stadt's *What's New*, which contained old-style standards and torch songs. He encourages Streisand to give up mundane commerciality in favor of material that would "do justice to her thrilling dramatic soprano." See "Mature Stars Seek the Formula for Mass Appeal," *New York Times*, 11 November 1984, 2:23–24.

Chapter 5

Coming Full Circle: Back to the Concert Stage

... at moments I've appreciated the sound of my voice, but ... unfortunately, I take it for granted, too. ... I must never do that because it's a God-given gift.[1]

The thing basically is that I was ready to sing. I was ready ... to face this kind of fear.[2]

For the opening song of her 1985 *The Broadway Album*, Barbra Streisand asked Stephen Sondheim to revise the lyrics of "Putting It Together" to make them applicable to music. The song originally was written for Sondheim's *Sunday in the Park with George*, and in that show it expresses the frustration of a painter who tries to remain true to the purity of his creative ideas while dealing with life's realities and art as commerce. Through these revisions, Barbra could express musically the real-life struggle she faced in advance of the release of this collection of showtunes; she saw reality as the basis for the song's message. In what must have felt to Streisand like history repeating itself, even with her catalogue of twenty years worth of financially successful albums, some record executives were wary of the audience's receptiveness toward this kind of repertoire.

The Broadway Album is what the title implies, with one possible exception. The inclusion of a medley of "I Loves You, Porgy" and "Porgy, I's Your Woman Now" from *Porgy and Bess* is surprising because that show often is called an opera rather than a Broadway musical. But by now the public and her record label had come to expect the unexpected from Streisand. Furthermore, her selection of material reflects historical diversity; the songs are drawn from shows written as early as the 1920s (*Showboat*) and from those as recent as the 1980s (*Sunday in the Park with George* was produced in 1984).

Because many of the other songs on the album are from the creative mind of Stephen Sondheim, it might have been entitled *Streisand Sings Sondheim . . . and Others*. Sondheim certainly became one of the most prolific and influential American composers for the Broadway stage during the latter half of the twentieth century, so it was appropriate to finally bring the two artists together—if not on the stage, at least in the studio.[3] Sondheim's way with pithy texts and Streisand's unique abilities to interpret stories and enunciate musical lines had the potential for a fine pairing. By drawing on contemporary Sondheim and historical musical theatre, Streisand acknowledged both the past and the present simultaneously. In typical fashion, she was coming full circle—but rather circuitously. She was aware of the paradox in her literature choice, remarking that she was breaking new ground with old material.[4]

The past and present also were combined in the album's production and musical team. Peter Matz (who had arranged and conducted her earliest 1960s solo albums)[5] is named frequently among *The Broadway Album* liner credits for his efforts as arranger, conductor, and producer, but Richard Baskin (Barbra's suitor and collaborator at that time) also receives multiple credits. Streisand's name is listed as producer and vocalist, of course, but she is also credited as an arranger.[6] David Foster, a keyboardist on earlier Streisand albums (such as *Songbird*), provided her with an elaborate arrangement of "Somewhere" from *West Side Story*, which she also recorded as a music video under the direction of William Friedkin.[7] Continuing the coordination of old and new, Foster's arrangement uses modern sound technology, but most of the other songs were recorded in front of a full orchestra, an attempt to create an old-fashioned "live-" or "cast-" album feeling.[8] (As was typical over the years, the sound of Barbra's breathing was not edited out, adding another "live" quality to the mix.) Finally, the liner photographs also may reflect the past and present. Barbra is pictured twice on the stage of an empty theatre, perhaps symbolizing that she had "come home," but only in a private way.

All of the Streisand song types are represented on *The Broadway Album*, but the dividing line between categories is especially vague. As usual, songs that allow strong characterizations are the most prominent. Many of her expected vocal techniques also are evident; a prominent fast vibrato in all registers of her voice also is heard.

"Putting It Together" mixes characterization with autobiographical ideas resulting from the revisions Sondheim provided.[9] The song begins with a recitative-like opening sung while spoken dialogue from other "characters" is interspersed. It then expands into several tuneful, but rather fast, sections that are full of intricate words; the wordiness and the free form are hallmarks of the lyricist's style. A chorus of sorts (the text is not identical on repetitions) appears intermittently and contains the few long notes of the song. The chorus also exhibits Streisand's tendency toward phrase over-lapping. The word *art* occurs frequently and is sung as "ah-(r)t," with almost no hint of the "r" sound. Video excerpts showing Streisand singing this song indicate that she creates the sound by dropping her jaw, as would be expected in standard vocal production. In contrast, for the word *girl* her mouth position is more horizontal than vertical; subsequently, the "r" sound becomes increasingly prominent and nasal. The paucity of long tones causes those that are present to stand out, and the animation of her vocal mechanism makes every sound audible; for example *life* becomes "lah-i-ee-ehf." The Streisand/Matz arrangement of the accompaniment adds to the frantic or frustrated feeling of "Putting It Together" through several con-trasting layers, from sweeping strings to active rhythm lines.

The next song on the album provides remarkable contrast. "If I Loved You," by Rodgers and Hammerstein II, is a love ballad with words that beg for interpretation. Barbra commented that the most important word of the short AABA song is *if*, and that the singer must deal with it thought-fully.[10] She also colors several other words, including *loved, easy,* and *mist*. Text and musical phrases are sometimes overlapped (+ means no breath taken, ^ indicates breath taken): "Round in circles^I'd go+Longin' to tell you,^but afraid and shy,^I'd let my golden chances^pass me by.+Soon you'd leave me."[11] Streisand's control of pitch, breath, and dynamic gra-dations is clear during the final few measures where she descends from an intense high and loud note on *know* to a sudden soft note on *you* just moments later. (Similar control is noticeable during her medley from *The King and I* on the same album.) The final repetition of the title words is sung with silent space between words ("If^I^loved you") to place addi-tional emphasis on her purposely ambiguous reading of *if*. However, even with the space, her smooth timbre creates a feeling of connectedness and phrase. The accompaniment, like others of the collection, often sets Barbra against woodwinds, especially double reeds, in her same register. The blend is effective.

Autobiographical and advocacy songs include "Not While I'm Around" from *Sweeney Todd* and the medley "Pretty Women/The Ladies Who Lunch"[12] from *Sweeney Todd* and *Company,* all written by Sondheim. Streisand also sang "Not While" for her son, Jason, on her 1994 tour. In both cases she used her soft, breathy tone (until the final section) to elicit the gentleness of a lullaby. The dynamics and her mouth shape again affect the sound of vowels: near the end, *time* is heard with a sustained "long i" sound (the first half of the diphthong) and intense timbre, while shortly thereafter the same vowel on *I'm* is heard as "ah-(e)m" with a soft, clear timbre. These songs, like some others on the album (especially "Being Alive"), rightfully reflect a mid-life Streisand, who naturally has changed her outlook and priorities as she matures. Similar comments might be made about her version of "Send in the Clowns," for which Sondheim wrote some additional lyrics (for a return to the bridge) and approved location changes for others. Barbra's performance and the accompaniment (with lush cello and English horn countermelodies) justify placement of the song in the lyric-song category. Word coloring, rubato liberties, and dynamic contrasts abound, and they are set against her soft, breathy tone, which is warmed with wide and fast vibrato. Her treatment of the word *clowns* has her vocalize either the *n* or the *ow*.

"Adelaide's Lament" from *Guys and Dolls* provides additional contrast on *The Broadway Album*. At first hearing, it sounds much like the Barbra of years before with a nasal, strongly New York accent (some of her spoken "character" lines recall *I Can Get It for You Wholesale*, and the arrangement of "Lament" was done by Sid Ramin, who had orchestrated "Miss Marmelstein"). However, repeated listening draws attention to several vocal details. Barbra's nasal characterization is appropriate for the congested sound Adelaide needed at that point, but near the end of this performance, on the louder, higher notes used for *mood* and *(per)-son*, Streisand's later open, fuller and darker tone is clear, and the accent is gone. The nasality and coughing (some of the latter likely added on a different track) suggest that Streisand can maintain a full tone through almost any character effect. This capability already was familiar through her tearful performances of "My Man" in *Funny Girl* or "With One More Look at You" in *A Star Is Born*.

Despite the skepticism of some in advance of the album's debut, *Variety* ran the headline "Streisand Vaults RIAA Hurdles; 'Broadway' Races to Triple-Plat" on 5 February 1986, a mere three months after its release. The writer also reported that radio-play of individual tracks was not widespread, but that album sales were brisk—a typical situation for Streisand recordings. Many reviews of the album were published (see bibliography), and the vast majority were positive. Authors welcomed Barbra back to Broadway repertoire and remarked on the continued beauty of her vocal tone, the presumed ease of her technique, and the depth of her interpretations. Rod McKuen, writing for *Stereo Review*, stated that this recording placed Streisand ahead of Frank Sinatra as "the artist with the longest span of No. 1 albums in the history of *Billboard's* Top Ten Albums charts."[13] Barbra was awarded a Grammy as Best Pop Female Vocalist for *The Broadway Album* (her competition was Tina Turner, Cyndi Lauper, Madonna, and Dionne Warwick), and she noted that it came twenty-four years after winning her first Grammy in the same category. In her acceptance speech she commented that it was particularly "gratifying" to be praised for work on this type of repertoire, which she felt reaffirmed the quality of the material.[14] In a final convergence of old and new, it was during this time that Martin Erlichman resumed duties as Streisand's manager.[15]

In the summer of 1986, several people received a tape-recorded invitation to attend dinner and a concert on 6 September at Barbra Streisand's Malibu home; Streisand herself would be the featured entertainment in an event designed to raise money in support of Democratic congressional candidates. The concert was billed as her "first full-length concert in twenty years," but it was by invitation only, and attendees were asked to contribute $5,000 per couple to the political fund (a fact she later tentatively joked about in her comments between songs). The concert attracted considerable press, perhaps more for the fact that Barbra was singing than for the cause the singing supported. While she had displayed social awareness previously, this occasion launched Streisand more visibly and forthrightly into the political arena—as an activist, not as a candidate. The nuclear accident at Chernobyl earlier that year served as the catalyst that brought Barbra to the realization that the drawing power of her voice might assist in creating a safer world (as visualized by those of like political and social leanings). Her desire to help overpowered her hesitancy to perform publicly.

For those not invited to the *One Voice* concert, HBO television, CBS/Fox music video, and Columbia Records provided the next-best options. HBO aired a videotape of the concert (produced by Streisand, Martin Erlichman, Dwight Hemion, and Gary Smith) in December 1986, which subsequently was made available for commercial purchase.[16] An album from the concert, produced by Richard Baskin, was released the following spring.[17] Barbra's proceeds from the event went to her newly established Streisand Foundation, which supports non-profit groups involved with anti-nuclear activities, environmental concerns, and civil liberties and human rights issues.[18] Some of her thoughts on these topics served as verbal segues (written by Streisand and Alan and Marilyn Bergman) between songs;[19] thus, in a general way, the entire album might be placed in the autobiographical and advocacy category.

The concert videotape begins with panoramic shots of the countryside, excerpts from a sound check and her audio invitation, comments from celebrities as they arrived (many of whom, including Bette Midler, had never heard Barbra in concert), and portions of Robin Williams's show-opening monologue. Then a very modern, electronic, eight-piece instrumental combo begins the ethereal introduction of "Somewhere" from Streisand's Broadway album. Ever theatrical, she slowly emerges from a haze of smoke. An awkward moment ensues as she is forced to continue singing even though the audience is sustaining its enthusiastic ovation. Although it does not severely affect Streisand's sound, the horizontal shape of her mouth (which comes from grinning while trying to sing during the applause) is noticeable—noticeable because once the audience has quieted her usual vertical mouth and flat tongue are seen and the timbre changes slightly. During another moment in the concert, the actress lights a candle and sings "Papa, Can You Hear Me?" from *Yentl*, and the largely industry-based audience applauds warmly, perhaps in an effort to ameliorate her

Oscar snub years earlier. The concert scene she creates is similar to that in the film, but her verbal introduction establishes the focus on "father figures" the world has lost to violence. The scene and the song end with darkness as she blows out the candle and all lights are cut.

Only three of the thirteen songs presented in the *One Voice* video are not found on earlier Streisand albums, although it is always interesting to hear her new performances of older material. Oddly, one song from the video is omitted from the album—her dramatic reading of "Send in the Clowns." The three new songs actually are quite old: "It's a New World" was written by Harold Arlen and Ira Gershwin in the 1950s, "Over the Rainbow" was written by Arlen and E. Y. Harburg in 1939, and "America, the Beautiful" began its entry into American song lore in the 1920s. Streisand remarks that she was hesitant to sing Judy Garland's "Rainbow" signature song, but Barbra does the song justice with her own personalized and heartfelt version of the optimistic text, complete with its less-familiar opening verse. She also comments on her joy in singing different material, which is particularly interesting since Streisand had not recently presented many concerts where repetition would be common. Two duets with Barry Gibb (from the *Guilty* album but with slightly different arrangements since backup singers were used in the studio) provided style and sound contrast. A summarization of analytical points concerning the concert follows.

- In this setting, Streisand improvises a greater number of short melodic decorations than likely would be found on studio versions of the same songs. These occur especially during the later sections of a song, although the basic interpretive choices remain consistent; see "Somewhere," "Evergreen," and "Something's Coming."

- Several words end with a closed-mouth, nasal sound, whether that "n" sound is part of the actual word (*somehow* becomes "some-hown" and the final *here* of "Send in the Clowns" contains a brief "n" and then simply dissipates), and she continues to vocalize consonants (the word *people* in shorter settings has pitch on the *l*; in longer settings, a mixture of "ah" and "eh" is held for the second syllable; it then ends with a stop of air after a quick flip of the tongue to a short "l" sound).

- Streisand visually takes on character in live presentation, no matter the other musical traits of a song ("Evergreen" as compared to "Something's Coming"). This especially is evident by watching her eyes at the beginning of and during "Send in the Clowns," which received extended applause upon conclusion. Her duet with Barry Gibb on "What Kind of Fool" is choreographed with slight gestures as was her 1980 Grammy performance with Neil Diamond of "You Don't Bring Me Flowers."

- The sound quality of this outdoor recording usually is admirable, but the contemporary sounds of the synthesized accompaniments[20] may or may not enhance the arrangements. "The Way We Were" in particular is presented with a stronger beat and wailing electric guitar lines that Barbra answers with a belt tone;

"Guilty" also seems to have a brighter tempo and a crisper sound than heard on the album of the same name.

- Several of her phrases seem shorter than usual and include fewer long-held tones ("Evergreen" and "Send in the Clowns"), but there is some overlap of textual phrase with musical phrase ("there's a land that I heard of+once^in a lullaby" from "Over the Rainbow").[21]

- She creates shadow vowels at the ends of words, which often extends them (*tree* becomes "tree-ah"); the animation of her jaw, lips, and tongue are pronounced and aid her clean diction.

- Streisand's finesse with timbral changes and controlled dynamic gradations (sudden or sweeping) consistently is evident, as is her fast vibrato in all ranges except when the dynamic level is extremely soft. She does not sing any strong belt songs during the concert until "Happy Days Are Here Again," which comes near the end. She begins "America" with no accompaniment and uses a child-like breathy tone.

- For variation, Streisand alters the melodic line on repeats of verses or musical sections (during *lovers*, which begins the second verse of "People," the second syllable is dropped several steps instead of being raised a step as in the printed music. In "Over the Rainbow," the octave leap that usually begins the final A section is omitted and replaced by a repeated high note—after being overlapped from the end of the bridge text, i.e., *me* connected to *somewhere* with both syllables of the latter on the same pitch).

- Barbra is beginning to decorate a melody note by preceding it once or twice with the note just above, sometimes called "the upper neighbor" (heard on *fly* in "Over the Rainbow"), a technique that will soon become more pronounced.

- She ends many words simply by stopping the air, a technique made even more effective by pulling the microphone away in a dramatic gesture (if at the end of the song or phrase).

- In comparison with the 1968 video from *A Happening in Central Park*, Streisand's posture is more erect in 1986, and her hands and arms do not flail about as dramatically. The Malibu evening might have been humid and slightly windy, but she seems to have developed a habit of lightly brushing her hair away from her forehead.

The 1986 concert closed with "America, the Beautiful," arranged by Randy Kerber, who also served as conductor, keyboard player, and backup singer. He borrowed phrases from both the second and third verses of the published text for the middle section of this arrangement, bringing together notions of heros with mercy and mending national flaws. The audience was invited to sing along on the last section, a repeat of the familiar first verse, with Barbra improvising melody and rhythms, flavored by some gospel inflection, above the crowd. Some critics (of the recording and of the video) assailed her preachy speaking, but most welcomed her concert singing (see bibliography).

In 1988 Columbia released Streisand's *Till I Loved You* album, a collection of studio material with a decidedly middle-of-the-road sound. Its songs manifest several styles and the work of several producers, arrangers, lyricists, and composers (including Barbra). Her colleague from the early 1970s, Burt Bacharach, is represented as composer and arranger on three selections. The wrapper for this album (which was one of the last to be available as both a phonograph album and a compact disc) took advantage of her recent Broadway and concertizing success by including a cover sticker that read, "The Greatest Female Vocalist of the Century!"

Barbra was going through some relationship changes in the late 1980s, and this is reflected in a variety of ways in much of the *Till I Loved You* repertoire. For example, actor Don Johnson sings a duet with her on the title song[22] and provides backup vocal harmony on "What Were We Thinking of?" The two stars had a short, but widely publicized, relationship at the time.[23] Several of the other songs contain lyrics about the difficulty of making relationships work and the effort they require ("Why Let It Go?", "Some Good Things Never Last," and "Two People"). Other songs take a cheerful or contented view of love ("On My Way to You" and "You and Me for Always"). Typical of this period of Streisand's career, the album also is personalized by her words of thanks in the liner notes.

The reflective (and mature or experienced) nature of some of these texts allow greater characterization or interpretation than many contemporary pop lyrics, which always is an advantage with Streisand's approach.[24] For example, characterizations are heard on the "Till I Loved You" duet (which otherwise is a ballad) and "All I Ask of You" from *Phantom of the Opera* (which otherwise exhibits sweeping lyric-song qualities). Similarly, slight characterization is noticeable on the one advocacy-like song of the set, "The Places You Find Love" by Quincy Jones. Its text, a lesson on the true source of happiness, is delivered in a story-like fashion, and Barbra's gospel inflections are supported by a celebrity backup group that includes Luther Vandross, Dionne Warwick, Jennifer Holliday, and James Ingram.

The similarity of the lyrics does not, however, suggest musical and accompanimental sameness throughout. There are tunes with moderate to bright tempos, active rhythmic layers with a backbeat, and synthesized sounds ("The Places" and "What Were"). There also are slower, orchestrally accompanied ballads ("On My Way to You" by Michel Legrand and Alan and Marilyn Bergman). The album contains several relatively long songs; in fact, only four are less than four minutes in length. Unlike extended songs from Streisand's earlier recordings (those on the *Guilty* album or "The Main Event/Fight" and "No More Tears"), the length in this case is not created simply by repeats, long fades, or instrumental interludes; instead, the texts are expansive. Typical of this pop-song style period, several songs receive a harmonic boost from a modulation upward during the second half and many are quite free in form (AABAB for "Why Let," and irregular phrase and section lengths in "On My Way").

Several specific points about Streisand's vocal technique deserve mention. Barbra seems to have been influenced by the accents Don Johnson placed on several words during "Till I Loved You" (heard on the word *possibly*, for example) and "What Were We Thinking of?" She produces a sound similar to his in the latter on *saddest* and at other points. Writing for the *New York Times*, Stephen Holden suggested that Johnson has a Southern-rock quality in his sound; perhaps this is the trait Barbra absorbed.[25]

During the course of the album, Streisand's tendency to decorate a melodic pitch with its upper neighbor becomes more pronounced. Sometimes just one short reference to the added note is heard before it is slurred to the main note. At other times there are multiple references to the decorating pitch, perhaps D-C-D-C, where each of the first three notes are of equal length and the final main note is sustained, as in Example 4. Occasionally the first note of such a set of four notes is protracted slightly to create a rhythm relationship that could be written as Example 5. These varied approaches can be heard on the final hum of "All I Ask of You"; on *heart*, *fast*, and *go* of "Why Let It Go?"; and on *know*, *free*, and *last* of "Some Good Things Never Last." In contrast, "On My Way to You" ends with Streisand on a long "oo" sound for *you*. Her tone is rich, and it slowly fades away so that it is somewhat unclear as to exactly when she stops making sound, in part because that pitch is continued by an instrument of like timbre. The section in question totals about twenty-three seconds, with the transitional area beginning about eighteen seconds through. Whatever the length, the phrase is interesting—the blend of the instrumental pitch with her voice is remarkable.

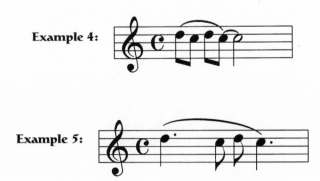

Example 4:

Example 5:

Andrew Lloyd Webber's melody for "All I Ask of You" stretches Streisand's mature low range, particularly on the words *true* and *too*. Those round, easy vowels help her sustain a pure, strong tone in that register, and on *shelter* she reverts to her typical "shel-tah(r)," which makes a smooth "ah" vowel for the low-pitched second syllable. Barbra's ability to casually decorate or color even the shortest of notes is heard by carefully listening to the descending line beginning with "share each day with me" at the harmony change.[26] The line goes by so quickly that a listener might not realize what has happened, but both *each* and *with* are colored slightly.

Overall, *Till I Loved You* reflects very little of Streisand's belt sound; the extant higher notes generally are produced with the head voice. "Some Good Things" exhibits her propensity for adding an "h" sound before some vowel sounds that occur in the middle of words on slurs. However, Barbra's performance makes it clear that there is not a usual or predictable place for this to happen: it is not consistently done with certain vowels more than others, nor in one type of rhythmic setting over another, nor with particular location of a word within a phrase. Some melodies, including Lloyd Webber's and her own "Two People," require her to traverse wide melodic intervals, which she does with accuracy and consistent timbre and tone.

Between 1989 and 1991 Streisand recorded several new songs, but none appear on a typical album (or by now, compact disc). Her 1989 compact disc entitled *A Collection: Greatest Hits . . . and More* contains ten tracks borrowed from albums issued between the mid-1970s and *Till I Loved You*. In fact, two of the ten had been the "new" material on her last "best of" set, *Memories*. But *A Collection* also has its own new material; two selections that Columbia described as "tender love ballads" reflecting a "bittersweet mood."[27] The liner features photographs reflecting the work of Native American artisans, a message about care of the earth from Barbra, and commentary (included at her request) from Earth Communication Office.[28] Once again she used an album (in this case, the liner more than the repertoire) to promote her feelings on important issues.

The two new ballads on *A Collection* are "We're Not Makin' Love Anymore" by romantic ballad singer Michael Bolton and Diane Warren, and "Someone That I Used to Love" by Michael Masser and Gerry Goffin. The lyrics of the two have enough in common that some joint analysis is practical. Streisand colors several words for effect whether they are particularly descriptive words (*motion* and *stranger* among others). Her penchant for leaping up a wide interval to emphasize a textual or musical moment is heard on *alright* and *refused*. Her approach to the word *love* varies from "lah(vn)" to "luhv" to "lahv" to "la-uh(v)n" depending on the length of the pitch, the number of pitches sung on the word, its location in the phrase, and the dynamic level. The accompaniments create the most distinction between the two songs. "We're Not" has a heavy beat with occasional sweet strings floating above, and technology permits Streisand to almost sing a duet with herself as she fades one phrase while a new one begins. This approach adds to the characterization of the lyric. In contrast, "Someone" has a much lighter beat and a piano introduction that allows parlando delivery of the repeated-note melody that opens the verses.

Two newly recorded songs also appear on the soundtrack from Streisand's 1991 film *The Prince of Tides*, which she starred in and directed. Its liner notes clearly state, however, that neither song actually is heard in the film, not even under titles or credits. Barbra stated in several publicity interviews for the film and in the liner that she did not want Streisand-the-singer to distract from Streisand-the-actress playing the role of psychiatrist Susan Lowenstein. "Places That Belong to You" was written by James Newton Howard (who scored the film) and Alan and Marilyn Bergman. Its lyric summarizes the emotional points of the plot, and its imagery and orchestration are rich, like the film and the score. Barbra's vocalization begins with her soft, breathy tone, but later the mood and the melodic line cause her to open to a full sound using mostly head voice rather than her strongest belt quality. Her vibrato is prominent in both her middle and high registers, and it is especially noticeable on the soft, breathy final *you*. The lyric contains one potentially tricky spot where the Bergmans place in proximity several short phrases centered around the word *was*. A sophis-ticated singer like Streisand, who has precise diction and subtle interpretive skills, can make the passage work, deftly navigating the twists in meaning, but the section challenges the listener to think through all the thoughts. A music video of the song, which included scenes from the movie (minus the spoken text), was made, but it did not receive substantial air time.

Streisand's son, Jason, a burgeoning actor, played her son in *The Prince of Tides*. According to the soundtrack liner notes, a birthday gift from Jason to Barbra of Billie Holiday's recording of "For All We Know" was the impetus for the song's inclusion in the film.[29] An instrumental version was used to underscore one scene of the film, and Streisand thought the original lyric was fitting for the film's story, so she recorded it as the second vocal on the soundtrack. The accompaniment has a kind of polished cab-aret quality to it; brushes on the snare drum establish the rhythmic foun-dation and the interlude features a breathy, vibrato-filled saxophone solo. Again, the vocal interpretation progresses from a soft, breathy opening to a belt sound with considerable melodic decoration and back to a soft, quiet ending. Undoubtedly, the addition of two Streisand songs to the soundtrack helped its sales; "For All We Know" also was used as one of the closing songs for her 1994 tour concerts.

A similar sales technique was used in 1996 with the soundtrack to *The Mirror Has Two Faces*, another film starring and directed and produced by Streisand. The genesis of the film's original music is complicated. It was "composed and adapted" by Marvin Hamlisch, although the "love theme" and some of the incidental instrumental music was composed by Barbra. Her love theme also inspired "All of My Life," another song in her cata-logue with lyrics by the Bergmans. But similar to the situation in *The Prince of Tides*, this song is not heard in *Mirror*—it was added to the soundtrack (also produced by Streisand) as a "bonus track."[30] The nature of the *Mirror* story called for contemporary pop music as well as opera and jazz excerpts and instrumental background music. The film's pop music includes "The Power Inside of Me" performed by pop crooner Richard Marx (and heard in the movie) and a duet sung by Streisand and Bryan Adams (heard under the credits). Adams's raspy voice is familiar to top-40 listeners, and he has seen chart success with other movie theme songs. Their duet, "I Finally Found Someone," was a collaboration from Streisand, Hamlisch, Adams, and R. J. Lange. Marvin Hamlisch reported that a second song was in contention for the film's theme song, but "It Doesn't Get Better Than This" did not prevail against the Streisand/Adams duet.[31] "I Finally Found Someone" did well enough on the singles charts to give Barbra at least one top-10 hit in each of the last four decades.

In 1991 Streisand and Columbia, by then associated with Sony, celebrated the longevity of Barbra's career and the popularity of her recordings by releasing a retrospective boxed set entitled *Just for the Record*. The collection comprises four compact discs (two with material from the 1960s and one each representing the 1970s and 1980s) and a detailed booklet written by Barbra (containing program notes, dedications, historical information, lists of awards and honors, and liner credits). Together they serve as a kind of autobiography,[32] and in one sense, the set simply continues the trend she began in the 1970s toward revealing personal information through recordings. As mentioned before, it is always rewarding to study the album art on Streisand's releases. In this case, the theme is pink roses. The roses pictured on the 1960s discs are a bud and a bud just beginning to open, the rose photographed for the 1970s disc is slightly more unfurled, and the rose marking the 1980s is in full bloom. Barbra concludes the booklet by thanking the public for its faithful listening.

The first 1960s disc actually begins with a recording that pre-dates the 1960s and Streisand's professional career: she recorded "You'll Never Know" in 1955 in the Nola Recording Studios in New York City.[33] Her performance already displays certain vocal characteristics that will remain a part of her style for decades to come, including an ease with vocal production (remarkable for a thirteen year old), good control of dynamics, full and rich tone (albeit youthful), clean diction (including a sophisticated breath break between the vowel sounds connecting *away* and *and*), and personalized interpretations and arrangements. Even slight inflections are heard on the words *just, now,* and *way* among others; they are similar to those sung many years later on "All I Ask of You." Streisand's musical and textual phrases of "You'll Never Know" at times are not aligned in the traditional manner, foreshadowing Barbra's future (for example, "haven't I told^you so+a million or more times"[34]). Nonetheless, the weakness of her high notes and the inconsistency of her vibrato divulge her youthfulness.

The rest of disc 1 consists of songs and dialogue from Streisand's early television and night-club appearances and solo and cast albums. The concert tracks in particular remind the listener of her early enthusiasm and brash technique. As would be expected, the repertoire emphasizes character songs and belt/torch numbers. The animation of her vocal mechanism is heard on many words, particularly in "Happy Days Are Here Again," and hindsight suggests that her lower range is not yet fully developed (on "Keepin' Out of Mischief Now," for example). Barbra's ability to present texts with rhythmic elasticity, yet to guide them cleanly through harmony changes, is notable coming from such an inexperienced singer (for example, on "Moon River" and "Nobody's Heart"). A touch of comedy is added with "I Hate Music," which she presents with her child-like nasal sound. Contrast comes quickly with her sensitive reading of "Spring Can Really Hang You Up the Most." Several of these performances are accompanied only minimally, which is not a drawback, and some have a jazz-inspired rhythm section and style. Although many of the selections were not recorded in a studio, the recording quality generally is good. It is interesting to hear the audience react to this as-yet-unknown singer and to hear Streisand's impassioned charactizations during several numbers (such as "Lover, Come Back to Me").

The second *Just for the Record* disc from the 1960s features material from performances that made Streisand a household name: Broadway's *Funny Girl*, the television specials, and her earliest musical films. Adding to the autobiographical nature of the collection are other personal recordings. These include a tape of Barbra's mother singing "Second Hand Rose" and Streisand's duet with Harold Arlen of "Ding-Dong! The Witch Is Dead" from his *Harold Sings Arlen (with Friend)* album. The selections from *Funny Girl* reveal Streisand's young and pathos-filled sound, but contrast again comes with her controlled rendition of "I'm Always Chasing Rainbows," which features several leaps up during *rainbows* and varied phrasings of the titular words. For listeners already familiar with Streisand's early albums, the inclusion on *Just for the Record* of the little-known "You Wanna Bet" is a welcome surprise. The performance is instructive for hearing how her voice developed and how her musical surroundings changed during the first five years of her career. Barbra's rendition clearly exhibits growing dynamic and vocal control and more sophisticated, elaborate accompaniments. Naturally, her mature timbre is not yet evident, but her wide palette of tonal color is.

The 1970s disc begins with two selections from a 10 March 1970 recording session that never appeared on commercial albums: "The Singer" and "I Can Do It."[35] The text of the former is particularly insightful in light of Streisand's interest in literature with personal meaning. Its text is about the frustrations a person can feel when living in the glare of the public spotlight—when there is a feeling that the audience does not really know, or perhaps care about, the real-life person underneath a performer's professional veneer. A rather rough "boom-chick" accompaniment with a decidedly German-cabaret sound belies the poignancy of the text. Switching quickly from a 1960s disc to this one indicates how much Barbra's voice mellowed over the decade; her lower register became considerably more controlled, but she ably moved freely to her head voice for some high notes ("You're the Top" and "Since I Fell for You"). The 1970s disc also documents some of Streisand's film and recording-studio work and other concert or television appearances. Material issued on the boxed set but not found on other albums includes her duet with Ryan O'Neal of "You're the Top" from *What's Up Doc?* (an otherwise non-musical film) and her duet with Ray Charles, "Cryin' Time," that was omitted from the *Barbra Streisand and Other Musical Instruments* soundtrack. The latter shows the muddiness that can result when two distinctive, interpretive singers try to sing unison rhythms.

Barbra's association with Stephen Sondheim's music is most directly linked to her 1985 Broadway set, but *Just for the Record* includes a 1974 recording of his "There Won't Be Trumpets" that also had gone unreleased. Similarly, "What Are You Doing the Rest of Your Life?" and alternate or "demo" versions of other songs highlight her continued professional relationship with Alan and Marilyn Bergman and Michel Legrand. In this manner, consumers were acquiring both a historical record of Streisand's singing and some previously unreleased material, the same approach that was used with her "greatest hits" albums. However, although "Stoney End" represents her foray into soft-rock, most of the songs on the 1970s disc could be described as love ballads, belt or torch songs, and character songs, none of which reflect much rock influence. In other words, *Just for the Record* does not contain complete documentation of Barbra's transitional and experimental period.[36] Some of her soulful sound, which is characteristic of the 1970s portion of her career, is heard, as is her ability to place her own stamp on a song associated with another singer. For example, many listeners remember "Close to You" as a light-pop love ballad that became a hit for Karen and Richard Carpenter. Barbra's version is more lush and slower—one interpretation might be that it is being sung as the private thoughts of a woman to her absent man. This approach creates layers of meaning in the manner of a theatre song, but perhaps more than the text can withstand.

Some of Streisand's eclecticism of the 1980s and her return to her musical-theatre roots are evident on the final disc of *Just for the Record.* It, too, contains some unreleased material, including an alternate text of "The Way We Were" entitled "The Way We Weren't" and "I Know Him So Well" from *Chess*, which had been considered for *The Broadway Album.* Perhaps in an effort to erase any misconception about Streisand's perceived Hollywood power, the final disc also contains excerpts from an audition tape made to pitch *Yentl* to studio executives. Even on this non-studio tape, the fullness of Barbra's mature tone, her precise diction, and her control of timbre and dynamics are clear, although some of the highest notes are a bit thin. The fullness of her lower register is evident on "I Know Him So Well" and others. Although several song types are found on the 1980s disc, it exudes the feeling of autobiography that would be expected from the later years of her career.

In the same vein as the popular duets between Natalie Cole and her late father and Hank Williams Jr. and his late father, Streisand's *Just for the Record* concludes with her singing a duet with her own 1955 recording of "You'll Never Know." The duet portion is brief, probably because the thirteen-year-old Barbra has a slightly wobbly pitch center and an inconsistent vibrato that do not match the 1988 Barbra. In this version, the song is extended to include a second verse and repeats of the chorus (in an arrangement by Rupert Holmes). It exhibits late-Streisand improvisation and timbre variations from soul to belt with a characteristically fast, but controlled, vibrato.

Much was written about the release of *Just for the Record*. Its appearance preceded the 1991 holiday shopping season, the premiere of Streisand's movie *The Prince of Tides*, and her fiftieth birthday the following April. Critics noted, among other things, that the sheer length of her successful recording career deserved recognition, but that this set did not signal the end of the story (see bibliography). Several expressed opinions that her vocal technique and timbre had matured nicely, but that a loss of spontaneity (largely from being confined to the studio) and an over-emphasis on technological perfection minimized the energy on recent recordings. A few were surprised that "perfectionist" Streisand allowed the audience to hear less-than-perfect recordings; rehearsal imperfections during "What Are You Doing the Rest of Your Life?" and "Evergreen" are left intact. In an interview with Steve Kmetko in 1991, Streisand said that she preferred the mellow nature of her 1990s voice compared to that of previous years, noting that formerly her vocal sound was somewhat brash and laden with a Brooklyn accent.[37] All of these comments take on added interest as shortly she would venture back on to the public concert stage. The high price of *Just for the Record* (from about $60 to $80) did not deter fans—the set was certified platinum, but a shorter version of the collection, called *Highlights from Just for the Record*, also was issued. Streisand was awarded the Grammy Legend Award from the National Academy of Recording Arts and Sciences in 1992, the year after *Just for the Record* was released. She was introduced on the occasion by Stephen Sondheim, who commented on her remarkable voice and her unfailing musical instincts. Barbra responded by thanking the Academy, Martin Erlichman, the composers and lyricists of her songs, and her fans "who have stayed with me as the musical tastes of the country changed from decade to decade." She praised them for remaining faithful "when I attempted to change with the times and . . . when I came back home."[38]

In some ways, Streisand's next album, *Back to Broadway*, combined the musical styles of *The Broadway Album* and *Till I Loved You*. As indicated by its title, this 1993 collection also contains songs from Broadway shows written across the decades, but several are updated into contemporary-pop or jazz-like arrangements, especially "Luck Be a Lady" and "Speak Low." Once again, the conventional has taken on an air of unconventionality, and modern and historical sounds are combined as the credits list synthesizer players and programmers as well as featured players of traditional instruments. David Foster, who created her arrangement of "Somewhere" on *The Broadway Album*, arranged and produced several cuts on *Back to Broadway*. It also is Barbra's first full-length compact disc where the person responsible for the "Digital Vocal Editing" (Dave Reitzas) is credited. Although the sound might be influenced by the digital recording technology, Streisand's attention to every vocal detail and the continuing maturation of her voice, especially its low register, stand out clearly.

Like those that accompany many post-1970s Streisand albums, the liner notes for *Back to Broadway* were written by Barbra, and they provide insight into her repertoire selection process and her total involvement in the record-making process.[39] She comments that she wanted a biting, angry sound for "Everybody Says Don't" like that which she hears in music of Stravinsky or Bartók, and that this lyric particularly resonates with much of her career experience (hence it becomes both a character song and an autobiographical song). Similarly, she wanted harmonies of greater complexity than those in the original composition of "I've Never Been in Love Before," a love ballad. "Speak Low" was a song she recalled from her childhood, and "Children Will Listen" is meaningful because of its message about how children develop under the sometimes-unwitting influence of adults (therefore signaling its label as an advocacy song).[40] Streisand's comments about the need to play a character while singing the strong melody and text of "With One Look" affirms her approach. Equally interesting is her revelation that she recalled singing "Luck Be a Lady" in her early nightclub act but was unaware that she had never recorded it. Barbra also writes that she is not uncomfortable singing this song that many might think more appropriate for a man. This statement confirms what has been evident, but perhaps unspoken, for much of her career: she often gravitates towards repertoire that convention might assign to male singers. Looking back over her recordings, a list of Streisand's "man" songs includes: "Sam, You Made the Pants Too Long"; "Starting Here, Starting Now" that David Shire had written with Robert Goulet in mind; "Superman"; "Pretty Women"; and now this tune from *Guys and Dolls*. This observation is intended only to support the idea that, although she selects her repertoire carefully, with characterization considerations always at the forefront, she also has an eye toward upsetting the notion of the "expected."

Back to Broadway opens with "Some Enchanted Evening" from *South*

Pacific. The song begins slowly with minimal accompaniment to allow her to establish the setting. The drama and her intensity build, and Streisand employs considerable rubato tempo and improvised melodic decoration. Her habit of using the upper neighbor to decorate pitches, especially at the end of a phrase, is heard on the words *try, own,* and *(a)-lone.*[41] Like many theatre songs, this one ends quietly, as it began. The lively, layered arrangement by Bill Ross of "Everybody Says Don't" provides immediate contrast. Disjunct string lines (formed from Barbra's countermelody ideas) and syncopated brass and percussion enhance her piqued enunciation of the wordy text. Sharp final consonants (some followed by a shadow vowel), vocal growl, and heavy accents abound, and her word sculpting is heard on triphthongs in *poise* and *noise.* She does not resort to her most powerful belt timbre, but her tone is strong throughout.

Two duets are included among the selections: "Music of the Night" with Michael Crawford, Streisand's colleague from *Hello, Dolly,* and a medley of "I Have a Love" and "One Hand, One Heart" with a singer she long admired, Johnny Mathis. "Music of the Night" is especially creative in its unconventionality, because even though the song is a duet on this album, it was not originally performed as a duet in *Phantom of the Opera.* (On the other hand, "Move On," heard as a solo on this disc, *was* a duet in *Sunday in the Park with George.* Similarly, she recorded "All I Ask of You," from *Phantom* and found on her *Till I Loved You* album, as a solo even though it occurred primarily as a duet between Christine and Raoul in that show.)

Michael Crawford and Johnny Mathis both have unique timbres bringing into play Barbra's timbral adaptability,[42] although the Crawford/Streisand pairing on "Music of the Night" is probably the more effective of the two partnerships. It requires both singers to work throughout their respective ranges and to vary timbres as the song progresses. They take turns with true harmony parts, and Streisand sometimes adds a bit of an edge or intensity and a stronger vibrato when they sing simultaneously.

Three specific words from the Crawford/Streisand duet illustrate Barbra's focus on minute details: she colors the word *sensation* with a brief and slight quiver-like inflection; on the word *power* in the second half of the song, she switches to a belt tone (for it and the title words that follow) to add strength; and her long-held *night* before the end sounds as "nah-e-t(eh)" with strong enunciation of the *t* (but later on the soft ending, that word recurs and she places a gentle but clear *t* on the end). Crisp final consonants (such as *k,* where a listener can almost hear the back and sides of Barbra's tongue operate, and *t*) also are heard in "With One Look," but they usually are not followed by extended shadow vowels.

Vocal inflections also occur during the jazz-like arrangement of "Speak Low," where Barbra significantly alters the AABA notated melody (here extended by repetition of the last A and a coda) with each return of A, obliterating the limited-pitch quality of Kurt Weill's original tune.[43] Slight decorations are added to the words *always* and *is*, but they are so brief that it is hard to distinguish exactly what happens. They sound like a brief catch in the throat, but her ease with the technique gives even these miniscule additions full tone.[44] On the other hand, some brief decorative notes included by the composer are omitted in her performance (such as those notated for the word *our*).[45] Rhythmic elasticity abounds in "Speak Low," where both the written opening melodic interval of a sixth (the hook on the title words) and the motivic triplets are altered or non-existant in Streisand's rendition. This elasticity especially is noticeable at the bridge, where Barbra holds the highest note of the song for at least three beats rather than making it part of a quarter-note triplet group. She stays true to the harmonic phrase, however, by shortening other notes so that the four-bar segment remains intact. In the second four-bar phrase, she chooses ascending pitches rather than the written descending triplet, which otherwise would have been a sequence to the opening group.

George and Ira Gershwin's ballad "The Man I Love" also receives a contemporary, jazz-like treatment on *Back to Broadway*.[46] Its instrumentation and style suggest a cabaret band, albeit a sophisticated, large one. Streisand's rhythmic maneuverings are heard during the bridge of the song, which is written to begin on beat 1. She, however, places the first melody note off the beat. At other times she creates a triplet- or compound-rhythm feeling against duple accompaniment or drags words printed in one measure into the next, always able to adjust to the harmonic changes without unduly altering the tune.[47] Atypically, she does not include the opening verse ahead of the AABA refrain.

Andrew Lloyd Webber's sweeping melodies and dramatic characters give Streisand a chance to show off her range of vocal timbres and her ability to quickly adjust dynamics, as evidenced in her characterization of "As If We Never Said Goodbye."[48] She takes a quasi-classical approach to the long vowel sounds in this song, staying longer on the front half of the diphthong, in *way* for example. The second syllable of *goodbye* comes across as "bah-i-(ee)" or "bah-eh" with a slight nasal "n" sound in the mix. Her phrasing of the title words also is interesting: a breath often occurs between *if* and *we*, and another is placed after *said*. This allows her to carry the musical line from *goodbye* across to whatever word then follows. Barbra's approach to the climactic section, focused on the word *last*, is to vocalize the "l" sound briefly at the beginning, making the following vowel sound come across as a syncopated, stronger note heard after beat 1. Her strong chest sound is apparent in the lower range of the song (as it is on "With One Look"), and her higher belt sound has added passion and intensity appropriate to the story. However, throughout this compact disc, Streisand's high notes on certain vowels, especially those that are either more horizontally shaped or formed further back in the throat (such as *one*, which sounds like "wun"), have a tinge of thinness or reediness about them. This may indicate a natural mellowing and lowering of her voice with age. Barbra's presentation of the word *you* places length on the "y" sound (like "ya-oo"), which creates the illusion that she is sliding into the main pitch more than she really is; the same phenomenon is noticeable on "Children Will Listen." Sometimes she chooses to slide into pitches for effect, as heard on "Luck Be a Lady."

Back to Broadway marked the fiftieth album in Streisand's long singing career and the first since she renewed her Columbia/Sony music and film contract for a reported $60 million. Critics were mixed in their reviews of her singing and the success of the two duets (see bibliography). Several noted that Barbra continued to borrow material from the same shows and composers that were represented on *The Broadway Album* of 1985. They encouraged her to be more adventuresome in her theatre repertoire choices. Nevertheless, in the aftermath of other successes, *Back to Broadway* debuted at the top of the charts, giving Streisand claim to the accolade as the "only artist to have No. 1 albums in the '60s, '70s, '80s, and '90s."[49] Fred Bronson concluded that "Streisand's talent transcends time," noting that her first album in the 1960s charted along side those by Andy Williams and Al Martino, while the *Back to Broadway* album competed with the Stone Temple Pilots and Dr. Dre. But the hype over this album's release and its success was minor compared to what would follow.

Most fans of Barbra Streisand in the 1980s likely felt that they might never see her perform in person. She was deeply involved in film production, she clearly stated that she did not wish to return to the Broadway stage, and her rare concert engagements usually were for select audiences at political or social-cause fund raisers. Then, in the fall of 1993, the unexpected happened—naturally. The owners of the under-construction MGM Grand Hotel and Casino in Las Vegas announced that Barbra Streisand would be the premiere act for the fifteen-thousand-seat "Garden" arena of the giant complex.[50] Even more surprising was the fact that tickets for *Barbra: The Concert* would go on sale to the public! Because everyone knew this would be a major event, promoters and her management made arrangements to have the first day of ticket sales (no other days likely would be needed) occur on a Sunday, hoping to avoid interruption of telephone systems during the business week. This was a wise move; one newspaper reported that the MGM Grand received more than a million phone requests in the first 24-hour period after sales began—the original 26,000+ seats were gone in no time.[51]

Because her performances were so rare, Streisand's concerts in Las Vegas attracted more than the usual media attention—her appearance there was covered as front-page news by the *Las Vegas Sun*. Having attended the second of the two concerts in person (and being in and around the MGM Grand the day of the first), it was interesting to compare my own observations with those that I later heard or read.[52] As one example, an article in *US* magazine reported that so many cameras were confiscated from attendees that a pile "practically took over the MGM Grand's lobby."[53] If the writer's reference is to the hotel lobby, the statement raises doubt since that lobby is several minutes walking distance away from the MGM Grand Garden arena—with the casinos and a food court in between. And during the time I stood in line to go through the metal detectors that led to concert seating (actually there were about a dozen lines to speed the process along, an apparent improvement from the first night), I saw only three or four persons asked to leave a camera in a side room where it could be claimed after the show (instructions had been given as early as ordering the tickets about the "no cameras" policy). Additionally, negative or sarcastic comments appeared in the press because the concert started almost an hour behind schedule, but this delay appeared to have as much to do with the new MGM Grand's parking arrangements and celebrity-audience accommodations as anything Barbra could or should have controlled.

Barbra: The Concert was arranged in halves, like acts of a show—a comfortable plan for someone with theatrical background. The first act was autobiographical in nature (although it was not clear if every word of every story was factual[54]); the second more concert-like with some of the large stage furniture that created an "at home" feeling for Act 1 removed.[55] Streisand selected "As if We Never Said Goodbye" (re-texted to be applicable to a singer rather than an actress) as the opening number.[56] The song and its blocking started the evening off with a clear affirmation of Barbra's acting and directing skills. She entered upstage left on a balcony and slowly made her way toward the center of the stage. As the music and text reached their climax in a reference to coming "home," Streisand stood front and center singing in full voice. The "director" had given the "singer" a grand moment, and two minutes into the program the audience was on its feet with enthusiastic applause.[57] Streisand engaged no backup singers or dancers, but her elegant stage and a screen that lowered from above (for better vision at a distance, duets with Marlon Brando and with herself on videotape, and other video clips) served as her stage partners. The considerable technology on display was, as would be expected, well rehearsed and used with precision, a credit to the large crew. Occasionally her costuming (one outfit per half) assisted with choreography, and she participated in a short comic bit with Mike Myers as the "Linda Richman" character from *Saturday Night Live*. During the second half, her political and social beliefs were the basis for the between-songs banter, and she introduced some guests in the audience, including Virginia Clinton Kelley (President Clinton's mother in her last public appearance) and her own mother, Diana Kind (the second night).

Barbra called on several of her friends and long-time colleagues to help select the repertoire, plan the show's format and text, and assist with the myriad details involved in both her Las Vegas concerts and the subsequent tour. From her own recording catalogue, they had more than five hundred songs from which to choose (see Appendix B), a fact noted by Marvin Hamlisch in his tribute to Streisand included in *The Concert* Piano-Vocal-Guitar selections (see bibliography). Alan and Marilyn Bergman helped write the dialogue between songs, and Hamlisch conducted the 64-piece orchestra. In an interview given while the tour was in Washington, D.C., Hamlisch remarked that he took the job simply because Streisand is "the best."[58] He also explained that he watched her on closed-circuit television during each performance (since his back was toward her), which enabled him to be right with her on phrasing and tempo, and that the concert repertoire and order was changed slightly from night to night.[59] Although the entire show was scripted (the script projected on monitors to which Streisand could refer), it was presented by a seasoned, well-rehearsed actress who made it sound spontaneous, drawing attention to that ever-present notion of artistic contradiction discussed in chapter 1. Barbra's rapport with the audience was comfortable; she often responded wittily to shouts from individuals during moments that were not scripted. Her spoken New York accent seemed to come and go as often as it does for character purposes when she sings.

The concert repertoire was selected to fit the two-act plan (although it changed considerably from Las Vegas to the spring tour). Streisand reached back to many of her earlier hits ("People" and "On a Clear Day"). She also included recent material (songs from *The Broadway Album*), songs new to her (such as "The Man That Got Away," a Judy Garland torch song by Harold Arlen), different arrangements of older material ("Happy Days Are Here Again" is more optimistic and "bluesy" than usual), and one brand new song, "Ordinary Miracles," by Marvin Hamlisch and the Bergmans.[60] Barbra introduced the song by saying that the text (which is about how positive transformation can result from simple gestures and love) was particularly meaningful to her. During the second concert in Las Vegas, Barbra slipped slightly on the words of "Evergreen." This touch of humanity, her quick retort about making an error on words of her own song, and her smooth recovery brought a wave of applause from the crowd. Generally, her vocal abilities were displayed with no trickery or gimmicks, and her stage blocking and facial expressions added to the total package.[61] She produced a consistent timbre over her entire range (but with great color variation from song to song). She held the long, soft endings of "Evergreen" and "Someday My Prince Will Come" with solid pitch and tone, even though an occasional loud and high-pitched note or phrase seemed to be held for less time than she might have liked. Barbra's large, open mouth and throat and animated vocal apparatus clearly were visible, as was her ability to sustain musical tone with her teeth nearly shut. She ran the gamut of repertoire from belt/torch song to lyric song, most imbued with characterization (it was possible to see her "get into character" on some songs like "You Don't Bring Me Flowers") or personal meaning ("Not While I'm Around" was dedicated to her son, and "I'm Still Here" contained lyric revisions to be applicable to her).[62] Several climactic moments were built into the music and the show, and the audience responded, as though on cue, each time.

The darker, more mature sound of Streisand's voice was particularly evident to the ear memory on songs from the earlier part of her career, and past hits also confirmed that once she has a reading set in her mind, it changes only slightly over the years. As one example, her phrasing of the unusual word *valentining* in "He Touched Me" remains consistent: she breathes between the syllables *-len* and *-tin*. Likewise, attendees familiar with her earlier performances would notice a more regal carriage (and more standard vocal posture) and less extension of her arms, as also was noted with *One Voice* in 1986. Barbra sings in almost any position (seated, lounging over a chair, crossed legged), but she usually ends up standing if the song requires a louder belt sound.

Streisand produced several different vocal timbres and styles, including some elements of soul or gospel during "Can't Help Lovin' That Man." She tinted words with vocal quivers and growls and with elaborate (for her) or simple melodic decorations. Barbra's skill with the microphone enhanced her clean diction and dynamics shadings (although her controlled breath support assists)—she often moved her whole body toward or away from it so that the motion becomes part of the blocking or characterization.[63] Compared to its prominence on her studio recordings, Streisand's breathing was not fully audible during the concert or on the subsequent videotapes and compact discs. Perhaps the truly "live" nature of the concert erased the need for that touch of intimacy applied to phonograph recordings or compact discs.[64] Her ability to simply stop sound by stopping air is easier to verify when watching her sing; she has developed some sort of vocal "follow through," probably from mental focus, which assures the feeling of continuity through an otherwise broken phrase. Marvin Hamlisch observed that, despite all her attention to details (both music and textual) and her love of rehearsing, at times Streisand seems unaware of her own musical prowess. After one especially moving Act 1 in New York, he rushed to her to share his excitement only to have her genuinely inquire as to what all the excitement was about.[65]

With foresight and marketing acumen, the Streisand camp and Sony/ Columbia made many types of souvenirs available at the concerts. A large photograph-laden program sold for $20–25, and other items included posters, tee shirts, hats, mugs, and jackets, many reportedly designed by Barbra.[66] For those who did not get everything they wanted at the concert, Sony Signatures issued a mail-order catalogue, although it stated that some items sold at the concerts were no longer available.

The success (both musical and personal) of the two-night stand in Las Vegas led to a full-fledged concert tour during the late spring and summer of 1994. Streisand began the tour in London, where she had spent considerable time during the filming of *Yentl*, with four shows, the first on 20 April. Two nights in the Washington, D.C. area (an acknowledgement of her increasing political awareness) then followed. She performed three times in Detroit in mid-May (actually at the Palace of Auburn Hills, just outside of Detroit). The Detroit concerts were a surprise to many, but that city had hosted Barbra in the early 1960s on her first out-of-town club performance, and she wanted to thank her supporters there by returning. Other tour cities included Anaheim and San Jose in California and her hometown, New York City. A few of the original Anaheim dates had to be rescheduled when Streisand became ill, but the planned number were completed after the New York stint was finished. Each venue had a seating capacity of fifteen to twenty thousand and could accommodate the stage set up and other lighting, staging, and sound requirements (including carpeting). In each location there was a scramble for the tickets that were priced from $50 to $350; additional dates were added to the original docket at some sites.[67] Several prime seats also were allotted to various charities; they were permitted to sell the tickets at $1000 each, keeping the additional money as a donation. Likewise, Barbra gave proceeds to other charities or schools (for support of music programs) in each city.[68]

The 17 May 1994 concert in Detroit provided me with further analytical opportunity and a means of comparison, especially in light of Hamlisch's comments about the rehearsal process and changes from night to night; several observations follow. The personalized lyrics of "I'm Still Here" were further revised (and some lines cut) as the tour progressed, and "Everybody Says Don't" was shortened within the opening medley. Her duet with Marlon Brando on "I'll Know" contained more vocal improvisation from Streisand than was heard in Las Vegas or on subsequent videotape or compact disc performances.[69] Apparently the drum-set and bass players were allowed more freedom on "People" as the tour progressed. During the Detroit performance, the drum line is similar to the standard "boom-chick" pattern heard supporting her 1960s performances, but the 1994 video and compact-disc recordings have elaborate drum and bass lines—so much more elaborate that at times the clarity of the beat seems lost. The arrangement of "What Is This Thing Called Love?," heard both in Las Vegas and Detroit but not included on the video or compact disc, also has a complicated percussion part. The song was arranged in segments as a character song, but the accompaniment seemed overdone, with Barbra's voice almost lost in all the activity. I noticed the strength of her low register and her freedom to move smoothly into her pure head voice on "He Touched Me" and "Can't Help Lovin' That Man," respectively. The second-half concert was revised to include a powerhouse finale from *Yentl* with Barbra singing a duet with her Yentl character.

Several media outlets carried reviews of the performances and of the compact disc set, videotape, and television specials that eventually followed (see bibliography). Many took the opportunity to recap Barbra's career, to assess her place in history, to air their thoughts on her between-song commentary and salary, and to comment on the audience they observed. Regarding one performance in New York, Jon Pareles noted that Streisand did not rely on "syllable-torturing melismas" like some 1980s and 1990s pop stars, and that, while several crescendos and musical climaxes were built into the arrangements, most of the time Streisand employed "tender restraint."[70]

One of the few technical comments Streisand reportedly made after the tour was: "It's very exhausting physically. It's a lot of breathing; you have to be in pretty good shape. And I don't work out vocally. I don't practice."[71] When asked later, during an interview published on the Internet, if she felt it a "burden" to have such a demand for her singing, Streisand responded, "It was . . . before I did this concert tour, where I was feeling there was pressure in terms of wanting to give back to my fans. . . . It's not a burden anymore."[72]

In 1997 Streisand released her most personal collection of songs to date—interview comments over the years since *Yentl* suggested that such a collection probably was inevitable as she sought deeper meaning in her life. Her liner notes and many of her public statements explained that *Higher Ground* was inspired by the music sung at the funeral of Virginia Clinton Kelley, with whom Barbra had developed a strong friendship. While the set is intended to speak "to the hearts of all persons of faith,"[73] once again the repertoire is anything but predictable. The messages and musical styles represented span a wide range. With or without a spiritual connection, the repertoire suggests familiarity through the inclusion of material from Broadway shows (*Carousel*) and from Marvin Hamlisch and Alan and Marilyn Bergman ("Leading With Your Heart," named after Kelley's autobiography). Some well-known and traditional sacred texts are present (although usually in new settings and with improvised melodic alterations), such as "I Believe" and "Deep River." "Avinu Malkeinu" ("Our Father, Our King") and the title cut represent less-familiar and clearly sacred works. Streisand provides contrast with heartfelt pop songs that display typical contemporary pop traits: multiple verse/chorus form, a strong backbeat, and a mid-point modulation. According to Barbra, "At the Same Time" calls for unity among peoples and care of our earth; its tender-but-imperative message is enhanced by the addition of a children's choir to the arrangement. Streisand's duet with pop-song superstar Celine Dion, "Tell Him," attracted considerable attention. Barbra sings the role of an older, more experienced woman assuaging the hesitancy about love expressed by a younger woman. The song's connection to the album's theme is made by way of Barbra's prediction of Virginia Kelley's likely encouragement to boldly embark on new relationships. The most personal song of the group is "If I Could," which Barbra sings for her son. Her sensitive performance might make some listeners feel as though they are intruding on a very private moment. Authors often are given the advice to "write what you know"; Barbra seems to be singing what she knows in this case—no acting needed.

Traditional orchestral accompaniments support some songs; others are arranged in a contemporary-pop style using acoustic and electronic and programmable instruments. This contrast is evident within the medley of "I Believe" and "You'll Never Walk Alone." Arrangers from past Streisand albums, including Jeremy Lubbock, William Ross, and Marvin Hamlisch, contributed to *Higher Ground*. "On Holy Ground" was arranged by Mervyn Warren, and it mixes traditional black gospel techniques with a Hollywood studio style.[74] The song begins with Barbra and minimal accompaniment from a Hammond B-3 organ and piano on verse 1; a backup choir joins with "ahs" at the first chorus. The second verse and chorus are stronger, and a backbeat is provided by the tambourine. At this point, the choir takes over presentation of the text while Streisand provides echo embellishments, mostly with her upper mix-belt timbre. The improvisations get increasingly elaborate, as would be expected in the style, but contrary to the customary lengthy vamp-style endings in black-gospel performance, the song swells to a dramatic close with full choir, strong instrumental ensemble, and belting soloist. Streisand's sound occasionally projects a strained edge when singing loudly in her high range.

Most of the arrangements on *Higher Ground* feature Streisand's warm lower register. Her diction on some songs is less pop-like than on other albums, and occasionally a word ending with *er* has a non-nasal "r" sound included rather than her customary "ah" ending. This technique occurs in "Deep River" as does her use of her pure head voice on high notes (on the words *over* or *promise*).[75] Although hints of some folk-instrument sounds are heard in "The Water Is Wide," which is grouped with "Deep River," Barbra uses her more classical-style diction rather than folk dialect. Her tendency to decorate melody notes with the upper neighbor is heard during "You'll Never Walk Alone," "If I Could," and "Circle," among others. Her technique of adding an "h" sound before vowels on slurred notes is perhaps stretched too far during the soft ending of "At the Same Time," even becoming distracting in the oft-slurred melody of "Everything Must Change."

The duet between Celine Dion and Barbra indicates that the former's range is higher and that her vibrato can be faster than Streisand's. They take turns with the harmony and echo passages, but the darker quality of Barbra's timbre allows for easy identification of her sound even if the lyrics do not make it clear. As the two singers end the song together, Barbra adroitly adds a catch-like inflection on *let*, which shows she still has remarkable command of nuances; the technique that makes her voice readily identifiable, and for many singers, enviable.[76]

Only a few reviewers chose to write about *Higher Ground*, and Barbra did more publicity than usual for the album. If sales numbers (because of the album's serious theme) were a concern, the concern was unwarranted. Streisand's faithful fans caused the album to chart number 1 upon its release in November 1997. SoundScan numbers indicated that it sold between two-hundred and four-hundred thousand copies during each of its first eight weeks.[77] More than 5 million copies of *Higher Ground* were sold world-wide by April 1999.

As Barbra enters what might be expected to be the twilight of her singing years (although assuming the expected is often a guarantee of something else with her—she announced on an America Online interview on 2 November 1998 that she was beginning work on a new album,[78] and shortly thereafter she agreed to sing one concert on New Year's Eve, 1999), she rightfully can boast of a long and successful recording career—nearly half of her 50+ albums are certified platinum, and she was ranked thirty-first on the VH-1 cable channel's "100 Greatest Women of *Rock and Roll*" [italics added] in 1999. Her oeuvre exhibits a variety of repertoire from many of the styles of popular music significant during her lifetime. While her voice can take on chameleon-like characteristics and her acting abilities enhance text interpretation, Streisand's primary focus has been on songs that mean something to her or that can be dramatized. This approach and her natural vocal talents have reaped their rewards. Popular song artists are expected to add their own personality to their recordings, but Streisand carried that idea to a different level. The girl who had wanted to be an actress had not only become one through song, she also established the interpretive and technical standards against which others would be judged. And in the process she brought considerable satisfaction to her customers, her listening audience.

NOTES

1. Barbra Streisand, interview by Larry King, *Larry King Live*, CNN television, 7 June 1995.

2. Barbra Streisand, interview by Barbra Walters, *20/20*, ABC television, 19 November 1993.

3. Streisand recorded "There Won't Be Trumpets" by Stephen Sondheim in 1974, but it was not released until 1991 on *Just for the Record*. It was combined in a medley with "A Quiet Thing," and the pair apparently caused Barbra to begin

thinking about recording a collection of Broadway songs. See Barbra Streisand, accompanying booklet for *Just for the Record*, compact disc 44111 (Sony Music Entertainment, 1991), 57. His "Small World" appears on her *Color Me Barbra*. See the discography.

4. Streisand commented in detail about the inception and production of this album on a publicity show aired 11 January 1986 on HBO entitled "Putting It Together, The Making of *The Broadway Album.*" (It was released later for home video purchase.) Similarly, substantial information is provided in the liner notes of the album as written by Alan and Marilyn Bergman on Barbra Streisand, *The Broadway Album*, compact disc 40092 (Columbia, 1985) and in Stephen Holden, "Barbra Streisand: 'This Is the Music I Love. It Is My Roots',"*New York Times*, 10 November 1985, 2:1, 23. Several remarks from these sources are paraphrased for use along with my analytical observations. In the video, Streisand states that she purposely became more involved with the technical aspects of recording during this experience. She learned, among other things, why the physical location of the track on the record disc affected her recorded voice from moment to moment. She also was flattered when William Friedkin, the interviewer, described several of the songs as "sound pictures," which again draws attention to the notion of acting the song.

5. In an interview in *Billboard*, Matz revealed that they recorded enough material to make a two-record set, but that Columbia nixed the idea. ("I Know Him so Well" ended up on *Just for the Record*.) See Paul Grein, "Producer Enjoys 'Broadway' LP's Success," *Billboard* (1 March 1986): 42. Peter Matz later worked with opera singer Samuel Ramey on his *Samuel Ramey Sings Rodgers and Hammerstein* album.

6. This appears to be her first official credit as arranger, but as noted previously, her liner notes for *Lazy Afternoon* and comments from composer/conductor David Shire suggest that she already had been contributing ideas for her arrangements.

7. See Bob Doerschuk, "Barbra Streisand's Synthesizer Wizards Take 'Somewhere' to the Stars," *Keyboard* (February 1986): 17. Doerschuk mentions that Streisand seems to "enjoy confounding her fans' expectations," and quotes Foster as saying that no printed music of the arrangement existed for a long time. It was created through overdubbing layers around Barbra's demo tape of her vocal ideas. Other technical information about the equipment used is included as well.

8. Opinions vary as to whether the album successfully recreates the feeling of a "live" album. Although it generally received good reviews, and its sales figures were beyond what was expected, some people continued to prefer the more spirited sound of Streisand's earlier style. For example, composer David Shire, who had worked with Barbra in the 1960s, noted that *The Broadway Album* clearly "was made in the studio." He suspected Streisand wanted both perfection and spontaneous excitement—which he suggested was impossible. David Shire, interview by author, Muncie, Indiana, 4 March 1998.

9. Interestingly, in response to a request for an interview about his work with Streisand, Mr. Sondheim commented that he had no helpful comments because he wrote songs for characters, not for a specific singer's style. Stephen Sondheim, New York, New York, to Linda Pohly, Muncie, Indiana, typewritten letter signed, 25 August 1997. Other related information is found in Craig Zadan, *Sondheim & Co.* (New York: Harper and Row Publishers, 1989), 288–293. For example, Streisand

is quoted as saying that an earlier arrangement of "Not While I'm Around" led her to an interpretation as a lover singing it to a lover. The mother/child idea (as used on the album) came with a simpler setting.

10. "Putting It Together, The Making of *The Broadway Album*," Barwood Films, CBS/Fox Home Video, 1986.

11. Lyric excerpt of "If I Loved You" by Richard Rodgers and Oscar Hammerstein II. Streisand does not sing the familiar dialect noted on the word *longin'*, which was appropriate for the show in which the song originally was included (*Carousel*). She clearly sings "longing."

12. In "Putting It Together, The Making of *The Broadway Album*," Streisand comments on how her reading of the lyrics of "Pretty Woman" evolve during the track, touching on envy and resolution. Her interpretation is enhanced by the breadth of her timbral palette heard on this lengthy, sectional song. Likewise she mentions that she recorded three different arrangements of "Can't Help Lovin' That Man" from *Showboat*. The "Making of" videotape contains excerpts from one that has a jazz-like arrangement with a faster tempo and more syncopation than the love-ballad style released on the album. Her vocal performance on the unused cut has a decidedly cabaret blues sound as well. The album version is modeled after the 1951 Ava Gardner film rendition (there actually sung by Annette Warren), but with Stevie Wonder added as guest harmonica player. Jerome Kern had written a repetitive, stepwise melodic line (half and whole steps) for the chorus, but Streisand decorates several long pitches with a slurred leap upward.

13. Rod McKuen, review of *The Broadway Album*, in *Stereo Review* (April 1986): 69–70. McKuen also points out that the album was not recorded digitally, even though released in both album and compact-disc formats. Digital recordings and compact discs were just beginning to be commonplace at this time. Streisand's career has spanned several changes in recording and film-making technology. "Adelaide's Lament" is included only on the compact-disc format.

14. Barbra Streisand, acceptance remarks, "The Twenty-Ninth Annual Grammy Awards," CBS television, 24 February 1987.

15. Paul Grein, "Erlichman Back as Streisand's Manager," *Billboard* (15 February 1986): 78.

16. Steve Schneider wrote of the remarkable contract arranged between Martin Erlichman and HBO executives regarding the concert and the video. HBO helped with some advance money; Erlichman and Streisand retained final edit and approval; and if approved, HBO was granted exclusive opportunity to buy broadcast rights (at an unreported but assumed-to-be-high price). The Streisand camp was interested in a cable outlet, in part, because the show would not be interrupted by commercials and because cable networks usually have larger budgets for special events. See "Streisand Returns to TV, on Her Terms," *New York Times*, 21 December 1986, 2:30.

17. By September of 1987, *One Voice* was certified gold, giving Barbra her thirtieth such album and ranking her first in that category to date. She was followed by Elvis Presley and the Rolling Stones, each with 28 gold albums. See "USA Snapshot," *USA Today*, 14 September 1987, 1D.

18. According to a chart published in *Variety*, by 1996 the Streisand Foundation had contributed more than $10 million to various causes. Her other philanthropic

and political activities also are outlined. See Beverly Walker, "A Citizen First," *Variety* (21 October 1996): S48, S50.

19. The writing is thoughtful in the manner in which political concerns are connected to a particular song's history or its use in the concert. For example, "The Way We Were," from a movie plot set in the 1930s through the 1950s, is introduced by way of comments on Franklin Delano Roosevelt's presidency.

20. Barbra introduces the band during the show, and remarks how they can make a few pieces sound like many. She also comments on Nyle Steiner and his invention, the EVI, which appears to be a wind-blown electronic instrument that can sample sounds ranging from flute, to oboe, to cello.

21. "Over the Rainbow," by Harold Arlen and E. Y. Harburg.

22. Johnson perhaps is not quite as accurate as Streisand with pitches, particularly when in his low range. This is heard when comparing the melody at the end of his verse 1 (starting with *could*) with the end of her verse 2 (beginning with *but*).

23. Streisand returned the favor by singing backup for "What If It Takes All Night" on Johnson's *Let It Roll* album (Epic, 1989). She also appeared as a "passerby" in one episode of his popular television series *Miami Vice*.

24. Roy Hemming suggests the album has a "romantic story line" tracing the ups and downs of relationships. See his review of *Till I Loved You*, in *Stereo Review* (March 1989): 111. I do not see the grouping to be that linear, but we agree on the overriding theme of the lyrics.

25. Stephen Holden, "Barbra Streisand and the Showstopper Syndrome," *New York Times*, 6 November 1988, 2:29. Holden also sees a vague storyline about love and relationships in the album.

26. "All I Ask of You," music by Andrew Lloyd Webber, lyrics by Charles Hart, additional lyrics by Richard Stilgoe.

27. "A Collection Greatest Hits . . . and More" [internet on-line]; available from http://www.music.sony.com/Music/ArtistIn . . . raStreisand_ACollectionGreatestHits .html; Internet; accessed 8 July 1997. This article also lists Barbra's album sales figures to date; approximately 52 million Streisand albums had been purchased by fans around the world since the early 1960s. Columbia expected some of her early material to be reissued on compact disc beginning in the fall of 1989. (See bibliography for reviews of some of the reissued items.) Some authors criticized Streisand for releasing so many "greatest-hits" type sets in such a short timespan, suggesting more new material was needed. This album, like her other compilations, nevertheless sold well.

28. On 22 April 1990, Streisand appeared as the closing singer on an ABC television special celebrating Earth Day. Streisand's song "One Day" was written for the occasion by her friends the Bergmans and Michel Legrand. It has not appeared on commercial recordings.

29. Barbra Streisand, *The Prince of Tides*, cassette tape 48627 (Columbia, 1991), liner.

30. *The Mirror Has Two Faces*, compact disc 67887 (Columbia, 1996), liner.

31. Larry King, "Making Music to Reflect 'Mirror'," *USA Today*, 21 October 1996, 4D. "It Doesn't Get Better Than This" has some similarity, especially in its angular melody, to "All of My Life." The "unused" song is available on Barbra Streisand, compact disc, *Rarities* vol. 1B (private release by *Barbrabilia*, Arlington Heights, Illinois, 1997).

32. For purposes herein, each disc of *Just for the Record* could have been discussed along with other recordings from the same time period. I examine them collectively as one means of summarizing Streisand's singing career through the 1980s.

33. Barbra Streisand, accompanying booklet for *Just for the Record*, compact disc 44111 (Sony Music Entertainment, 1991), 7. As mentioned in chapter 1, Streisand recorded two selections that day, as did her mother, Diana Kind.

34. "You'll Never Know," by Mack Gordon and Harry Warren.

35. Barbra Streisand, accompanying booklet for *Just for the Record*, compact disc 44111 (Sony Music Entertainment, 1991), 45.

36. Chris Willman comes to a similar conclusion. See "The Last of Her Kind Remains a Mystery," *Los Angeles Times*, 22 September 1991, CAL:61. Willman also discusses Streisand's comments (in the *Just for the Record* booklet, page 88) about "You'll Never Know," *The Prince of Tides*, and her need to deal with her own "inner child."

37. Barbra Streisand, interview with Steve Kmetko, *CBS This Morning*, CBS television, aired in segments the week preceding 25 December 1991.

38. Barbra Streisand, acceptance remarks for Grammy Legend Award, "The Thirty-Fourth Annual Grammy Awards," CBS television, 25 February 1992.

39. Barbra Streisand, *Back to Broadway*, compact disc 48119 (Columbia, 1993), liner.

40. She also sang "Children Will Listen" in a concert that was part of the inaugural festivities for Bill Clinton's first term as president.

41. The upper-neighbor pitch decoration also is heard on her hum at the end of "Children Will Listen," and on *love* in "The Man I Love."

42. Henry Pleasants has noted Streisand's ability to take on certain aspects of the sounds of other singers when doing a cover song, but here the same seems to apply to duet partners. See *The Great American Popular Singers* (New York: Simon and Schuster, 1974), 362. The melody of "I Have a Love" is quite angular, forcing the singer to be agile and precise with wide intervals. Streisand and Mathis seem to blend best when he is in what might be called his "belt" mode.

43. For an analysis of the melody and harmony as written by Weill, see Allen Forte, *The American Popular Ballad of the Golden Era, 1924–1950* (Princeton, New Jersey: Princeton University Press, 1995), 269–274.

44. This catch sound also is heard in "I've Never Been in Love Before" as the title words appear near the end.

45. The printed music for "Speak Low" is available from Chappell and Co., Inc., New York.

46. George Gershwin was already at the forefront of adding richer harmonic color to his songs in the mid-1920s; in Streisand's arrangement the rhythms and instrumentation add further modernization. For more on the influence of Gershwin and Jerome Kern on popular song harmony, see Charles Hamm, *Yesterdays: Popular Song in America* (New York: W. W. Norton and Co., 1979), 364–369. The printed music of "The Man I Love" is available from New World Music Corporation.

47. I thank composer Paul Chihara for his observations about this song.

48. The song is from Lloyd Webber's show *Sunset Boulevard*, which had not yet opened on Broadway at the time of the release of Streisand's album. Several

singers recorded songs from *Sunset Boulevard*. A comparison is found in David Finkle, "Ready for Her Close-Up," *Village Voice* (26 March 1996): 64, 66.

49. Fred Bronson, "Back to Broadway and Back to No. 1," *Billboard* (17 July 1993): 120. See also Anne Ayers, "Streisand 'Back' at the Top," *USA Today*, 8 July 1993, 1D. The chart-topping albums included *People* from the 1960s, *A Star Is Born* among others from the 1970s, and *Guilty* and *The Broadway Album* from the 1980s. A pre-release listening party was held in New York on 14 May 1993; see Irv Lichtman, "Big Col Blitz Backs Barbra's 'Back to B'way'," *Billboard* (12 June 1993): 1, 87.

50. It was announced in articles by Pauline Yoshihashi, "Streisand to Play MGM Grand Casino for Possible Record $20 Million Haul," *Wall Street Journal*, 4 October 1993, B3; and David J. Fox, "Is Streisand Changing the Tides?," *Los Angeles Times*, 6 November 1993, F1. The latter also contained the phone number to call for tickets beginning at 9 a.m. the following Sunday, 7 November. Earlier, when the concerts were still a rumor, one writer queried as to whether Streisand would have to cross a picket line to perform. At that time the MGM Grand was not unionized, which might have caused an interesting dilemma for outspoken political-liberal Streisand. See Michael Fleming, "Will Babs Cross the Line?," *Variety* (16 August 1993): 4. This did not become an issue in the press at the time of the concerts.

51. Robert Macy, "Streisand Fans Clamor for Tickets," *Detroit News*, 31 December 1993, 5A; Vernon Silver, "People Who Need Barbra," *New York Times*, 26 December 1993, 9: 4. Vernon reports that 12,805 tickets were sold for each night, then 600 more were released in mid-December. One source told him that most ticket requests came from the Los Angeles area, but that the MGM reported it got calls from all fifty states and from Canada and England, "even though there was no advertising in those countries."

52. My comments about the concert tour often will be in first person because I attended one show in Las Vegas and one later in Detroit. The personal perspective is important—I do not believe I would attempt analysis of Streisand's vocal style in this depth without the experience of seeing her perform in person (although much of the analysis is of necessity subjective, no matter the media source, and perspectives could be as numerous as attendees). Written reminiscences of performers and composers at work have been common and valuable throughout music history. See for example Charles Burney, *An Account of the Musical Performances in Westminster Abbey and the Pantheon, March 26, 27, 29; and June the 3rd and 5th, 1784*, in *In Commemoration of Handel* (London: T. Payne and G. Robinson, 1785; reprint Amsterdam: F. A. M. Knuf, 1964); Wilhelm Jerger, ed. *The Piano Master Classes of Franz Liszt, 1884–1886: Diary Notes of August Gollerich* (Bloomington: Indiana University Press, 1996). Additional seating for Streisand's Las Vegas concerts apparently became available after 7 November. I got my tickets by calling an 800 number given in a full-page MGM advertisement (with the headline "It Just Doesn't Get Any Grander Than This") in the *USA Today* of 8 November 1993. Upon my inquiry about ticket availability (assuming they were all gone), the operator reported that a few more had just been made available following a reconfiguration of the seating chart. The price range approximated $1000, $800, $500, $300, and $150, but tickets were not available in every range. I ordered two at $300 each, and they arrived by certified mail in mid-December following a letter

from the MGM Grand confirming the purchase. They were multi-colored and featured the photograph of Barbra from the cover of *Back to Broadway*. The seats proved to be quite good—center of the arena (no side-angle view) but toward the back. A large drop-down screen helped vision; the sound was very good.

53. Ryan Murphy, "No Comment," *US* (March 1994), 31.

54. For example, during the tour concerts that followed in the spring and summer of 1994, Barbra referred to a meeting she had with Prince Charles in Los Angeles in the mid-1970s, but she likely was incorrect about the year. This also is noted in Allison J. Waldman, *The Barbra Streisand Scrapbook* (New York: Citadel Press, 1995), 182.

55. This format is similar to what Streisand used on previous tours and in Las Vegas decades earlier. A summary of her 1966 performance in Newport, Rhode Island, mentions a large orchestra seated behind a scrim, no use of backup singers or dancers, and a concert format interspersed with comic monologues. See Gardner Dunton, "Barbra's First of Four One-Nighters," *Variety* (3 August 1966): 52. A reviewer of her 1969 performance at the International Hotel in Las Vegas (where $15 was charged for dinner and the 55-minute show) observed that she did not present a typical nightclub act, that she used a 37-piece orchestra, that she had come to Las Vegas a week in advance for rehearsal, and that she was very nervous about returning to sing in front of an audience. See " 'This Is Work' Says Barbra," *Billboard* (4 October 1969): SC-9.

56. As If We Never Said Goodbye" begins with the character questioning her own fright. In my observation, the words were more than lyrics—they were reality. Streisand seemed to hold on very tightly to the microphone with one hand and the balcony rail with the other, almost embarrassed by the welcoming applause that held up her opening words. (Here the problem uncovered in *One Voice*, where she had started to sing off stage and then had to continue through extended applause, was rectified.) Relaxation seemed to begin with the following medley, especially on the belted B section of "Don't Rain on My Parade." Jim Feldman found that moment to be especially exciting. He wrote, "When Streisand cut loose on the payoff phrase . . . with abandon, it hit home that . . . I was finally in the presence of the greatest and most commanding singer I could ever possibly imagine." See "Simply, Streisand," *Village Voice* (18 January 1994): 73. I had a similar reaction and still am moved by that section of the song when hearing the compact disc or watching the videotape.

57. That same moment in her original rendition of "As if We Never Said Goodbye" (on Streisand's *Back to Broadway* album) provides an interesting comparison. On the album the climactic note is a second or two less in length. A greater rubato was added during the tour performance to accommodate the anticipated audience reaction.

58. Marvin Hamlisch, interview with Mary Matlin and Maureen Orth, *Equal Time*, CNBC television, 11 May 1994.

59. This reordering is evident on the "BJS Detroit #1 Cue Sheet 5/17/94" that numbers each song and spoken segment. After proceeding quite regularly by number, it jumps from number 20 to 43B/C to 22/23. This shows that "Evergreen" was moved from late in the show in Las Vegas to the first half in Detroit. The cue sheet also confirms that the video operator (for segments with Brando from *Guys and Dolls* or for the psychiatrist/patient scene) had specific verbal cues from her script,

much like in a play, to know when to start the playback ("chemistry" then a blink for Brando; "patient or doctor" for the psychiatrist sequence). I thank Anthony Andrich of *Barbrabilia* magazine for allowing perusal of the cue sheet.

60. Her varied recorded performances of "Ordinary Miracles" each contain one moment where her tendency to not coordinate text and musical phrases does not work in her favor. She takes a big breath separating *extraordinary* (a modifier) and *way* even though they are the end of a prepositional phrase preceding a verb. She also adds a melisma to *way*, which makes the word difficult to understand. The intent might be to put emphasis on the modifier, but the concommitant musical line does not lend itself to this plan. On the other hand, her ability to change dynamic levels with great control is heard as she ellides the end of one phrase into the next between *wonder* and *endless*.

61. Roy Hemming, writing for *Stereo Review*, disagreed in his assessment of the compact disc set, suggesting that she sometimes used "vocal tricks" to "camouflage technical frailties that have crept into her voice as she's gotten older." See (January 1995): 133. Although many critics hailed her concert performances, several expressed dissatisfaction with the compact discs, especially regarding some of her habitual vocal techniques, her political commentary, and their perception of the recording's focus on the adoration her fans display toward her (see bibliography).

62. Alan and Marilyn Bergman describe this as her ability to "inhabit" a song. See their written remarks included in the Piano-Vocal-Guitar selections from *The Concert* listed in the bibliography. They also confirm the notion that the concert format was intended to focus on her life and her beliefs.

63. Credit also must go to the tour's sound engineers. For information, see Shaun Considine, "As If She Never Said Goodbye," *TV Guide* (20–26 August 1994): 10–17; liner notes from *Barbra: The Concert* compact disc 66109 (Columbia, 1994).

64. This notion came to me during one specific moment on *The Concert* videotape. Streisand audibly breathes in (through her nose—unusual for a singer) during the quiet ending of "The Man That Got Away." That instance made the lack of breath sounds in other places noticeable.

65. Ann On-Line, "Interview with Marvin Hamlisch" [internet on-line]; available from http://www.annonline.com/interviews/960711; Internet, accessed 19 November 1997. Hamlisch also revealed that Streisand does not think much about her technique, and does not use vocal exercises or a vocal coach.

66. One of the concert mugs often is visible on Rosie O'Donnell's desk during her television show on NBC. A similar catalogue flyer was available during and after the subsequent tour; it also included ordering information for her compact discs and movies on video. The program for the tour was similar to the one sold at the Las Vegas concerts. The tour version includes a message from Barbra that explains how the tour grew out of the success of Las Vegas and revised credits to include the names of the trucking and travel assistants, etc. The credits reveal that the members of the rhythm section and basic orchestral players (like "first violin" and "first woodwind") traveled with Streisand.

67. See Alan Bisbort, "Waiting for Barbra," *Washington Post*, 6 May 1994, B5. In Detroit the procedure was to get a numbered wrist band from an appropriate ticket outlet on a given day. The following Sunday, wrist-band wearers were to arrive at the same location at noon, where they would be called by number to buy up to four tickets. Cash was preferred, and the tickets clearly stated the ban on

cameras and recording devices. Later, upon entrance to the arena corridor, patrons again were given a flyer that stated the rules. Among them were instructions on going through the security check points and a warning that entrance and exit to the hall would be permitted only between songs (refreshments were sold in the corridor, but few people moved about). Tickets for the first two shows sold out in fifty-nine minutes, and a third show was added. The local newspaper carried several extensive articles about Streisand just before and during her time in the area. (See Amber Arellano, "Streisand Fans Beg, Plead and Pay," *Detroit Free Press*, 28 March 1994, 1E; Mike Martindale, "High Note: Streisand Tickets Just a Memory," *Detroit News*, 28 March 1994, 1A, 8A.) Ticket scalping was a problem according to several entertainment magazines and news shows and as noted in Brenda Ingersoll, "That's the Ticket! Many Banking on Streisand," *Detroit News*, 3 April 1994, C: 1, 5. Letters to the editor following some negative reports usually were pro-Streisand; her fans are faithful and vocal. See *Entertainment Weekly* (6 May 1994): 4.

68. Not all of the charity tickets sold well, see "Hey Big Spenders," *Detroit News*, 11 May 1994, 5D; Marc Peyser, "Charity Case," *Newsweek* (9 May 1994): 72. A chart summarizing Streisand's philanthropic and social giving and her political appearances is found in *Variety* (21 October 1996): S48.

69. There are actually three versions of the 1994 concert videotape. The first two are taken from a July 1994 Anaheim show that was aired by HBO television in August 1994, which was later issued by Columbia Music Video. However, copies of that tape sold by Blockbuster Video contained a "bonus track" of "What Are You Doing the Rest of Your Life," which eventually led to some legal wrangling. The third version was aired on CBS television (which brought Streisand an Emmy award in 1996). It contained a spliced-in medley of Disney songs she sang in Las Vegas. Additionally, the two-compact-disc (or two-cassette-tape) set from the tour is a fourth version, having been taped in New York City in June 1994. Therefore, a devoted fan really needs to own all versions to have as much repertoire as possible and to hear varied performances.

70. Jon Pareles, "In New York, Streisand Is a Hometown Hero," *New York Times*, 22 June 1994, B3.

71. Michael Shnayerson, "A Star Is Reborn," *Vanity Fair* (November 1994): 154. In the same article (which covers pages 150–159 and 190–194), the author reveals that Streisand rebuffed criticism of her use of TelePrompTers with the statement that without them she would not have done the concerts, that she was financially responsible to pay for $20 million of tour expenses (including the cost of a full orchestra, a touring rarity), and that she began to fear or resent the length of the tour—because it was exhausting. This might be related to the same feeling she had years before on Broadway with *Funny Girl*. Once the rehearsal period is over, the "set" show got tedious in its repetition.

72. "Mr. Showbiz: Barbra Streisand," [internet on-line]; available from http://www.mrshowbiz.com/interviews/344_4.html; Internet; accessed 24 February 1998. Streisand announced in April 1999 that she would sing one concert at the MGM Grand to usher in the new millennium. Ticket prices range from $500 to $2500; they sold out in record time.

73. Barbra Streisand, *Higher Ground*, compact disc 66181 (Columbia, 1997), liner 3. The liner also contains comments about the sessions from Jay Landers, who

served in the past as the Artist and Repertoire person for Streisand's albums, but who is listed on this disc as Executive Producer (with Barbra).

74. The title is sometimes listed as "Holy Ground," and different print and re-corded versions exchange references to "God" and "Jesus." Streisand's performance uses the former. A line from Exodus 3:5 is the basis for the song. Geron Davis composed the song in the early 1980s, and sheet music is available from Meadow-green Music Co.

75. When compared to what musicologist and librarian Wayne Shirley calls the "Standard Version" of "Deep River," Streisand uses some of her characteristic var-iation techniques. She stretches some notes into a following measure, shortening subsequent notes to make up the time; she uses octave displacement on certain pitches (especially later in the song); and she significantly alters the melodic line (especially on the B of the AABA form). She implies a fermata on *Lord*, which is not found in many printed versions. See Wayne Shirley, "The Coming of 'Deep River'," *American Music* 15, no. 4 (Winter 1997): 493–534.

76. Celine Dion reported that Streisand recorded her track first, and then Dion added her track. The two women later got together to record a video of the song. Celine Dion, interview by Larry King, *Larry King Live*, CNN television, 4 April 1998.

77. "The Barbra Streisand Music Guide: For All We Know," [internet on-line]; available from http://members.aol.com/barbramusc/forallwe.html#Concerts & Pub-lic Appearances; Internet; accessed 24 February 1998.

78. *A Love Like Ours* was released in the fall of 1999. (See discography and bibliography.)

Chapter 6

A Road Well Traveled: Conclusions

> *Larry King*: We have a whole room full of guests tonight . . . a legendary singer, . . . an Oscar winner, . . . an Emmy winner, . . . and a multiple Golden Globe recipient. . . . They are all here as one—Barbra Streisand.
>
> *Barbra Streisand*: You just scared me with that intro. I've got a lot to live up to now, right?[1]

Streisand's answer to King in 1992 was given with a hint of both playfulness and sincerity. Interestingly, her reaction was similar to her response nearly thirty years earlier upon receiving countless accolades after the Broadway premiere of *Funny Girl*.[2] Barbra's comments are understandable. Is it always possible for performers, even those possessed of great talent, to live up to the expectations of an audience or of critics? Similarly, how does a performer maintain a level of excellence and a commitment to personal goals in a business that continually embraces its perception of what will be new, different, exciting, and profitable?

Barbra Streisand seems to have been as successful as anyone in the often-destructive, fickle, and ever-evolving entertainment arena by remaining true to her own visions of success and her own thoughts on how to approach a project. The twin philosophies evident in the early part of her career remain intact: *I'll do it my way, no matter the consequences* and *Keep them wanting more.* Typical of the duality or contradiction apparent in her life, these forthright and confident-sounding philosophies are balanced by equally prominent images of insecurity and vulnerability as well as a desire and need to be headed toward a new mission or goal.[3] Stephen Holden wrote, "A fundamental contradiction in the Streisand personality is that[,] even while finding endless faults in past accomplishments, she has never been afraid to forge ahead and take huge risks."[4] In many ways, Barbra is the CEO and president of a large and diverse, multi-million-dollar conglomerate whose only commodity really is herself. When faced with that potentiality and responsibility, one must either find unusual strength or suffer haunting consequences. As she has said, "I don't know which is worse, the fear of failure or the fear of success."[5]

Her ability to simultaneously project strength and vulnerability, simplicity and complexity, and intimacy and overpowering talent might be the very thing that both attracts and repels Barbra's public and critics.[6] These conflicts, and her constant struggle to find answers about herself, often are reflected in the titles of articles written about her: "A Superstar's Struggle 'to Become a Woman' " (*McCall's*, April 1975), "Streisand at 40, Taking the Gamble of Her Life" (*Ladies' Home Journal*, April 1982), "The Barbra Streisand Nobody Knows" (*Esquire*, October 1982), "Streisand, the Way She Really Is" (*Life*, December 1983), "Barbra's New Direction" (*Ladies' Home Journal*, February 1992), "Barbra's Quest for the Best" (*TV Guide*, 20–26 August 1994), and "A Star Is Reborn" (*People*, 31 May 1993; and the same title in *Ladies' Home Journal*, November 1976). This short list points to another area of incongruity. Streisand is in a business where publicity is paramount and where, in promotion of her products, she courts the media. On the other hand, she loathes inconsistency or inaccuracy on the part of reporters and frequently professes to enjoy her work more than her stardom. Similarly, she fights for privacy in her personal life, yet uses her work (both song and film) to offer glimpses into her life, her beliefs, and her thoughts.

With that in mind, Barbra apparently has developed an understanding of her place in the world and of the benefits (some would say power) and responsibilities that attend fame. She knows how to act like a star, while at the same time exposing a side of herself that is down-to-earth and seemingly quite shy.[7] Questions could arise as to the truth or reality of that dual image—is it real or created for public consumption? In Streisand's case, it is quite possible that both are true—she is real and yet created. Her youth was spent envisioning her career, and all of her adult life has been spent living it.

These thoughts are important because they have an impact on Barbra's singing and recording career, the primary topics at hand. What follows is a recap of her singing techniques and repertoire choices; a summary of reactions toward her from critics, colleagues, and fans; and an assessment of her place among other popular-song singers and in popular-song history.

There has been remarkable consistency in Streisand's vocal technique over the years. She, of course, followed the basic parameters of popular song as previously outlined: using a microphone, focusing on text, and taking liberties with melody and rhythm.[8] She never has been a harbinger of new musical developments; instead, her innovation centered around new and very personal approaches to her material. Barbra's early Broadway style was influenced by jazz (although without an emphasis on scat singing), and her later pop style was marked by an awareness of gospel and soul sounds (minus extreme melismatic filigree). Her unique approach to phrasing, where the textual and musical phrases often do not coincide, probably is the most outstanding feature of her performances and is the technique most difficult for others to emulate effectively. As has been described earlier, her highly developed vocal and mental follow-through supports graceful phrasing even during dramatic moments that contain choppy rhythms or broken melodic segments. Critics and vocal teachers note Streisand's attention to clean diction and its influence on the whole of popular music. This approach adds a flavor of classical music to her style and to popular music, even though it would be misleading to suggest that she specifically uses classical-style pronunciations. Bill Reed, a New York singing teacher who specializes in teaching a theatrical style, assessed Streisand's influence in this way: "She helped legitimize pop singing. . . . [and] she was influential in making a pop style more acceptable and prominent on Broadway." Author Paul Evans agreed, writing that she, "enunciated more properly than any other pop singer."[9]

Barbra has experienced some of the natural vocal changes that can be expected with age. Her range has lowered slightly,[10] and the bottom end has gotten stronger and more rich in tone. Streisand's earlier nasal sound has mellowed, but her consistent production of sound in the facial mask still influences her tone. Despite this forward focus, significant nasality can creep back into her voice on certain vowel sounds, for characterization purposes, or during belt moments.[11] Streisand's ability to move smoothly, without an audible break, between vocal tessituras, timbral sounds, and styles sets her apart from many pop vocalists who have a pronounced shift point. Her fast, narrow vibrato is distinctive; in later years it has become more noticeable in all registers but remains most prominent during high-pitched and loud phrases. Streisand's understanding of the importance of breath support to fine singing and her refined control of her breath supply enhance her efforts with interpretive phrasing, dynamic gradations, and timbral coloring. In fact, her ability to adroitly change the color and mood of her voice enables her to be an actress in each song through text painting or word coloring—an approach in which she strongly believes. These characteristics lead to "the cultivation of a personal sound," which is a hallmark of all influential popular-music performers.[12] In Barbra's case, her wide timbral spectrum ranks second only to her unique phrasing as her most identifiable skill.

Those who have worked with her in the studio frequently acknowledge Barbra's fine-tuned sense of pitch and harmony. It allows her freedom of invention as she maneuvers through a melodic line. This freedom affects and supports her penchant to drastically alter rhythms and to vary them upon repetition of musical sections or textual lines. There does not seem to be a formulaic rhythmic pattern of variation in her recordings, but she consistently avoids singing squarely on the beat. This contributes to a feeling of unease in some of her 1970s soft-rock selections.

On the other hand, Barbra's keen attention to the rehearsal process and minute musical details creates a "set" version of many selections. Individual concert performances might bring spontaneous and minor changes in phrasing, timing, or melodic decoration (those who conducted for her attest to this), but even songs performed over a span of many years retained many of the same vocal characteristics and interpretations ("On a Clear Day," for example). Streisand has developed certain idiosyncratic techniques, perhaps the most recent being the use of the upper neighbor tone as a decoration or harmonic suspension at the end of a phrase. Still, her recording from age thirteen ("You'll Never Know") establishes vocal mannerisms that she continued to use in her mid-fifties. These traits are described in detail in the preceding chapters. Similarly, Barbra's tendency to present a song as a story with development lends itself to a formal structure in which the opening text often is sung in a recitative or parlando fashion. Greater lyrical and emotional elements come into play as the song progresses. Although some listeners and critics occasionally note that Streisand's technique and stylings harbor flaws, one characteristic of musical genius is the ability to use that which seems like a flaw to artistic and unique advantage.[13]

Streisand has had the good luck, foresight, industry stature, and business savvy to work with the persons and the technology that enhance her own gifts and style. Most of the time, unless the accompaniment was allowed to become too cumbersome, her arrangers achieved a sense of balance between creative instrumentation and a focus on her voice. The clarity and distinctive overall timbre of Streisand's voice help in this regard. Her musical prowess, her understanding of her capabilities, and her experience allow Barbra to offer useful contributions to arrangements and orchestrations. Her desire to be involved with the totality of a product and her attention to detail would be hazardous without creative vision and musical wherewithal.[14] Although the use of a microphone is an expected part of popular-music performance, Streisand's subtle and comfortable use of the mike provides a point of study for young singers. As has been noted previously, some listeners prefer her more youthful sound and interpretations, finding them more spontaneous and refreshing when compared to the more emotionally refined and technically perfected performances of Barbra's later recordings. It is interesting to ponder how much of her own vocal perfection is further perfected by digital technology. Some listeners (not just of Streisand's music) prefer what they hear as a more realistic and human sound on the older vinyl album format.

The overriding factor in Streisand's repertoire selection has been the search for lyrics that allow characterization. She has had considerable control over her repertoire from the beginning, but her choices do not always conform to expectations. The song categories established in earlier chapters (character songs, love ballads, lyric songs, torch or belt songs, and advocacy and autobiographical songs) allow organization of the material and provide a means of focusing discussion, despite the evolution of musical styles (from classic to contemporary pop, for example) over the years. Character songs and belt or torch songs received most of Barbra's attention in the 1960s, while love ballads and advocacy/autobiography songs came into prominence since the 1970s. Other performers (Paul Robeson, for example) have taken painful career risks when they spoke out on political issues, but Streisand's incorporation of her political and social beliefs into her music does not appear to have adversely affected the strength of her fan base. Lyric songs, which usually do not receive much radio broadcast time, are a regular part of Barbra's recording productivity.

An increased feeling of maturity in the nature and tone of the texts Streisand selected to sing became apparent as Barbra reached her late forties and fifties ("Tell Him" for example). Other songs that disappeared from Streisand's repertoire over the years include those that tell of a youngster trying to make it in the tough show-business world ("I'm the Greatest Star" and "I've Been Here") and some that she refers to as "dependent victim" songs.[15] Her partnerships with other popular singers provided vocal contrast from song to song and duet to duet and perhaps opened new marketing doors. Her individualistic interpretations of many familiar songs have made her versions stand apart from those of other singers ("America, the Beautiful," "Happy Days Are Here Again," "Over the Rainbow"), and her stamp on her signature songs caused others to shy away from performing them with regularity ("People," "The Way We Were," "Evergreen"). Streisand's overt dramaticism and her refined technique require texts and tunes that can withstand her musical and interpretive acumen. These issues are the most common sources of criticism regarding her singing.[16]

In public settings, the visual aspect of Streisand's singing is as important as her musical style and technique. Her body language and facial expressions, those of a seasoned actress, enhance her musical interpretations. During a concert, the attention remains on her as a singer, not on peripheral costumes and set, choreography, or backup musicians. Although a story line might be woven through the repertoire as a means of unifying the whole, it does not become the primary focus. Her natural physical features (large open resonation cavities) create and enrich her tone and pitch production, but she also uses her tongue, jaw, and lips to good advantage. In other words, she seems to have good vocal technique whether she can describe what that is or how she sings from a physiological standpoint.[17] Similarly, despite Streisand's comments that she does not read music, she uses musical terminology correctly in interviews and on liner notes, she speaks knowingly of other styles and composers (mostly classical), and she apparently has learned over the years to play a modicum of guitar and piano. Barbra may not command the myriad details of music theory, but she possesses the tools necessary to complement her work.

All of these musical features and concepts contribute to Barbra's artistic stature, and her commercial viability belies the norm where frequent touring and radio exposure are the expectation. The consistency of her style and her disregard for (or only passing acknowledgement of) many of the newer musical trends, which otherwise were prominent during the course of her career, make her success even more remarkable. By following her own instincts she forged a new path, but it was a newness achieved by way of an older style. Although they do not tell the whole story, the long list of awards and accolades she has garnered from the popular-music industry are testament to the buying-public's interest in her work.

It is difficult to ascertain where, by whom, and how Streisand was musically influenced in her youth. In the 1990s she stated on numerous occasions that her favorite singer is Johnny Mathis. Over the years she has revealed that she listened to Joni James on *Your Hit Parade* and that she considers Judy Garland, Aretha Franklin, Joni Mitchell, Lee Wiley, Ethel Waters, and Billie Holiday each to have fine singing talents.[18] But Barbra never has credited any direct influence, and her unique skills and sound make it impractical to point to one clear model. The names that frequently are mentioned in a comparison with Streisand are, of course, Judy Garland, Edith Piaf, and Ethel Merman, but the similarity seems to stem more from their emotional approach than their musical technique.[19] Some authors remarked briefly on influences that they hear in individual Streisand performances or during certain periods of her recording career. For example, in 1963, Truman Capote compared Streisand to Bea Lillie and Billie Holiday. The fact that those singers were dissimilar in style points to his perception of Streisand's versatility.[20]

Several entertainers over the years (as diverse as comedienne Marilyn Michaels, contemporary Christian singer Sandi Patti, and male impersonators) have performed imitations of Streisand. Michaels's approach (as seen on *The Ed Sullivan Show*) was more physical than musical, although she did approximate Streisand's nasal belt sound and Brooklyn accent. Patti, a well-trained, high soprano, included a brief imitation of Streisand as part of a comedy segment around the song "Jesus Loves Me" on her *More Than Wonderful* cassette.[21] She intertwines that song with "People" and seems to focus on Streisand's abilities to hold long tones and make drastic dynamic changes. Patti also scoops and slides into pitches (much more than Barbra), uses a nasal belt for high and loud passages, elongates shadow vowels, and places an "h" sound before vowels that change pitch in her mimickery. Overall, Patti sounds vaguely like Streisand from the early

1970s mixed with a hint of Patti LaBelle or Aretha Franklin. A singer named Hynden Walch also did an imitation of Streisand (and Garland and Piaf) in a Chicago stage show called *The Rise and Fall of Little Voice*. In an article about the show, Walch is quoted as saying, "I'd never imitated anybody. . . . What I learned is that it involves a switch in what singers call placement . . . Streisand's is actually the healthiest sound, very consistent, coming through her nose finally, but starting down deep, in her diaphragm, a good way to sing."[22]

Several singers also have been influenced more seriously by Streisand. Upon the release of Streisand's *A Happening in Central Park*, Burt Korall noted that Lainie Kazan (who had been an understudy in *Funny Girl*), Lana Cantrell, and Barbara Minkus all took "root in [Streisand's] emotional, all-stops-out style."[23] And in 1973, Colman Andrews drew a connection between Barbra's approach to "Something So Right" (on her *The Way We Were* album) and what he anticipated the song might be like in the hands of Gladys Knight. He labeled Knight "the black Barbra Streisand."[24] For many years popular-song singer Julie Budd has been compared to Streisand—to Budd's benefit and detriment.[25] Her singing career continued in the late 1990s when a headline suggested she was "Like a Baby Streisand All Grown Up." Stephen Holden, who has reviewed many Streisand albums (see bibliography), suggests that their musical resemblance stems from phrasing "lyrics with an elevated diction that measures every syllable by the weight of its consonants." He also notes that Budd can change vocal color for dramatic purposes and that both singers "love to belt."[26] Similar thoughts were voiced by Don Heckman, who also has critiqued both singers. Heckman observed that the similarities between the two, first noticed in the 1970s, were "still front and center" in the 1990s.[27]

Of the popular-music and theatre singers new to the scene in the late 1990s, perhaps Linda Eder was the one who rightfully could claim the strongest connection to Streisand's style and ability. This fact was noted in an article entitled "Passing the Torch," in which the writer claimed that, "like Ethel Merman, Judy Garland, and Barbra Streisand, Eder has more voice than most mere mortals."[28] He also suggested that Eder has a fresh sound not encumbered with an "ever-shrinking arsenal of vocal mannerisms," a trait he associated with Streisand. In my own analysis, I hear the greatest similarity between the two when Eder is in her middle-range (she has a higher soprano range and greater concomitant head-voice sound). On her recording of "Someone Like You,"[29] Eder delivers a recitative-like opening, clear and fast vibrato, octave leaps for emphasis, and controlled dynamic contrasts (especially at the end)—all of which are Streisand traits. In an appearance on *Live with Regis and Kathie Lee* on NBC television in 1997, Linda performed "No One Knows Who I Am" from *Jekyll and Hyde*, a Broadway show in which she starred. In that visual setting, differences between the two women were noticeable. For example, Eder does not seem to be as comfortable as Streisand with using a hand-held micro-phone; Linda moved it about for sound/technique purposes, but the con-tinual movement became distracting. Eder does not use as much facial expression to underscore the emotion of the lyric as does Streisand—an approach that some viewers might prefer. The younger singer executed clean diction (especially making miniscule breaks between *who*, *I*, and *am* of the titular words) and had substantial nasality on her higher, louder notes (a sound which might have been formed as the back of her tongue arched) during her well-received performance. Both traits are typical of Streisand's sound, whether the production process is similar.

Streisand's stature in popular song also is indicated by how many times non-American singers are compared to her. For example, Alla Pugacheva, Russia's leading pop star beginning in the mid-1970s, has sold more than 100 million records and is "often likened to Barbra Streisand, Liza Min-nelli, or [Bette] Midler."[30] The link seems to be based on Pugacheva's "fiery temperament, womanly suffering and soul." Her career is thought to be hampered by the fact that pop music "still flows mainly . . . from the West to the East." A similar statement can be made about Greek songstress Nana Mouskouri, whose record sales and amazing productivity (450 albums) exceed other female singers worldwide. She is compared to Streisand more in terms of longevity and commercial success than with regard to singing technique.[31]

Several connections between the styles and careers of Streisand and Frank Sinatra are evident even though there are also significant differences. Re-cordings from both singers display highly unique interpretive skills with considerable emphasis on the lyrics. Upon Sinatra's death in May 1998, Susan Stamberg offered a reminiscence of Sinatra on National Public Ra-dio's *Morning Edition*.[32] She suggested that a listener who wanted to try to understand what was special about a Sinatra vocal line should try to sing along with him. That attempt would show that usually one cannot match him—Frank will be momentarily ahead and then behind and then ahead and so forth.[33] Stamberg concluded that through his attention to detail, his musical skill, and his appealing persona, Sinatra was the first popular singer to think of himself as an artist. Barbra Streisand easily in-herited that mantle and some of that style but molded it her own way.

Streisand's critics and professional colleagues have had varied opinions as to her abilities, the artistic merits of her work, and her strong personality traits. I address the first two topics throughout this study. Regarding the latter, Streisand often has pointed to interviews she gave that were positive and complimentary but that never were published.[34] She concludes that negative or controversial press makes better (or more profitable) copy than positive articles. These experiences make her hesitant to give interviews, particularly those that can be edited to alter context. This situation leads to a conflict about which she has been questioned. The paucity of her public appearances contributes to a sense of mystique, which might be beneficial, but also can be interpreted as a kind of aloofness, disinterest, or harshness.[35] In fact, an interview on the Internet from 1998 begins, "Let's face it, Barbra Streisand scares people." The writer goes on to note that, for many people, she is " 'too' something: too controlling, too Jewish, too politically active, too vain."[36] Streisand responds to criticism of her desire to control all aspects of her work by stating that it is her obligation to her audience to care about everything that affects the product. Beyond music and film, Streisand also is direct in stating her opinions concerning social and political issues, which has elicited caustic and sarcastic remarks from members of the press who might view political commentary to be the sole domain of professional politicians and journalists. Columnist Margaret Carlson pondered why Streisand seems to evoke more furor than other celebrities associated with political and social causes. Carlson concluded that Barbra was a victim of "her clout as the virtual ATM [automated bank teller machine] of Democratic politics."[37]

Several authors suggest that Streisand's widespread appeal, in large part (whether the appeal is positive or negative), comes from those indescribable and indefinable characteristics of a "star." As early as 1963, writers inquired as to what made Barbra so special and offered varied analyses. A critic for *Variety* wrote that, "Miss Streisand is that rarity who has both cult and crowd appeal, probably because she caters to neither. A one-of-a-kind talent, her stage image is a bag of paradoxes."[38] Other authors believed that the attraction of her talents, personality, and material were heightened by the marketing plan of Martin Erlichman, who saw the need to avoid overexposure.[39] In 1963 Erlichman also had tried to pinpoint his client's appeal. He came to his conclusion not thinking as a manager but "as a man," in comparing her charm to that of Charlie Chaplin, "the little fellow [that] people wanted to help."[40]

In the middle years of Streisand's career, when writing about American female pop vocalists, Aida Pavletich observed,

More than an actress or singer, [Barbra] is a personality whose force makes her a leader. As a singer she can be moving, poignant, or embarrassing, but she does not take embarrassment upon herself; she has made it evident that there is no need to apologize for aspirations, a factor even her fiercest critics must respect.[41]

Much later, authors still were trying to analyze Streisand's appeal. Susan Whitall described her as "an entity beyond this mortal coil, a pop culture goddess," and a self-made personality who broke the mold of expectation, who "became beautiful through sheer force of will, magnetic through sheer force of personality."[42] An editorial at the time of Barbra's 1994 tour appearance in London began with the headline: "Funny Star, The Love of Celebrities Cannot Be Explained, Only Enjoyed." The author suggested that "stardom lies in sympathy for the flawed and vulnerable 'ordinary' person perceived behind the glitter of the superstar."[43] Similarly, in an article entitled "She's Worth Her Weight in Barbra," William Grimes pondered why fans paid so much to attend her concerts. He observed that, even though many American consumers were in a penny-pinching mood, they seemed unfazed at paying significant amounts of money to see her in person: "Why? There is no convincing answer." But he surmised that she is "an inspirational figure to the unsung millions who felt like outcasts."[44] Even Streisand's nay-sayers recognize her ability to make things happen— usually her way. Andrew Sarris, in a review of *Yentl*, professed to being "a notorious nonworshipper of Barbra from time immemorial," but acknowledged that "she may one day be remembered as the last female star in Hollywood with the leverage to make a movie happen."[45] More directly, Joe Queenan did not find anything to compliment about the phenomenon of Streisand's star image. He wrote, "But herein lies much of her appeal. Streisand embodies everything that is tacky and cheap and hopelessly corny and unsophisticated about Middle America."[46] These examples represent the varied opinions and approaches of pundits, critics, and professional writers, but in the final analysis, each listener and movie-goer has to make an individual assessment of Barbra's merits as an entertainer, and those opinions have and will speak volumes.[47]

Recently, particularly since the souvenir barrage of *Barbra: The Concert*, Streisand memorabilia has been plentiful among collectors, and a Streisand museum opened in San Francisco in 1996.[48] Indeed, cottage industries have blossomed among those who wish to buy, sell, and trade Streisand artifacts. The commercial aspect of popular music never can be separated from its artistic side;[49] buying and selling collectibles may be an extension of that situation. The multiplicity of Streisand's endeavors, her financial success, and her career longevity also have caused her to be branded by *Vanity Fair* as part of "the New Establishment," an establishment based on power in the Information Age.[50] Her progression into the musical establishment (after a rebellious beginning) was discussed earlier; this new label pertains to the whole of her career and her persona, and recalls the notion of Streisand as the CEO of a large conglomerate.

From the perspective of Streisand's legion of fans, the reasons for their faithful admiration likely are as varied as the fans themselves. Certainly there has been a long-time connection between Barbra and the gay community (if it is reasonable to assume uniform opinion in any group). But there also has been a connection between that community and Judy Garland, Bette Midler, Liza Minnelli (Judy's daughter), and others.[51] As issues of gender, sexuality, and ethnicity are discussed in the media, additional attention has been paid to the varied nature of Streisand's constituency. Two non-Streisand mainstream films contain scenes depicting her role as an icon among gay men and transvestites: *In & Out* starring Kevin Kline and Tom Selleck in 1997,[52] and *To Wong Foo, Thanks for Everything! Julie Newmar* starring Patrick Swayze in 1995. The former is the story of a high school drama teacher who is thought to be homosexual, in part because of his love of Streisand movies. The latter features cross dressers who, in one scene, listened to Streisand's "Gotta Move" as they traveled toward a better life, teaching residents of a small, isolated town a valuable lesson about people along the way. When queried by Kevin Sessums about her appeal among gay fans, Streisand reportedly wondered if it might have something to do with the ease with which she can be imitated or "I guess because I was so odd."[53]

Streisand's fan base also is linked to her own Jewish heritage and her cognizance of issues important to women (although we must again acknowledge that there can be as many opinions about Streisand within those populations as there are members). From the beginnings of her career, she did not hide her ethnic background—she flaunted it through her looks, her name, her style, and her choice of material. Barbra's interest in this aspect of her life seems to have reached a new height with *Yentl* in the 1980s. Her Jewish background and her position as a potential role model have been a subject for commentary over the years.[54] Similarly, she has successfully breached a male-dominated system (particularly in the film industry) and has spoken out on her beliefs in the abilities and resources women possess.[55] In a lengthy review of Streisand's 20 June 1994 concert in New York, Camille Paglia commented on the music and on the myth of Streisand, her stardom, the concert environment, and the audience. Paglia wrote, "The rich range of New York Jewish society turned out in force," and later, "She had literally grown into her nose: that bravely preserved ethnic badge." Her conclusion was that Barbra "remains one of the great symbols of modern woman, independent, self-directed, always in process."[56]

Yet Streisand has a wider appeal in the popular media and with the general public. She was referenced frequently on the late-1990s CBS television situation comedy *The Nanny*, and a surprise appearance by Streisand in a Mike Myers/Linda Richman segment of NBC television's *Saturday Night Live* in 1992 left guests Madonna and Roseanne, two other unique talents, almost speechless.[57] Among Streisand's fans from within her professional circles, two outspoken supporters are Kathie Lee Gifford and Rosie O'Donnell. Gifford attended one of Barbra's New Year's 1993–1994 Las Vegas concerts, and upon return to her *Live with Regis and Kathie Lee* on NBC television, Gifford commented on her admiration of Streisand's talents and fortitude. Barbra was a guest on O'Donnell's talk show in 1997 after O'Donnell launched an impassioned but good-natured, on-air campaign to entice Streisand to appear. Rosie, whose late mother also had admired Streisand, found Barbra to be "warm and kind."[58]

Although surprised by the immediate success of Streisand's *The Broad-*

way Album in 1985, Columbia Records executives planned to keep the album's momentum going by repeating "its initial marketing campaign," which sought "to reach older, higher-income consumers."[59] A Columbia market survey revealed that forty percent of the album's buyers ranged in age from 26 to 35, while thirty-five percent of the buyers were from 36 to 50 years of age. Most of these consumers were located in America's northeast and midwest, although worldwide sales were brisk as well. However, some industry insiders were skeptical as to whether a strategy that emphasized a middle-of-the-road album would be sustained across the market, noting that with Streisand, buyers were "buying a legend." One indication of Barbra's worldwide influence is found in a brief interview transcript published in *Music at the Margins: Popular Music and Global Cultural Diversity*, a compilation of articles. The informant, an Indonesian-Dutch musician named Anya, who hoped to become a professional singer, revealed that she liked music that has "emotion" and that she learned her technical skills from listening to "Barbara [*sic*] Streisand and Karen Carpenter."[60]

On the other hand, Streisand has had chart success beyond her usual Middle-of-the-Road or Adult Contemporary categories. A *Billboard* article by Paul Grein contains a list of other charts on which Streisand has registered, if only briefly: "No More Tears" made it to the top of the disco chart (where "The Main Event/Fight" and "Shake Me, Wake Me" also had done well); her duet with Neil Diamond, "You Don't Bring Me Flowers," made it onto the country chart; and *Classical Barbra* was listed for months on the classical chart.[61] Grein also suggests that Streisand "helped open the door to album acceptance for female artists," and that one of the most intriguing facets of her career "has been the way she's always been able to bounce back from intermittent lulls."

Streisand's place in popular-song history is, like many things about her, difficult to ascertain with absolute clarity. She has broken most of the usual rules for success in popular music. She generally does not perform to promote new albums, and she never has been on the cutting edge of style development. The early years of her career are marked by unconventionality when comparing her style and repertoire to others her age. In 1969, Burt Korall wrote, "Crazy? Like a fox. A contemporary artist yet a throwback, Barbra Streisand was camp even before 'camp' became fashionable."[62] In a retrospective on her career, David Patrick Stearns wrote, "Streisand was clearly not just another girl with a big voice . . . she emerged as the Marlon Brando of pop music. . . . It's characteristic that even as a newcomer Streisand refused to play by the rules."[63] Critic Peter Reilly agreed, stating,

For sixteen years she's been making albums that make only passing nods to contemporary musical styles and that continue to reflect one musician, one singer, one actress at different points in her career. That in itself is against the rules. One Must

Change with the Times [*sic*] has always been the dictum of the entertainment world.[64]

After nearly four decades in the popular-song spotlight, a feature article on Streisand's career opened with the headline: "A True American Original." The author concluded, "One method that Streisand has used to achieve this kind of timelessness is by associating herself with greats of yesteryear and thereby placing herself in a long cultural tradition."[65] He goes on to report that Clive Davis, the president of Arista Records, believed that Streisand "always reinvents herself to provide the fresh and unpredictable" and that she also "has a sense of history and of the classics." This statement is supported by a 26 December 1997 *USA Today* article that began: "Music '97 Rich in Diversity."[66] Therein, Edna Gundersen reported that the music industry had a rebound year in 1997 with a 5.2 percent increase in recording sales. She also quoted the president of the Recording Industry Association of America as saying, "When you've got a year that has success with Hanson, Streisand, 2Pac, and Erykah Badu, the feeling is you've got something for everyone." The importance of this diversity is its potential to attract new audiences (and in Streisand's case, new generations of fans), and it ties directly to the multiplicity, eclecticism, and inclination toward personalization so important in Barbra's career.

Barbra Streisand's importance stems from her ability to be successful by doing things her own way, from her innate and learned musical gifts, and from her ability to blend the traditional with a sense of newness. Additionally, critics and observers over the years never failed to mention the importance of Streisand's charisma in front of an audience. While that experience may cause her anxiety, her rapport, from whatever source she draws upon, is undeniable. According to Streisand's representative, Martin Erlichman, she plans one day to pen an autobiography.[67] Likely she will recount her varied experiences and successes and her view of her contributions to the world.[68] As part of that process, we can hope that Barbra will incorporate reminiscences and details about the behind-the-scenes aspects of her singing and recordings. Comments and perspectives from her long-time musical colleagues would add additional insight; they have been witness to artistry at the most basic level. As early as 1964, Leonard Feather wrote that the best compliment he could pay Streisand was to say that "she sounds like a combination of Barbra Streisand, Barbra Streisand, and Barbra Streisand."[69] More than thirty-five years later, that statement is still a compliment and still the best description of her singing.

NOTES

1. Barbra Streisand, interview by Larry King, *Larry King Live*, CNN television, 6 February 1992.

2. Barbra Streisand, interview with unidentified reporter, compact disc, *Rarities* vol. 5 (private release by *Barbrabilia*, Arlington Heights, Illinois, 1997); and Joanne Stang, "She Couldn't Be Medium," *New York Times*, 5 April 1964, 10:3.

3. During a question and answer session on America Online on 2 November 1998 Streisand was asked about the lessons of life she has learned over the years. Included in her answer were her beliefs that you shouldn't accept other's opinions too readily, that you should listen to your own sense of truth, and that you should love your neighbor as yourself.

4. See Stephen Holden, " 'This Is the Music I Love. It Is My Roots'," *New York Times*, 10 November 1985, 2:1, 23.

5. Barbra Streisand, interview by Mary Turner, "The Legend of Barbra Streisand," produced by Westwood One, phonodisc A2S1779 (Columbia Records, 1983). Certainly the diversity of her talents contribute to her success and popularity, and her multiple endeavors keep her in the public eye.

6. Paul Evans wrote that, "Streisand's appeal [musically] was based on a tension of self-assurance and vulnerablity [sic]—she'd descend from an almost light-operatic delivery to a Brooklyn-girl chumminess, provoking both adoration and sympathy." See Anthony DeCurtis and James Henke, eds., *The Rolling Stone Record Guide* (New York: Straight Arrow Publishers, Inc., 1992), s.v. "Barbra Streisand," by Paul Evans.

7. See Molly Haskell, *New York Times*, 9 March 1975, 2:1. Haskell writes, "Around Streisand, too, there is a 'must-see' mystique. . . . She acts—and has always acted—like a star." Haskell goes on to point out several other traits of Streisand's stardom, many related to her film work.

8. These conventions are discussed in Henry Pleasants, *The Great American Popular Singers* (New York: Simon and Schuster, 1974), 38–48.

9. Reed recalled a poll that stated that some 38% of American women would like to be singers. In his experience many want to sound like Streisand, finding her music to be "harmless," the type with which people identify. Bill Reed, interview by author, telephone, Muncie, Indiana, 24 June 1997. Anthony DeCurtis and James Henke, eds., *The Rolling Stone Record Guide* (New York: Straight Arrow Publishers, Inc., 1992), s.v. "Barbra Streisand," by Paul Evans.

10. In 1994 Whitney Balliett wrote, "Streisand is a contralto with a couple of octaves at her command, and she wows her listeners with her shrewd dynamics . . . and the singular Streisand-from-Brooklyn nasal quality of her voice." See "Showcase Barbra Streisand," *The New Yorker* (20 June 1994): 70–71.

11. Streisand has mentioned that she has a deviated septum (when the membrane separating the two nasal passages is off center), calling it one of "God's little tricks." Barbra Streisand, interview by Oprah Winfrey, *The Oprah Winfrey Show*, ABC television, 11 November 1996. For vocalists this can have a variety of meanings and results, see Anthony Jahn, "Nasal Surgery for Singers," *The New York Opera Newsletter* (July/August 1998): 13. Without fully knowing Streisand's condition, a deviated septum might influence her sound and could make her more prone to sinus infections. Thanks to Professor John Hines and baritone Vaughn Bryner for their comments. For more information, see Richard Miller, *The Structure of Singing* (New York: Schirmer Books, 1986); William Vennard, *Singing: The Mechanism and the Technic*, rev. ed. (New York: Carl Fischer, 1967). In addition to a deviated septum, Barbra also has remarked that she hears high-pitched frequencies,

those in the supersonic range, a phenomenon often called tinnitus. See Lawrence Grobel, "Playboy Interview: Barbra Streisand," *Playboy* (October 1977): 90. This condition would have to be analyzed by specialists to determine its impact, if any, on Streisand's singing or hearing related to music.

12. Michael Campbell, *And the Beat Goes On* (New York: Schirmer Books, 1996), 20.

13. This definition of musical genius was suggested by Jan Swafford in a critique of George Gershwin on National Public Radio's *Performance Today* hosted by Martin Goldsmith, 30 July 1998.

14. Several anecdotes about her perceived excessive attention to musical details have been bandied about for years. That story will have to be told by insiders.

15. Streisand made this comment during her z1994 tour concerts, but she nonetheless sang "My Man," a song that would fit the "dependent victim" description.

16. See specific comments in various chapters. Will Friedwald summarizes his reaction to her style by stating that she uses her formidable technique to cover her true feelings. See Will Friedwald, *Jazz Singing* (New York: Scribner, 1990), 336.

17. In an interview on the French television show *A La Una* during a promotional tour for *Yentl* in 1984, Streisand remarked that someone once asked her how she held long notes. She did not have an answer, but the question caused her to think about the process. She then had to go to a doctor to learn about the physical aspects of breathing so that she could get back to doing it without thinking about it.

18. A study of several recordings by Joni James revealed that she had a fast vibrato, often slightly decorated melody notes, and slid into melody notes. Although these also are traits of some Streisand recordings, there is not enough consistent similarity in technique to draw any conclusions, and Streisand's overall sound and dramatic interpretations are markedly different from James's. My efforts to listen to other *Hit Parade* singers and best-selling popular-song singers of the 1950s did not uncover other clear influences on or similarities with Streisand. Even if similarities between Barbra and another singer were discovered, Streisand would have to verify that she indeed listened to that performer before a substantive point could be made.

19. A review of a ten-album set by Edith Piaf summarizes much of her style and appeal. See John L. Wilson, review of *Pathé FSX 154–163*, in *High Fidelity* (December 1965): 125.

20. "Bea, Billie, and Barbra," *Newsweek* (3 June 1963): 79.

21. The Sandi Patti cassette is C3818 (Impact Records, 1983).

22. See Sid Smith, "A Powerhouse," *Chicago Tribune*, 6 January 1994, 5:6.

23. Burt Korall, "Her Name Is Barbra," *Saturday Review* (11 January 1969): 108–109.

24. Colman Andrews, review of *The Way We Were*, in *Creem* (June 1973): 66–67.

25. When Budd was age fourteen, Gene Lees reviewed her *Wild and Wonderful*, in *High Fidelity* (November 1969): 143. His negative comments about Budd are based on his dislike of several of Streisand's mannerisms. During the late 1960s, Lees preferred the vocal stylings of Peggy Lee. See "The Consumate Artistry of Peggy Lee," *High Fidelity* (July 1968): 96.

26. Stephen Holden, "Like a Baby Streisand All Grown Up," *New York Times*,

16 September 1997, E5. Holden also has reported that a young male Australian singer named David Campbell has been compared favorably to Streisand, see "He's an All-Australian Boy," _New York Times_, 31 October 1997, E:41. See also Don Heckman, "Budd Needs to Find Own Voice," _Los Angeles Times_, 23 October 1997, CAL:48.

27. I heard Budd speak and sing at the Frank Sinatra Conference held at Hofstra University in November of 1998. I concur with Holden's assessment of her musical strengths but found her public persona too much like Streisand's to avoid comparison (as though Julie was doing an imitation of Brooklyn Barbra).

28. Howard Reich, "Passing the Torch," _Chicago Tribune_, 4 May 1997, 7:13. Howard Cohen also notes strong similarity between Eder and Streisand in "Another Streisand?," _Kansas City Star_, 7 June 1997, E:10.

29. "Someone Like You" is from _Jekyll and Hyde_ and is found on cassette tape 60416–4-RC (RCA Victor, 1990).

30. Alessandra Stanley, "Most Famous Singer in Russia, but 'Invisible' in the West," _New York Times_, 23 April 1997, C:9, 13.

31. Don Heckman, "Greece's Ambassador of Global Goodwill," _Los Angeles Times_, 4 June 1997, F:1.

32. The segment aired on NPR's _Morning Edition_ on 15 May 1998. Stamberg pointed out other characteristics of Sinatra's style that sound as if Streisand's name could have been substituted into the discussion: clean diction, personalized and honest text interpretations, good vocal technique, unique phrasing and rhythms. Stamberg also remarked that Sinatra could make a 32-bar song sound like a three-act play, a statement applied to Barbra on the liner of _The Second Barbra Streisand Album_. See a similar analysis in Richard Ackelson, _Frank Sinatra: A Complete Recording History of Techniques, Songs, Composers, Lyricists, Arrangers, Sessions, and First-Issue Albums_ (Jefferson, North Carolina: McFarland & Co., Inc., 1992), chapter 2. But Ackelson also writes that, "The voice came from nature, but Sinatra augmented it with extensive training and study" (page 19). That would mark a clear difference between Streisand and Sinatra.

33. Several speakers at the Frank Sinatra Conference held at Hofstra University in November of 1998 referred to Sinatra's phrasing and lyrics. For example, Peter C. Woodward, in a talk entitled "Aspects of Sinatra's Rhythmic Phrasing," noted that Frank developed a sort of "antecedent/consequent" approach where the first part of a phrase might "float" rhythmically speaking, while the later portion more clearly locked into the beat and tempo on key words.

34. Streisand remarked on this situation on _The Oprah Winfrey Show_, ABC television, 11 November 1996.

35. Conversation centered around this topic during Streisand's appearance on _The Oprah Winfrey Show_, ABC television, 11 November 1996, and in an interview with film critic Gene Shalit on _Today_, NBC television, segments aired the week of 20 November 1987. At the time of the release of _Just for the Record_, columnist Chris Willman stated that, in her younger days, Barbra had "seemed knowable," but that in 1991 she was a "powerful and publicly polite but slightly removed figure." See "Last of Her Kind Remains a Mystery," _Los Angeles Times_, 22 September 1991, CAL:61.

36. "Mr. Showbiz: Barbra Streisand." [internet on-line], available from http://www.mrshowbiz.com/interviews/344_1.html; Internet; accessed 24 February 1998.

See also Luaine Lee, "Never the Hollywood Dumpling, Streisand Still Does Things Her Way," *Detroit News*, 11 November 1996, 4C.

37. Margaret Carlson, "Of Barbs and Barbra," *Time* (13 February 1995): 51. Streisand continued her support of Democratic candidates during the 1998 election. She appeared on America On-Line *Live* on 2 November 1998 to encourage those who logged on to vote and to answer questions about her political views. She also voiced her continued support for President Bill Clinton during his impeachment dilemma.

38. "Mister Kelly's, Chi," *Variety* (19 June 1963): 56.

39. "What Makes a Barbra Special?," *Business Week* (20 May 1967): 64, 67–70. In the article Martin Erlichman also predicted that Streisand would be "a $100-million business" earning about $3 to $4 million per year for about thirty years (he underestimated) and that soon we would have "TV cartridges that you can play at home" where her early specials could be viewed years later (he was correct). He also is quoted as saying, "The main thing is to guard her against too much public exposure as a performer. She demands a lot from an audience. And people can take only so much of it at a time." See Thomas B. Morgan, "Superbarbra," *Look* (5 April 1966): 54–63, especially page 59.

40. Pete Hamill, "Good-bye Brooklyn, Hello Fame," *The Saturday Evening Post* (27 July 1963): 22–23. When writing about her 1994 London concerts, Robert Sandall combined the notion of the marketing advantages of the "scarcity of her live performances" with a conclusion that "at current prices, some may begin to feel the lack of warmth which lies at the heart of the phenomenon called Barbra Streisand." See "The Price of Fame," *Sunday Times* (London), 24 April 1994, 10: 6, 7. My own view is that she is somewhat reclusive and private (for personal, security, and marketing reasons) but that the concert tour was her way of trying to more personally reach out to her faithful fans. My observations of the audience's reactions indicate that she was successful notwithstanding high ticket prices.

41. Aida Pavletich, *Sirens of Song: The Popular Female Vocalist in America* (New York: Da Capo Paperback Press, 1980), 41–42. The author also states that a certain amount of "vulgarity is the essence of popular music" (because of its intended accessibility) and that Streisand achieves this while being both popular and musical.

42. Susan Whitall, "The Sound and the Furor," *Detroit News*, 13 May 1994, D1, 10.

43. See *Times* (London) 20 April 1994, 17.

44. William Grimes, "She's Worth Her Weight in Barbra," *New York Times*, 3 April 1994, 4:4. Another article begins, "She is, really, the last star," and the author asks many of the same questions and draws many of the same conclusions as Grimes. See Randall Short, "Desperately Needing Streisand," *New York* (27 June–4 July 1994): 92–93. Anne Janette Johnson quotes J. Curtis Sanburn, a contributor for *Harper's Bazaar*, as saying, her "star quality makes for a driven, creative dynamo; the biggest, most powerful performer in Hollywood. She's big because she keeps building on her talent, and we respond with surprise and recognition each time she gives us something new, yet distinctly Barbra." In *Contemporary Musicians*, vol. 2 (Detroit: Gale Research, Inc., 1989), 224–226.

45. Andrew Sarris, "Yentl Schmentl—Sing, Barbra," *Village Voice* (29 November 1983): 55. Sarris deals with the issue of inequality between the sexes in the

production of the movie and with financial aspects of Hollywood's movie-making industry, which are beyond the scope of this study. Streisand has commented that she does not feel the same kind of prejudice against women in the music industry. See Barbra Streisand, interview by Larry King, *Larry King Live*, CNN television, 6 February 1992.

46. Joe Queenan, *If You're Talking to Me, Your Career Must Be in Trouble* (New York: Hyperion, 1994), chapter 10:"Sacred Cow."

47. It is always interesting to read letters sent to editors after Streisand has been featured in a magazine article. Although detractors make their feelings known, Barbra's supporters are active and vocal in their response to written comments. Even as early as 1964, fans replied to the cover article in *Time* (one of her first) expressing delight that she was getting widespread attention and that the author did an admirable job in introducing the public to a complicated young woman. See *Time* (17 and 24 April 1964): 25 and 9 respectively. Following an extensive photograph layout and story about Streisand's marriage to James Brolin in the 20 July 1998 issue of *People Weekly*, a number of fans and detractors wrote letters. Several are printed in the 10 August issue, page 6.

48. Carey Goldberg, "Barbra, Gorgeous! You Have A Shrine," *New York Times*, 21 May 1996, A:12. One visitor to the museum is quoted as saying the reason for Streisand's popularity is her ability to achieve her goals despite the skepticism of many. The owner of the establishment agrees, stating that her success in overcoming "adversity and prejudice" is the key. Another author reported later that Streisand memorabilia did not sell as well as many had hoped. See David Laurell, "Selling Streisand: Benefit Auction of Barbra Memorabilia Stirs Emotions but Falls Below Expectations," *Popular Culture Collecting* (July 1997): 12–16. Laurell nonetheless noted the loyalty of those who collect Streisand material whether they ever have any personal contact with her. He reported that some fans commented that their relationship is with her work and with her commitment to it. See also Steve Hockensmith, "Singing Her Praises" and "People Who Need Barbra," *Chicago Tribune*, 31 August 1995, 5:1, 2.

49. The impossibility of separating the commercial and creative sides of rhythm and blues is discussed in David Sanjek, "One Size Does Not Fit All: The Precarious Position of the African American Entrepreneur in Post-World War II American Popular Music," *American Music* 15, no. 4 (Winter 1997): 535–562, especially page 538.

50. "The New Establishment," *Vanity Fair* (October 1994): 209–245. Streisand's name is joined on the list by those of others from the entertainment industry including David Geffen, Michael Eisner, Michael Ovitz, Oprah Winfrey, Steven Spielberg, and Ted Turner.

51. An article entitled "Freeze Frame, Faces in Time: Three Dramatic Divas" in *Biography* (May 1998) discusses Midler, Minnelli, and Streisand on page 10. Each woman's biographical summation concludes with the statement: "Icon of gay culture." See also Robert Plunket, "Farewell, Judy; Hello, Madonna," *New York Times*, 19 June 1994, 2:23.

52. See Rita Kempley, " 'In & Out': Closet Encounters," *Washington Post*, 19 September 1997, C:1, 7.

53. Quoted in Kevin Sessums, "Queen of Tides," *Vanity Fair* (September 1991): 228.

54. Marcia Pally takes another line of thinking: "Streisand [in *Yentl*] is an advertisement for American Jewish sensibilities. . . . It follows a long line of films meant to mollify both Jewish paranoia and gentile anti-Semitism." See "Kaddish for the Fading Image of Jews in Film," *Film Comment* (January–February 1994): 49–55.

55. In 1992 Streisand commented on these issues in a particularly pointed manner during the keynote speech she delivered upon her induction into the Women in Film Hall of Fame. The text of the speech was reprinted in her 1994 tour concert program.

56. Camille Paglia, "The Way She Was," *The New Republic* (18 and 25 July 1994): 20–22.

57. A similar observation was recounted by Michael McWilliams in "Hello, Gawjuss," *Detroit News*, 28 December 1993, C:1,6. He wrote that the moment "proved that Streisand is the diva's diva, the one who invented the formula for the contemporary female superstar."

58. Jeannie Williams, "Streisand Lives Up to O'Donnell's Dreams," *USA Today*, 21 November 1997, D:2. Near the end of the show an interesting moment occurred when Rosie, an enthusiastic-if-not-always-precise singer, began to sing "People" to her guest. Streisand briefly gestured with her hand for Rosie to raise her pitch and lower the volume, but quickly abandoned the quest for correctness and enjoyed the moment. Streisand has not sung on this type of show for decades.

59. Irv Lichtman, "Renewed Push Set for Streisand," *Billboard* (1 February 1986): 88.

60. See *Music at the Margins* (Newbury Park, California: Sage Publications, 1991), 250–252. The interview was translated into English by Paul Rutten.

61. Paul Grein, "Streisand's 20-Year Blitz," *Billboard* (16 April 1983): 6, 98. Many years earlier a writer had credited Barbra with indirectly helping the album sales of other "distaff attractions" such as Nancy Wilson, Ethel Ennis, Gale Garnett, Damite Jo, Eydie Gorme, Teri Thornton, Doris Day, and Patti Page. See "Barbra Streisand Pacing Field with Five Gold Disk Albums," *Billboard* (6 February 1965): 12.

62. Burt Korall, "Her Name Is Barbra," *Saturday Review* (11 January 1969): 108–109.

63. Daniel Patrick Stearns, "Barbra at $350 a Ticket," *A & E Monthly* (August 1994): 26–30.

64. Peter Reilly, "Streisand: Half Street Kid, Half Dowager Empress," *Stereo Review* (March 1979): 114.

65. John Voland, "A True American Original," *Variety* (21 October 1996): S46, 50.

66. See *USA Today*, 26 December 1997, D:1, 2.

67. Martin Erlichman, telephone conversation with Linda Pohly, Muncie, Indiana, 12 May 1998. She also announced in the fall of 1998 that she was beginning work on a new compact disc to be entitled *Barbra . . . in Love*. The single "I've Dreamed of You" from the new compact disc was released in June 1999 and introduced on the *Rosie O'Donnell Show*. The whole disc, retitled *A Love Like Ours*, was issued in October 1999 (see discography).

68. This is an important goal for her. Streisand told Barbara Walters that she felt a need to be of service to the world as a way of enriching her soul, and when

asked how she would like to be remembered—as an actress, singer, political activist, etc., Barbra replied "all of the above," and as someone who "contributed something to the world." Barbra Streisand, interview with Barbara Walters, *20/20*, ABC television, 19 November 1993.

69. Leonard Feather, "Wild Girl, Wild Sound," *Melody Maker* (1 February 1964): 12.

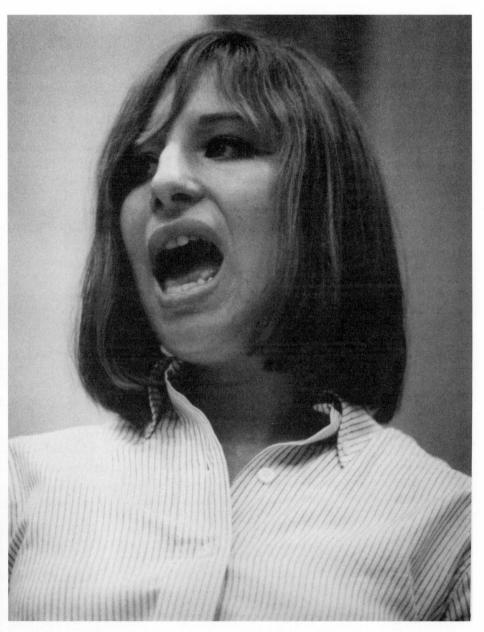

A recording session c. 1963

Performing at the Hollywood Bowl in 1963

On Stage as Fanny Brice in Funny Girl *singing "His Is the Only Music That Makes Me Dance"*

A Happening in Central Park *1967*

As Fanny Brice in the film version of Funny Girl *singing "My Man"*

On stage in Las Vegas in 1972

At the piano as Esther Hoffman on the set of A Star Is Born *1976*

In the studio working on Yentl 1983

A Grammy Award in 1987 for The Broadway Album

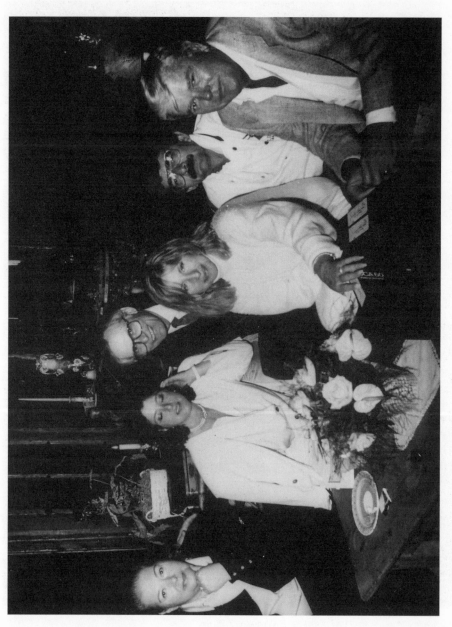

After the One Voice concert in 1986 with colleagues including Alan and Marilyn Bergman

Barbra: The Concert *in New York City 1994*

Discography

This list provides information on the contents of all of Barbra Streisand's solo albums and compact discs (hereinafter called "albums") and those from films and musical theatre shows in which she was a featured singer. The album titles are listed in chronological order along with label name and catalogue number(s), date of issue, and producer and arranger names. Song titles and other relevant song information then follows; the contents and format will be described shortly. Following the album title, other pertinent information is provided, such as whether the album is from a show or movie. Soundtracks from films in which Streisand starred but on which she does not sing (such as *The Owl and the Pussycat* or *Nuts*) are not listed.

Columbia has been Streisand's record label throughout her solo recording career; her voice occasionally is heard on other labels as a cast member of a show or film. The label catalogue number is provided for varying formats (phonodisc, compact disc, cassette); they are for issues in the United States and were garnered from the recordings whenever possible. In other instances, the label number was obtained from publications by familiar companies such as Schwann. The issue dates given are taken from the album liner whenever possible; I also consulted Streisand's accompanying booklet for her *Just for the Record* boxed set and the discography published in "The Legend of Barbra Streisand," *Billboard* (10 December 1983): BS-15. Only the date of the original issue is provided. Some of her early albums have been reissued on compact disc as is evident from the CD catalogue numbers provided for albums originally released before compact disc technology was available. Occasionally information about the producer and arranger was not provided on the recording or liner notes, and it is therefore not included herein. No distinction is made between levels of production credit, such as "executive" or "co-".

Streisand's *Just for the Record* boxed set is exceptional in many ways: it was released in 1991 but contains material from a span of years, some tracks included therein never were released elsewhere, occasionally the *Just for the Record* version of a song pre-dates the originally issued album version, and some tracks are repeats from other Streisand albums. The reader should refer to the alphabetic list of song titles in Appendix B for information on the album location of various versions (of these and other songs) and their chronology.

The titles of songs recorded on each album are listed following the main album information. The titles are organized alphabetically rather than by the song's placement on the album (the placement can change from recorded format to recorded format). However, songs that are part of a medley (and therefore might not be complete) are grouped at the end of each album list. Some song titles have been standardized where they are inconsistent from album to album; see, for example: Love theme from "A Star Is Born" (Evergreen), which is more commonly referred to as "Evergreen." Titles of songs released on the *Just for the Record* boxed set are followed by a date indicating their original recording date. Other information about each song also is included:

version (followed by a number)—Barbra has recorded some songs several times; this number indicates which chronological version is found on a particular album (identical version numbers indicate a repeated track),

ensemble—indicates the song is sung by a show or film ensemble of which Streisand was a part (show or movie songs in which she does not sing are omitted),

live—signals a track that was recorded "live" in a concert setting instead of in the studio if this is not clear from the album title.

Barbra Streisand has recorded and has had significant chart success with several duets; duet partners (not associated with a cast character) are named following the song title. The discography song list also provides lyricist and composer credits. This information has been taken directly from an album or compact disc whenever possible. When incomplete information was provided, I sought documentation from other sources including Streisand's *Just for the Record* booklet and *Popular Music: An Annotated Index of American Popular Songs* in several volumes edited by Nat Shapiro or Bruce Pollock. Nevertheless, some first names, in particular, remained unverifiable. If no composer or lyricist is named anywhere on the recording and the information could not be confirmed elsewhere, the term "unavailable" or "traditional" appears. If Barbra's name appears as producer or composer in the liner information, it is printed in **bold** in this list for visual aid. Because Streisand has recorded so many theatre songs, the title of the appropriate show follows the composer/lyricist names. This information was garnered from Streisand's album liners and from sources such as Stanley Green, *Broadway Musicals Show by Show*.

Following the song information is a paragraph about the album. It includes commentary on the album's repertoire content, its place in Streisand's productivity and life, personnel who worked on the album, musical highlights on the set, critics' reactions, or the album's musical or technological history and context. More detailed information is found in the preceding historical and analytical chapters.

An alphabetical arrangement of the album titles is provided in Appendix A along with the chronology number from the discography for cross reference. An alphabetical list of all the songs Barbra Streisand has recorded for commercial albums then follows as Appendix B. It also includes the album chronology numbers for cross reference to the discography. The album numbers for songs recorded or issued multiple times are listed so that repeated tracks of the same version appear together. Album numbers for subsequent versions then follow. Appendix C lists other recordings on which Barbra has performed as well as videos featuring her singing.

Streisand has commented more than once (see liner notes for *Back to Broadway* and the accompanying booklet for *Just for the Record*) that it is hard for her to keep track of all that she has sung, recorded, and released. These lists attempt to organize that vast quantity of material.

ALBUMS IN CHRONOLOGICAL ORDER

1. *I Can Get It for You Wholesale* (cast album)

Label and Number: Columbia, compact disc CK 57374, cassette CT 53020
Date: April 1962
Producer: Goddard Lieberson
Arranger: Lehman Engel, Sid Ramin

Ballad of the Garment Trade (ensemble); Harold Rome
I'm Not a Well Man (ensemble); Harold Rome
Miss Marmelstein (version 1); Harold Rome
What Are They Doing to Us Now? (ensemble); Harold Rome

This show, produced by David Merrick, opened on Broadway at the Shubert Theatre on 22 March 1962 and ran for 300 performances. The plot, set in the 1930s New York Garment District, was based on a novel by Jerome Weidman. Although Streisand had a minor part in the show, her success in the role of Miss Marmelstein caused a stir and brought her to the attention of a wider New York audience. Harold Rome wrote "Miss Marmelstein" and "What Are They Doing to Us Now?" to showcase Barbra's vocal and comedic talents. These and the other two songs that involved Barbra all fit under my character song heading (see chapter 2). Although Streisand was just barely 20 years of age and essentially an untrained vocalist, Rome's songs allowed her to show off her clean diction, varied timbral palette, and youthful energy. Arranger Sid Ramin first came to wide-spread attention as an arranger for the score to Leonard Bernstein's *West Side Story* in 1957. *Wholesale* also introduced Streisand to her future husband, Elliott Gould, who had one of the male leads in the show. She irritated some in the management by her inventive "biographical" entries for the playbill (writing that she was born in Madagascar rather than Brooklyn, for example). Barbra would work again with persons affiliated with this show: Harold Rome also wrote the music for *Pins and Needles* (#2 below), and Herbert Ross, the choreographer, directed the musical numbers for the film *Funny Girl*. Streisand was performing on and off at the Blue Angel supper club in New York while *Wholesale* was in production.

2. *Pins and Needles* (cast album)

Label and Number: Columbia, compact disc CK 57380, cassette CT 57380

Date: May 1962

Producer: Harold Rome, Elizabeth Lauer, Charles Burr

Arranger: Elise Bretton, Stan Freeman

Doing the Reactionary (ensemble); Harold Rome

Four Little Angels of Peace (ensemble); Harold Rome

Nobody Makes a Pass at Me; Harold Rome

Not Cricket to Picket; Harold Rome

Sitting on Your Status Quo (ensemble); Harold Rome

What Good Is Love?; Harold Rome

The revue *Pins and Needles*, about the struggles of union workers in the post-Depression era, began as an amateur show performed by members of the International Ladies' Garment Workers' Union in the mid-1930s. It grew into a Broadway show under this title in 1937. Harold Rome provided the music, and Rome, Arthur Arent, Marc Blitzstein (an influential American opera composer), Emanuel Eisenberg, and Charles Friedman wrote the skits. Barbra Streisand became involved as the lead singer in the twenty-fifth anniversary production in 1962. Although she would become renowned years later for her involvement in political and social issues, this Streisand recording is remembered more for its further introduction of her vocal talents than for its social statement. Barbra's solo, "Nobody Makes a Pass at Me," is reminiscent of her solo "Miss Marmelstein" (see #1 above) in compositional and performance style. By way of contrast, "What Good Is Love?" affords her the opportunity to sing a blues-inflected torch song as she might have performed in a club setting. Her strengths as an impassioned belter are evident. The character nature of the other songs (filled with humor and sarcasm) allowed her to project her acting and singing skills simultaneously. In May of 1962, Barbra was invited to sing for President Kennedy in Washington.

3. *The Barbra Streisand Album*

Label and Number: Columbia, stereo phonodisc CS 8807, monaural CL 2007, cassette PCT 8807, compact disc CK 57374

Date: February 1963

Producer: Mike Berniker

Arranger: Peter Matz

Come to the Supermarket (In Old Peking); Cole Porter

Cry Me a River (version 2); Arthur Hamilton

Happy Days Are Here Again (version 2); Jack Yellen, Milton Ager

I'll Tell the Man in the Street; Lorenz Hart, Richard Rodgers; *I Married an Angel*

Keepin' Out of Mischief Now (version 2); Andy Razaf, Thomas "Fats" Waller

Much More; Harvey Schmidt, Tom Jones; *Fantasticks*

My Honey's Lovin' Arms (version 1); Herman Ruby, Joseph Meyer

Sleepin' Bee, A (version 2); Truman Capote, Harold Arlen; *House of Flowers*

Soon It's Gonna Rain; Harvey Schmidt, Tom Jones; *Fantasticks*

Taste of Honey, A; Ric Marlow, Bobby Scott

Who's Afraid of the Big Bad Wolf? (version 2); Ann Ronell, Frank E. Churchill

The efforts of Streisand's manager, Martin Erlichman, paid off when she signed her first solo recording contract with Columbia records. Barbra's contract allowed her to select her own material, and she gravitated toward the theatre songs and standards she had been singing in New York clubs, which contrasted with the repertoire most singers her age were recording for albums at that time. She sang character songs ("Who's Afraid of the Big Bad Wolf?"), belt or torch numbers ("Cry Me a River"), and lyric songs with long sweeping melodies and classically oriented accompaniment ("I'll Tell the Man in the Street"). While Streisand's Broadway sound continues to predominate, her jazz-influenced style also can be heard on songs such as "My Honey's Lovin' Arms." Her individualized approach to rhythm, tempo, and text characterization is introduced through her now-familiar, slow-tempo arrangement (by Ken and Mitzi Welch) of "Happy Days Are Here Again." Although the songs in this collection already were familiar to Streisand, the arrangements for the album were created and conducted by Peter Matz, whom she called upon at the suggestion of composer Harold Arlen. Some of the arrangements heard on the album are significantly different than those released by Columbia as singles ("Happy Days," for example). *The Barbra Streisand Album* brought Barbra her first Grammy Award in 1964.

4. *The Second Barbra Streisand Album*

Label and Number: Columbia, stereo phonodisc CS 8854, monaural CL 2054; compact disc CK 57378, cassette CT 57378

Date: August 1963

Producer: Mike Berniker

Arranger: Peter Matz, Peter Daniels

Any Place I Hang My Hat Is Home (version 1); Johnny Mercer, Harold Arlen; *St. Louis Woman*

Down With Love; E. Y. Harburg, Harold Arlen; *Hurray for Love*

Gotta Move (version 1); Peter Matz

I Don't Care Much; Fred Ebb, John Kander

I Stayed Too Long at the Fair (version 1); Billy Barnes

Like a Straw in the Wind; Harold Arlen

Lover, Come Back to Me (version 2); Oscar Hammerstein II, Sigmund Romberg; *The New Moon*

My Coloring Book (version 1); Fred Ebb, John Kander

Right as the Rain; E. Y. Harburg, Harold Arlen; *Bloomer Girl*

When the Sun Comes Out (version 2); Ted Koehler, Harold Arlen

Who Will Buy?; Lionel Bart; *Oliver*

Following the immediate success of Streisand's first album, Columbia quickly issued *The Second Barbra Streisand Album*, which also was arranged and conducted by Peter Matz. Peter Daniels, who accompanied her club engagements, is credited with providing "Additional Materials." Five songs of the set are by Harold Arlen, who frequently is named among Streisand's favorite composers. Writing for the *New Grove Dictionary of American Music*, Larry Stempel commented that Arlen's musical style "shows an affinity with black musical expression," and that several of his shows, including *Bloomer Girl* and *St. Louis Woman*, were written for black casts or shows that had black singing characters. Although Barbra's first two solo albums were released within months of each other, the second exhibits her increasing interpretive experience and vocal control. (Some listeners found her additional control to be a negative aspect. John Indcox, writing for *High Fidelity Magazine*, found the album "an almost unrelieved bore." See the bibliography.) Her most prominent vocal characteristics during this period include: fast vibrato; bright, forward, nasal timbre; rhythmic flexibility around the beat; and altered tone color and word painting for characterization of lyrics. Streisand's technique of mismatching lyric and musical phrase points is beginning to be evident. The style and length of some of the numbers make it obvious that the repertoire was chosen for album sales instead of radio play ("My Coloring Book" exceeds four minutes). In the months surrounding the release of her second album, Barbra was seen and heard nationally on *The Ed Sullivan Show* and *The Judy Garland Show*.

5. *The Third Album*

Label and Number: Columbia, stereo phonodisc CS 8954, monaural CL 2154, compact disc 57379, cassette CT 57379

Date: February 1964

Producer: Mike Berniker

Arranger: Ray Ellis, Sid Ramin, Peter Matz, Peter Daniels

As Time Goes By; Herman Hupfeld

Bewitched (Bothered and Bewildered); Lorenz Hart, Richard Rodgers

Draw Me a Circle; Young

I Had Myself a True Love (version 2); Johnny Mercer, Harold Arlen; *St. Louis Woman*

It Had to Be You; Gus Kahn, Isham Jones

Just in Time; Betty Comden, Adolph Green, Jule Styne; *Bells Are Ringing*

Make Believe; Oscar Hammerstein II, Jerome Kern

My Melancholy Baby; Watson, George A. Norton, Ernie Burnett

Never Will I Marry; Frank Loesser; *Greenwillow*

Taking a Chance on Love; John Latouche, Ted Fetter, Vernon Duke; *Cabin in the Sky*

As evidenced in the list of names and show titles above, Streisand continued to look to theatre composers for the repertoire of *The Third Album*. Nevertheless, a more subdued sound permeates the album, and more love ballads find their way onto the vinyl. For example, Barbra's child-like gentle tone is heard on her performance of "Just in Time" arranged by Leonard Bernstein. Her individualized approach to specific words, coloring them for interpretive effect—even when the required technique takes her away from standard vocal tone production—is especially evident on "Never Will I Marry." On songs such as "It Had to Be You" she sings the verse that other singers might omit (heading straight to the more popular chorus) to help establish an acting or story context. "Draw Me a Circle" would be used again later on her television special *Color Me Barbra*. This album remained high on the sales charts for several weeks even as Barbra was opening in her first starring role on Broadway in *Funny Girl*.

6. *Funny Girl* (cast album)

Label and Number: Capital, phonodisc STAO 2059; Angel, compact disc ZDM 7 64661 25

Date: April 1964

Producer: Dick Jones

Arranger: Buster Davis, Ralph Burns

Cornet Man; Jule Styne, Bob Merrill

Don't Rain on My Parade (version 1); Jule Styne, Bob Merrill

His Love Makes Me Beautiful (version 1, ensemble); Jule Styne, Bob Merrill

I Want to Be Seen With You Tonight (ensemble); Jule Styne, Bob Merrill

I'm the Greatest Star (version 1); Jule Styne, Bob Merrill

Music That Makes Me Dance, The (version 1); Jule Styne, Bob Merrill

People (version 1); Jule Styne, Bob Merrill

Rat-tat-tat-tat (ensemble); Jule Styne, Bob Merrill

Sadie Sadie (version 1, ensemble); Jule Styne, Bob Merrill

Who Are You Now?; Jule Styne, Bob Merrill

You Are Woman (ensemble); Jule Styne, Bob Merrill

This cast album is one of the few Streisand recordings that is not on the Columbia label. It, of course, is from the Broadway show that made Barbra a theatre star and helped to secure her role in the movie of the same name (although an actress's move from a stage role to the same film part was not always guaranteed as will be noted with *Hello, Dolly* later). *Funny Girl* went through a long gestation period (Mary Martin and Anne Bancroft were considered for the lead), several rewrites, and a multitude of songs, all of which apparently was exciting to the young star. When it finally was set, *Funny Girl* ran for 1,348 performances at the Winter Garden Theatre. Although originally meant to be co-produced by David Merrick, who produced *I Can Get It for You Wholesale*, *Funny Girl* was produced by Ray Stark, the real-life son-in-law of the story's subject, Fanny Brice. Stark also would produce Barbra's first movies. Barbra stayed with the show until Christmas of 1965 when she left to recreate the role in London. Mimi Hines had the unenviable task of following Barbra at the Winter Garden. (Jule Styne reminisces about *Funny Girl* in *Jule, The Story of Composer Jule Styne* by Theodore Taylor.)

The songs created by Styne and Merrill (Stephen Sondheim at one time had been courted for lyricist) showcase Barbra's talents in a variety of styles from the ballad "People," which became one of her signature songs, to the gutsy, show-within-a-show "Cornet Man." Her belt powers are heard on "Don't Rain on My Parade," while her comic side is evident in "You Are Woman." Compare this album's contents with #14 below to see which songs were retained and which were replaced in the movie version of *Funny Girl*. The most obvious omission here is "My Man," which was a hit for Fanny and later for Barbra. Fanny Brice and Barbra Streisand were both successful singer/actresses, but their vocal style was not similar. Streisand exhibits considerably more technical finesse and timbral variety. Barbra was nominated for the Tony Award for her role in *Funny Girl*, but lost to Carol Channing, star of *Hello, Dolly*.

7. People

Label and Number: Columbia, stereo phonodisc CS 9015, monaural CL 2215, cassette PCT 09015, compact disc CK 09015

Date: September 1964

Producer: Robert Mersey

Arranger: Peter Matz, Ray Ellis

Absent Minded Me; Jule Styne, Bob Merrill

Autumn; Richard Maltby Jr., David Shire

Don't Like Goodbyes; Truman Capote, Harold Arlen

Fine and Dandy; Kay Swift, Paul James; *Fine and Dandy*

How Does the Wine Taste?; Matt Dubey, Harold Karr

I'm All Smiles; Michael Leonard, Herbert Martin; *The Yearling*

Love Is a Bore; Sammy Cahn, Jimmy Van Heusen

My Lord and Master; Oscar Hammerstein II, Richard Rodgers; *The King and I*

People (version 2); Jule Styne, Bob Merrill

Supper Time; Irving Berlin; *As Thousands Cheer*

When in Rome (I Do As the Romans Do); Carolyn Leigh, Cy Coleman

Will He Like Me? (version 1); Sheldon Harnick, Jerry Bock; *She Loves Me*

This title takes advantage of Barbra's success with the hit ballad from *Funny Girl* and is the only solo album (not related to a show) of the early years of her career whose title does not contain her name in some way. (Appendix B shows that she has recorded "People" several times for inclusion on other albums.) Otherwise this album continues the rather subdued quality noted on *The Third Album* and contains fewer character songs than earlier sets, even though many of the songs are from theatre music teams. That is not to say that there is no variety in the repertoire; compare her feisty "Love Is a Bore" with the more mellow "Fine and Dandy." Composer David Shire worked with Streisand several other times in the future

as conductor (*Simply Streisand*) and composer ("What About Today?").
Barbra received another Grammy Award (Best Vocal Performance—Female) for "People."

8. *My Name Is Barbra* (television special)

Label and Number: Columbia, phonodisc CS 9136, cassette PCT 00168, compact
disc CK 09136

Date: May 1965

Producer: Robert Mersey

Arranger: Peter Matz

I Can See It (version 1); Tom Jones, Harvey Schmidt; *Fantasticks*

I've Got No Strings; Leigh Harline, Ned Washington

If You Were the Only Boy in the World; Clifford Grey, Nat D. Ayer

Jenny Rebecca; Carol Hall

My Man (version 2); Maurice Yvain, Channing Pollock; *Ziegfeld Follies*

My Name Is Barbara [*sic*]; Leonard Bernstein

My Pa; Michael Leonard, Herbert Martin; *The Yearling*

Someone to Watch Over Me; George Gershwin, Ira Gershwin; *Oh, Kay!*

Sweet Zoo; J. Harris

Where Is the Wonder?; Michael Barr, Dion McGregor

Why Did I Choose You? (version 1); Michael Leonard, Herbert Martin; *The Yearling*

medley:

    I'm Five; M. Schafer

    Kid Again, A.; Johnny Melfi, Roger Perry

My Name Is Barbra was unusual for its day in its format, having three
segments (or acts) and no guest stars. The subsequent album is not exactly
a soundtrack from the special (which aired on 28 April 1965), but it includes songs from both the childhood and concert segments of the show.
In fact, about half of the album's material was not part of the special
(which had featured some of her "old hits" like "People" that already had
been issued on albums), but the new songs are added in a related thematic
manner. For example, the lyric song "Jenny Rebecca" is grouped with the
other childhood songs, "A Kid Again" and "I'm Five." On side 2 the listener hears songs with more adult themes. "My Man," which purposely
was omitted from *Funny Girl* because of its close association with Fanny
Brice, was included on the special and on this album. Streisand never has
sung all of the lyrics of that song, part of which reveal that the "man" of
the song beats the woman singer. Although of French origin, "My Man"

became a hit for Fanny Brice as part of the 1921 *Ziegfeld Follies. My Name Is Barbra* brought Streisand her first Emmy Awards, and in the 1980s it was released as a home video (see Appendix C). In an introduction to the video, Streisand mentions that "My Name Is Barbara," by Leonard Bernstein, was not written for her. She also recalls that she had to watch the first airing of the special from her dressing room backstage in *Funny Girl.* As a point of comparison, the stereo version of the album was advertised as costing $4.79 in 1965; the monaural version cost a dollar less. Readers interested in Streisand memorabilia and collectibles should consult internet sources like those listed in the bibliography. In addition to the Emmys she received for the special, Streisand also won another Grammy for the album.

9. *My Name Is Barbra, Two . . .* (television special)

Label and Number: Columbia, phonodisc CS 9209, cassette PCT 00102, compact disc CK 09209

Date: October 1965

Producer: Robert Mersey

Arranger: Peter Matz, Don Costa

All That I Want; N. Wolfe, F. Forest

He Touched Me (version 1); Ira Levin, Milton Schafer

How Much of the Dream Comes True?; J. Barry, T. Peacock

I Got Plenty of Nothin' (version 1); George Gershwin, Ira Gershwin, DuBose Heyward; *Porgy and Bess*

Kind of Man a Woman Needs, The; Michael Leonard, Herbert Martin

No More Songs for Me; Richard Maltby Jr., David Shire

Quiet Night; Richard Rodgers, Lorenz Hart; *On Your Toes*

Second Hand Rose (version 1); Grant Clarke, James F. Hanley; *Ziegfeld Follies*

Shadow of Your Smile, The; Paul Francis Webster, Johnny Mandel

Where's That Rainbow?; Lorenz Hart, Richard Rodgers

medley:

　Best Things in Life Are Free, The (version 1); B. G. DeSylva, Ray Henderson, Lew Brown; *Good News*

　Brother, Can You Spare a Dime?; E. Y. Harburg, Jay Gorney

　Give Me the Simple Life (version 1); Harry Ruby, Rube Bloom

　I Got Plenty of Nothin' (version 2); George Gershwin, Ira Gershwin, DuBose Heyward; *Porgy and Bess*

　Nobody Knows You When You're Down and Out (version 1); Jimmie Cox

　Second Hand Rose (version 2); Grant Clarke, James F. Hanley; *Ziegfeld Follies*

The long medley included on this album is from the second segment of Streisand's first television special, *My Name Is Barbra*. It was filmed in the Bergdorf-Goodman department store, setting up conflict between the surroundings and the songs' lyrics. Notice that the album also contains full-length versions of some of the songs that appear incomplete in the medley. Like "My Man," "Second Hand Rose" had been a hit decades earlier for Fanny Brice.

10. *Color Me Barbra* (television special)

Label and Number: Columbia, stereo phonodisc CS 9278, monaural CL 2478, cassette PCT 9278, compact disc CK 09278

Date: March 1966

Producer: Joe Layton, Dwight Hemion

Arranger: unavailable

C'est Si Bon (It's So Good); Jerry Seelen, A. Harnez, Henri Betti

Gotta Move (version 2); Peter Matz

Minute Waltz, The; Lan O'Kun

Non, C'est Rien; Michel Jourdan, Armand Canfora, Joss Baselli

One Kiss; Oscar Hammerstein II, Sigmund Romberg; *The New Moon*

Starting Here, Starting Now (version 1); Richard Maltby Jr., David Shire

Where Am I Going?; Dorothy Fields, Cy Coleman; *Sweet Charity*

Where or When?; Lorenz Hart, Richard Rodgers; *Babes in Arms*

Yesterdays; Otto Harbach, Jerome Kern; *Roberta*

medley:

  Animal Crackers in My Soup; Ted Koehler, Irving Caesar, Ray Henderson

  Funny Face; Ira Gershwin, George Gershwin

  I Love You; unavailable

  I Stayed Too Long at the Fair (version 2); Billy Barnes

  I've Grown Accustomed to Her Face; Alan Jay Lerner, Frederick Loewe

  Let's Face the Music and Dance; Irving Berlin

  Look at That Face (version 1); Anthony Newley, Leslie Bricusse; *The Roar of the Greasepaint—The Smell of the Crowd*

  Sam, You Made the Pants Too Long (version 1); Sam M. Lewis, Victor Young, Fred Whitehouse, Milton Berle

  Small World; Stephen Sondheim, Jule Styne

  That Face; Alan Bergman, Lew Spence

  They Didn't Believe Me; Herbert Reynolds, Jerome Kern

Were Thine That Special Face; Cole Porter; *Kiss Me Kate*

What's New Pussycat?; Hal David, Burt Bacharach

Material from Streisand's second television special, *Color Me Barbra*, appears on the album of the same name. For this show, one segment was filmed (with new color cameras, reflecting both the advances in the technology of the day and the reason for the title) in the Philadelphia Museum of Art and a second as a circus sequence. The music from the latter comprises the medley included herein. A year and a half later, in October 1967, CBS aired Streisand's third television special, *The Belle of 14th Street*. It did not receive the critical acclaim of her first two, but some of the music recorded for its vaudevillian theme was included years later on Barbra's *Just for the Record* boxed set (#44). The repertoire on *Color* has many ties to Barbra's past and future: Peter Matz is represented here as composer—he had conducted and arranged her first albums; she sings a French-language song leading to her next solo album; Stephen Sondheim, whose music will play an important role on *The Broadway Album* of 1985, is represented for the first time in her work; Alan Bergman's name appears not paired with his future wife, Marilyn (they were responsible for Streisand's hit "The Way We Were"); and Barbra will appear in 1971 on a television special with Burt Bacharach. "Sam You Made the Pants Too Long" is actually a parody (by Whitehouse and Berle) of "Lawd, You Made the Night Too Long."

11. *Je m'appelle Barbra*

Label and Number: Columbia, stereo phonodisc CS 9347, monaural CL 2547, compact disc CK 9347, cassette PCT 9347

Date: October 1966

Producer: Ettore Stratta

Arranger: Michel Legrand, Ray Ellis

Autumn Leaves; Johnny Mercer, Jacques Prevert, Joseph Kosma

Clopin Clopant; Bruno Coquatrix, Pierre Dudan, Kermet Goell

Free Again (version 1); Robert Colby, Michel Jourdan, Armand Canfora, Joss Barelli

I Wish You Love; Albert A. Beach, Charles Trenet

I've Been Here; Earl Shuman, Michel Vaucaire, Charles Dumont

Le Mur; Michel Vaucaire, Charles Dumont

Love and Learn; Norman Gimbel, Eddy Marnay, Michel Legrand

Ma Première Chanson; **Barbra Streisand**, Eddy Marnay

Martina; Hal Shaper, Michel Legrand

Once Upon a Summertime; Johnny Mercer, Eddy Marnay, Eddie Barclay, Michel
  Legrand

Speak to Me of Love; Bruce Sievier, Jean Lenoir

What Now My Love?; Carl Sigman, P. Delanoe, Gilbert Becaud

"Ma première chanson" (My First Song) is of interest on this album
because it is the first song for which Streisand received composer credit.
Her most successful composition, "Evergreen," will become a hit ten years
later. The song "Le Mur" was written for French chanteuse Edith Piaf, but
she died before recording it. "I've Been Here" is the English version of "Le
Mur," and both are included on this set. Streisand's long association with
composer/conductor/arranger Michel Legrand (*Yentl* #38) begins on this
album as well. In his review of this album, Morgan Ames laments that
Streisand's style and repertoire choices have "set off an unpleasant melee
of sobbing, shrieking girl singers," but suggests that it also has strengthened
trends in orchestral arranging (see bibliography). Despite the French title
and some French-language songs, the repertoire is typical for this period of
Barbra's recording career: character songs, belt or torch songs, lyric songs,
and love ballads (see chapter 2 for a description of these song types). Perhaps her constituency shied away from the title, or fans were looking for
something new from Streisand. She couldn't be expected to maintain the
pace and success with which she began only four years earlier, but this
album was her least successful to date. In 1966 Barbra completed her
Funny Girl obligation in London and went on a short American concert
tour in the summer. In December she gave birth to her son, Jason.

12. *Simply Streisand*

Label and Number: Columbia, stereo phonodisc CS 9482, monaural CL 2682,
  compact disc CK 9482, cassette PCT 9482

Date: October 1967

Producer: Jack Gold, Howard A. Roberts

Arranger: Ray Ellis, David Shire

All the Things You Are; Oscar Hammerstein II, Jerome Kern; *Very Warm for May*

Boy Next Door, The; Hugh Martin, Ralph Blane; *Meet Me in St. Louis*

I'll Know (version 1); Frank Loesser; *Guys and Dolls*

Lover Man (Oh Where Can You Be?) (version 1); Jimmie Davis, Roger J. Ramirez,
  Jimmy Sherman

Make the Man Love Me; Dorothy Fields, Arthur Schwartz; *A Tree Grows in Brooklyn*

More Than You Know (version 1); Billy Rose, Edward Eliscu, Vincent Youmans

My Funny Valentine; Richard Rodgers, Lorenz Hart; *Babes in Arms*

Nearness of You, The; Ned Washington, Hoagy Carmichael

Stout-hearted Men; Oscar Hammerstein II, Sigmund Romberg; *The New Moon*

When Sunny Gets Blue; Jack Segal, Marvin Fisher

Simply Streisand begins a period of transition, although on this album it is evident more in vocal style and arrangement than repertoire. David Shire, conductor for the set, suggests that the title sets the mood—simplicity. However, it was coming at a time in American history when change was the watch word, and life was anything but simple. Barbra had secured her place in showbiz history in a flurry of successful activity. She had become an actress on stage and through song literature, but at a mere 25-years-of-age, where would she go next? The vocal style on this album reflects a growing maturity heard in her more refined tone (less brash belting) and controlled technique. It is supported by simpler accompaniments. "Lover Man" exhibits brief moments of soul-influenced sound and ends with improvisatory repetition, traits not common to the popular-song standards of her usual repertoire. Further contemporary pop sound is heard in the gentle backbeat of "The Nearness of You," providing a glimpse down one path she would explore.

13. *A Christmas Album*

Label and Number: Columbia, stereo phonodisc CS 9557, monaural CL 2757, compact disc CK 9557, cassette PCT 9557

Date: October 1967

Producer: Jack Gold, Ettore Stratta

Arranger: Marty Paich, Ray Ellis

Ave Maria; Charles Gounod, Ray Ellis

Best Gift, The; Lan O'Kun

Christmas Song, The (Chestnuts Roasting on an Open Fire); Mel Torme, Robert Wells

Have Yourself a Merry Little Christmas; Hugh Martin, Ralph Blane

I Wonder as I Wander; John Jacob Niles, Ray Ellis

Jingle Bells (New Adaptation); James S. Pierpont, Marty Paich, Jack Gold

Lord's Prayer, The; Albert Hay Malotte, Ray Ellis

My Favorite Things; Oscar Hammerstein II, Richard Rodgers; *The Sound of Music*

O Little Town of Bethlehem (New Adaptation); Phillips Brooks, Lewis H. Redner, Jack Gold

Sleep in Heavenly Peace (Silent Night) (version 1); Franz Gruber, Ray Ellis

White Christmas; Irving Berlin

This phase of Streisand's recording career also finds her exploring a wider variety of repertoire (see #12 above). Although it is not uncommon for solo artists to record albums of Christmas music, some people might have been surprised to find Barbra, who never hesitated from reflecting her Jewish heritage, doing so. Moreover, the repertoire on this album does not focus on the secular side of the season and, in fact, includes some songs that technically are not related to the holiday ("The Lord's Prayer"). The arrangements provide contrast that supports Barbra's vocal flexibility—"Jingle Bells" is sung at breakneck speed with some New York accent and jazz style interpolated. Her penchant for leaping up an octave from traditionally notated melodies frequently is heard. Nevertheless, Streisand approaches several of the pieces with more classically oriented diction and tone. "The Best Gift" suggests the final category for organizing her repertoire: autobiographical or advocacy songs (see chapter 3). It reflects the emotion of her son's recent birth. The album has been available for purchase for more than 30 years (being reissued in the 1990s on compact disc) and parallels the staying power of Streisand's vocal career. The original record jacket reflects changes in recording technology by listing only the stereo phonodisc catalogue number; monaural had become passé.

14. *Funny Girl* (film)

Label and Number: Columbia, phonodisc BOS 3220, compact disc CK 03220, cassette JST 20034

Date: July 1968

Producer: Jack Gold

Arranger: unavailable

Don't Rain on My Parade (version 2); Bob Merrill, Jule Styne

Funny Girl (version 1); Bob Merrill, Jule Styne

His Love Makes Me Beautiful (version 2, ensemble); Bob Merrill, Jule Styne

I'd Rather Be Blue Over You (Than Happy With Somebody Else); Billy Rose, Fisher

I'm the Greatest Star (version 3); Bob Merrill, Jule Styne

My Man (version 3); Maurice Yvain, Channing Pollock; *Ziegfeld Follies*

People (version 4); Bob Merrill, Jule Styne

Roller Skate Rag (ensemble); Bob Merrill, Jule Styne

Sadie, Sadie (version 2, ensemble); Bob Merrill, Jule Styne

Swan, The; Bob Merrill, Jule Styne

You Are Woman, I Am Man (ensemble); Bob Merrill, Jule Styne

Barbra Streisand achieved one of her childhood goals when she stepped in front of the cameras to begin work on the film version of *Funny Girl* produced by Ray Stark and directed by William Wyler. Capitalizing on

Streisand's stage and recording success, Columbia Pictures launched a major advertising campaign to promote the movie even before its completion, offering advanced box-office tickets. Their efforts were fruitful, and her film debut brought Barbra an Academy Award for Best Actress; her see-through outfit at the event garnered almost as much attention as her award. She had earned multiple Emmys and Grammys and now an Oscar well before her thirtieth birthday. Political events of the day in the Middle East brought the film additional notoriety since the male lead opposite Jewish Streisand was Egyptian Omar Sharif. As noted with the cast album of the show (#6 in discography), some of the Styne/Merrill songs were retained from Broadway, and others were omitted or replaced. A comparison of Barbra's vocals on the two albums is instructive for hearing how her voice had matured with less stridency and how her confidence as a more subtle actress was evolving (see especially "You Are Woman, I Am Man"). Interestingly, most reviews of the movie neglected to comment on Streisand's singing as though its quality was unquestioned (see chapter 3). A writer for *The New Yorker* (16 November 1968) observed that the soundtrack was very much a "solo performance" since there are few production numbers and little musical emphasis on other cast members. It ranked number 8 on the top-10 album list of 1969. Reflecting the media options of the day, the soundtrack was available as a stereo phonodisc, a 4-track or 8-track stereo tape cartridge, or a 4-track reel-to-reel stereo tape. In addition to "People" and "My Man," "Don't Rain on My Parade" became a Streisand signature song and is found on several albums (see Appendix B).

15. *A Happening in Central Park* (live)

Label and Number: Columbia, phonodisc CS 9710, compact disc CK 09710, cassette PCT 09710

Date: September 1968

Producer: Jack Gold

Arranger: unavailable (possibly Nick Perito)

Cry Me a River (version 3); Arthur Hamilton

Happy Days Are Here Again (version 4); Jack Yellen, Milton Ager

He Touched Me (version 2); Ira Levin, Milton Schafer

I Can See It (version 2); Harvey Schmidt, Tom Jones; *Fantasticks*

Love Is Like a New Born Child; O. Brown Jr.

Marty the Martian; J. Harris

Natural Sounds; Lan O'Kun; *The Juggler*

People (version 3); Bob Merrill, Jule Styne

Second Hand Rose (version 3); Grant Clarke, James F. Hanley; *Ziegfeld Follies*

Sleep in Heavenly Peace (Silent Night) (version 2); Franz Gruber, Ray Ellis

Value (version 2); Jeff Harris; *Another Evening With Harry Stoones*

This album is Streisand's first "live" concert album; the material comes from her 17 June 1967 free concert in New York's Central Park, a performance given while she was on a short break from filming *Funny Girl* in California. The concert set a record for its day with an estimated 135,000 persons in attendance. In addition to issuing an album, Streisand's marketing team also released videotaped footage of the concert as a television special for CBS (available in the 1990s on home video). As would be expected, the album is a sort of "greatest hits" collection since the audience was treated to songs already popular in Streisand's oeuvre. What was new for many listeners was hearing Streisand the comedienne deliver comic monologues and displaying her rapport with an audience. Other new material included the songs "Love Is Like a Newborn Child" (Barbra's own son was just months old) and "Natural Sounds." Always providing the unexpected, Streisand also included her rendition of "Sleep in Heavenly Peace" ("Silent Night") on the humid summer evening; she later suggested her emphasis was on "peace." Phil Ramone, who had a long career as a sound man and who produced some of Streisand's work in the 1970s, was responsible for the sound at the concert venue, which some reviewers of the album criticized as uneven (see bibliography).

16. *What About Today?*

Label and Number: Columbia, phonodisc CS 9816, compact disc CK 47014, cassette CT 47014

Date: July 1969

Producer: Wally Gold

Arranger: Peter Matz, Don Costa, Michel Legrand

Alfie; Hal David, Burt Bacharach

Ask Yourself Why; Alan Bergman, Marilyn Bergman, Michel Legrand

Goodnight; John Lennon, Paul McCartney

Honey Pie; John Lennon, Paul McCartney

Little Tin Soldier; J. Webb

Morning After, The; David Shire, Richard Maltby Jr.

Punky's Dilemma; Paul Simon

That's a Fine Kind o' Freedom; Martin Charnin, Harold Arlen

Until It's Time for You to Go; Buffy Sainte-Marie

What About Today?; David Shire

With a Little Help From My Friends; John Lennon, Paul McCartney

A glance at the list of contemporary composers represented on this album suggests further why this period of Streisand's recording career can be labeled transitional or experimental. Columbia Records, in fact, suggested in its promotion of *What About Today?* that Barbra was moving into the rock world—in hindsight an exaggeration. The credits indicate that several of the composers and arrangers involved also reflect her musical past—Peter Matz, Michel Legrand, David Shire, and Harold Arlen. Some of the arrangements exhibit this mix of traditional with new, juxtaposing a light backbeat with sweet orchestral strings. In the final analysis, much of Streisand's musical style and vocal approach remain consistent between past albums and this one. It appears that the message of the lyrics is what has changed. Interestingly, the most socially pointed song texts ("Ask Yourself Why," "That's a Fine Kind of Freedom," and "The Morning After") of the album come from the more traditional theatrically oriented composers of the group. Two songs on this album from the fertile minds of Lennon and McCartney are presented as playful character songs. The third, "Goodnight," is a gentle ballad.

17. *Hello, Dolly* (film)

Label and Number: 20th C. Fox, phonodisc DTCS 5103

Date: December 1969

Producer: unavailable

Arranger: unavailable

Before the Parade Passes By (ensemble); Jerry Herman

Dancing (ensemble); Jerry Herman

Finale (ensemble); Jerry Herman

Hello, Dolly (version 1, ensemble); Jerry Herman

It Takes a Woman (Reprise); Jerry Herman

Just Leave Everything to Me; Jerry Herman

Love Is Only Love; Jerry Herman

Put on Your Sunday Clothes (ensemble); Jerry Herman

So Long, Dearie; Jerry Herman

Certainly a dichotomy is evident between the contemporaneous lyrics of Streisand's *What About Today?* album above and her role as the mature Dolly Levi in the film version of *Hello, Dolly*. Barbra had lost the Tony Award to Carol Channing several years earlier (see #6); now it was ironic that Streisand was signed to play Channing's character in one of the last "old-fashioned" Hollywood musicals. (Thirty years later the issue of casting Streisand was still being debated. Following an airing of the film, American Movie Classics television sponsored an on-line opinion poll about who should have played the film role of Dolly. Streisand received several adamant votes of confidence, but Doris Day, Lucille Ball, Debbie Reynolds, and of course, Carol Channing also were suggested. AMC's "Corner Table" [internet on-line]; available from www.amctv.com; accessed 17 February 1999). The movie was directed by song-and-dance man Gene Kelly. Michael Crawford and Tommy Tune both had secondary roles in *Hello, Dolly*, but went on to greater fame in musical theatre years later. Crawford reached a peak in his career through his portrayal of the phantom in Andrew Lloyd Webber's *The Phantom of the Opera*; he joined Barbra for a duet on her 1993 *Back to Broadway* (#46). The movie version of *Hello, Dolly* contains many of the songs from the stage show, but "Just Leave Everything to Me," which introduces Dolly and her meddling ways to the film audience, and the decision-time ballad "Love Is Only Love" were added. They show different sides of Barbra's vocal skills—clean fast comic diction and poignant, rhythmically free lyric interpretation. This cast album features more ensemble work and more solos from other cast members than does *Funny Girl*. A highlight for Streisand and for listeners is her duet with legend Louis Armstrong. *Hello, Dolly* is one of only a few Streisand albums that is not certified gold in record sales.

18. *Barbra Streisand's Greatest Hits*

Label and Number: Columbia, phonodisc KCS 9968, compact disc CK 9968, cassette JCT 00852

Date: December 1969

Producer: Robert Mersey, Ettore Stratta, Jack Gold, Warren Vincent

Arranger: Peter Matz, Michel Legrand, Don Costa

Don't Rain on My Parade (version 2); Bob Merrill, Jule Styne

Free Again (version 1); Robert Colby, Michel Jourdan, Armand Canfora, Joss Barelli

Gotta Move (version 1); Peter Matz

Happy Days Are Here Again (version 4, live); Jack Yellen, Milton Ager

He Touched Me (version 1); Ira Levin, Milton Schafer

My Coloring Book (version 1); Fred Ebb, John Kander

My Man (version 2); Maurice Yvain, Channing Pollock; *Ziegfeld Follies*

People (version 2); Jule Styne, Bob Merrill

Sam, You Made the Pants Too Long (version 2); Sam M. Lewis, Victor Young, Fred Whitehouse, Milton Berle

Second Hand Rose (version 1); Grant Clarke, James F. Hanley; *Ziegfeld Follies*

Why Did I Choose You? (version 1); Michael Leonard, Herbert Martin; *The Yearling*

"Greatest hits" albums are not uncommon in the popular music world, but it is relevant to note that, of the eleven songs included in this set, only one, "People," registered on the top-10 singles charts. Streisand's marketing strength relied on albums—not singles or even touring and top-40 radio broadcast time. In a sales strategy that Barbra would repeat over the years, *Greatest Hits* contains one number ("Sam, You Made the Pants Too Long) that was not found in its entirety on any other album (it appears in part during a medley on *Color Me Barbra* and was issued as a single). On 7 February 1970, *Billboard* included *Barbra Streisand's Greatest Hits* as one of its Spotlight Picks along with albums by Aretha Franklin (soul), James Brown (soul/funk), Chicago (progressive rock), and Bill Deal and the Rhondels (singles hits). In 1969 Streisand also performed briefly at the International Hotel in Las Vegas; some of that material was issued on *Just for the Record* in 1991 (#44).

19. *On a Clear Day You Can See Forever* (film)

Label and Number: Columbia, compact disc CK 57377, cassette CT 57377

Date: July 1970

Producer: Wally Gold

Arranger: Nelson Riddle

Go to Sleep; Burton Lane, Alan Jay Lerner

He Isn't You; Burton Lane, Alan Jay Lerner

Hurry, It's Lovely Up Here; Burton Lane, Alan Jay Lerner

Love With All the Trimmings; Burton Lane, Alan Jay Lerner

On a Clear Day (You Can See Forever) (Reprise) (version 1); Burton Lane, Alan Jay Lerner

What Did I Have That I Don't Have?; Burton Lane, Alan Jay Lerner

The reincarnation story of *Clear Day* provided Streisand the opportunity to play a variety of characters with contrasting dialects and personalities— compare "Go to Sleep" with "He Isn't You." Several songs exhibit her skill with detailed tone coloring to enhance individual words or phrases ("Hurry It's Lovely" or "What Did I Have?," for example). Unlike *Hello, Dolly*, this soundtrack clearly features Barbra; Yves Montand is the only other cast member heard. The show's title song was a hit for Streisand; she has recorded at least three different versions of it (see Appendix B), and a collectible single is extant that has a substantially different orchestral accompaniment and vocal arrangement (see chapter 3). Morgan Ames, writing for *High Fidelity Magazine*, felt that the stand-alone success of the soundtrack album was a credit to Nelson Riddle's arrangements (see bibliography). Harry Stradling, who was responsible for the photography of all three of Streisand's early film musicals and who Barbra admired, died shortly after this production. It was directed by Vincente Minnelli, the father of Liza and one-time husband of Judy Garland. In the following year, Streisand's first non-musical film was released. A soundtrack from *The Owl and the Pussycat* was issued by Columbia, but it does not include any singing from Barbra. Her audience was ready for the comedy and story-line variety *Owl* provided. In June 1971 *Mad Magazine* writers had suggested that Barbra's films were beginning to look and sound the same; they published a satire entitled "On a Clear Day You Can See a Funny Girl Singing 'Hello Dolly' Forever." Barbra sensed the need for more control, too; she and Paul Newman and Sidney Poitier formed First Artists Production Co., Ltd. in June of 1969.

20. *Stoney End*

Label and Number: Columbia, phonodisc KC 30378, compact disc CK 30378, cassette PCT 30378

Date: October 1970

Producer: Richard Perry

Arranger: Gene Page, Perry Botkin Jr., Claus Ogerman

Free the People; Barbara Keith

Hands Off the Man (Flim Flam Man); Laura Nyro

I Don't Know Where I Stand; Joni Mitchell

I'll Be Home; Randy Newman

If You Could Read My Mind; Gordon Lightfoot

Just a Little Lovin' (Early in the Mornin'); Barry Mann, Cynthia Weil

Let Me Go; Randy Newman

Maybe; Harry Nilsson

No Easy Way Down; Gerry Goffin, Carole King

Stoney End (version 1); Laura Nyro

Time and Love; Laura Nyro

Richard Perry's credit as producer signals the significant change in style heard on this album as do the names of contributing arrangers and composers. Streisand had experimented previously with a rock-oriented sound (singles "Our Corner of the Night" and "Frank Mills" from *Hair*), but this album exhibits a more marked entrance into the soft-rock or folk-rock arena. Stronger backbeats, electronic instrument sounds, and more frequent use of back-up singers clearly are evident. The title song of the album did well on singles sales charts. Nevertheless, many of Barbra's vocal techniques and interpretive methods remain consistent from previous albums, the possible exception being that she uses less of her belt sound here. While these songs were not written for use in shows, Streisand still approaches some as songs with character-development possibilities ("Hands Off the Man"). She seems most comfortable with and strongest on those that have a slight gospel or bluesy feel in the arrangement ("Just a Little Lovin"). In March of 1971, Barbra appeared as a guest on *The Burt Bacharach Special* on CBS television. They sang a duet of "They Long to Be Close to You," which was a number-1 hit for the Carpenters in the summer of 1970 (see #44). The following summer Barbra Streisand was divorced from Elliott Gould.

21. *Barbra Joan Streisand*

Label and Number: Columbia, phonodisc KC 30792, compact disc CK 30792, cassette PCT 30792

Date: August 1971

Producer: Richard Perry

Arranger: Nick DeCaro, Fanny, Dick Hazard, Kenny Welch, Peter Matz, Gene Page, Richard Perry, Head

Beautiful; Carole King

I Mean to Shine; D. Fagen, W. Becker

I Never Meant to Hurt You; Laura Nyro

Love; John Lennon

Mother; John Lennon

Since I Fell for You (version 1); Buddy Johnson

Space Captain; M. Moore

Summer Knows, The; Alan Bergman, Marilyn Bergman, Michel Legrand

Where You Lead (version 1); Carole King, Toni Stern

You've Got a Friend; Carole King

medley:

House Is Not a Home, A; Hal David, Burt Bacharach

One Less Bell to Answer; Hal David, Burt Bacharach

Barbra Joan is the second Streisand album produced by Richard Perry, and it continues to reflect the style transition noted previously. Liner credits also reveal a greater number of females associated with this album's creation, although that did not continue as a trend in Streisand's recording productivity. Additional soul- or gospel-influenced sound is heard here, and Billy Preston plays the organ on some selections. Contrast is provided by gentle ballads such as John Lennon's "Love." Perhaps a hint of autobiography is suggested in "Mother" and "Space Captain." Barbra does not completely abandon her earlier style, however, as noticed in the 1940s torch song "Since I Fell for You" and the Peter Matz arrangement of the Bacharach/David medley. As the movie-industry technique of associating contemporary pop songs with non-musical films was becoming more wide spread, "The Summer Knows" represents one of the first contemporaneous film songs Barbra recorded that was not from a movie in which she starred. It allowed her to work with the Legrand/Bergman/Bergman team that would be even more prominent in her career in the 1980s and 90s. *Barbra Joan* received the December 1971 *Stereo Review* "Recording of Special Merit" designation for her skill in interpreting a variety of musical styles. One of the most interesting aspects of the original album issue is the cover art. Barbra uses the professional spelling of her first name above a photograph of her that reflects uncertainty, while the back cover photograph shows a contented or childlike Streisand with her name spelled Barbara— the spelling used in her youth.

22. *Live Concert at the Forum* (live)

Label and Number: Columbia, phonodisc KC 31760, compact disc CM 31760
Date: October 1972
Producer: Richard Perry
Arranger: Don Hannah, Don Costa, Peter Matz, Claus Ogerman, Gene Page

Didn't We?; Jimmy Webb
Don't Rain on My Parade (version 3); Bob Merrill, Jule Styne
My Man (version 4); Maurice Yvain, Channing Pollock; *Ziegfeld Follies*
On a Clear Day (You Can See Forever) (version 2); Alan Jay Lerner, Burton Lane
People (version 5); Bob Merrill, Jule Styne
Starting Here, Starting Now (version 2); Richard Maltby Jr., David Shire
Stoney End (version 2); Laura Nyro
medley:
  Make Your Own Kind of Music (version 1); Barry Mann, Cynthia Weil
  Sing (version 1); Joe Raposo
medley:
  Sweet Inspiration (version 1); Dan Penn, Spooner Oldham
  Where You Lead (version 2); Carole King, Toni Stern
medley:
  Happy Days Are Here Again (version 5); Jack Yellen, Milton Ager
  Sing (version 2); Joe Raposo

Barbra had participated in a peace concert in 1968 and her *What About Today?* album featured lyrics with social commentary, but she had not yet made significant political statements. That situation changed when she agreed to be the final singer in a concert to raise money for the presidential campaign of Senator George McGovern in 1972. The concert also featured James Taylor and Carole King, who had two albums in that year's top 10. Streisand's performance resulted in her first concert album since *Happening* in 1968 (#15). The autobiography and advocacy category of her repertoire becomes even more prominent during the concert: she sang one of Jason's favorite songs from *Sesame Street*. Otherwise much of the repertoire might be classified as "greatest hits," although some songs sound updated with more contemporary instrumentation. Her arrangement of "Sweet Inspiration" begins with a slow, lyric verse and then (following "Where You Lead") launches into an up-tempo soul-style segment. The song originally was recorded by the Sweet Inspirations, which included Cissy Houston, and did well on the 1968 R & B chart. That ensemble also sang backup for Aretha Franklin and Elvis Presley. Streisand performs "Sweet Inspiration" at a slightly faster tempo than heard on the group's original performance. During 1972 two more of her films were released: *What's Up Doc?* and *Up the Sandbox* (from First Artists). A theme song was recorded for *Sandbox*, but it was dropped from the film. The recording appears on *Just for the Record* (#44).

23. *Barbra Streisand and Other Musical Instruments* (television special)

Label and Number: Columbia, phonodisc KC 32655, compact disc CK 32655, cassette PCT 32655

Date: October 1973

Producer: Martin Erlichman

Arranger: Ken Welch, Mitzie Welch

Auf dem Wasser zu singen; Franz Schubert, Ken Welch, Mitzie Welch

By Myself (version 2); Howard Dietz, Arthur Schwartz

Come Back to Me; Alan Jay Lerner, Burton Lane; *On a Clear Day*

Don't Ever Leave Me; Jerome Kern, Oscar Hammerstein II; *Sweet Adeline*

I Never Has Seen Snow; Harold Arlen, Truman Capote; *House of Flowers*

Sweetest Sounds, The; Richard Rodgers; *No Strings*

medley:

   Don't Rain on My Parade (version 4); Jule Styne, Bob Merrill; *Funny Girl*

   Glad to Be Unhappy; Richard Rodgers, Lorenz Hart; *On Your Toes*

   I Got Rhythm; George Gershwin, Ira Gershwin; *Girl Crazy*

   Johnny One Note; Lorenz Hart, Richard Rodgers; *Babes in Arms*

   One Note Samba; Antonio Carlos Jobin, N. Mendonca, Jon Hendricks

   People (version 6); Jule Styne, Bob Merrill; *Funny Girl*

Piano Practicing; Lan O'Kun

Second Hand Rose (version 4); Grant Clarke, James F. Hanley; *Ziegfeld Follies* medley:

Make Your Own Kind of Music (version 2); Barry Mann, Cynthia Weil

World Is a Concerto, The; Ken Welch, Mitzie Welch

This is a soundtrack of sorts from one of the less successful of Streisand's specials made for television—although the production team still included Dwight Hemion, Joe Layton, and Martin Erlichman (who appears as the washing machine player in the concerto). During the Friday, 2 November 1973 CBS special, she sang several new songs, but some of the material might be described as new, ethnic stylings of old hits. From a vocal technique point of view, the most interesting performance is "I Never Has Seen Snow" (see comments in chapter 3). Peter Reilly observed that the production might have been overdone but that one of Barbra's "gifts" was the ability to make something rehearsed in detail sound improvised and "spontaneous as ever" (see bibliography). *TV Guide* reported that Jack Parnell conducted the orchestra, and another eclectic singer Ray Charles joined Barbra as a guest star. Their duet of "Crying Time" was not released on this soundtrack but was included on her 1991 *Just for the Record* (#44).

24. *Barbra Streisand: The Way We Were*

Label and Number: Columbia, phonodisc PC 32801, compact disc CK 57381, cassette CT 57381

Date: January 1974

Producer: Tommy LiPuma, Marty Paich, Wally Gold

Arranger: Nick DeCaro, Marty Paich

All in Love Is Fair (version 1); Stevie Wonder

Being at War With Each Other; Carole King

Best Thing You've Ever Done, The; Martin Charnin

I've Never Been a Woman Before; T. Baird, R. Miller

Pieces of Dreams; Alan Bergman, Marilyn Bergman, Michel Legrand

Something So Right; Paul Simon

Summer Me, Winter Me; Alan Bergman, Marilyn Bergman, Michel Legrand

Way We Were, The (version 2); Alan Bergman, Marilyn Bergman, Marvin Hamlisch

What Are You Doing the Rest of Your Life? (version 1); Alan Bergman, Marilyn Bergman, Michel Legrand

medley:

How About Me?; Irving Berlin

My Buddy; Gus Kahn, Walter Donaldson

The title of this album sometimes appears without Streisand's name in front of the movie/song title, but the double name is one way to distinguish it from the film soundtrack (#25). (The black caftan she wears in the cover photo originally was planned as a costume for *The Way We Were* but was discarded.) The repertoire of this set clearly shows that Barbra was not headed down a soft-rock path wearing blinders. Rather, her recordings would find her exploring an eclectic assortment of popular song. She brought her theatrical approach to melody-based, contemporary pop ballads, which were newly written but reminiscent of pre-rock standards. She recorded material that would suit a club or concert stage at the same time she was retreating from live vocal performance. This album features a single of the theme song "The Way We Were," but its arrangement is by Marty Paich rather than Marvin Hamlisch (who arranged it for use with the movie). Otherwise the thick harmonies and sensitive lyrics of the Legrand/Bergman/Bergman threesome are contrasted with the styles of Stevie Wonder, Carole King, and Paul Simon. A writer for *Creem* found Simon's "Something So Right" to be the best crafted song of the album (see bibliography). The song also shows Streisand's growing comfort with melismatic embellishment, although she never decorates melodies as much as several popular female singers of the 1980s and 1990s. Most of the songs included on this recording fit in either the love ballad or torch song categories and, therefore, allow Barbra to use her polished, mature timbre to color words and vary dynamics.

25. *The Way We Were* (film)

Label and Number: Columbia, phonodisc KS 32830, 8 track SA 32830, cassette ST 32830

Date: January 1974

Producer: Fred Salem

Arranger: Marvin Hamlisch

Way We Were, The (version 1); Alan Bergman, Marilyn Bergman, Marvin Hamlisch

Way We Were, The (Reprise); Alan Bergman, Marilyn Bergman, Marvin Hamlisch

Of primary interest on this soundtrack is Streisand's recording of the film's theme song. It eventually reaped an Academy Award and a Grammy for its creators and a number-1 hit for Barbra—her first since "People" ten years earlier. Although Marvin Hamlisch had worked as a rehearsal pianist for *Funny Girl* on Broadway, Streisand and Hamlisch had not worked together since. This film co-starred Robert Redford, was directed by Sydney

Pollock, and has remained one of Streisand's most popular movies. It also brought her an Academy Award nomination as Best Actress. According to *The Top Ten* by Gilbert and Theroux, the other top singles of 1974 following Streisand's ballad were "Come and Get Your Love" by Redbone, "Seasons in the Sun" by Terry Jacks, "Show and Tell" by Al Wilson, and "Love's Theme" from the Love Unlimited Orchestra.

26. *ButterFly*

Label and Number: Columbia, phonodisc PC 33005, 8 track CK 33005, compact disc CK 33005, cassette PCT 33005

Date: October 1974

Producer: Jon Peters

Arranger: Tom Scott, John Bahler, Lee Holdridge

Cryin' Time (version 2); Buck Owens

Grandma's Hands; Bill Withers

Guava Jelly; Bob Marley

I Won't Last a Day Without You; Paul Williams, Roger Nichols

Jubilation; Paul Anka, J. Harris

Let the Good Times Roll; L. Lee

Life on Mars; David Bowie

Love in the Afternoon; B. Weisman, E. Sands, R. Germinaro

Simple Man; Graham Nash

Since I Don't Have You; Lennie Martin, Joseph Rock, John Taylor, James Beaumont, Janet Vogel, Joseph Verscharen, Walter Lester

Barbra's personal life is clearly reflected in the production of this album. She was just beginning a long relationship with Jon Peters, who is credited as producer, and several photographs of the two adorn the liner. The list of composers represented also shows her continued interest in a variety of repertoire from old standards to reggae-influenced material to a song by country performer Buck Owens to the gospel-inflected "Jubilation." In fact, many of the arrangements exhibit hints of gospel style, similar to those heard on her previous soft-rock albums, or jazz inflections, which, in part, were brought to Barbra from the experience of arranger Tom Scott. On the other hand, some reviewers remarked that "I Won't Last a Day Without You" was the best performance on the album because it allowed Barbra to create an emotional story within a pop ballad setting. Confirming the notion of variety they also noted the influence of Aretha Franklin in Streisand's gospel/soul sounds. Ben Gerson wrote that she always has been a precise singer but that some of this material suffers from too much precision (see bibliography). This album is ranked gold by the Record Industry Association of America, but Streisand commented to Larry King in February of 1992 that it is the one she might like to withdraw from circulation. In 1974 Barbra's next film, a romantic comedy, *For Pete's Sake*, was released; it was produced by her manager, Martin Erlichman, under the Rastar (Ray Stark) banner. She had met Jon Peters when he was asked to design a wig for her character, Henrietta. Barbra recorded a theme song, entitled "For Pete's Sake Don't Let Him Down," for the film, but it has never appeared on a Streisand album.

27. *Funny Lady* (film)

Label and Number: Arista, phonodisc AL 9004

Date: March 1975

Producer: Peter Matz

Arranger: Peter Matz

Am I Blue?; Grant Clarke, Harry Akst

Blind Date (ensemble); Fred Ebb, John Kander

How Lucky Can You Get? (ensemble); Fred Ebb, John Kander

I Found a Million Dollar Baby (In a Five & Ten Cent Store); Billy Rose, Mort Dixon, Harry Warren

I Got a Code in My Doze; Billy Rose, Arthur Fields, Fred Hall

If I Love Again; Jack P. Murray, Ben Oakland

Isn't This Better?; Fred Ebb, John Kander

It's Gonna Be a Great Day; Billy Rose, Edward Eliscu, Vincent Youmans

Let's Hear It for Me; Fred Ebb, John Kander

More Than You Know (version 2); Billy Rose, Edward Eliscu, Vincent Youmans

So Long, Honey Lamb (ensemble); Fred Ebb, John Kander

medley:

   I Like Him/I Like Her (ensemble); Fred Ebb, John Kander

   It's Only a Paper Moon (ensemble); Billy Rose, E. Y. Harburg, Harold Arlen

Funny Lady is the film sequel to Streisand's first movie about the life (partially fictionalized) of Fanny Brice; it is rather traditional in its storyline and musical style and provides great contrast to Barbra's next film venture (see #30). Herbert Ross, who had been the choreographer and musical director for *Funny Girl*, also directed and choreographed *Lady*. This film completed Barbra's film commitment to producer Ray Stark; the soundtrack is one of a handful of Streisand albums not on the Columbia label. Some new music was written for the movie, while other songs were borrowed from the film's time period and from Billy Rose, the real-life second husband of Fanny Brice. Those familiar with the movie recall that Billy proposes to Fanny by way of a model of Casa Mañana, part of the set he planned for use at the Texas Centennial. (The Centennial was a big success, and in real life Fanny Brice visited the production in 1936. Billy Rose's papers are held by the New York Public Library.) The score of *Funny Lady* brought Barbra and Peter Matz back together as did a premiere viewing and concert at the Kennedy Center in Washington, which was presented as an ABC television special and as a benefit for the Special Olympics. (The show did not do well in television ratings; regular fare of the day such as "All in the Family," "Good Times," "Kojak," "The Waltons," and "M*A*S*H" all ranked substantially higher.) For fans that missed Barbra's stage work, some of the show-within-a-show sequences of this movie might fill that need vicariously; the score certainly allowed her to display her varied interpretive skills from ethnic/comic teaser to torch dramatist to gospel-inspired belter. Ben Vareen, who portrayed *Ziegfeld Follies* star Bert Williams, and James Caan, as Billy Rose, also are heard on the soundtrack. Omar Sharif returned to the movie in a few scenes as Nick Arnstein but is not heard on the album.

28. *Lazy Afternoon*

Label and Number: Columbia, phonodisc PC 33815, compact disc CK 33815, cassette PCT 33815

Date: October 1975

Producer: Rupert Holmes, Jeffrey Lesser

Arranger: Rupert Holmes

By the Way (version 1); **Barbra Streisand**, Rupert Holmes

Child Is Born, A; Alan Bergman, Marilyn Bergman

I Never Had It So Good; Paul Williams, Roger Nichols

Lazy Afternoon (version 1); John LaTouche, Jerome Moross; *Golden Apple*

Letters That Cross in the Mail; Rupert Holmes

Moanin' Low; Howard Dietz, Ralph Rainger; *The Little Show*

My Father's Song; Rupert Holmes

Shake Me Wake Me (When It's Over); Brian Holland, Lamont Dozier, Eddie Holland

Widescreen; Rupert Holmes

You and I; Stevie Wonder

Unlike some of her other albums, this one finds Barbra in the hands of one primary arranger, Rupert Holmes, even though the repertoire is varied again in style. The arrangements exhibit a mix of contemporary pop techniques with lush orchestral/electronic settings. Several of the lyrics contain developmental possibilities that allow Barbra to work as an actress. Holmes wrote one of the songs in partnership with Barbra and wrote another to reflect her thoughts about her father, who had died when she was a baby. Streisand provided such information through the autobiographical liner notes. Her performance of the disco-like "Shake Me, Wake Me" shows that she can sing squarely on the beat when necessary. Otherwise the mood of the songs is mostly characterized by the title track. *Audio* magazine's 1976 review of the album mentions that it is available in "quadraphonic" sound for $7.98; it also could be purchased in the 8-track and cassette formats. Her success among her legion of fans continued to be reflected by her receipt of the People's Choice Award of 1975 for both Favorite Movie Actress and Favorite Female Singer.

29. *Classical Barbra*

Label and Number: Columbia, phonodisc M 33452, compact disc MK 33452, cassette MT 33452

Date: February 1976

Producer: Claus Ogerman

Arranger: Claus Ogerman

Après un rêve; Gabriel Fauré, Romain Bussine

Beau Soir; Claude Debussy, Paul Bourget

Brezairola; Joseph Canteloube

Dank sei dir, Herr; George F. Handel, Claus Ogerman

I Loved You; Claus Ogerman, Alexander Pushkin

In Trutina; Carl Orff

Lascia Ch'io Pianga; George F. Handel, Giacomo Rossi

Mondnacht; Robert Schumann, Joseph von Eichendorff

Pavane; Gabriel Fauré, Claus Ogerman

Verschwiegene Liebe; Hugo Wolf, Joseph von Eichendorff

Streisand's eclecticism is nowhere more evident than on her album of classical songs, which she reportedly considered entitling *Classical Barbra: A Work in Progress*. (She had begun work on and recorded the songs several months before the album was issued.) Claus Ogerman, who had previously worked with her on contemporary pop albums (see #20 and #22), served, for better or worse, as producer and arranger (and composer in one instance). Full orchestral arrangements are provided even for some songs that were originally written for voice and piano. As can be observed in the bibliography of reviews that follows, considerable print space was devoted to assessing this collection. Because of the repertoire, periodicals such as *Opera News* provided a review even though its writers usually would ignore Streisand's recordings. Her selection of material is interesting in that it centers around popular repertoire of this milieu; many listeners might be familiar with the songs. She sings in several languages with the emphasis on French, a language she had sung on *Je m'appelle Barbra* in the mid-1960s (see #11). In general her vocal style seems subdued, focusing on a rather pure and soft tone color. Many years later, Streisand was said to have commented on the rhythmic discipline needed to sing classical songs—even though on some of these selections she varies from the printed notation more than a typical classical vocal instructor would allow (*New York Times*, 10 November 1985, 2:1). Crossing over traditional lines (some would say barriers) of musical style was not new—consider Marilyn Horne or Leonard Bernstein, but it would become more commonplace in subsequent decades. In hindsight this album confirms how Streisand puts her own stamp on any repertoire (a trait of popular song) and how she brought a greater sense of classical finesse to popular-song performance technique.

30. *A Star Is Born* (film)

Label and Number: Columbia, phonodisc JS 34403, compact disc CK 57375, cassette CT 57375

Date: November 1976

Producer: **Barbra Streisand**, Phil Ramone

Arranger: unavailable

Everything; Rupert Holmes, Paul Williams

I Believe in Love; Kenny Loggins, Alan Bergman, Marilyn Bergman

Lost Inside of You (version 1, ensemble); **Barbra Streisand**, Leon Russell

Love Theme From "A Star Is Born" (Evergreen) (version 1); **Barbra Streisand**, Paul Williams

Love Theme From "A Star Is Born" (Evergreen) (Reprise) (version 2, ensemble); **Barbra Streisand**, Paul Williams

Queen Bee; Rupert Holmes

Woman in the Moon, The; Paul Williams, Kenny Ascher

medley:

    Watch Closely Now; Paul Williams, Kenny Ascher

    With One More Look at You; Paul Williams, Kenny Ascher

This soundtrack, for which Barbra is listed as producer (her first such credit), was released in advance of the movie as a means of promotion. Streisand's version of the film was the third (she is listed as Executive Producer, Jon Peters as Producer); there also is a 1932 non-musical production and one from 1954 starring Judy Garland. Eventually Streisand's album would become the number-five top seller of 1977, the theme song would reach number three for the year, and "Evergreen" would bring another Academy Award to Streisand, this time as composer along with Paul Williams. As a love ballad it contradicts the rock world of the film's story, and it developed out of guitar lessons Streisand took in preparation for the film. "Evergreen" also garnered Barbra additional Grammy Awards as both Song of the Year and Best Pop Vocal Performance—Female. Rupert Holmes, who arranged and conducted her *Lazy Afternoon* album (#28), also contributed to this score. Phil Ramone, who was responsible for the sound on *A Happening in Central Park* (#15), was involved in recording sound for some scenes in this movie as well. Ramone later told the story of how Barbra was received by one of the rock audiences attending a concert they produced to get footage for the film: "the crowd just melted. . . . It was one of the most spontaneous and creative moments you could experience" (*Billboard*, 11 May 1996, PR-24). The film did well at the box office despite several negative reviews and pre-release press reports. Kris Kristofferson played the male lead opposite Streisand; Elvis Presley had been asked to play the role in what turned out to be the final years of his life—a life with tragic similarity to the movie's plot.

31. *Streisand Superman*

Label and Number: Columbia, phonodisc PC 34830, compact disc CK 34830, cassette PCT 34830

Date: June 1977

Producer: Gary Klein

Arranger: Nick DeCaro, Larry Carlton, Jack Nitzsche, Charlie Calello

Answer Me; **Barbra Streisand**, Paul Williams, Kenny Ascher

Baby Me Baby; Roger Miller

Cabin Fever; Ron Nagle

Don't Believe What You Read; Ron Nagle, **Barbra Streisand**, Scott Matthews

I Found You Love; Alan Gordon

Love Comes From Unexpected Places; Kim Carnes, Dave Ellingson

Lullaby for Myself; Rupert Holmes

My Heart Belongs to Me (version 1); Alan Gordon

New York State of Mind (version 1); Billy Joel

Superman (version 1); Richie Snyder

For this album, Barbra returned to contemporary pop and began to use music (and album liner notes) to more directly let her followers know what was on her mind. "Don't Believe What You Read" was written at her request (and she also receives composer credit) to answer a press story that she allowed birds to fly around inside her home. Contemporary social issues also are reflected in lyrics such as "Cabin Fever." "My Heart Belongs to Me" was successful as a single and helped boost album sales to a platinum rating. Several reviewers of this album commented on Streisand's need for intelligent lyrics to match her interpretive tendencies and sophisticated technique; they found few in this set. Likewise they began to notice the loyalty of Barbra's fan base whether her material matched her talents or not. Peter Reilly wrote, "[F]or if the phenomenon that is Streisand *could* be finally explained, wouldn't we be robbing ourselves of a lot of future joy and amazement?" (see bibliography).

32. *Songbird*

Label and Number: Columbia, phonodisc JC 35375, compact disc CK 35375, cassette PCT 35375

Date: May 1978

Producer: Gary Klein

Arranger: David Wolfert, Gene Page, Jerry Hey, Larry Williams, Alan Gordon, Nick DeCaro, James Newton Howard, Bill Reichenbach, George Michalski, Niki Oosterveen, Larry Carlton, John Tropea, Lee Holdridge

Deep in the Night; H. Miller, E. Merriam

Honey, Can I Put on Your Clothes?; J. Monte Ray, J. Leiber, M. Stroller

I Don't Break Easily; B. Roberts

Love Breakdown; Alan Gordon

Man I Loved, A; Niki Oosterveen, George Michalski

One More Night; S. Bishop

Songbird (version 1); Dave Wolfert, Stephen Nelson

Stay Away; Kim Carnes

Tomorrow; Charles Strouse, Martin Charnin; *Annie*

You Don't Bring Me Flowers (version 1); Neil Diamond, Alan Bergman, Marilyn Bergman

This is the second album in a row produced by Gary Klein, and it continues with contemporary pop songs, many with a danceable beat. Among the long list of arrangers engaged for this effort is James Newton Howard, who later would compose the score for Streisand's movie *The Prince of Tides*. As always, belt or torch songs are included ("Deep in the Night" and "Stay Away"), and some material clearly is not designed for radio play ("Honey, Can I Put on Your Clothes?" is more than five minutes in length). Her version of the familiar "Tomorrow" is quite different (easy and relaxed) than performances listeners might know as sung by a child in the show *Annie*. Streisand's solo version of "You Don't Bring Me Flowers" is included and allows her to exhibit her dramatic ballad strengths; her more famous duet version (with Neil Diamond) appears on her next collection.

The same month *Songbird* was released Barbra sang on a television special marking the 30th anniversary of the founding of Israel.

33. *Barbra Streisand's Greatest Hits, Volume 2*

Label and Number: Columbia, phonodisc FC 35679, compact disc CK 35679, cassette FCT 35679

Date: November 1978

Producer: **Barbra Streisand**, Phil Ramone, Gary Klein, Charlie Calello, Bob Gaudio, Tommy LiPuma, Marty Paich, Richard Perry

Arranger: Charlie Calello, Larry Carlton, Nick DeCaro, Alan Lindgren, Marty Paich, Don Hannah, Gene Page

All in Love Is Fair (version 1); Stevie Wonder

Love Theme From "A Star Is Born" (Evergreen) (version 1); **Barbra Streisand**, Paul Williams

Love Theme From "Eyes of Laura Mars" (Prisoner); Karen Lawrence, John Desautels

My Heart Belongs to Me (version 1); Alan Gordon

Songbird (version 1); Dave Wolfert, Stephen Nelson

Stoney End (version 1); Laura Nyro

Superman (version 1); R. Snyder

Way We Were, The (version 2); Marvin Hamlisch, Alan Bergman, Marilyn Bergman

You Don't Bring Me Flowers (version 1, duet Neil Diamond); Neil Diamond, Alan Bergman, Marilyn Bergman

medley:

  Sweet Inspiration (version 1, live); Dan Penn, Spooner Oldham

  Where You Lead (version 2, live); Carole King, Toni Stern

Streisand ended the decade of the 1970s on a musical high note. She had three songs on the 1979 top-40 list: "You Don't Bring Me Flowers" (the duet version included here), "The Main Event," and "No More Tears" (see the following two albums). Few could argue her continued success and her ability to adjust to the times without losing the essentials of her musical identity. Many years later, Barbra's stature in the pop-rock world of the 1970s was acknowledged in a textbook on rock and roll. Authors Michael Campbell and James Brody discussed her leadership in the "gold record" category (over the Beatles and Elton John) and the importance of "pop-oriented stars" in the musical landscape of the time (*Rock and Roll: An Introduction*, New York: Schirmer Books, 1999).

Following the marketing strategy introduced with her earlier "greatest hits" album (#18), this one contains material not previously released: the

"Flowers" duet and the theme song from *The Eyes of Laura Mars*, a film produced by Jon Peters and starring Faye Dunaway. Peters continued to make a name for himself as a movie producer—among his hits was *Batman*. *Volume Two* also achieved a platinum sales rating and is different from her first "hits" set in its inclusion of several songs that did well as singles including "Evergreen," "The Way We Were," and "Stoney End." See my comments in chapter 4 about Streisand's televised duet with Diamond on the Grammy Awards show in 1980. Barbra and Neil received a Grammy in the Best Pop Vocal Performance by a Duo or Group for their recording.

34. *The Main Event* (film)

Label and Number: Columbia, phonodisc JS 36115, compact disc CK 57376, cassette CT 57376

Date: June 1979

Producer: Gary LeMel, Bob Esty

Arranger: Bob Esty

Main Event, The (Ballad); Paul Jabara, Bruce Roberts

Main Event, The/Fight (version 1); Paul Jabara, Bruce Roberts, Bob Esty

Main Event, The/Fight (Short Version); Paul Jabara, Bruce Roberts, Bob Esty

This soundtrack is instructive for comparing Barbra's style with contrasting versions of the same song! The "short version" became a big disco hit and was popular in aerobic classes. The movie reunited Streisand with Ryan O'Neal, who was paired with her in *What's Up Doc?* in 1972. This was Barbra's final film for First Artists; it also was owned in part by her production and development company, Barwood (Barbra + Hollywood).

35. *Wet*

Label and Number: Columbia, phonodisc FC 36258, compact disc CK 36258, cassette FCT 36258

Date: October 1979

Producer: Gary Klein

Arranger: Lee Holdridge, Greg Mathieson, David Foster, Bill Champlin, Lalo Schifrin, Bruce Roberts, Paul Jabara, Luther Waters, Nick DeCaro, Charlie Calello

After the Rain; Alan Bergman, Marilyn Bergman, Michel Legrand

Come Rain or Come Shine; Johnny Mercer, Harold Arlen; *St. Louis Woman*

I Ain't Gonna Cry Tonight; Alan Gordon

Kiss Me in the Rain; S. Farina, L. Ratner

Niagara; Marvin Hamlisch, Carole Bayer Sager, Bruce Roberts

No More Tears (Enough Is Enough) (version 1, duet Donna Summer); Paul Jabara, Bruce Roberts

On Rainy Afternoons; Alan Bergman, Marilyn Bergman, Lalo Schifrin

Splish Splash; Bobby Darin, Jean Murray, **Barbra Streisand**

Wet; Dave Wolfert, S. Sheridan, **Barbra Streisand**

Wet brought Barbra and Gary Klein back together, but the repertoire is more diverse than the other albums he produced for her in the 1970s. Again a whole stable of arrangers was employed, some used only for the various layers common in pop studio arrangements. All of the songs on the album make some reference to water; two come from the pens of the Legrand/Bergman/Bergman team. In the following year, Barbra sang at an ACLU benefit/tribute to her friends the Bergmans. (She sang "The Way We Were" and a discarded song from that film that never was recorded. It was included later on her retrospective boxed set, #44). Streisand is also reunited with material from Marvin Hamlisch, Paul Jabara (from "The Main Event"), and Harold Arlen. Her duet with Donna Summer was significantly different in style than her duet with Neil Diamond, but both were very successful. Streisand fans are well aware of the story regarding the teaming of Streisand and Summer; apparently Donna was a favorite singer of Barbra's son, Jason. Summer's *Bad Girls* album was a top seller of 1979. The sheet music from "Kiss Me in the Rain" was published by Cortlandt Music, Emanuel Music Corp. (Barbra's company named after her late father), and Bandier-Koppelman, Inc. The notation of the rhythm, likely an attempt to notate her performance, shows the recitative-like or parlando manner with which she approaches texts, especially a verse leading to a refrain, although her recording contains even more metric fluidity than shown in the notation.

36. *Guilty*

Label and Number: Columbia, phonodisc FC 36750, compact disc CK 36750, cassette FCT 36750

Date: October 1980

Producer: Barry Gibb, Albhy Galuten, Karl Richardson

Arranger: Albhy Galuten, Barry Gibb, Peter Graves

Guilty (version 1, duet Barry Gibb); Barry Gibb, Maurice Gibb, Robin Gibb

Life Story; Barry Gibb, Robin Gibb

Love Inside, The (version 1); Barry Gibb

Make It Like a Memory; Barry Gibb, Albhy Galuten

Never Give Up; Barry Gibb, Albhy Galuten

Promises; Barry Gibb, Robin Gibb

Run Wild; Barry Gibb, Robin Gibb

What Kind of Fool? (version 1, duet Barry Gibb); Barry Gibb, Albhy Galuten

Woman in Love (version 1); Barry Gibb, Robin Gibb

Like her *Lazy Afternoon* album of 1975, *Guilty* put Barbra in the care of one primary composer/arranger. In this case it was Barry Gibb of the Bee Gees, who was at the peak of his career with albums such as *Saturday Night Fever* and *Spirits Having Flown*. His success continued with *Guilty*, and Barbra has acknowledged it as her most successful album to that time. Barry appeared with her several years later for her *One Voice* concert, which was eventually issued as an album (#41) and video. The lyrics of the songs on *Guilty* are not as story-line oriented as much of the repertoire Streisand usually seeks, and the accompaniments are multi-layered with extensive electronic sounds, complex percussion, and lyric strings (see chapter 4). "Woman in Love" did well on the singles charts even though, according to Barry Gibb, Streisand originally had reservations about the "liberationist" nature of the lyric. Gibb also reported that all of the songs on the album were written for Barbra except "The Love Inside" (*Billboard*, 28 February 1991). At that year's Grammy Awards, the title song won for Best Pop Vocal Performance by a Duo or Group with Vocal; Barbra and Barry also delighted the audience by making the Grammy presentation in the Rock Vocal—Male category. This "presenter" role was not common for Streisand, but the Streisand/Gibb duo award actually had been presented during the pre-telecast part of the show, so the pair otherwise would not have had television exposure that evening. After the applauding audience quieted, Barbra asked Barry if he felt *guilty*. He said he didn't and wondered why she asked. She quipped that she felt like she was *cheating on Neil Diamond!* (see #33). "Guilty" and "Woman in Love" also were listed on the BMI "Most Performed Songs of 1980," and "Woman" charted number 1 in Canada, Britain, Australia, Holland, Belgium, Israel, South Africa, Norway, and Austria (*Billboard*, 6 December 1980).

37. *Memories*

Label and Number: Columbia, phonodisc TC 37678, compact disc CK 37678, cassette TCT 37678

Date: November 1981

Producer: Andrew Lloyd Webber, Bob Gaudio, Gary Klein, Charlie Calello, **Barbra Streisand**, Phil Ramone, Barry Gibb, Albhy Galuten, Carl Richardson, Marty Paich, Charles Koppelman

Arranger: unavailable

Comin' In and Out of Your Life (version 1); Richard Parker, Bobby Whiteside

Lost Inside of You (version 2); Leon Russell, **Barbra Streisand**

Love Inside, The (version 1); Barry Gibb

Love Theme From "A Star Is Born" (Evergreen) (version 1); **Barbra Streisand**, Paul Williams

Memory (version 1); Andrew Lloyd Webber, T. S. Eliot, Trevor Nunn; *Cats*

My Heart Belongs to Me (version 1); Alan Gordon

New York State of Mind (version 1); Billy Joel

No More Tears (Enough Is Enough) (version 1, duet Donna Summer); Paul Jabara, Bruce Roberts

Way We Were, The (version 2); Marvin Hamlisch, Alan Bergman, Marilyn Bergman

You Don't Bring Me Flowers (version 1, duet Neil Diamond); Neil Diamond, Alan Bergman, Marilyn Bergman

Four tracks are repeated on this collection from *Barbra Streisand's Greatest Hits, Vol. 2* (#33), while several other songs were "hits" in the interim years. Three new songs round out the set: "Memory" from *Cats* (a lyric song); a belt number "Comin' In and Out of Your Life"; and a solo version of the love ballad "Lost Inside of You," which had been sung as a duet with Kris Kristofferson in *A Star Is Born*. Critic Peter Reilly suggested that readers would have to decide whether $6 to $9 was reasonable to pay for only a few minutes of new material on the phonodisc, cassette, or 8-track; he revealed he'd pay up to $50 for the "Memory" track alone (see bibliography).

38. *Yentl* (film)

Label and Number: Columbia, phonodisc JS 39152, compact disc CK 39152, cassette JST 39152

Date: 1983

Producer: **Barbra Streisand**, Alan Bergman, Marilyn Bergman, Phil Ramone, Dave Grusin

Arranger: Michel Legrand

No Matter What Happens; Michel Legrand, Alan Bergman, Marilyn Bergman

No Matter What Happens (Studio Version); Michel Legrand, Alan Bergman, Marilyn Bergman

No Wonder; Michel Legrand, Alan Bergman, Marilyn Bergman

No Wonder (Part Two); Michel Legrand, Alan Bergman, Marilyn Bergman

No Wonder (Reprise); Michel Legrand, Alan Bergman, Marilyn Bergman

Papa, Can You Hear Me? (version 2); Michel Legrand, Alan Bergman, Marilyn Bergman

Piece of Sky, A (version 2); Michel Legrand, Alan Bergman, Marilyn Bergman

This Is One of Those Moments; Michel Legrand, Alan Bergman, Marilyn Bergman

Tomorrow Night; Michel Legrand, Alan Bergman, Marilyn Bergman

Way He Makes Me Feel, The; Michel Legrand, Alan Bergman, Marilyn Bergman

Way He Makes Me Feel, The (Studio Version); Michel Legrand, Alan Bergman, Marilyn Bergman

Where Is It Written? (version 1); Michel Legrand, Alan Bergman, Marilyn Bergman

Will Someone Ever Look at Me That Way? (version 1); Michel Legrand, Alan Bergman, Marilyn Bergman

In between her movies *The Main Event* and *Yentl*, Streisand took her first supporting role in the film *All Night Long*, a non-musical comedy starring Gene Hackman (non-musical, but audiences did get to hear Barbra's Cheryl character sing country western while playing the electric organ!). She played a blond-wigged, "Valley" wife who got involved with a man going through a mid-life crisis. The film was not commercially successful and provides great contrast (in both style and Streisand's involvement level) to her next project, *Yentl*. Barbra is the only singer heard on the soundtrack from her very personal film, since no other character in this "Film with Music" sings. That approach was determined by the story line in which the main character, Yentl, is living the secret of a young woman posing as a young man so she can attend a yeshiva. By having hers be the only singing voice, Yentl's inner thoughts are revealed to the observer through song rather than speech. To help her bring the musical part of her vision to fruition, Barbra called on her long-time friends and colleagues, Michel Legrand and Alan and Marilyn Bergman. The score eventually won an Academy Award, and the soundtrack, which some worried would be too "ethnic," is rated multi-platinum in sales. The album also contains two "studio" versions—arrangements with more contemporary rhythms and instrumentation than those used to create the "period" sound of the movie (although several critics wondered if the musical ethnicity of the score was clearly focused, see bibliography). The album and the film were released during the holiday shopping season of 1983, a common marketing strategy used with Streisand's products. The personal nature of and the controversy around *Yentl* caused Barbra to be listed as one of *People* magazine's "25 Most Intriguing People of 1982" (3 January 1983 issue), twenty years after she first came to the attention of the public and just after she celebrated her fortieth birthday.

39. *Emotion*

Label and Number: Columbia, phonodisc OC 39480, compact disc CK 39480, cassette OCT 39480

Date: 1984

Producer: Richard Perry, Bill Cuomo, Kim Carnes, Maurice White, Charles Koppelman, **Barbra Streisand**, Jim Steinman, Albhy Galuten, Richard Baskin

Arranger/Programmer: Peter Bliss, Bill Cuomo, Robbie Buchanan, Gary K. Chang, Maurice White, Martin Page, Brian Fairweather, Bobby Whiteside, Rory Dodd,

Holly Sherwood, Eric Troyer, Jim Steinman, Michel Colombier, Albhy Galuten, James Newton Howard, Lee Holdridge

Best I Could; Bobby Whiteside, Richard Parker

Clear Sailing; Peter McIan, Anne Black Montgomery

Emotion; Peter Bliss

Heart Don't Change My Mind; Diane Warren, Robbie Buchanan

Here We Are at Last (version 1); **Barbra Streisand**, Richard Baskin

Left in the Dark; Jim Steinman

Make No Mistake; He's Mine (duet Kim Carnes); Kim Carnes

Time Machine; Maurice White, Martin Page, Brian Fairweather

When I Dream; Michel Colombier, Kathy Wakefield, Richard Baskin

You're a Step in the Right Direction; John Cougar Mellencamp, **Barbra Streisand**

Streisand returned to contemporary pop for this album released on the heels of her successful film, *Yentl*. As noted in the list above, the album was produced, arranged, and programmed (an indication of how music technology was changing) by a host of participants, including Richard Baskin, Barbra's intermittent companion. The pair penned the love ballad "Here We Are at Last," and in the booklet she wrote to accompany *Just for the Record* (#44), Barbra reports that the melody originally was written for *The Main Event*. Of course, Kim Carnes already was a successful composer/performer in her own right ("Betty Davis Eyes") as was John Mellencamp. Maurice White was the driving force behind the eclectic big-band/rock/soul group Earth, Wind, and Fire, while Richard Perry and Albhy Galuten had contributed to earlier Streisand albums. She also made her first venture into the new media outlet, music videos, with "Left in the Dark" and the title track. Streisand's faithful legion of fans made the album a commercial success, but it was a disappointment to many critics following the material of *Guilty*. Barbra has had little to say about *Emotion*, especially since she was already thinking seriously about returning to her musical roots. Nevertheless, 1984 was an award-filled year for Barbra. She began to be recognized for her body of work and her overall contributions with such recognitions as The Women in Film Crystal Award, the National Organization of Women Courage Award, and the Scopus Award given by the American Friends of the Hebrew University.

40. *The Broadway Album*

Label and Number: Columbia, phonodisc OC 40092, compact disc CK 40092, cassette OCT 40092

Date: November 1985

Producer: **Barbra Streisand**, Peter Matz, Richard Baskin, Bob Esty, Paul Jabara, David Foster

Arranger/Programmer: **Barbra Streisand,** Peter Matz, Richard Baskin, Randy Waldman, Jerry Hey, Jeremy Lubbock, Rhett Lawrence, Alexander Courage, Michael
Boddicker

Adelaide's Lament (only on compact disc); Frank Loesser; *Guys and Dolls*

Being Alive; Stephen Sondheim; *Company*

Can't Help Lovin' That Man (version 1); Jerome Kern, Oscar Hammerstein II;
Showboat

If I Loved You (version 1); Richard Rodgers, Oscar Hammerstein II; *Carousel*

Not While I'm Around (version 1); Stephen Sondheim; *Sweeney Todd*

Putting It Together (version 1); Stephen Sondheim; *Sunday in the Park With George*

Send in the Clowns; Stephen Sondheim; *A Little Night Music*

Something's Coming (version 1); Leonard Bernstein, Stephen Sondheim; *West Side
Story*

Somewhere (version 1); Leonard Bernstein, Stephen Sondheim; *West Side Story*
medley:

   I Have Dreamed; Richard Rodgers, Oscar Hammerstein II; *The King and I*

   Something Wonderful; Richard Rodgers, Oscar Hammerstein II; *The King and I*

   We Kiss in a Shadow; Richard Rodgers, Oscar Hammerstein II; *The King and I*
medley:

   Ladies Who Lunch, The; Stephen Sondheim; *Company*

   Pretty Women; Stephen Sondheim; *Sweeney Todd*
medley:

   I Loves You, Porgy; George Gershwin, Ira Gershwin, DuBose Heyward; *Porgy
and Bess*

   Porgy, I's Your Woman Now (Bess You Is My Woman); George Gershwin, Ira
Gershwin, DuBose Heyward; *Porgy and Bess*

The Broadway Album is just what the title suggests: a collection of songs
from Broadway shows (although *Porgy and Bess* is usually labelled an
opera), an idea that Barbra had been thinking about for several years. Even
though she did not spend much of her acting career on the Broadway stage,
her musical roots were buried deep in its music. She had proven her ability
to be successful with contemporary pop hits ("Evergreen" and "Guilty,"
for example), but she was drawn to the greater interpretive possibilities of
standards and show tunes. Nevertheless, the literature on this album is
typically eclectic, drawing from shows spanning the 1920s through 1984.
Several of the songs are by Stephen Sondheim, who is known for his complicated, meaning-laden lyrics; in fact, he altered some lyrics for this project. Barbra turned to her colleague of the 1960s, Peter Matz, to be
conductor and arranger, but she also relied on the talents of younger, up-
and-coming musicians such as David Foster (*St. Elmo's Fire*). All of the
song types previously described (see chapter 2) are heard on *The Broadway*

Album. Autobiographical thinking is found in "Putting it Together," "If I Loved You" is a love ballad, "Adelaide's Lament" is a character song (it appears only on the CD as that format was becoming more popular), her rendition of "Send in the Clowns" qualifies as a lyric song, and Barbra's belt power is exhibited in "Can't Help Lovin' that Man" and "Porgy I's Your Woman Now." Only "Somewhere" received much radio broadcast, but the album quickly scaled the charts and was ranked multi-platinum, despite the widely reported skepticism of some Columbia executives who feared there was not a market for this repertoire. The following spring Barbra was again awarded the Grammy for Best Pop Vocal–Female, twenty-four years after she had won in that category for the first time. By the end of 1986, the album had done well enough to rank sixth for the year behind *Whitney Houston, Music from Miami Vice, Brothers in Arms* by Dire Straits, *5150* by Van Halen, and *Afterburner* by ZZ Top. The attention to musical detail heard on Barbra's album reflects the conflict that many listeners face. Some prefer the more gutsy brash interpretations and tone of Streisand's early years, while others marvel at the supple, rich timbre and vocal technique (finesse, control, and nuance) heard on her later recordings. In 1999 her medley from *The King and I* was reissued as part of a Sony compact disc (SK 63386) that featured music from an animated version of that story. Streisand's next project was the dramatic court-room film, *Nuts*, written by Tom Toper. Barbra is credited with writing its score, but its soundtrack contained no vocal selections.

41. *One Voice* (live)

Label and Number: Columbia, phonodisc OC 40788, compact disc CK 40788, cassette OCT 40788

Date: 1987

Producer: Richard Baskin

Arranger: unavailable

America the Beautiful; Katherine Lee Bates, Samuel A. Ward

Guilty (version 2, duet Barry Gibb); Barry Gibb, Robin Gibb, Maurice Gibb

Happy Days Are Here Again (version 6); Jack Yellen, Milton Ager

It's a New World; Ira Gershwin, Harold Arlen

Love Theme From "A Star Is Born" (Evergreen) (version 3); **Barbra Streisand**, Paul Williams

Over the Rainbow (version 1); Harold Arlen, E. Y. Harburg

Papa, Can You Hear Me? (version 3); Michel Legrand, Alan Bergman, Marilyn Bergman

People (version 7); Bob Merrill, Jule Styne

Something's Coming (version 2); Leonard Bernstein, Stephen Sondheim; *West Side Story*

Somewhere (version 2); Leonard Bernstein, Stephen Sondheim; *West Side Story*

Way We Were, The (version 3); Marvin Hamlisch, Alan Bergman, Marilyn Bergman

What Kind of Fool? (version 2, duet Barry Gibb); Barry Gibb, Albhy Galuten

Barbra made her political stance very clear with her first concert performance in many years. The concert was held at her home in Malibu for an invited audience that paid $5,000 per couple to attend, with proceeds going to support Democratic candidates in the 1986 elections (see chapter 5). Material from that event was released as this album and as a video; part of the resultant income went to the Streisand Foundation, which supports causes close to Barbra's heart. The album is in many ways a "greatest hits" collection since she sings several of her signature songs. On the other hand, it also includes some songs she had never recorded before ("Over the Rainbow"). Barry Gibb agreed to sing with her on two duets from her successful *Guilty* album, which he had produced and composed (#36). Generally the critics praised her singing but found her political commentary (used to tie the songs together) tiresome. Some of the accompanimental arrangements are slightly different on this album than on previously issued tracks since a full orchestra was not employed for the outdoor setting. "The Way We Were" in particular receives an alternative treatment. The video version of the concert contains "Send in the Clowns," which was omitted from the album. In September of 1987 *One Voice* reached gold status, giving Streisand her thirtieth such album.

42. *Till I Loved You*

Label and Number: Columbia, phonodisc OC 40880, compact disc CK 40880, cassette OCT 40880

Date: 1988

Producer: Quincy Jones, **Barbra Streisand**, Phil Ramone, Burt Bacharach, Carole Bayer Sager, Denny Diante

Arranger/Programmer: Rhett Lawrence, Randy Kerber, Larry Williams, Glen Ballard, Clif Magness, Quincy Jones, Jerry Hey, Patrick Williams, Randy Waldman, Phil Ramone, Burt Bacharach, Jeremy Lubbock, Scott Cutler

All I Ask of You (version 1); Andrew Lloyd Webber, Charles Hart, Richard Stilgoe; *The Phantom of the Opera*

Love Light; Burt Bacharach, Carole Bayer Sager

On My Way to You; Michel Legrand, Alan Bergman, Marilyn Bergman

One More Time Around; Burt Bacharach, Carole Bayer Sager, Tom Keane

Places You Find Love, The; Clif Magness, Glen Ballard

Some Good Things Never Last; Mark Radice

Till I Loved You (duet Don Johnson); Maury Yeston; *Goya*

Two People; **Barbra Streisand**, Alan Bergman, Marilyn Bergman

What Were We Thinking of?; Scott Cutler, Antonina Armato

Why Let It Go?; Alan Hawkshaw, Alan Bergman, Marilyn Bergman

You and Me for Always; Burt Bacharach, Carole Bayer Sager

Barbra's brief relationship with actor Don Johnson might be the most memorable aspect of this contemporary pop album. He sang the title duet with her and sang backup on "What Were We Thinking of?" She returned the favor by singing backup on "What If It Takes All Night?" on his 1989 Epic album *Let It Roll*. The music for "Two People" had been written by Streisand for the score of her film *Nuts*; lyrics were added later by the Bergmans. Supporting the notion that Streisand did not rely on radio play of singles to promote her albums, most of the songs on this set exceed four minutes in length. Several critics again commented on the strength of her vocal skills, but lamented the lack of material strong enough to support them (the exception in this case being "All I Ask of You"). This criticism came despite the fact that many of the recording industry's biggest names were involved in producing, arranging, and composing the album. In 1988 Barbra was recipient of the People's Choice Award as "All-Time Favorite Musical Performer" selected from a slate that included Frank Sinatra and Kenny Rogers. In her pre-recorded acceptance remarks she commented that she did not take the choice of the people lightly, connecting the award to the lyrics of her hit song from 1964, "People."

43. *A Collection: Greatest Hits and More*

Label and Number: Columbia, compact disc CK 45369, cassette OCT 45369

Date: 1989

Producer: Narada Michael Waldon, Barry Gibb, Albhy Galuten, Karl Richardson, Phil Ramone, Andrew Lloyd Webber, Bob Esty, Michael Masser, Rupert Holmes, Jeffrey Lesser, Dave Grusin, David Foster

Arranger: Narada Michael Waldon, Bob Esty, David Foster

All I Ask of You (version 1); Andrew Lloyd Webber, Charles Hart, Richard Stilgoe; *The Phantom of the Opera*

By the Way (version 1); **Barbra Streisand**, Rupert Holmes

Comin' In and Out of Your Life (version 1); Richard Parker, Bobby Whiteside

Guilty (version 1, duet Barry Gibb); Barry Gibb, Maurice Gibb, Robin Gibb

Main Event, The/Fight (version 1); Paul Jabara, Bruce Roberts, Bob Esty

Memory (version 1); Andrew Lloyd Webber, T. S. Eliot, Trevor Nunn; *Cats*

Someone That I Used to Love; Gerry Goffin, Michael Masser

Somewhere (version 1); Leonard Bernstein, Stephen Sondheim; *West Side Story*

Way He Makes Me Feel, The (Studio Version); Michel Legrand, Alan Bergman, Marilyn Bergman

We're Not Makin' Love Anymore; Michael Bolton, Diane Warren

What Kind of Fool? (version 1, duet Barry Gibb); Barry Gibb, Albhy Galuten

Woman in Love (version 1); Barry Gibb, Robin Gibb

The repetitive nature of this collection received considerable attention from critics (see bibliography), but Barbra was again steeped in a film project, *The Prince of Tides*. Only two songs of *A Collection* are new: "We're Not Makin' Love Anymore" and "Someone That I Used to Love" (perhaps both reflecting the state of her personal relationships at that time). Sony, the parent company of Streisand's label Columbia, issued a lengthy promotional statement about the album (actually a compact disc by now) on its web site as the internet became more prominent in American life. The company also announced that several of her earlier albums would be reissued as compact discs in 1989. The amount of material a CD can accommodate compared to a 33 rpm phonodisc becomes clear when this is done. The songs from two early albums would likely fit on one CD, but of course that is not a wise marketing strategy for a singer with such a loyal customer base. *A Collection* reached platinum status in spite of its repetitiveness. In 1990 Streisand appeared on a television show entitled "The Earth Day Special," which was produced by Richard Baskin. She concluded the show with "One Day," a song by Michel Legrand and the Bergmans. It has not appeared on any of her subsequent albums.

44. *Just for the Record*

Label and Number: Sony/Columbia, compact disc C4K 44111, cassette C4T 44111

Date: 1991

Producer: **Barbra Streisand**, Martin Erlichman

A "Highlights from *Just for the Record*" also was released (in 1992): compact disc CK 52849, cassette CT 52849

Any Place I Hang My Hat Is Home (1963, version 1); Harold Arlen, Johnny Mercer; *St. Louis Woman*

Be My Guest (1963, duet Judy Garland); Mel Torme

Between Yesterday and Tomorrow (1973); Michel Legrand, Alan Bergman, Marilyn Bergman

Can You Tell the Moment? (1973); Michel Legrand, Alan Bergman, Marilyn Bergman

Cry Me a River (1962, version 1, live); Arthur Hamilton

Cryin' Time (1973, version 1, duet Ray Charles); Buck Owens

Ding Dong the Witch Is Dead (1966, duet Harold Arlen); Harold Arlen, E. Y. Harburg

Don't Rain on My Parade (1968, version 2); Jule Styne, Bob Merrill; *Funny Girl*

Funny Girl (1968, version 1); Jule Styne, Bob Merrill; *Funny Girl*

God Bless the Child (1974); Arthur Hertzog Jr., Billie Holiday

Guilty (1980, version 1, duet Barry Gibb); Barry Gibb, Robin Gibb, Maurice Gibb

Happy Days Are Here Again (1962, version 1); Milton Ager, Jack Yellen

Hatikvah (1978); Naphtali Herz Imber

He Touched Me (1965, version 1); Milton Schafer, Ira Levin

Hello, Dolly (1969, version 1, ensemble); Jerry Herman; *Hello Dolly*

Here We Are at Last (1984, version 1); **Barbra Streisand**, Richard Baskin

House of Flowers (1966); Harold Arlen, Truman Capote; *House of Flowers*

I Can Do It (1970); Johnny Worth

I Had Myself a True Love (1962, version 1, live); Harold Arlen, Johnny Mercer; *St. Louis Woman*

I Hate Music (1962, live); Leonard Bernstein

I Know Him So Well (1985); Benny Andersson, Bjorn Ulvaeus, Tim Rice; *Chess*

I'm Always Chasing Rainbows (1967); Harry Carroll, Joseph McCarthy; *Irene*

I'm the Greatest Star (1965, version 2, live); Jule Styne, Bob Merrill; *Funny Girl*

If I Close My Eyes (1972); Billy Goldenberg, Alan Bergman, Marilyn Bergman

If I Loved You (1985, version 1); Richard Rodgers, Oscar Hammerstein II; *Carousel*

Keepin' Out of Mischief Now (1962, version 1, live); Thomas "Fats" Waller, Andy Razaf

Lost Inside of You (1976, version 1, ensemble); **Barbra Streisand**, Leon Russell

Love Theme From "A Star Is Born" (Evergreen) (1976, version 1); **Barbra Streisand**, Paul Williams

Lover, Come Back to Me (1962, version 1, live); Sigmund Romberg, Oscar Hammerstein II, *The New Moon*

Miss Marmelstein (1962, version 1); Harold Rome; *I Can Get It for You Wholesale*

Moon and I, The (1981); Michel Legrand, Alan Bergman, Marilyn Bergman

Moon River (1961); Henry Mancini, Johnny Mercer

My Honey's Lovin' Arms (1963, version 1); Joseph Meyer, Herman Ruby

My Man (1965, version 1, live); Maurice Yvain, Channing Pollock; *Ziegfeld Follies*

Nobody's Heart (Belongs to Me) (1962, live); Richard Rodgers, Lorenz Hart

On a Clear Day (You Can See Forever) (Reprise) (1969, version 1); Burton Lane, Alan Jay Lerner; *On a Clear Day*

Over the Rainbow (1986, version 1, live); Harold Arlen, E. Y. Harburg; *The Wizard of Oz*

Papa, Can You Hear Me? (1981, version 1); Michel Legrand, Alan Bergman, Marilyn Bergman

People (1964, version 2); Jule Styne, Bob Merrill; *Funny Girl*

Piece of Sky, A (1981, version 1; 1983, version 2); Michel Legrand, Alan Bergman, Marilyn Bergman

Putting It Together (1985, version 1); Stephen Sondheim; *Sunday in the Park With George*

Since I Fell for You (1971, version 1); Buddy Johnson

Singer, The (1970); Walter Marks

Sleep in Heavenly Peace (Silent Night) (1968, version 2, live); Franz Gruber, Ray Ellis

Sleepin' Bee, A (1961, version 1); Harold Arlen, Truman Capote; *House of Flowers*

Spring Can Really Hang You Up the Most (1962); Tommy Wolf, Fran Landesman

Starting Here, Starting Now (1966, version 1); David Shire, Richard Maltby Jr.

Stoney End (1970, version 1); Laura Nyro

They Long to Be Close to You (1971, duet Burt Bacharach); Burt Bacharach, Hal David

Value (1962, version 1, live); Jeff Harris; *Another Evening With Harry Stoones*

Warm All Over (1988); Frank Loesser; *The Most Happy Fella*

Way We Were, The (1973, version 1; 1980, version 2); Marvin Hamlisch, Alan Bergman, Marilyn Bergman

Way We Weren't, The (1980); Marvin Hamlisch, Alan Bergman, Marilyn Bergman

We've Only Just Begun (1971); Roger Nichols, Paul Williams

What Are You Doing the Rest of Your Life? (1972, version 2, duet Michel Legrand); Michel Legrand, Alan Bergman, Marilyn Bergman

When the Sun Comes Out (1963, version 1); Harold Arlen, Ted Koehler

Who's Afraid of the Big Bad Wolf? (1962, version 1); Frank E. Churchill, Ann Ronell

You Don't Bring Me Flowers (1980, version 2, live, duet Neil Diamond); Neil Diamond, Alan Bergman, Marilyn Bergman

You Wanna Bet (1965); Cy Coleman, Dorothy Fields

You'll Never Know (1955); Harry Warren, Mack Gordon

You'll Never Know (1988, duet **Barbra Streisand**); Harry Warren, Mack Gordon

You're the Top (1972, duet Ryan O'Neal); Cole Porter; *Anything Goes*

medley:

By Myself (1963, version 1); Arthur Schwartz, Howard Dietz

It All Depends on You (1963, duet Judy Garland); Ray Henderson, B. G. De-Sylva, Lew Brown

Lover Come Back to Me (1963, version 3); Sigmund Romberg, Oscar Hammerstein II; *The New Moon*

Hooray for Love (1963, duet Judy Garland); Harold Arlen, Leo Robin

I Like New York in June; How About You? (1963, duet Judy Garland); Burton Lane, Ralph Freed

medley:

Happy Days Are Here Again (1963, version 3, duet Judy Garland); Milton Ager, Jack Yellen (Judy also sings Get Happy)

medley:

Any Place I Hang My Hat Is Home (1965, version 2); Harold Arlen, Johnny Mercer; *St. Louis Woman*

Best Things in Life Are Free, The (1965, version 1); Ray Henderson, B. G. DeSylva, Lew Brown; *Good News!*

Give Me the Simple Life (1965, version 1); Rube Bloom, Harry Ruby

Nobody Knows You When You're Down and Out (1965, version 1); Jimmie Cox

Second Hand Rose (1965, version 2); James F. Hanley, Grant Clarke; *Ziegfeld Follies*

medley:

I Stayed Too Long at the Fair (1966, version 2); Billy Barnes

Look at That Face (1966, version 1); Anthony Newley, Leslie Bricusse

medley:

Good Man Is Hard to Find, A (1967); Eddie Green

Some of These Days (1967); Shelton Brooks

medley:

In the Wee Small Hours of the Morning (1969, live); David Mann, Bob Hilliard

When You Gotta Go (1969); Anthony Newley, Herbert Kretzmer

medley:

Quiet Thing, A (1974); John Kander, Fred Ebb

There Won't Be Trumpets (1974); Stephen Sondheim

In 1991 Columbia, by then associated with Sony, released a 4-compact-disc boxed set that, with the lengthy accompanying booklet written by Barbra, became the closest thing extant to a Streisand autobiography. The first two discs represent the 1960s, the second the 1970s, and the final disc the 1980s; a careful observer will note how the rose theme pictured on the discs symbolizes the budding and blooming of Barbra's singing career. Although the set contains many repeated tracks from earlier recordings, it also contains a substantial number of never-before-issued tracks. Among the highlights are Streisand's first recording from age 13, "You'll Never Know" (which is then repeated as a duet with 49-year-old Barbra on the final disc); a recording by Streisand's mother, Diana Kind, of "Second Hand Rose"; material from her 1963 guest appearance on *The Judy Garland Show* and other early television and club performances; "The Way

We Weren't," a song cut from the film; and several tracks from over the years that never were placed on albums (which can be identified in Appendix B by searching for those titles that are followed only by #44). Despite its high price, the set did well enough during the holiday shopping season of 1991 to be ranked platinum. One previously unreleased track, "Warm All Over," was nominated for a Grammy that year. Successive listening to the chronological discs clearly indicates how Streisand's voice has darkened and mellowed over the years, and how many of her basic vocal techniques and repertoire choices have remained consistent. The latter is slightly exaggerated in this instance by the fact that her light rock or contemporary pop repertoire is only minimally represented in the collection. Although known for her perfectionist tendencies, informal or demo recordings are included as well ("What Are You Doing the Rest of Your Life?"). Fortunately for Streisand fans, as reviewer Ernie Santosuosso put it, the collection "merely concludes the chapter, not the book" of Barbra's singing life (see bibliography). The following year Streisand was the recipient of the Grammy Legend Award, which was presented to her at the ceremony by Stephen Sondheim.

45. *The Prince of Tides* (film)

Label and Number: Columbia, compact disc CK 48627, cassette CT 48627

Date: 1991

Producer: **Barbra Streisand**, James Newton Howard

Arranger: Brad Dechter, Marty Paich, Humme Mann, Johnny Mandel

For All We Know (version 1); J. Fred Coots, Sam M. Lewis

Places That Belong to You; James Newton Howard, Alan Bergman, Marilyn Bergman

This soundtrack contains two vocals, neither of which were heard during the film. "Places" summarizes the mood of the movie, and the studio released a publicity video of it. An instrumental version of "For All We Know" underscored one scene; Streisand thought the original lyrics also complemented the film's story, so she included her version of the song on the soundtrack. "For All" also was used as a closing number during Streisand's concert tour of 1994 (see below). The male star of *Prince* was Nick Nolte, and Barbra served as star, director, and producer. Her son, Jason (then in his mid-twenties), played her son in the film and received positive critical reviews for his efforts. He escorted his mother to the Academy Awards that year where the film had garnered six nominations including Best Picture. Nolte won in the category of Best Actor.

46. *Back to Broadway*

Label and Number: Columbia, compact disc CK 44189, cassette CT 44189

Date: 1993

Producer: David Foster, **Barbra Streisand**, Andrew Lloyd Webber, Nigel Wright

Arranger: Johnny Mandel, David Foster, Bill Ross, **Barbra Streisand**, Andrew Pryce Jackman, Andrew Lloyd Webber, John Cameron, David Cullen, Jonathon Tunick, Billy Byers, Jeremy Lubbock, Michael Starobin

As If We Never Said Goodbye (version 1); Andrew Lloyd Webber, Don Black, Christopher Hampton; *Sunset Boulevard*

Children Will Listen; Stephen Sondheim; *Into the Woods*

Everybody Says Don't (version 1); Stephen Sondheim; *Anyone Can Whistle*

I've Never Been in Love Before; Frank Loesser; *Guys and Dolls*

Luck Be a Lady; Frank Loesser; *Guys and Dolls*

Man I Love, The; George Gershwin, Ira Gershwin; *Lady Be Good*

Move On; Stephen Sondheim; *Sunday in the Park With George*

Music of the Night, The (duet Michael Crawford); Andrew Lloyd Webber, Charles Hart, Richard Stilgoe; *The Phantom of the Opera*

Some Enchanted Evening; Richard Rodgers, Oscar Hammerstein II; *South Pacific*

Speak Low; Kurt Weill, Ogden Nash; *One Touch of Venus*

With One Look; Andrew Lloyd Webber, Don Black, Christopher Hampton, Amy Powers; *Sunset Boulevard*

medley:

I Have a Love (duet Johnny Mathis); Leonard Bernstein, Stephen Sondheim; *West Side Story*

One Hand, One Heart (duet Johnny Mathis); Leonard Bernstein, Stephen Sondheim; *West Side Story*

Although a companion in theme to her 1985 *The Broadway Album*, this collection is significantly different in tone and style. Several of the standards have been contemporized by pop or jazz-like arrangements ("Luck Be a Lady," for example). David Foster, who arranged the outer-space sound of "Somewhere" on *The Broadway Album*, arranged and produced several of these tracks. In the liner notes Streisand confirms her acting approach to lyrics interpretation in her comments about "With One Look" and indicates that she was heavily involved in arranging some of the accompaniments. The two duets on this album are nostalgic; Johnny Mathis had always been one of her favorite pop singers, and Michael Crawford played a secondary lead in her film *Hello, Dolly*. Streisand's ability to adjust timbre according to the interpretive or musical situation comes into play when balancing the contrasting timbres of her duet partners' voices (see chapter 5). Lloyd Webber's "As If We Never Said Goodbye" will appear again on her next album with the lyrics rewritten to apply to her return to the concert stage. His compositional style (sweeping melodies, lush orchestrations, and dramatic characters) compliments her vocal skills. *Back to Broadway* was Streisand's fiftieth album for Columbia, and came just after she renewed her contract with them for a reported $60 million, a price range associated at that time with younger pop-music superstars, Madonna and Michael Jackson. (To reach fifty Columbia counted some film soundtracks that do not feature her singing and some "Highlights from" sets.) *Back to Broadway* debuted at number one, bumping Janet Jackson from that spot. Two events from her personal life attracted considerable press attention around the time of this album's release: her brief friendship with tennis player Andre Agassi and her appearance in Washington, D.C. at the White House Correspondents' Association dinner.

47. *Barbra: The Concert* (live)

Label and Number: Columbia, compact disc C2K 66109, cassette C2T 66109

Date: 1994

Producer: **Barbra Streisand**, Jay Landers

Arranger: Marvin Hamlisch (with several orchestrators)

Barbra: The Concert—Highlights also was released (in 1995): compact disc CK 67100, cassette CT 67100

As If We Never Said Goodbye (version 2); Andrew Lloyd Webber, Don Black, Christopher Hampton, Amy Powers; *Sunset Boulevard*

Can't Help Lovin' That Man (version 2); Jerome Kern, Oscar Hammerstein II; *Showboat*

For All We Know (version 2); J. Fred Coots, Sam M. Lewis

Happy Days Are Here Again (version 7); Milton Ager, Jack Yellen

He Touched Me (version 3); Ira Levin, Milton Schafer

I'll Know (version 2); Frank Loesser; *Guys and Dolls*

Lazy Afternoon (version 2); John LaTouche, Jerome Moross; *Golden Apple*

Love Theme From "A Star Is Born" (Evergreen) (version 4); **Barbra Streisand**, Paul Williams

Lover Man (Oh Where Can You Be?) (version 2); Jimmie Davis, Roger J. Ramirez, Jimmy Sherman

Man That Got Away, The; Harold Arlen, Ira Gershwin

My Man (version 5); Maurice Yvain, Channing Pollock; *Ziegfeld Follies*

Not While I'm Around (version 2); Stephen Sondheim; *Sweeney Todd*

On a Clear Day (You Can See Forever) (version 3); Burton Lane, Alan Jay Lerner; *On a Clear Day*

Ordinary Miracles; Marvin Hamlisch, Alan Bergman, Marilyn Bergman

People (version 8); Jule Styne, Bob Merrill; *Funny Girl*

Somewhere (version 3); Leonard Bernstein, Stephen Sondheim; *West Side Story*

Way We Were, The (version 4); Marvin Hamlisch, Alan Bergman, Marilyn Bergman

Will He Like Me? (version 2); Sheldon Harnick, Jerry Bock; *She Loves Me*

You Don't Bring Me Flowers (version 2); Neil Diamond, Alan Bergman, Marilyn Bergman

medley:

 Don't Rain On My Parade (version 5); Jule Styne, Bob Merrill; *Funny Girl*

 Everybody Says Don't (version 2); Stephen Sondheim; *Anyone Can Whistle*

 I'm Still Here; Stephen Sondheim; *Follies*

medley:

 Once Upon a Dream; S. Fain, J. Lawrence

 Someday My Prince Will Come; Larry Morey, Frank Churchill

 When You Wish Upon a Star; Leigh Harline, Ned Washington

medley:

 Papa, Can You Hear Me? (version 4); Michel Legrand, Alan Bergman, Marilyn Bergman

 Piece of Sky, A (version 3); Michel Legrand, Alan Bergman, Marilyn Bergman

 Where Is It Written? (version 2); Michel Legrand, Alan Bergman, Marilyn Bergman

 Will Someone Ever Look at Me That Way? (version 2); Michel Legrand, Alan Bergman, Marilyn Bergman

Many people who follow Streisand's career were surprised but thrilled when her management announced she would present two public concerts for the opening of the MGM Grand Hotel and Casino in Las Vegas over New Year's 1993–94. The rush for tickets and their prices set records. Barbra felt comfortable enough with her success in Las Vegas that she launched her first concert tour in decades the following spring. She sang in London, Detroit, Washington (D.C.), two sites in California, and New York City. The concerts were produced by Barbra and Martin Erlichman for J.E.G. productions, which likely stands for Jason Emanuel Gould, her son. *Barbra: The Concert* eventually was released as a two-compact disc set; a video (in 2 different versions, each different from that on the compact discs); a cable television concert, which won two Emmy Awards; and a network television special (see chapter 5). She designed the concert around the format of a theatre show, which allowed her to use her sense of drama, directorial experience, and musicianship to present a total artistic package. The first act was (for the most part) autobiographical, while Act 2 was more concert like but with considerable dialogue introducing and linking the repertoire. Barbra sang many of her familiar signature songs such as "Evergreen," "On a Clear Day," "The Way We Were," and "People" (composer Jule Styne attended two of the New York concerts; only a few months later he died), but incorporated several new pieces into the mix as well (recall that the compact disc and video versions are not identical). "Ordinary Miracles," about the power of individual contributions to humanity, was written for the occasion by her friends the Bergmans and Marvin Hamlisch. (He also agreed to serve as musical director for the Vegas performances and the tour, conducting a 60+ piece orchestra—an expensive rarity.) Other new material included "The Man That Got Away," a torch song Judy Garland sang in her version of *A Star Is Born*; Lloyd Webber's "As If We Never Said Goodbye" with lyrics altered to fit Barbra's entrance onto the stage; and a medley of Disney songs dedicated to her goddaughter. She selected material spanning her career, but stayed away from some of her soft rock material (such as "Stoney End," see similar comments with #44 above). In advance of the Vegas shows and tour, many people wondered whether she would include any duets, since they had been among her most popular hits (with Donna Summer, Neil Diamond, Barry Gibb). She did and she didn't. She had no in-person partners, but sang with Marlon Brando and with herself on two video clips from *Guys and Dolls* and *Yentl* respectively. The rarity of her public performances over the years attracted the press to every concert. Most reviewers welcomed her back to the concert stage by complimenting her vocal skills, her rapport with an audience, and her attention to details; several found her personalized and political dialogue between songs to be self-indulgent (see bibliography). At this point she was known as a staunch supporter of President Bill Clinton and of Democratic politics. (Her visibility in this arena brought an invitation to speak at the Kennedy School of Government at Harvard University in 1995.) For many listeners, the real joy in hearing the concert recording stems from the spontaneity instilled by the "live" event. Barbra's voice retains its more mature timbre, and her technique and control are exceptional, but more of Streisand's early emotional style also is evident than on some recent studio recordings.

48. *The Mirror Has Two Faces* (film)

Label and Number: Columbia, compact disc CK 67887

Date: 1996

Producer: **Barbra Streisand**

Arranger: Marvin Hamlisch

All of My Life; **Barbra Streisand**, Marvin Hamlisch, Alan Bergman, Marilyn Bergman

I Finally Found Someone (duet Bryan Adams); **Barbra Streisand**, Marvin Hamlisch, R. J. Lange, Bryan Adams

Like *The Prince of Tides* soundtrack (#45), this album contains two vocals by Streisand, although this time one (her duet with Bryan Adams) was used to accompany the film's final credits. It was released as a single and did well enough to give Barbra at least one top-10 hit in each decade since the 1960s. The film was not a smash at the box office, but veteran actress Lauren Bacall, cast as Barbra's film mother, received considerable positive notice, and the role brought Bacall a Golden Globe Award. Barbra did not receive any personal Academy Award nominations for her efforts as star, producer, and director. Nevertheless, her appearance at the awards show that year attracted attention because she once again seemed snubbed by the Academy and because she was escorted by her future husband, James Brolin. Despite being ignored by the Academy, Barbra received that year's ShowEast Filmmaker of the Year Award.

49. *Higher Ground*

Label and Number: Columbia, compact disc CK 66181, cassette CT 66181

Date: 1997

Producer: **Barbra Streisand**, Arif Mardin, Walter Afanasieff, David Foster, Mervyn Warren, Jeremy Lubbock, Jay Landers

Arranger/Programmer: Jeremy Lubbock, William Ross, David Foster, Walter Afanasieff, Simon Franglen, Mervyn Warren, Scott Frankfurt, Dan Shea, Arif Mardin, Marvin Hamlisch, William David Brohn

At the Same Time; Ann Hampton Callaway

Avinu Malkeinu; Max Janowski

Circle; Jud Friedman, Cynthia Weil

Everything Must Change; Bernard Ighner

Higher Ground; Steve Dorff, George Green, Kent Agee

If I Could; Ronald L. Miller, Kenny Hirsch, Martha V. Sharron

Leading With Your Heart; Alan Bergman, Marilyn Bergman, Marvin Hamlisch

Lessons to Be Learned; Allan Rich, Dorothy Sea Gazeley, Marsha Malamet

On Holy Ground; Geron Davis

Tell Him (duet Celine Dion); David Foster, Linda Thompson, Walter Afanasieff

medley:

    I Believe; Ervin Drake, Irvin Graham, Jimmy Shirl, Al Stillman

    You'll Never Walk Alone; Richard Rodgers, Oscar Hammerstein II; *Carousel*

medley:

    Deep River; traditional

    Water Is Wide, The; traditional

The funeral of President Bill Clinton's mother, Virginia Kelley, who had a short-lived but close friendship with Streisand, was the inspiration behind this album of mostly inspirational songs. At that service Barbra heard a gospel singer present "On Holy Ground," which made her decide that she would like to record it. Other selections on the set have personal meaning as well and are typically eclectic in their messages. "If I Could" is sung for Barbra's son, "Leading With Your Heart" has a title borrowed from Virginia Kelley's autobiography, and "Tell Him" is a duet outlining the wisdom an older woman has gained about relationships. "Avinu Malkeinu" ("Our Father, Our King") obviously reflects Streisand's heritage. The album entered the charts at number 1. As she has since the 1970s, Barbra wrote the liner notes so that listeners would understand the connections she felt with the repertoire. By this time, Streisand was in her mid-fifties, and her vocal timbre exhibits a dark, rich quality. Celine Dion's popularity at the time ("My Heart Will Go On" from the film *Titanic*) helped draw attention to their duet, for which the parts were recorded individually. Dion reported to Larry King (4 April 1998, CNN television) that Barbra recorded her track first and then Celine added hers. (The two got together later to make a video of the song for publicity purposes.) Sony announced that a premiere satellite broadcast of "Tell Him" would be sent to all U.S. radio stations and international radio markets at 9 PM Eastern time on 7 November 1997. The duet brought Barbra her first British top-10 hit in nearly twenty years. In a review of "Tell Him," British pop-music scholar Simon Frith observed that Streisand still was a star "presence," while Dion was more of a "populist." He found their vocal timbres and style to be complementary, but their approach to lyrics contrasting—Streisand's inviting awe, Dion's "reassuringly ordinary"; Streisand imposing herself on a song, Dion shaped by the song (see *Village Voice*, 16 December 1997, 87).

50. *A Love Like Ours*

Label and Number: Columbia, compact disc 69601

Date: September 1999

Producer: **Barbra Streisand**, Walter Afanasieff, David Foster, Richard Marx, Tony Brown, Arif Mardin, Jay Landers

Arranger/Programmer: William Ross, Jorge Calandrelli, Walter Afanasieff, Greg Bieck, David Foster, Richard Marx, Felipe Elgueta, Arif Mardin, Steve Skinner, Marvin Hamlisch, Peter Hume, Bruce Roberts, Jeremy Lubbock, Ralph Burns

If I Didn't Love You; Bruce Roberts, Junior Miles

If I Never Met You; Tom Snow, Dean Pitchford

If You Ever Leave Me (duet Vince Gill); Richard Marx

Island, The; Alan Bergman, Marilyn Bergman, Ivan Lins, Vitor Martins

Isn't It a Pity?; George Gershwin, Ira Gershwin

It Must Be You; Steve Dorff, Stephony Smith

I've Dreamed of You; Rolf Loveland, Ann Hampton Callaway

Just One Lifetime; Melissa Manchester, Tom Snow

Love Like Ours; Alan Bergman, Marilyn Bergman, Dave Grusin

Music That Makes Me Dance, The; Jule Styne, Bob Merrill; *Funny Girl*

Wait; Alan Bergman, Marilyn Bergman, Michel Legrand

We Must Be Loving Right; Roger Brown, Clay Blaker

The inspiration for this September 1999 compact disc was Streisand's marriage to actor James Brolin in July 1998; therefore, the whole set might fall under the autobiographical repertoire category, even though contrasting musical styles are evident (see Chapter 2). Barbra's liner notes reveal that some of the CD's music was, in fact, heard at their wedding, and on the 15 November 1999 broadcast of the *Rosie O'Donnell Show*, Barbra said that she "wanted to make a record that just celebrated love and marriage." Already by that time, the set had reached platinum in sales. (The first single from the album, "I've Dreamed of You," was released earlier in the summer of 1999, perhaps in time to take advantage of sales for the summer wedding season.)

Careful perusal of the names associated with the composition and arrangements of the songs indicates that, even with this specific and personal theme in mind, Streisand again sought repertoire from both long-familiar and contemporary sources (Gershwin compared to Marx). Her pairing with country star Vince Gill adds another to her lengthy duet list—each partner contrasting significantly in style; their performance video received substantial broadcast time on country-music video channels, providing an expanded audience for Streisand. She had had previous modest success on a country-music chart in 1978 with her duet with Neil Diamond on "You Don't Bring Me Flowers."

Streisand's re-make of "The Music That Makes Me Dance" allows a listener to compare her voice and interpretive approach over a long time span. The most noticeable change from the original cast-album performance (see Appendix B) comes at the end. The 1999 version does not keep Barbra as long on high-pitched belt notes. In general, the tone or atmosphere of the set is gentle. This is most clearly evident on "We Must Be Loving Right," where her finesse with timbre and inflection project simultaneous ease or nonchalance *and* precision or focus. Streisand uses her belt powers, and there are wide dynamic contrasts throughout, but no up-tempo or feisty character songs are present—ballads and lyric songs predominate. Barbra states in the liner that she prefers to sing live with an orchestra and that most of the songs herein were recorded in that manner. More than one reviewer commented that the arrangements often were excessive, a criticism they have made with some previous albums (see bibliography). On the other hand, her rendition of Gershwin's "Isn't It a Pity?" received justifiable praise.

In the fall of 1999 Barbra was also planning and rehearsing with Marvin Hamlisch for her Millennium New Year's concert in Las Vegas. She reported to Rosie O'Donnell two items of particular interest: that she would have to begin singing regularly days in advance of the concert to get her voice in shape since she does not practice and that they were considering adding a second performance because of ticket demand. This demand likely was fueled in part by comments from Barbra about her thoughts on retiring (NBC's *Today*, 22 September 1999) and from Martin Erlichman that this might be her last concert (Streisand's web site, accessed 1 October 1999; see bibliography). Time will tell if other compact discs will be forthcoming in Streisand's long and prestigious vocal career.

Albums Alphabetical by Title with Discography Chronology Number

Songs Alphabetical by Title with Discography Chronology Number(s)

Absent Minded Me, 7

Adelaide's Lament, 40 (only on compact disc format)

After the Rain, 35

Alfie, 16

All I Ask of You, 42, 43

All in Love Is Fair, 24, 33

All of My Life, 48

All That I Want, 9

All the Things You Are, 12

Am I Blue?, 27

America the Beautiful, 41

Animal Crackers in My Soup, 10

Answer Me, 31

Any Place I Hang My Hat Is Home, 4, 44; appears a second time on 44 as version 2

Après un Rêve, 29

As If We Never Said Goodbye, 46; version 2, 47

As Time Goes By, 5

Ask Yourself Why, 16

At the Same Time, 49

Auf dem Wasser zu Singen, 23

Autumn, 7

Other Recordings and Videos

Barbra Streisand is heard on several singles that were not issued as album tracks, on special albums that do not feature her, and on albums where she is a guest performer with some other featured singer. A selective list (alphabetic by song title) follows. The "Other Details" column includes information such as date of issue, arranger, album chronology number (see discography), etc. Information on these and other singles and their continued availability can be found on some internet sites that discuss Streisand memorabilia such as The Barbra Streisand Music Guide (see Bibliography including the address for her own web site) or in Stephen Thacker, "Her Name Is Barbra," *The Record Collector* (October 1997): 77–85. Some of the singles have been reissued on "fan-club" recordings such as those on the Kismet label in the 1980s and those from *Barbrabilia* in the 1990s.

Song Title	Album Title (or Single)	Label	Other Details
Child Is Born, A	*For Our Children*	Disney	1991: benefit AIDS; also on 28
Ding, Dong the Witch Is Dead	*Harold Sings Arlen (with Friend)*	Columbia	duet; April 1966; also on 44
House of Flowers	*Harold Sings Arlen (with Friend)*	Columbia	arr. Matz; April 1966; also on 44
I Finally Found Someone	single (side 2, Evergreen in Spanish)	Columbia	1996; duet with Bryan Adams; also on 48

I Got Plenty of Nothin'	*Zenith Salutes the Broadway Musicals*	Columbia	1960s
I've Got a Crush on You	*Frank Sinatra Duets*	Capital	1993
King and I medley	*The King and I* animated version	Sony	1999; reissue from *The Broadway Album* (40)
Left in the Dark/Here We Are at Last	single	Columbia	1984; also on 39
Love Theme From "A Star Is Born" (Evergreen)	*Diana, Princess of Wales: Tribute*	Columbia/Sony	1997; repeat version
Quiet Night	*American Popular Song*	CBS/Smithsonian	1984; also on 9
several songs (repeats from 13)	*Season's Greetings from Barbra Streisand*	Columbia	other performers: Nabors, Day, Kostelanetz
Silent Night	*Best of the Great Songs of Christmas*, album 10	Columbia	1970s, on 13
What If It Takes All Night	*Don Johnson Let It Roll*	Epic	1989, she sings background only

Several videotapes feature Streisand's singing; movie musicals in which she starred are not listed. See the bibliography for information concerning other books about Streisand, some of which contain filmographies.

Title	Label Information	Other Details
Putting It Together: The Making of the Broadway Album	CBS/FOX 710150 (1985)	Aired as HBO special
Barbra: The Concert	Columbia Music Video 29V-50117 (1994)	Aired as HBO special; another version aired on CBS (1995)
Color Me Barbra	CBS/FOX 3518 (1986)	1966 television special
Funny Girl *30th Anniversary Video*		Available from *Barbrabilia*, 1997
Grammy's Greatest Moments, Vol. 1	A*Vision Entertainment 50740–3	Contains 1980 duet with Neil Diamond
Happening in Central Park, A	CBS/FOX 3520 (1987)	Taped for television special 1967

I Remember Barbra	Third Degree Productions (1981)	Kevin Burns, 22 min., available Library of Congress
Judy Garland and Friends	Warner Reprise Video, Warner Bros. 338293 (1991)	Contains 1963 duets with Streisand
Music That Makes Me Dance, The		Available from *Barbrabilia*, 1997; contains individual performances of some unreleased material
My Name Is Barbra	CBS/FOX 3519 (1986)	1965 television special
One Voice	CBS/FOX 515050 (1986)	Aired as HBO special

Several album-length recordings of material not issued commercially by Streisand's label have been available through "fan-club" outlets over the years. A selective list of these recordings follows; many are now considered collectibles. The liners usually contain little or no credits and production information.

Title	Label Information	Other Details
After Hours	Kismet K-1012 (1985)	studio work on "The Main Event" and "No More Tears"
Beginnings	Kismet K-1010 (1985)	The Tonight Show, 1961–62
Flashback	Kismet K-1004 (1984)	Jack Paar Show, Garry Moore Show, other songs
Magic Moments	Kismet K-1008 (1985)	several songs from 1960s and 1970s
Memories Are Made of This	Kismet 1001 (1984)	Burt Bacharach Special; "The Way We Were" studio work
On Broadway	Kismet K-1016 (1985)	"On Broadway" studio work plus other unreleased material
Rarities Vol. 1A, Vol. 1B	available from *Barbrabilia* (1997)	singles collection
Rarities Vol. 2A, Vol. 2B	available from *Barbrabilia* (1997)	concert performance 24 July 1994, Anaheim, CA; other

Rarities Vol. 3A, Vol. 3B	available from *Barbrabilia* (1997)	concert performance 17 May 1994, Detroit, MI
Rarities Vol. 4	available from *Barbrabilia* (1997)	club performance 1963, hungry i, CA
Rarities Vol. 6	available from *Barbrabilia* (1997)	alternate soundtracks

Reference Bibliography

RECORDING REVIEWS

This portion of the bibliography lists reviews of Streisand's album-length recordings in chronological order by recording. The title of each recording appears at the left margin and can be referenced in the Discography and Appendix A. The bibliography includes only reviews that the author personally has seen; entries are not reiterated from secondary sources. More citations are listed for recordings released since the 1970s because reviews of popular music were not written as commonly before that time, and because automated indexing systems now make the material more accessible. An occasional gap occurs where no reviews are available, such as for *The Main Event*, which was reviewed as a movie but not as a soundtrack. Reviews of movie, stage, or television performances generally are not listed here, but reviews of related cast albums or soundtracks are (see "Other Reviews" below). Some reviews are of reissues (such as early albums re-released on CD format) as will be evidenced by their dates.

Compilations of reviews of Streisand's recordings also are available in sources such as:

DeCurtis, Anthony, and James Henke, eds. *The Rolling Stone Album Guide*. New York: Straight Arrow Publishers, Inc., 1992. S.v. "Barbra Streisand," by Paul Evans.

Erlewine, Michael, Vladimir Bogdanov, and Chris Woodstra, eds. *All Music Guide to Rock*. San Francisco: Miller Freeman Books, 1995. S.v. "Barbra Streisand," by William Ruhlman.

Grimes, Janet, ed. *CD Review Digest Annual*. (Vols. 4, 5, 7). Voorheesville, New York: The Peri Press, 1990, 1991, 1994.

Marsh, Dave. *The New Rolling Stone Record Guide*. New York: Rolling Stone Press, 1983. S.v. "Barbra Streisand" by Stephen Holden.

The Barbra Streisand Album

Indcox, John F. Review of *The Barbra Streisand Album*. In *High Fidelity* (June 1963): 84.

Korté, Steve. Review of *The Barbra Streisand Album*. In *CD Review* (February 1990): 72.

The Second Barbra Streisand Album

Indcox, John F. Review of *The Second Barbra Streisand Album*. In *High Fidelity* (December 1963): 104.

The Third Album

Korté, Steve. Review of *The Third Album*. In *CD Review* (February 1990): 72.

Wilson, John S. Review of *The Third Album*. In *High Fidelity* (May 1964): 86.

Funny Girl (cast album)

Ditsky, John. Review of *Funny Girl*. In *Fanfare* (November/December 1989): 509.

Wilson, John S. Review of *Funny Girl*, Original Broadway Cast. In *High Fidelity* (July 1964): 75.

People

Wilson, John S. Review of *People*. In *High Fidelity* (January 1965): 94.

My Name Is Barbra

Review of *My Name Is Barbra*. In *High Fidelity* (September 1965): 118.

Color Me Barbra

Wilson, John S. Review of *Color Me Barbra*. In *High Fidelity* (July 1966): 92–93.

Je m'appelle Barbra

Ames, Morgan. Review of *Je m'appelle Barbra*. In *High Fidelity* (February 1967): 124.

Simply Streisand

Review of *Simply Streisand*. In *Billboard* (28 October 1967): back cover.

A Christmas Album

Review of *A Christmas Album*. In *Billboard* (18 November 1967): back cover.

A Happening in Central Park

Korall, Burt. Review of *A Happening in Central Park*. In *Saturday Review* (11 January 1969): 108–109.
Lees, Gene. Review of *A Happening in Central Park*. In *High Fidelity* (February 1969): 126.
Reed, Rex. Review of *A Happening in Central Park*. In *Stereo Review* (February 1969): 128.
Review of *A Happening in Central Park*. In *The New Yorker* (16 November 1968): 131.

Funny Girl (film)

Lees, Gene. Review of *Funny Girl*. In *High Fidelity* (November 1968): 144, 146.
Review of *Funny Girl*. In *The New Yorker* (16 November 1968): 132–133.

What About Today?

Reed, Rex. Review of *What About Today?* In *Stereo Review* (November 1969): 140.

On a Clear Day You Can See Forever

Ames, Morgan. Review of *On a Clear Day You Can See Forever*. In *High Fidelity* (October 1970): 136.

Barbra Streisand's Greatest Hits

Review of *Barbra Streisand's Greatest Hits*. In *Billboard* (7 February 1970): back cover.

Stoney End

Dubro, Alec. Review of *Stoney End*. In *Rolling Stone* (1 April 1971): 50.
Heckman, Don. Review of *Stoney End*. Undated newspaper clipping. Personal collection of Linda Pohly.
Reed, Rex. Review of *Stoney End*. In *Stereo Review* (June 1971): 79–80.
Sharos, David. Review of *Stoney End*. In *Chicago Tribune*, 11 June 1996, 5:5.

Barbra Joan Streisand

Ames, Morgan. Review of *Barbra Joan Streisand*. In *High Fidelity* (December 1971): 118.

Holden, Stephen. Review of *Barbra Joan Streisand*. In *Rolling Stone* (6 January 1972): 66.

R. R. Review of *Barbra Joan Streisand*. In *Stereo Review* (December 1971): 132, 134.

Review of *Barbra Joan Streisand*. In *Audio* (October 1972): 90.

Live Concert at the Forum

Landau, Jon. Review of *Live Concert at the Forum*. In *Rolling Stone* (21 December 1972): 62.

Reilly, Peter. Review of *Live Concert at the Forum*. In *Stereo Review* (March 1973): 89–90.

Review of *Live at the Forum* [*sic*]. In *Saturday Review* (January 1973): 53.

Review of *Live Concert at the Forum*. In *Melody Maker* (3 February 1973): 22.

Sharos, David. Review of *Live Concert at the Forum*. In *Chicago Tribune*, 11 June 1996, 5:5.

Barbra Streisand and Other Musical Instruments

Reilly, Peter. Review of *Barbra Streisand and Other Musical Instruments*. In *Stereo Review* (July 1974): 93.

Barbra Streisand: The Way We Were

Andrews, Colman. Review of *Barbra Streisand: The Way We Were*. In *Creem* (June 1973): 66–67.

Holden, Stephen. Review of *Barbra Streisand: The Way We Were*. In *Rolling Stone* (11 April 1974): 62.

Landau, Jon. Review of *Barbra Streisand: The Way We Were*. In *Rolling Stone* (6 June 1974): 68.

ButterFly

Bookspan, Martin. Review of *Butterfly*. In *Consumer Reports* (August 1975): 515.

Gerson, Ben. Review of *Butterfly*. In *Rolling Stone* (2 January 1975): 64.

Marranca, Bonnie. Review of *Butterfly*. In *Crawdaddy* (February 1975): 83.

Reilly, Peter. Review of *Butterfly*. In *Stereo Review* (April 1975): 86.

Review of *Barbra Butterfly* [*sic*]. In *National Catholic Reporter* (24 January 1975): 12.

Funny Lady

Reilly, Peter. Review of *Funny Lady*. In *Stereo Review* (July 1975): 70–71.

Lazy Afternoon

Bregman, Steven H. Review of *Lazy Afternoon*. In *Listening Post* (March 1976): 25.
De Van, Fred. Review of *Lazy Afternoon*. In *Audio* (July 1976): 69.
Holden, Stephen. Review of *Lazy Afternoon*. In *Rolling Stone* (15 January 1976): 52–53.
Reilly, Peter. Review of *Lazy Afternoon*. In *Stereo Review* (February 1976): 89.

Classical Barbra

Bernheimer, Martin. Review of *Classical Barbra*. In *Los Angeles Times*, 8 February 1976, CAL:1, 60.
Bretton, Elise. Review of *Classical Barbra*. In *High Fidelity* (February 1977): 149.
Davis, Peter G. Review of *Classical Barbra*. In *Viva* (July 1976): 39–40.
Freeman, John W. Review of *Classical Barbra*. In *Opera News* (3 April 1976): 56.
Gould, Glenn. Review of *Classical Barbra*. In *High Fidelity* (May 1976): 73–75.
Horowitz, IS. Review of *Classical Barbra*. In *Billboard* (6 March 1976): 74.
McLellan, Joseph. Review of *Classical Barbra*. In *Detroit News*, 28 March 1976, 4H.
Porter, Stan. Review of *Classical Barbra*. In *Encore American & Worldwide News* (5 April 1976): 41.
Rich, Alan. Review of *Classical Barbra*. In *New York* (8 March 1976): 79.
Rockwell, John. Review of *Classical Barbra*. In *Rolling Stone* (3 June 1976): 77, 79.
Willis, Thomas. Review of *Classical Barbra*. In *Chicago Tribune*, 4 April 1976, 6:6–7.

A Star Is Born

Reilly, Peter. Review of *A Star Is Born*. In *Stereo Review* (March 1977): 110.
Tucker, Ken. Review of *A Star Is Born*. In *Rolling Stone* (24 February 1977): 66.

Streisand Superman

Dodds, Richard. Review of *Streisand Superman*. In *Times-Picayune* (New Orleans), 11 July 1977, 1:18.
Duffy, Mike. Review of *Streisand Superman*. In *Detroit Free Press*, 21 July 1977, B:6.
Hilburn, Robert. Review of *Streisand Superman*. In *Los Angeles Times*, 5 July 1977, IV:9.
Hilburn, Robert. Review of *Streisand Superman*. In *Los Angeles Times*, 1 January 1978, CAL:60, 62.
Marsh, Dave. Review of *Streisand Superman*. In *Rolling Stone* (11 August 1977): 68.
Reilly, Peter. Review of *Streisand Superman*. In *Stereo Review* (October 1977): 92.
Riegel, Richard. Review of *Streisand Superman*. In *Creem* (November 1977): 68.

Roberts, John Storm. Review of *Streisand Superman*. In *High Fidelity* (October 1977): 166.
Tiegel, Eliot. Review of *Streisand Superman*. In *Billboard* (9 July 1977): 98.

Songbird

Blume, Dave. Review of *Songbird*. In *Los Angeles Times*, 9 July 1978, CAL:85.
Hirshberg, Jennefer. Review of *Songbird*. In *Washington Post*, 2 July 1978, F:4.
Holden, Stephen. Review of *Songbird*. In *Rolling Stone* (27 July 1978): 68.
Morgan, Albert. Review of *Songbird*. In *City* (August 1978): 52.
Reilly, Peter. Review of *Songbird*. In *Stereo Review* (September 1978): 147.
Zieja, Dan. Review of *Songbird*. In *Detroit Free Press*, 17 June 1978, 11A.

Barbra Streisand's Greatest Hits, Volume 2

Blume, Dave. Review of *Barbra Streisand's Greatest Hits, Volume 2*. In *Los Angeles Times*, 17 December 1978, 138–139.
Reilly, Peter. Review of *Barbra Streisand's Greatest Hits, Volume 2*. In *Stereo Review* (March 1979): 114.

Wet

Blume, Dave. Review of *Wet*. In *Los Angeles Times*, 11 November 1979, CAL:79.
Holden, Stephen. Review of *Wet*. In *Rolling Stone* (7 February 1980): 80.
Kresh, Paul. Review of *Wet*. In *Stereo Review* (February 1980): 106, 109.
Mayer, Ira. Review of *Wet*. In *High Fidelity* (January 1980): 105–106.

Guilty

Feldman, Jim. Review of *Guilty*. In *Village Voice* (31 Dec.–6 Jan. 1981): 55–56.
Grein, Paul. Review of *Guilty*. In *Los Angeles Times*, 5 October 1980, 92.
Harrington, Richard. Review of *Guilty*. In *Washington Post*, 28 September 1980, K:7.
Hilburn, Robert. Review of *Guilty*. In *Los Angeles Times*, 9 November 1980, CAL: 68.
Holden, Stephen. Review of *Guilty*. In *Rolling Stone* (11 December 1980): 56.
McFarlin, Jim. Review of *Guilty*. In *Detroit News*, 30 November 1980, 8D.
Reilly, Peter. Review of *Guilty*. In *Stereo Review* (December 1980): 103–104.

Memories

Reilly, Peter. Review of *Memories*. In *Stereo Review* (April 1982): 68.

Yentl

Berman, Leslie. Review of *Yentl*. In *Rolling Stone* (2 February 1984): 50–51.
Case, Brian. Review of *Yentl*. In *Melody Maker* (7 April 1984): 31.

McFarlin, Jim. Review of *Yentl*. In *Detroit News*, 13 November 1983, 1E, 6E.
Reilly, Peter. Review of *Yentl*. In *Stereo Review* (February 1984): 92.
Review of *Yentl*. In *US* (5 December 1983): 57.

Emotion

Grein, Paul. Review of *Emotion*. In *Los Angeles Times*, 14 October 1984, CAL: 67.
Holden, Stephen. Review of *Emotion*. In *New York Times*, 11 November 1984, 2: 23.
McFarlin, Jim. Review of *Emotion*. In *Detroit News*, 9 December 1984, 1L, 6L.
Musto, Michael. Review of *Emotion*. In *US* (3 December 1984): 62.
Novak, Ralph. Review of *Emotion*. In *People* (November 1984): 24.

The Broadway Album

Bosworth, Patricia. Review of *The Broadway Album*. In *Working Woman* (March 1986): 160.
Davis, Francis. Review of *The Broadway Album*. In *Rolling Stone* (16 January 1986): 48–49.
Hume, Ann C. Review of *The Broadway Album*. In *Atlanta* (April 1986): 24.
Kordosh, J. Review of *The Broadway Album*. In *Creem* (April 1986): 29.
McFarlin, Jim. Review of *The Broadway Album*. In *Detroit News*, 29 December 1985, F:3.
McGuigan, Cathleen. Review of *The Broadway Album*. In *Newsweek* (23 December 1985): 77.
McKuen, Rod. Review of *The Broadway Album*. In *Stereo Review* (April 1986): 69–70.
Sullivan, Dan. Review of *The Broadway Album*. In *Los Angeles Times*, 3 November 1985, CAL:52.
Travers, Peter. Review of *The Broadway Album*. In *People Weekly* (16 December 1985): 43, 47.
Weiss, Paulette. Review of *The Broadway Album*. In *Audio* (July 1986): 112–113.

One Voice

Grein, Paul. Review of *One Voice*. In *Los Angeles Times*. 19 April 1987, CAL:91–92.
Haller, Scott. Review of *One Voice*. In *People Weekly* (20 July 1987): 20–21.
Hemming, Roy. Review of *One Voice*. In *Stereo Review* (September 1987): 98.
Kart, Larry. Review of *One Voice*. In *Chicago Tribune*, 23 April 1987, 5:12.
Weiss, Paulette. Review of *One Voice*. In *Audio* (October 1987): 405.

Till I Loved You

Ditsky, John. Review of *Till I Loved You*. In *Fanfare* (May/June 1989): 448.
Grein, Paul. Review of *Till I Loved You*. In *Los Angeles Times*, 26 October 1988, 6:1, 8.

Hemming, Roy. Review of *Till I Loved You*. In *Stereo Review* (March 1989): 111.

Holden, Stephen. Review of *Till I Loved You*. In *New York Times*, 6 November 1988, II:29.

Novak, Ralph. Review of *Till I Loved You*. In *People Weekly* (5 December 1988): 23.

Preeo, Max O. Review of *Till I Loved You*. In *Show Music* (Winter 1988/89): 62.

Stearns, David Patrick. Review of *Till I Loved You*. In *USA Today*, 26 October 1988, D:4.

Weiss, Paulette. Review of *Till I Loved You*. In *Audio* (June 1989): 136.

A Collection: Greatest Hits and More

Hardy, Ernest. Review of *A Collection*. In *Cash Box Magazine* (25 November 1989): 36.

Preeo, Max O. Review of *A Collection*. In *Show Music* (Fall 1991): 43.

Waryncia, Lou. Review of *A Collection*. In *CD Review* (February 1990): 72.

Just for the Record

Brown, Joe. Review of *Just for the Record*. In *Washington Post*, 6 October 1991, G:5.

Gamerman, Amy. Review of *Just for the Record*. In *Wall Street Journal*, 30 October 1991, A:14.

Grein, Paul. Review of *Just for the Record*. In *Musician* (November 1991): 96.

Holden, Stephen. Review of *Just for the Record*. In *Detroit Free Press*, 23 September 1991, E:2.

Holden, Stephen. Review of *Just for the Record*. In *New York Times*, 22 September 1991, 2:28, 32.

Kaufman, Joanne. Review of *Just for the Record*. In *People Weekly* (11 November 1991): 23, 26.

Preeo, Max O. Review of *Just for the Record*. In *Show Music* (Winter 1991/92): 67–68.

Reich, Howard. Review of *Just for the Record*. In *Chicago Tribune*, 27 September 1991, 5:1, 3.

Review of *Just for the Record*. In *The Absolute Sound* (April 1992): 164, 166.

Santosuosso, Ernie. Review of *Just for the Record*. In *Boston Globe*, 27 September 1991, 35, 36.

Stearns, David Patrick. Review of *Just for the Record*. In *USA Today*, 23 September 1991, D:1.

Whitall, Susan. Review of *Just for the Record*. In *Detroit News*, 30 September 1991, E:1, 4.

Willman, Chris. Review of *Just for the Record*. In *Los Angeles Times*, 22 September 1991, CAL:61.

Wurtzel, Elizabeth. Review of *Just for the Record*. In *The New Yorker* (23 December 1991): 91–92.

Back to Broadway

Ames, Katrine. Review of *Back to Broadway*. In *Newsweek* (12 July 1993): 63.

Farley, Christopher John. Review of *Back to Broadway*. In *Time* (5 July 1993): n.p.

Harrington, Richard. Review of *Back to Broadway*. In *Washington Post*, 27 June 1993, G:6.

Heckman, Don. Review of *Back to Broadway*. In *Los Angeles Times*, 27 June 1993, CAL:60.

Holden, Stephen. Review of *Back to Broadway*. In *New York Times*, 27 June 1993, 2:26.

Hulbert, Dan. Review of *Back to Broadway*. In *Atlanta Journal/Atlanta Constitution*, 29 June 1993, D:9.

Morse, Steve. Review of *Back to Broadway*. In *Boston Sunday Globe*, 27 June 1993, 86.

Sandow, Greg. Review of *Back to Broadway*. In *Entertainment Weekly* (Summer 1993): 100–102.

White, Armond. Review of *Back to Broadway*. In *Village Voice* (10 August 1993): 65, 76.

Barbra: The Concert

Farber, Jim. Review of *Barbra: The Concert*. In *Entertainment Weekly* (7 October 1994): 75.

Hemming, Roy. Review of *Barbra: The Concert*. In *Stereo Review* (January 1995): 133, 135.

Henry, Derrick. Review of *Barbra: The Concert*. In *Atlanta Journal/Atlanta Constitution*, 1 October 1994, 21.

Holden, Stephen. Review of *Barbra: The Concert*. In *New York Times*, 25 September 1994, 2:34, 42.

Reich, Howard. Review of *Barbra: The Concert*. In *Chicago Tribune*, 16 October 1994, 13:34.

Stearns, David Patrick. Review of *Barbra: The Concert*. In *USA Today*, 23 September 1994, D:1.

Willman, Chris. Review of *Barbra: The Concert*. In *Los Angeles Times*, 25 September 1994, 64.

The Mirror Has Two Faces

Stearns, David Patrick. Review of *The Mirror Has Two Faces* soundtrack. In *USA Today*, 23 October 1996, D:1.

Strauss, Neil. Review of *The Mirror Has Two Faces* soundtrack. In *New York Times*, 21 November 1996, C:16.

Higher Ground

Farley, Christopher John. Review of *Higher Ground*. In *Time* (24 November 1997): 105.

Harrington, Richard. Review of *Higher Ground*. In *Washington Post*, 16 November 1997, G:13.

Helligar, Jeremy. Review of *Higher Ground*. In *People Weekly* (8 December 1997): 34.

A Love Like Ours

Campbell, Chuck. "Streisand's Latest Album Too Smug and Full of Herself . . . " Review of *A Love Like Ours*. In *Macomb Daily* (Michigan), 21 October 1999, 5C.

Okrent, Daniel. "Short Takes." Review of *A Love Like Ours*. In *Time* (27 September 1999): n.p.

Smith, Tim. "Shouting from the Roof Tops." Review of *A Love Like Ours*. In *The Star Press* (Muncie), 26 September 1999, 3E.

Stearns, David Patrick. "Listen Up." Review of *A Love Like Ours*. In *USA Today*, 28 September 1999, 4D.

OTHER REVIEWS

Included herein are citations for reviews of recorded singles and stage, concert, television, or videotaped performances. The list is not exhaustive.

Albertson, Chris. "The Streisand Specials" (Review of *My Name Is Barbra; Color Me Barbra* videos). In *Stereo Review* (May 1987): 121.

"Barbra a Smash in London 'Funny' " (Review of stage show). In *Variety* (20 April 1966): 65–66.

Barron, John. "The Main Event" (Review of several videos). In *Detroit News*, 12 October 1991, 20–21D.

Biro, Nick. "After Barbra—What Else?" (Review of Chicago concert). In *Billboard* (14 December 1963): 14.

Cagle, Jess. "Tea and Symphony" (Review of Washington, D.C. concert). In *Entertainment Weekly* (27 May 1994): 16.

Champlin, Charles. "Streisand: A Scintillating Show of Gifts" (Review of Las Vegas performance). In *Los Angeles Times*, 5 August 1969, IV:1, 4.

Cox, Dan. "Barbra Streisand" (Review of Las Vegas performance). In *Variety* (10 January 1994): 61.

Dale. "Cocoanut Grove, L. A." (Review of club performance). In *Variety* (28 August 1963): 53.

Dale, Steve. Review of *Barbra Streisand Collection* (five-volume set of various videos). In *Chicago Tribune*, 2 November 1990, 7:67–68.

Deni, Laura. (Review of Las Vegas performance). In *Billboard* (26 December 1970): 21.

DeVine, Lawrence. "Barbra in London" (Review of London concert). In *Detroit Free Press*, 21 April 1994, C1–2.

Dewar, Cameron. "Barbra Great as Fanny but Show Tedious Stuff" (Review of Boston opening of *Funny Girl*). In *Billboard* (25 January 1964): 10.

Feldman, Jim. "Simply, Streisand" (Review of Las Vegas performance). In *Village Voice* (18 January 1994): 61–62, 73.

Freedland, Nat. " 'Star Is Born' Is Realistic Story of Rock Pressures" (Review of film). In *Billboard* (8 January 1977): 32.

"Full Throttle" (Review of theatre performance). In *Newsweek* (6 April 1964): 76–77.

"Funny Girl" (Review of theatre performance). In *Variety* (1 April 1964): 80.

Gates, David. "Too Much Togetherness?" (Review of Frank Sinatra *Duets*). In *Newsweek* (8 November 1993): 79.

Goldstein, Richard. "Barbra: 'Art Isn't Easy' " (Review of HBO special). In *Village Voice* (14 January 1986): 39.

Gundersen, Edna. "Streisand, As if She Had Never Left" (Review of Las Vegas performance). In *USA Today*, 3 January 1994, 1D.

"Harrah's, Lake Tahoe" (Review of club performance). In *Variety* (18 September 1963): 60.

Hewes, Harry. (Review of theatre performance). In *Saturday Review* (14 April 1963): 28.

Hilburn, Robert. "Streisand Stage Return a Lustrous Vegas Event" (Review of Las Vegas performance). In *Los Angeles Times*, 3 January 1994, F1, 4.

Hinckley, David. "Babs: The Way She Is" (Review of Las Vegas performance). In *New York Daily News*, 2 January 1994, 13.

Holden, Stephen. "The Streisand Specials" (Review of videos). In *New York Times*, 11 January 1987, 2:30.

Jackson, Alan. "Diva Delights with a Mix of Mythology and Magic" (Review of London concert). In *Times* (London), 21 April 1994, 5.

Jarvis, Jeff. "Barbra Streisand in Putting It Together" (Review of HBO special). In *People Weekly* (6 January 1986): 11.

JOSE. "Nothing Could Follow Barbra's Freebie in Central Park Except Sanitation Dept." (Review of concert). In *Variety* (21 June 1967): 58.

Lichtman, Irv. Review of *A Happening in Central Park* and *One Voice* (videos). In *Billboard* (22 August 1987): 76–77.

MOR. "Mister Kelly's, Chi." (Review of club performance). In *Variety* (19 June 1963): 56.

Musto, Michael. "Yes, Barbra Was Like Butter" (Review of Las Vegas performance). In *Village Voice* (18 January 1994): 36.

Newman, Melinda. "Streisand's Pitch Perfect on Evergreens" (Review of Madison Square Garden, New York concert). In *Billboard* (2 July 1994): 14.

O'Connor, John J. "Streisand On Making Her Album" (Review of television special). In *New York Times*, 10 January 1986, C:26.

O'Connor, John J. "TV: Streisand's 'One Voice' on HBO" (Review of television special). In *New York Times*, 27 December 1986, 1:46.

"On the Rue Streisand" (Review of theatre performance). In *Time* (3 April 1964): 54.

Paglia, Camille. "The Way She Was" (Review of Madison Square Garden, New York concert). In *The New Republic* (18–25 July 1994): 20–22.

Pareles, Jon. "In New York, Streisand Is a Hometown Hero" (Review of New York concert). In *New York Times*, 22 June 1994, B3.

Peyser, Marc. "Happy Days Are Here Again—Again" (Review of Washington, D.C. concert). In *Newsweek* (23 May 1994): 64–65.

"Riviera, Las Vegas" (Review of club performance). In *Variety* (10 July 1963): 62.

Roberts, Chris. Review of "We're Not Makin' Love Anymore" (single). In *Melody Maker* (17 February 1990): 31.

Rolontz, Bob. "A World of Talent and Class" (Review of Basin St. club performance). In *Billboard* (25 May 1963): 14.

Rosenberg, Howard. (Review of *Earth Day 1990 Special* television special). In *Los Angeles Times*, 21 April 1990, F:1.

Siskel, Gene. "Grand Dame" (Review of Las Vegas performances). In *Entertainment Weekly* (14 January 1994): 18–20.

Sobel, Robert. "Streisand and Lopez Shine at NY Concerts" (Review of concert). In *Billboard* (21 August 1965): 16, 47.

Stearns, David Patrick. "Spontaneity Lets Singer Truly Shine" (Review of Washington, D.C. concert). In *USA Today*, 12 May 1994, 1D–2D.

"Streisand Show: The Way She Was—And Still Is" (Review of Las Vegas performance). In *Detroit News*, 2 January 1994, 5A.

Taubman, Howard. "Theatre: 'I Can Get It for You Wholesale' Opens" (Review of theatre performance). In *New York Times*, 23 March 1962, L:29.

Taylor, C. "AC." Review of "I've Dreamed of You" (single). In *Billboard* (10 July 1999): 17.

" 'This Is Work' Says Barbra" (Review of Las Vegas performance). In *Billboard* (4 October 1969): SC-9.

Tiegel, Eliot. (Review of Las Vegas performance). In *Billboard* (15 January 1972): 16.

Weatherford, Mike. "Streisand's Talent Overcomes Anxieties" (Review of Las Vegas performance). In *Las Vegas Review-Journal/Sun*, 2 January 1994, 5C.

Whitall, Susan. "A Delirious Night of Magnificent Music" (Review of Detroit concert). In *Detroit News*, 16 May 1994, A:1, 4.

Wickham, Vicki. "Super Streisand" (Review of television appearance). In *Melody Maker* (27 March 1971): 6.

Wilson, Tom. "Streisand Launches L. V.'s New International Hotel" (Review of Las Vegas performance). In *Billboard* (19 July 1969): 24.

SELECTIVE LIST OF BOOKS ABOUT BARBRA STREISAND

Of the more than twenty books indexed below, none is an "authorized" biography. Some of the books are mostly text, others feature photographs.

Abitan, Guy. *Barbra Streisand: Une femme libre*. Paris: O. Orban, 1979.

Bly, Nellie. *Barbra Streisand: The Untold Story*. New York: Pinnacle Books, Windsor Publishing Corp., 1994.

Brady, Frank. *Barbra Streisand: An Illustrated Biography*. New York: Grosset & Dunlap, 1979.

Carrick, Peter. *Barbra Streisand: Biography*. London: Robert Hale Limited, 1991.

Castell, David. *Barbra Streisand: A Biography*. New York: Confucian Press, 1981.

Castell, David. *The Films of Barbra Streisand*, 3rd ed. Bembridge: BCW Publishing, 1977.

Considine, Shaun. *Barbra Streisand: The Woman, The Myth, The Music.* New York: Delacorte Press, 1985.

Dennen, Barry. *My Life with Barbra: A Love Story.* Amherst, New York: Prometheus Books, 1997.

Edwards, Anne. *Streisand: A Biography.* Boston: Little, Brown and Company, 1997.

Eldred, Patricia Mulrooney. *Barbra Streisand.* Mankato, Minnesota: Creative Education, 1975. [juvenile]

Harvey, Donna K., and Jackson Harvey. *Streisand: The Pictorial Biography.* Philadelphia: Courage Books, 1997.

Jordan, René. *The Greatest Star: The Barbra Streisand Story, An Unauthorized Biography.* New York: G. P. Putnam's Sons, 1975.

Keenan, Deborah. *On Stage, Barbra Streisand.* Mankato, Minnesota: Creative Education, 1976. [juvenile]

Kimbrell, James. *Barbra, an Actress Who Sings: An Unauthorized Biography.* Boston: Branden Publishing Company, 1989.

Kimbrell, James. *Barbra, an Actress Who Sings,* vol. 2. Edited by Cheri Kimbrell. Boston: Branden Publishing Company, Inc., 1992.

Riese, Randall. *Her Name Is Barbra: An Intimate Portrait of the Real Barbra Streisand.* New York: Carol Publishing Group, 1993.

Ruhlmann, William. *Barbra Streisand.* Stamford, Connecticut: Longmeadow Press, 1995.

Signorelli-Pappas, Rita. *Barbra Streisand.* New York: Chelsea House, 1996. [juvenile]

Spada, James. *Barbra, the First Decade: The Films and Career of Barbra Streisand.* Secaucus, New Jersey: The Citadel Press, 1974.

Spada, James. *Streisand: Her Life.* New York: Crown Publishers, Inc., 1995.

Spada, James. *Streisand: The Woman and the Legend.* With Christopher Nickens. Garden City, New York: Doubleday & Company, Inc., 1981.

Swenson, Karen. *Barbra, the Second Decade.* Secaucus, New Jersey: Citadel Press, 1986.

Teti, Frank. *Streisand Through the Lens.* With Karen Moline. New York: Delilah, 1982.

Vare, Ethlie Ann, comp. *Diva: Barbra Streisand and the Making of a Superstar.* New York: Boulevard Books, 1996.

Waldman, Allison J. *The Barbra Streisand Scrapbook.* New York: Carol Publishing Group, 1995.

Winnert, Derek. *Barbra Streisand "Quote Unquote."* New York: Crescent Books, 1996.

Zec, Donald and Anthony Fowles. *Barbra: A Biography of Barbra Streisand.* New York: St. Martin's Press, 1981.

VOCAL SELECTIONS

The sources listed below provide the text and music for many of the songs Streisand has recorded, but the songs do not necessarily appear with notation approximating her performances. The list is not exhaustive.

Hello Barbra! Vocal Selections from *Hello, Dolly!* Edwin H. Morris and Company, Inc. (#E8436a).

Streisand, Barbra. Vocal Selections from *A Collection: Greatest Hits and More.* Cherry Lane Music, Port Chester, New York (#02507969).

Streisand, Barbra. Vocal Selections from *Back to Broadway.* Cherry Lane Music, Port Chester, New York (#02502132).

Streisand, Barbra. Vocal Selections from *Barbra: The Concert.* ed. Milton Okun. Cherry Lane Music, Port Chester, New York (#02502164), 1995.

Streisand, Barbra. Vocal Selections from *Till I Loved You,* ed. Milton Okun. Cherry Lane Music, Port Chester, New York (#02507944), 1989.

Streisand Guilty. Chappell and Co., Inc., New York. Distributed by Hal Leonard Publishing Corporation, Milwaukee, Wisconsin (#HL00306809), 1980.

Vocal Selections from *Funny Girl.* Chappell and Co., Inc., New York (#162250–122).

Vocal Selections from *On a Clear Day You Can See Forever.* Chappell and Co., Inc. New York.

Vocal Selections from *Yentl.* Columbia Pictures Publications, Hialeah, Florida (#TSF0049), 1983.

SELECTED INTERNET SITES AND SOURCES

These sites were accessible between 1997 and 1999. The life of an internet site often is not long. This list is provided for possible access information, but more importantly as an indication of Streisand's popularity among users of this form of communication. In November of 1998, Barbra announced the creation of her own web site during an interview on America Online. The address is www.barbra streisand.com.

AOL: BARJSBiLiA
Http://acs2.bu.edu:8001/~pimentel/bjsweb.html
Http://members.aol.com/barbramusc/index.html (Barbra Streisand Music Guide)
Http://members.aol.com/iluvbarbra/
Http://members.aol.com/jlbpub/
Http://members.aol.com/markjayeye/bjsfaq/index.html
Http://mgfx.com/BARBRA/
Http://tnef.com/barbra_streisand.html   (OR)   Http://www.fansites.com/barbra_ streisand.html
Http://www.ajbl.com/jpbarbra.html
Http://www.celebsite.com/people/barbrastreisand/index.html
Http://www.cyberramp.net/~thumper/ssbottom.html
Http://www.electra.com/barbra.html
Http://www.eonline.com/Facts/People/0,12,231,00.html
Http://www.ex.ac.uk/festival96/barbra.html
Http://www.geocities.com/Hollywood/Set/4824/
Http://www.hhs.nl/~v942549/simstr.htm
Http://www.kac.net/barbra (Later changed to Http://www.kac.net/yankee/barbra. htm)

Http://www.mrshowbiz.com/starbios/barbrastreisand/a.html
Http://www.music.sony.com/Music/ArtistInfo/BarbraStreisand (Later linked to Http://www.barbra-streisand.com/)
Http://www.netsrq.com/~dbois/streisan.html
Http://www.rockonthenet.com/artists/info/barbra.htm
Http://www.usc.edu/dept/DT/V127/N5/divbarbra.05d.html
Http://www.yahoo.com/Entertainment/Music/Artists/By_Genre/Rock_and_Pop/
Streisand_Barbra/

Selected Bibliography of Sources Cited

This bibliography enumerates significant sources cited in various chapters of *The Barbra Streisand Companion*; other sources, which were used less frequently, are given full citations in the Notes or in the text. Items listed in the Reference Bibliography, such as recording reviews or biographies, are not reiterated here.

Chagollan, Steve, ed. "Spotlight, ShowEast Filmmaker of the Year." *Variety* (21 October 1996): S37–S60.

Feather, Leonard. "Wild Girl, Wild Sound." *Melody Maker* (1 February 1964): 12.

Forte, Allen. *The American Popular Ballad of the Golden Era, 1924–1950*. Princeton: Princeton University Press, 1995.

Grobel, Lawrence. "Playboy Interview: Barbra Streisand." *Playboy* (October 1977): 79–107, 193–200.

Hamm, Charles. *Yesterdays: Popular Song in America*. New York: W. W. Norton and Co., 1979.

Hemming, Roy, and David Hajdu. *Discovering Great Singers of Classic Pop*. New York: Newmarket Press, 1991.

Marsh, Dave. *The New Rolling Stone Record Guide*. New York: Rolling Stone Press, 1983. S.v. "Barbra Streisand," by Stephen Holden.

Pleasants, Henry. *The American Popular Singers*. New York: Simon and Schuster, 1974.

Reed, Bill, voice teacher. Interview by author, 24 June 1997, Muncie, Indiana, telephone.

Shire, David, composer/conductor. Interview by author, 4 March 1998, Muncie, Indiana.

Streisand, Barbra. Accompanying booklet for *Just for the Record*. Compact disc 44111, Sony Music Entertainment, 1991.

Streisand, Barbra. Interview by Larry King. *Larry King Live*. CNN television, 6 February 1992 and 7 June 1995.

Streisand, Barbra. Interview by Rosie O'Donnell. *The Rosie O'Donnell Show*. NBC television, 15 November 1999.

Streisand, Barbra. Interview by Barbara Walters. *20/20*. ABC television, 19 November 1993.

Streisand, Barbra. Interview by Oprah Winfrey. *The Oprah Winfrey Show*. ABC television, 11 November 1996.

Streisand, Barbra. Several interviews. Compact disc *Rarities* vol. 5. Private release by *Barbrabilia*, Arlington Heights, Illinois, 1997.

Index

This index includes references from the chapters and the discography annotations. See Appendix A and Appendix B for lists of albums and songs with Discography chronology numbers.

About the Author

LINDA POHLY is Associate Professor of music history and musicology at Ball State University. She is a member of the Sonneck Society for American Music and the International Association for the Study of Popular Music.